MIND-LINES

Lines For Changing *Minds*

L. Michael Hall, Ph.D.
Bobby G. Bodenhamer, D.Min.

Foreword by Joseph O'Connor

Fifth Edition

MIND-LINES: *Lines For Changing Minds*
©1997 Hall and Bodenhamer
Copyright # Txu 814-870
Library of Congress, Washington, D.C.

First Edition: Sept. 1997
Second Edition: Oct. 1998
Third Edition: March, 2000
Fourth Edition, December, 2001
Fifth Edition, February, 2005

ISBN #890001155

Published by: **NSP: Neuro-Semantics Publications**
P.O. Box 8
Clifton, CO. 81520-0008 USA
(970) 523-7877

Printing Company: **Action Printing**
Jerry Kucera, Owner
516 Fruitvale Court, Unit C
Grand Jct. CO. 81504
(970) 434-7701
Actionpres@aol.com
Cover Designed and Created by *Candi Clark*

Neuro-Semantics® is the trademark name for the International Society of Neuro-Semantics. For more than 2000 pages of *free information*, see the web sites:

www.neurosemantics.com
www.runyourownbrain.com

CONTENTS

Foreword   5
Preface   7
Mind-Line Response to a Toxic Idea   13

PART I: THE LANGUAGE AS MAGIC FRAMEWORK   19
1. *Neuro-Linguistic "Magic"*   20
2. *Three Facets of Neuro-Linguistic Magic*   31
3. *Conversational Reframing Patterns*   57
4. *The Formula*   69

PART II: THE 7 DIRECTIONS FOR FRAMING   92
5. *Deframing*   93
6. *Content Reframing*   111
7. *Counter-Framing*   125
8. *Pre-Framing and Post-Framing*:   143
9. *Outframing*   165
10. *Analogous or Story Reframing*   197
11. *Let There Be More Magic (Building on the Magic)*   209

PART III: THEORETICAL FRAMEWORKS   226
12: *Unfolding Mind-Lines (Denis Bridoux)*   227
13: *Mind-Lines: The Theoretical Foundation*   247

PART IV: THE MIND-LINES WORKSHOP   264
14: *Into the Fray of Mind-Lining*   265
15: *Eight Things You Should Know About "Meaning"*   275
16: *How To Do What When*   287
17: *Getting Into A Magical State*   293
18: *Mind-Lines—Step-by-Step*   302
19: *The Mind-Lines Mind Map — Pascal J. Gambardella, Ph.D.*   316
20: *Super-Charging Beliefs with Mind-Lines*   322

Epilogue   327

Appendix A: Remodeling Our Cinematic Frames   328
Appendix B: The Meta-Model   334
Appendix C: The "Is" Biz   339
Index   340
Bibliography   343
Glossary   345
Neuro-Semantics   351
Authors   353
Books   355
Trainings   356

ACKNOWLEDGMENTS

As a model *Mind-Lines* emerged from combining the best of NLP's conversational reframing patterns with the best of Neuro-Semantics' revolutionary *Meta-States* model.

Mind-Lines arose by using the theoretic frameworks regarding the distinction between map and territory from *Alfred Korzybski's* General Semantics and the unique formulations of that distinction in the field of NLP (Neuro-Linguistic Programming) as developed by *John Grinder* and *Richard Bandler*.

It arose also as we incorporated the "sleight of mouth" patterns that *Robert Dilts* developed and formalized from the magic-like language patterns of Richard Bandler. It was Robert who originally used the metaphor of a sleight of hand magician and so designed the reframing patterns as "sleight of mouth" patterns. This became the basic model in classic NLP.

When I (MH) first learned the conversational reframing patterns from *Chris Hall* and her elegance with these as language patterns, I wrote about them in *The Spirit of NLP* (1996). Afterwards Dr. Bob and I totally re-modeled the NLP version using Meta-States to rigorously re-work the model and to create *Mind-Lines* as it exists in this book.

Along the way we have been significantly influenced by numerous other thinkers and modelers:
> *Alfred Korzybski,* founder of General Semantics.
> *Gregory Bateson,* who popularized the idea of frames, meta, working with meta-levels, and reframing.
> *Paul Watzlawick* and his colleagues who furthered Bateson's developments on framing and reframing.

With the introduction of the fourth edition, we included contributions of two individuals who have used this model, taught it, and assisted us in further developing it. Both also have contributed chapters:
> *Pascal J. Gambardella, Ph.D.* who designed so many of the diagrams and art work and chapter 19 on mind-mapping Mind-Lines.
> *Denis Bridoux* who has played a key role in the ongoing conceptualizations of Mind-Lines and who contributed the chapter on the Unfolding of Mind-Lines as well as the Realization outframe.

FOREWORD

Joseph O'Connor

If you thought *linguistics* had all the relevance and fascination of declining Latin irregular verbs on a wet Monday afternoon, then prepare for a pleasant shock. Fun to read, and valuable to use, this book invites you to *play with language*.

Language makes the bond between us, how we relate to each other and even if we do relate at all. How do we connect and understand anything? Through language. We all learn it, and how well do we use it?

My English Language school studies were confined to interpreting a Shakespeare play and being able to tell an intransitive verb from a transitive one. Heaven forbid that it should tell me how to use language with purpose, to play with it, to light linguistic fireworks that would burst with multiple meanings and dazzling eloquence in my listener's mind. Language lies deep level in our minds, we cannot **not** respond to it. Sticks and stones can break our bones but words can break our hearts. And they can also heal and inspire our spirits.

As you read this book, some of the power of language will become yours to command. Language both describes and prescribes, you have to accept certain ideas to understand what you hear. And as it directs your attention towards some things, it just as surely makes others invisible. You create whole new worlds every time you read a novel, and you will create meaning as you read this book. Words mean nothing without a listener, so as you come to understand how we make meaning from these intriguing black squiggles on the paper, and the sounds in our heads that are one way we represent language, you will have more freedom and choice about how you use it.

'The man looked at the woman and said "cheese".'
> What does that mean?
It depends on the context that surrounds it. Could this be a kitchen scene? Is he being insulting? Telling the punch line of a joke? Or is she taking his picture? Or perhaps it is an example of an ambiguous sentence with multiple meanings that I concocted to make a point? *Words have no meaning without a frame to put them in.* Isolated from a meaningful context, you can only shrug your shoulders and move on.

So what? So, if you want to be understood you need to set a frame that tells the other person how to understand what you are saying in the way you want it understood. And, when responding, it gives you ways to change and play with the frames, or lack of them, in what you hear to influence the conversation.

Now you have space to ask yourself, not just, 'What does this mean?' But, also, 'What could this mean? And finally maybe, 'What would I like this to mean?'

All credit to the authors for making this clear, showing the structure behind it, and how to use it in practice.

So if you are ever asked, what does this *really* mean? You can laugh, like a good Zen apprentice and tell a joke. Jokes work because they lead you into understanding a situation in one frame, then they pull it out from under leaving you suddenly in another. A story then, of a now prominent writer when he was a humble college student. He wrote in one of his English compositions, 'The girl tumbled down the stairs and lay prostitute at the bottom.'

In the margin, the teacher wrote, 'My dear sir, you must learn to distinguish between a fallen woman and one who has merely slipped!'

Joseph O'Connor
Co-Author of *Introducing NLP*
London, July 1997

PREFACE

Have you ever heard a line,
—a statement, verse, or idea—
that changed your life?

May, 1997

*We have found **a magical three-dimensional box.*** In it lies all kinds of wild and wonderful and even horrible things. It's a box in your mind. And in this box you will find all kinds of meanings, meanings that affect your mind and body, your entire neuro-semantic system.

Magicians have always worked with *magic boxes*. They put into and pull from their magic boxes all kinds of wild and crazy things—rabbits, scarfs, coins, tigers, and the list goes on.

We too are, or can be, mental magicians. We can pull from the magical box of the *human mind* all kinds of wild and crazy meanings. After all, that's what we do best, we *make* meaning. And we do so by using a very special *magic formula* that we keep inside our heads. It's with that formula that we box up meanings and create our realities. *You* have such a box in *your* mind and, in fact, you are using it right this very moment as you read this. Yet, while the human brain produces this magic box, the magic box transcends the brain.

In this book you will discover how to identify your magical formula box from which, and by which, you construct your heavens and your hells. Everyday you pull things out of your box to your weal and/or to your woe. You do it in your talk. You do it in your thoughts. It can totally devastate you and ruin your life—and it can make you more resourceful and vibrant and alive than you have ever dared imagine.
- What semantic magic did you pull out of it today?
- What magic will you learn to pull out of it tomorrow?
- Would you like more fun than pleasure?
- How about becoming a magician over that magic?

Here you will discover how you can use the structure of meaning as a formula for creating new and more enhancing magic to fill your life with more love, joy, faith, hope, and resourcefulness. Alright!

And, because everybody you meet also has *a magical formula* which governs the way they think and feel and relate, you will learn some very, very powerful magic in this book. You will discover magic for your use in interacting with others. You will learn magic that will enable you to change realities, alter the direction of life, change the past, restructure emotions, shift paradigms, leap logical levels at a single bound, jump off tall towers of terror in a single leap, utter mind-lines and see demons vanish and heavens spring into existence, and all before noon.

Does this interest you? Then come with us to explore and master your own personal neuro-linguistics and neuro-semantics. Yes, those are big words, and we will explain them in a bit. No need to fear words—especially those that promise to enrich your skills and make you a wiser and better human being. Here we aim to coach you in becoming a skilled magician so that you can use your meaning-making powers with grace and power.

Here also we will coach you in how to mine mind-lines around you every day so that you can change your mind for good about who's in charge of your brain. Once you change your mind about that, it's only a matter of practice and time before you'll develop top-notch expertise in running your own brain. Then you'll be able to make the changes you want, and keep the change as long as you desire. You will learn to become truly elegant and professional in the mind-lines you offer your associates, loved ones, and friends.

To tease your mind a little bit about the possibilities of *neuro-linguistic magic,* we have included an example here at the beginning (p. 13). Don't worry about the labels used to describe the Mind-Lines, you'll learn those later. Just allow yourself to enjoy *the "sleight of mouth" shifts* and notice which ones work most impactfully for you. The magic within language and language expressions depends on several factors: your present state, how and when someone delivers them, in what context, for what purpose, etc. Play around with them. See which ones work most powerfully with your friends.

By the way, if you haven't noticed, we have added a bit of humor in this popularization of neuro-linguistics. It was either that or bore ourselves with academically difficult concepts. We opted to have fun. We did that because we believe that we don't have to play the language game using the insights and formulations from Linguistics, General Semantics, or NLP in a boring or over-scholarly way. So come and enjoy the *play* with us. And bring along *your magic formula box.* You know, that stuff in your brain that generates the magic.

And with that, *let the wonder of magic begin!*

SECOND PREFACE
July, 1998

Mind-Lines made its advent nine months ago. Since that time, all of the attention and interest it has evoked, as well as all of the sales that it has produced, has left Bob and I not a little bit surprised and taken back. Yet thoroughly enjoying it.

Within a couple months of releasing the book, in fact, we began hearing about *NLP Study Groups* all around the USA taking up the study of the "sleight of mouth" patterns via this book.

Both of us also had opportunities in the fall and winter of 1997-98 to provide trainings in the Mind-Lines model. From that context as well as the interest of people writing and calling, we began working on *a supplement* to *Mind-Lines* to make it more applicable, understandable, and relevant.

With this newly revised edition, we have now included most of that material. What did we leave out? We did not include pages and pages of *mind-lines* from "real time exercises" applying *mind-lines* to education, business, therapy, personal development, marketing, etc. We have also left out a long presentation of the conversational reframing by Jesus of Nazareth—his *lines* for changing *minds*.

After the publication of *Mind-Lines,* we also had multiple reviewers, trainers, and readers comment about just how semantically packed they found the text of the book.
> "There's a lot of meat in that little book."
> "You have really packed that work. I find that I have to read and reread passages over and over—and still can keep on discovering insights."

Several suggested (wouldn't you know it!) that we rewrite it or create a manual to assist a person in *unpacking* the book so that they could then use it more effectively for developing their skills in conversational reframing. In the manual that we produced, we precisely aimed to unpack the magic. In this edition we have also incorporated many of the changes, insights, simplifications, and suggestions of readers. In doing so we believe we have made this volume much more practical, useful, and user-friendly.

Though we have simplified things considerably, created numerous new diagrams, a new *Mind-Lines Chart*, many more illustrations, we still recognize that this book can blow away the intellectually fragile. You have to have teeth for this one. It still necessitates that you do some pulling, biting, masticating, and digesting to get it. No soft baby food here!

Why So Semantically Packed?

When you begin to study *Mind-Lines*, it doesn't take long before you notice that you have entered into a realm that involves some complexity. What explains this complexity? Several things.

- First, via *Mind-lines* we enter into the uniquely human realm of meaning and the neuro-semantic structure of perceived reality.
- Second, this domain for most of us typically resides at a level *outside* of consciousness although we can easily bring it into consciousness.
- This realm of meaning also involves numerous linguistic, neuro-linguistic, and psycho-logics (the "logic" that we create within).
- This realm also involves numerous levels or layers because meaning involves thoughts-about-thoughts, thoughts about feelings, feelings about feelings, etc.
- This realm involves processes of reframing—the transformation of meaning, which occurs by setting new frames of reference.

We have made numerous changes: a new arrangement of the *mind-lines*. We moved the *Deframing* mind-lines so that they come first. We turned *Abstracting* into a catch-all category and moved it from being the first *Outframing* mind-line to one of the last ones. And from the first edition to the second we added four new chapters.

THIRD PREFACE
March, 2000

Lines can change minds. In the past couple years I have been introducing *Mind-Line trainings* by asking if participants have ever heard a single line that completely changed their mind? Not surprisingly, I have been hearing about all kinds of ideas that have revolutionized the lives of people. *Lines* can do that. New lines that package empowering beliefs can do just that. Lines that encode new enhancing insights can do that. And, if you express the *line* in a powerfully succinct and memorable way—presto!, magic happens.

When such *mind magic* occurs, new commands are sent to the autonomic and central nervous systems. These then, in turn, set off neurological responses and, in the end, a new felt reality springs into existence. This describes the way it is with us humans. We digest words. We metamorphize ideas. We metabolize concepts. We take the *stuff of mind* and consciousness and turn it into flesh—into muscle tensions or relaxations, into fight/flight responses, into neuro-transmitters, glandular reactions, ulcers, keen vision, and all kinds of things. That's what we mean by the terms *neuro-linguistics* and *neuro-semantics*.

We are a neuro-semantic class of life. We take the associative meanings and conceptual meanings that we create in our heads and we *embody* them in our whole being. We develop muscle-memory from these ideas and beliefs. Here lies the context with which we engage in the magic of Mind-Lines.

When you utter *lines that change minds*—you engage in a *meta-stating process.* I did not realize that when I first wrote Mind-Lines. Bob urged me in his powerful and encouraging way to begin thinking about the NLP "sleight of mouth" patterns. He thought it was time to straighten out that model and see if we could find any logical levels that might organize the structure. I didn't think we had anything significant to offer. But he used some of his "kick butt" therapy on me, and so I started.

Later, we discovered that the entire model of *Mind-Lines,* as a structured way to think about higher level conceptualizations (namely, "beliefs") were *meta-states.* After all, when you create a Mind-Line, you operate at a level *above* mere representation of thoughts. You operate in and from a meta-state, and you seek to induce new meta-state understanding in the recipient. When you learn this thoroughly—you will find this model to be a "piece of cake." You will also find your skills at Mind-Lining growing at an exponential rate. Consequently the new chapter that we have added in this third edition reflects that once you begin meta-stating, mind-lines are but the linguistic expression.

Meta-States therefore provides *the conceptual framework* for understanding and using *Mind-Lines*. So if you want to improve your ability at conversational reframing, learn the *Meta-States* model. *Mind-Lines*, as the linguistic expression of new frames that create new meanings, is a persuasion model. By it we use words and linguistic structures to enrich perception and perspective. We use lines to influence people's lives—our own and others.

In this third edition, we have added a chapter from Pascal Gambardella, Ph.D. who took the book and used it as a guide for an NLP study group in the Washington DC area. From that study, Pascal created and added numerous graphics to the Mind-Lines model that also incorporated other additions. A big thanks to him for the tremendous contribution with the new graphics.

Finally, as we prepared for this third edition, *Meta Publications* has just released Robert Dilts' latest book which deals with mind-lines, *Sleight of Mouth: The Magic of Conversational Belief Change* (1999). I have accordingly added some references to that excellent work.

FOURTH PREFACE
Yet another 100 pages has been added to the fourth edition along with a new Chapter by Denis Bridoux, *Unfolding Mind-Lines*. As we now look back on this work and its ongoing evolution, we realize that this book is actually the first *Neuro-Semantics book* and the foundation work that latter led to *Frame Games* (2000).

FIFTH PREFACE
What more can we add to introduce this ever-evolving book about communication, meaning, beliefs, change and transformation, and persuasion? Oh yes, we've added a new chapter, *Super-Charging Beliefs with Mind-Lines*. Not only can we use Mind-Lines to transform negative beliefs, now we can beef up any belief that we want to be more robust and vigorous.

Enjoy, discover, and experience the transformation! The world is at your command if you know and can use the power of framing and the seven forms of reframing that you will discover in this book. May your lines be truly magical in their transformative power and may you become shamelessly wealthy on the inside as you enjoy touching people with healing magic with your words!

MIND-LINING
A TOXIC IDEA

The following pages will enable you to discover and learn all about *a magical three-dimensional box.* This is where the magic of meaning occurs. Inside that box or cube we all have a neurological and linguistic formula that governs how we construct "meaning." This induces us into mind-body or neuro-semantic states. Then, throughout the text of this book you will discover how to find this *magic box,* how to understand it, how to transform it, and how to pull out *magical lines* from that box to conversationally reframe someone's thinking (even your own).

By the time you complete this work, you will have learned more than two dozen explicit ways to reframe beliefs, ideas, and understandings. This means that when you tune into your own internal dialogue of meaning-making, or when you listen to someone else's, and you hear ideas that poison the mind, disrupt the emotions, or sabotage effective living—*you now will have at least twenty-six ways to transform that conceptual reality.*

How about that? Talk about having more choices and options regarding *how to look at things!* Having at least twenty-six ways to frame your thinking will give you twenty-six choices and alternatives regarding how to *feel,* how to *respond,* and how to look at things. Talk about a mind-expanding model—that's *Mind-Lines.*

To encourage you to work through the theoretical chapters of this book to deepen your understanding and appreciation of *language* itself as magic and then to tackle the *reframing directions*, here is an example of how *lines* can transform our mind and life. You will find many other examples in this book to stimulate your playful creativity.

We offer this one here because many people operate from the *idea* that anything that blocks immediate success is "failure" and that means "Failure" with a big F. What foolishness! Here are twenty-six ways to put new frames around this idea that will expand your thinking and give you more ways to frame things. You really can't "run your own brain" if you don't know how to frame things to empower your efforts and to put positive spins on things.

26 Ways to Reframe "Failure"
There are some toxic ideas in the following statement. Can you detect them? What are they? What is the external event and what is the internal state?
"Whenever I don't succeed, it really bothers me. It makes me feel like

a failure. Not reaching my goals is such a bummer. I get depressed. No wonder I put things off and hesitate about other things. I just hate being a failure."

1) Specificity or "Chunking" Down

So you think you *are* a "failure," do you? As you think about something for which you feel like a failure, and define yourself as such, *how* do you know to do this? If you lost a job once, are you a failure? Twice? Three times? What standard are you using to make this judgment? How do you know to use *that* standard? When, where, and with whom did this occur? How do you represent this generalization of being a "failure?" What pictures, sounds, feelings, and words do you use to create this meaning? If I were to get a sneak peak into the mental theater of your mind—what would I see? How would I know to give it the same name that you have, that is, to call it "failure?" How do you represent the action of failing at one thing as "making" you a failure?

2) Sequencing a Strategy

So up until now, you have accepted the idea of viewing and defining yourself as "a failure." Help me understand this. *How specifically* do you know that failing at one thing on a particular day makes you "a failure?" What do you see first, then what do you say about that, and so on as you think about this? If I were someone from the Temporary Job Agency and I could take your place so that you could have a vacation from this, teach me *how to do this the way you do*. What would I have to think, see, hear, and feel?

3) Reframing the External Behavior

Are you sure this means "failure," could it just mean feedback? *Not* reaching some important goals really means that you now have some crucial information about how *not* to get there. So, with that in mind, you can feel free to explore new possible avenues, can you not?

4) Reframing the Internal State

How interesting that you say that. What I really find as a failure, and I mean Failure with a big **"F"** is when someone who does not reach a goal sits down to wallow in whining and refuses to try again. When the person rolls over in the mud and won't learn or try again, I'd call that a "failure." If you're still giving it a go, you are not a failure.

5) Reflexively Applying To Self

Does that mean if you don't reach your goal in presenting this limiting and painful belief to me, that just talking to me will turn you into an even bigger failure? You have to succeed at this communication or it will mean that and *that* only?

So as you think about not reaching a goal and labeling it as making you a "failure," I take it that you do this a lot? You take a specific instance and over-generalize it into a whole category? And you successfully do this, don't you? Would you like to fail at this success?

6) Reflexively Applying to a Listener

So with that way of thinking about things, if I don't succeed in coming up with a good way of responding and helping you with this limiting belief, I will also become a failure? In other words, my success or failure as a human being depends on succeeding in this conversation in just the right way? There's no room for experimenting, feedback, or dialogue?

7) Counter-Example Framing

When you think about some of your successes—and how good and resourceful you feel about them, you mean if you mispronounce a word, or fail in any aspect of any goal surrounding that goal, *that* would turn you into a failure? "Success" is that fragile of a thing and "failure" is that solid?

8) Positive Prior Intentional Framing

Reaching the goals that you set for yourself must mean a lot to you. I can imagine that you develop this perspective to protect yourself from messing things up and to push yourself to higher levels. Since you want that, don't you think that perhaps some other attitudes about failure might help you to really succeed in your goals?

9) Positive Prior Causation Framing

It strikes me that it's important for you to set and reach goals. So you probably have taken on this limiting belief because you have had some painful experiences in the past and you now want to protect yourself against such. Perhaps it was those experiences that actually seduced you into that limiting belief. What other beliefs could you build that you would find even more effective than this one?

10) First Outcome Framing

What results when you move through life defining experiences and yourself as "failures" just because you don't reach a goal in precisely the way you want to? Does this serve you well in setting and reaching goals or in feeling successful? Do you like those negative unresourceful feelings?

11) Outcome of Outcome Framing

Imagine going out, say five or even ten years from now, after you have defined every unsuccessful attempt at reaching a goal as turning you into a "failure," and then living from *that "failure" identity* and feeling unresourceful … what will come out of that? Will you take on many risks? What other outcomes emerge when you feel like a "failure" and take that into your future?

12) Eternity Framing

When I think about this, I wonder what you will think when you look back on this belief about failure when you step over into eternity, and I wonder how you will think and feel about this limiting belief that you used in moving through life?

13) Model of the World Framing

It really is an interesting way to think about events because it overloads them with so much meaning! Do you know where you got this way of mapping about "one un-success equals failing?" Do you know that most people don't use that map to torture themselves?

14) Criteria and Value Framing

When you think about your values of enjoying life, appreciating people, doing your best, experimenting, learning, etc., do you not think of those values as more important than making a "success / failure" judgment about your actions?

15) Allness Framing

So since everybody has failed at something at some time in life, that must make everybody on this planet a "failure," a complete and absolute "failure," right?

16) Have-To Framing

So you *have to* frame your attempts at reaching a goal in this way? What would it feel like for you if you did not evaluate events in terms of success or failure? What would happen if you didn't do that? Suppose you framed attempts as experiments, feedback, or playing around?

17) Identity Framing

What an interesting belief about your self-identity—so totally dependent on your behaviors. Do you always *identify* people with their behaviors? Do you really consider that people *are* their behaviors and nothing more than their behaviors?

18) Ecology Framing

How enhancing do you find this belief when learning a new skill, trying a new sport, taking a risk, or practicing a new social behavior? Would you recommend this belief as a way for others to succeed with greater ease and positive feelings? Does it empower or limit your endeavors?

19) Other Abstractions Framing

The idea of "failure" really seems like a distressful and painful idea and yet you say that it really doesn't serve to enhance your actions or motivate you, so I'm just wondering if maybe this isn't a faulty map that just needs to *evaporate or vanish from the screen of your mind* because it isn't sufficiently real to be useful, but of course, if you allowed it to just *fade away* so that you focused more on using feedback for success, how would that empower you to get on with things?

20) Metaphoring and Storying Framing

1) So if you brush your hair but do not get every single strand of hair in just the right place, that also makes you a failure?

2) When my daughter Jessica turned nine months, she began the process of learning to walk, but she couldn't walk upon the first

attempt—nor upon the first hundred attempts. She constantly fell down and she would sometimes cry. But she would always get up and do it again. As she did, she learned more and she developed more strength in her legs, and more balance and movement, so that eventually she got the hang of it, and had a lot of fun in the process. And I wonder if this says anything that you can *take and apply to yourself now.*

There you have it—*twenty ways to play around with meaning and to alter the structure of reality!* And, given the introduction of Chapter 17, here are six more.

21) Both/And Framing

It sounds like so much of life is *either success or failure* and that there's hardly anything that you notice in-between. It seems like the boundary between what you call 'success' and 'failure' has hardly any distance so that you can step from one to the other in a moment. How useful would you find it to be able to measure *the degree* of these states? Or, perhaps, even better, to recognize that they can both occur at the same time?

22) Pseudo-Word Framing

So you're using this term "failure" with a lot of abandon and yet we haven't been able to actually point to any specific reference, either in the world or even in concept. Perhaps it's actually a pseudo-word that you've been tricked by the linguistic fraud of the label itself. Since it refers to nothing *real* or *tangible*, but only to a mapped construct in your mind, do you really need to use this non-referencing term?

23) Negation Framing

I know this isn't possible, but I'm just wondering what would it be like for you if you couldn't compute the meaning of "failure." As you think about 'failure' as a non-existing concept, as an experience you cannot experience, because you always get information and feedback, and discover how not to do something, I'm curious about how much more resourceful that would be.

24) Possibility and "As If" Framing

Since the state and experience of "failure" has been so unproductive and painful, take a moment to imagine the possibility of living in a world where being a "failure" could not occur, because you were so focused on always gathering more data about how to refine your actions ... now just pretend that you are there fully and completely and as you do, show me the face of that state, and the posture, and the breathing, good...

25) Systemic and Probability Framing

What's the probability that when you start this new project that you will totally and absolutely fail at it 100%, like someone who knew nothing at all about it? To what extent do you think you'll fail at it within the first 15 minutes? The first day? What about the first month? What are some of the other factors and contributing influences that could improve your odds at making this successful?

26) Decision Framing

Now that you have entertained several new ideas about this whole realm of succeeding and failing, what have you actually decided serves you best? What frame would empower you to get on with life, bounce with the ups and downs, and forever put yourself in a learning orientation? Have you decided to feed and nurture your mind on that idea? What one thing will you do today to begin this new way of moving through the world?

Lines can change minds. Lines can shift the meaning frames we give to experiences and ideas and can influence us in powerful ways. Lines can persuade us to think about things in ways that truly support our ongoing empowerment. So, in the following chapters, you will learn *how* such neuro-linguistic magic works and *how* to become *a master magician* of the word magic at your command.

PART I:

THE LANGUAGE

AS MAGIC

FRAMEWORK

"You don't need to take drugs
to hallucinate;
improper language
can fill your world with problems
and spooks
of many kinds."

Robert A. Wilson

Chapter 1

NEURO-LINGUISTIC MAGIC

"Magic is hidden in the language we speak.
The webs that you can tie and untie are at your command
if only you pay attention to what you already have
(language) and the structure of the incantations for growth."
Bandler and Grinder (1975)

The field of NLP (Neuro-Linguistic Programming) began in 1975 with the appearance of, *The Structure of Magic*. The subtitle that Richard Bandler and John Grinder gave it describes its emphasis, *"A Book about Language and Therapy."* That academic work made explicit something that we have known for a long, long time. Namely, the power of language to effect mind and emotion. They described the underlying structure behind the process of how words and symbols can have such seemingly *magical effects* upon people—upon minds, bodies, relationships, skills, understandings, health, etc.

But wait a minute.
*   *How* can mere words have *that pervasive of* an effect?
*   What forces, powers, principles, processes, mechanisms, etc. operate in the human mind-body system that explains such a powerful effect?

Bandler and Grinder found and experienced the *magic* of words in three diverse fields: Family Systems Therapy, Gestalt Therapy, and Ericksonian Hypnosis. Yet they *explained* the structure of the magic using the insights of other fields: General Semantics, Transformational Grammar, Cybernetics, and Cognitive Behavioral Psychology. Subsequently, they gave birth to a new movement which took up the term Alfred Korzybski introduced in 1936, *"neuro-linguistics."*

As a term, *neuro-linguistics* holistically summarizes *the mind-body connection* between language (words, symbols, etc.) and neurology. It specifies *how* our neurology (i.e., nervous system and brain) processes language and thereby responds to our languaging.

This begins to explain the seemingly *magical effects* that can occur within our "mind," "emotions," "body," etc. via the use of words. Words, while totally powerless to effect and change *external* reality, conversely have almost complete power to create, alter, change, destroy, and invent *internal* reality. We can say *"Abracadabra"* all we want to sides of mountains, doors, stalled cars, bank teller machines, and soda machines and do so until we turn blue in the face and nothing will happen (except the raising of our blood pressure). Rats!

But watch the explosion that can occur when you utter the tiniest little *idea* to a mind. For then, lo and behold, you can start a war, invent a new way of living, change your blood pressure, induce a deep state of depression, motivate yourself for higher levels of excellence, suffer psychosis, come to your "right mind," or create a million other magical effects in human experience.

If you have heard of Neuro-Linguistic Programming, then you have probably heard about, or perhaps even seen, some of the wonderful and marvelous NLP techniques. When most people think of NLP—those who know of it, think about the techniques of NLP that seem to work their magic rapidly and with surprising ease. Perhaps they have seen or heard about the ten-minute phobia cure.[1]

As a psychologist I simply could not believe that a person could "cure" (come on, get realistic!) a phobia in ten-minutes. My first response to that ideas was, "No way, that's impossible!"

Even after I read the instructions for re-structuring a person's neuro-linguistic coding (or internal program) for a phobia, I still couldn't see how it could work. "No way."

Then, I ran that Movie Rewind pattern with several people and to my utter surprise, while a minute prior to the process the person could make his or her neurology go into an absolutely freaked-out state of total panic and autonomic nervous system arousal by *just thinking* about some averse stimuli, a few minutes later, the person could *think about* the same object *and* remain calm and cool. It was incredible. I would even invite people to really try as hard as they could to freak out. But they couldn't.

Now I was really curious. What gives here? How can we explain this amazing transformation in human personality except by calling upon the gods?
- What processes drive these neurological responses?
- How do people get programmed, so to speak, inside their heads-bodies so that they can freak-out without a moment's notice, automatically,

regularly, systematically, and without even *thinking* about it consciously? That's really quite a skill!
• What internal program drives or runs this kind of thing?

It seems like a piece of magic when you think about it, doesn't it?
• *How* does the same person alter his or her internal program so that it subsequently operates in a completely new and different way?
• What languaging and symbolization would a person have to mentally entertain to pull off a different kind of behavior?
• How does the Movie Rewind pattern work to so completely transform a person's meanings and neurological responses?

Neuro-linguistics is a field that addresses these central questions about how we operate. NLP offers insights, models, and technologies for "running your own brain" more efficiently, effectively, and "magically."

When Bob and I began our journey into the field of NLP, we first put the emphasis on learning the techniques and applying them effectively. In doing this, we became technicians. Only later did we transmute into neuro-linguistic philosophers to the chagrin of our loved ones as we sought to understand how it all worked. In the process we became increasingly conscious of the power and use of language in creating change. Not a surprising turn of events. After all, NLP began with an in-depth understanding of *how language works in human neurology* in the first place, and how our languaging in a variety of *modes* creates our human "programs" for thinking, feeling, speaking, behaving, and relating. That's why it is *not* about linguistics, it is about *neuro*-linguistics, the languages that affect our states.

When we use *linguistics* here, we refer not only to the symbolic system of propositional language, but also to the *sensory-based languages* of the mind, that is, what we see, hear, feel, smell, and taste. We call this our *movie mind*. The jargon of NLP calls this "the VAK representational systems." Linguistics also includes metaphorical language (i.e., stories, narratives, metaphors, etc.), as well as mathematics, music, icons, and other symbolic systems.

While we separate linguistics from *neuro-linguistics,* even this is only a way of talking. As a verbal separation, we can do this only at the conceptual level, not the level of reality. In reality our mind-body-emotion system works as a whole. As neuro-linguistic creatures, what we say affects what we experience.

Neuro-Linguistic Creatures?
Ah, a new term! This term indicates that when we signal in our "mind," via various symbol systems (such as our linguistics), it always and inevitably affects in our "body." It can do none other. Mind-body is a system.

This explains *the hyphen*. The hyphen enables us to mentally and linguistically map a set of representations that structurally corresponds to the territory. Alfred Korzybski (1933/1994) invented this in his classical work, *Science and Sanity*. Using the hyphen prevents the elementalism of "mind" *and* "body" from misdirecting us in imagining that these are independent things. In 1936, he introduced the term *neuro-linguistic* and conducted *Neuro-Linguistic Trainings* using General Semantic processes.

And the point is? The point is that what we do "mentally" and "linguistically" activates neurological processes in our bodies. We are inescapably mind-body creatures.

> [Have you noticed our use of quotes around certain words such as "mind" "body," etc.? This Korzybskian device cues us that while we use a particular word to linguistically map something, it fails to adequately represent the territory. The *quotes* calls attention to the term as one with which we need to take special care.]

In this book we present many of the language patterns that you will find in the *Neuro-Linguistic model* and offer them as a way that we can increase our understanding in communication and competence in communicating with more elegance and skill. As you read and learn about how various **lines** for the **mind** *(mind-lines)* operate, we hope that you will enjoy discovering all of the magic these powerful language patterns offer.

In the process, we trust that you will develop a more intuitive understanding about how language works, how it works in neurology, how it constructs our internal "realities," and how it serves us as either a resource or a limitation. Yet the language patterns that you find here only represent the hem of the garment regarding the possibilities and opportunities of creating neuro-linguistic *magic*. As you go out to perform *magic* with the language you use with yourself and others, you can therefore maintain a wonderfully curious attitude about all of the yet-to-be-discovered patterns, can you not?

Life, Communication, Language

Life us a network of relationships. It involves relationships of relationships (we can relate to our relatings). Sometimes we use another big, fat, vague word in addition to *relationship* to describe this phenomenon. We use *communication*. Yet what do we actually mean by these words?

The critical NLP approach to language is to *de-nominalize* big, fat, vague nouns (or noun-like words) words and identify the underlying and hidden *verbs* lurking within.[2] This enables us to find a verb, a word that point to actions (movements, processes, things relating to one another). So, in the word "relationship," we have something in relation to another.

- But what? Who or what relates to what?
- When does this relating occur?
- In what way?
- How and for what purpose?

It's the same story with the term "communication." Hidden within this verb-turned-into-a-noun (or nominalization) a hidden verb lurks. Imagine that! Undoubtedly, some magician has waved a magic wand and presto, a set of movements and actions have been named and solidified, have become static, have stopped moving, and have become a statue-like *thing*—frozen in time and space. Wow! What word magic.

Now sometimes this works in powerful and wonderful ways to bless us. It encodes in a little tiny word a rich and extensive concept. Look at the first line in this section, "Life us a network of relationships." We there took two nominalizations (verbs turned into nouns) with a verb ("is") and a metaphor ("network") and tied them together to create an induction in the Land of Nominalizations. Let's examine the neuro-linguistics of this:

- How did it affect you?
- How did you make sense of that line?
- Where did it send you?

This symbolization, "Life us a network of relationships" represents a very high level abstraction of thought *about* a great many things. Talk about a generalization. It summarizes so much; it implies so much. I wonder what meanings you filled in when you first read those words. Hypnotic language pre-eminently works this way which we will get to in Chapter 9 about Metaphor.

- What specifically *relates* back and forth, and how and when, and in what network that makes up "life?"

"Relationship" only describes the unspecific process of one or more things relating (or interacting). *"Communication"* informs us that we *commune* some message (information, meaning) back and forth (*co*-mmunication). Ah, that sheds a little more light! As *information* moves from one thing to another, and/or passes back and forth between organisms or within facets (parts) of organisms—this describes "life."

To make this clear and precise we have to consider this abstract principle ("life us a network of relationships") in some particular context. Let's do this with the "life" of the human body.

Our sense receptors (eyes, ears, skin, taste buds, etc.) receive *input* of information from "the dance of electrons" out there in the process world of energy manifestations (we here describe the world in terms of modern physics).

From there, the neurology of our body *transforms* that information into nerve impulses and chemical "messages" that move along neuro-pathways. That *information* then experiences more *transformations* as it activates cells and cell assemblages in the cortex, which then passes that *information* on to appropriate "parts," whether the central nervous system, the autonomic nervous system, the immune system, etc.

Ah, *"life"*—the living, moving, information processing, sentient experience of "responding to the environment"—something that non-living, non-sentient things can't do—exists, functions, and operates by the *relating* and *communing* of messages. Okay, enough neuro-physiology, back to language.

Language Coding of Information

"Language" summarizes how we *encode*, in various symbolic formats, information. Actually we can and do encode information in various *modes* of awareness, modes or *modalities* that enable us to "communicate" to ourselves and others. The sensory modes that we mostly use to communicate involve using pictures, sounds, sensations (movements, touch), smells and tastes. These *sensory representational systems* make up our *movie mind*.

The encoding doesn't stop there. We can make many more specific *distinctions* using the representational systems. We can frame these modalities of sight, sound, sensation, smell, and taste with numerous qualities. These qualities create instructions for how to frame the internal cinema of our movie mind. NLP originally called these *"sub-modalities"* but we now know that they are meta-modalities to the sensory representations (see Appendix A and *Sub-Modalities Going Meta*, 2005).

Above and beyond the *sensory level* of representation we have sensory-based words (*Figure 1:1*). These empirically based terms encode or represent (as a symbol of a symbol) the information that we want to pass on about sights, sounds, sensations, smells, and tastes. We use sensory-based language to say such things as the following:

> "Would you turn around (K) and look (V) at the dirt on the carpet? Do you see (V) the dirt that forms the shape of *your* footprints? Now what do you have to say (A_d) about that?"

Notice the movie-like scenario which these words mentally evoke or the emotions that are stimulated. The sensory-based symbols is the basis of our movie mind and describe how we represent things in our mind. As a notational system, NLP uses the following basic *modalities*.

- **Visual** (pictures, sights, images)
- **Auditory** (sounds, noise, music, tones)
- **Kinesthetic** (sensations, physical feelings of the body)

- **O**lfactory (smells)
- **G**ustatory (tastes)

While we think of words as language, words actually enable us to evoke an even more basic language of the mind, our movie mind of sights (V), sounds (A), sensations (K), etc. Now we do not *literally* have a movie in our mind, let alone a movie screen in our "mind" or even pictures or sounds. In our head, we have neurons, neural pathways, neuro-transmitters, chemicals, assemblages, etc. At that level of experience it is all chemistry.

Yet we experience *the phenomena* of sights, sounds, and sensations. To us it *seems as if* we are seeing images, hearing sounds, and even re-experiencing sensations, smells, tastes, etc. This *phenomenological experience* describes how our move mind with all of its representations operate as a language code for consciousness, information, messages, and for thinking. So we *language* ourselves with sights, sounds, and sensations to "think" about and recall experiences.[3]

Figure 1:1
Levels of Abstracting

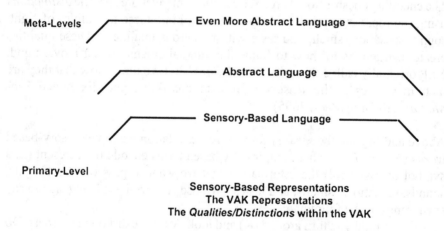

Let us now move up another level. Beyond the first languaging system of sense receptors which transduces external stimuli (information) into our bodies (creating before language awareness), we have our *neurological languaging* (the sensory signaling on the "screen" in our mind full of sights and sounds). After that we have *sensory-based words* (first level of *linguistic languaging*). After that we represent *abstract or non-sensory based language.*

Non-sensory based language refers to all language that becomes even more abstract as we delete more of the specific sensory information and generalize to a higher level. In this way we create a model of reality via these symbolic processes.

Figure 1:2
Meta-Levels

Language and Symbols
about
Lower level Modalities
(Working systemically and self-reflexively so that
it *feeds back* new data into the mind-body system)

Basic Level

Location of images	Location of sounds	Location of sensations
Distance	Distance	What
Snapshot-movie	# of Sound sources	Still or Moving
(Still — moving)	Music, Noise, Voice	Pressure
Number of images	Whose Voice	Area — Extent
Bordered/ Panoramic	Tone	Intensity
Color / Black-and-white	Volume (low to high)	Temperature
Shape, form	Clarity —Intelligibility	Moisture
Size	Pitch (low to high)	Texture
Horizontal & Vertical	Melody	Rhythm
Associated/ Dissociated		Smells
3D or Flat (2D)		Tastes
Brightness (from dull		Balance
to bright)		
Foreground/ background		
contrast		

Movie Mind
Our representational screen of consciousness
(sensed not actual)

Visual — Auditory — **Kinesthetic** — Olfactory — Gustatory
Sights —— Sounds — Sensations —— Smells —— Tastes

With more and more abstract language, we can now say or write things like the following. Read and enjoy:

> "Objective consideration of contemporary phenomena compels the conclusion that success or failure in competitive activities exhibits no tendency to be commensurate with innate capacity, but that a considerable element of the unpredictable must invariably be taken into account."

Did you like that? Thank George Orwell for that one (*Shooting an Elephant and Other Essays,* 1950). Pretty abstract, right? Sounds "intellectual," right? Did the question, "What in the world does he mean with all of that?" come to you while you read that? This is the danger of abstractions. Load up a sentence with too many nominalizations and then the mapping processes of deletion, generalization, and distortion (the three key modeling processes to be described later) leave us so high up the scale of abstraction that we can get lost in terms of understanding and have to invent our own meanings (i.e., hallucinate meanings) in an attempt to make sense of it.

Would you like to see the original piece from which Orwell created his "intellectual" abstraction? As you read the following, notice the original test in terms of its sensory-based referents, referents you can see, hear, and feel and use for your internal cinema of the mind.

> "I returned and saw under the sun that the race is not to the swift, nor the battle to the strong, neither yet bread to men of understanding, nor yet favor to men of skill; but time and chance happens to them all." (Ecclesiastes 9:11).

While we have some nominalizations in that one (most notably "time"), it basically presents *a sensory-based description of events* that we can see, hear, and feel. It offers us the kind of symbols that we can more easily use in signaling our brain to create an internal movie. It gives us lots of empirical words pointing to real-time nouns, things that we can actually represent. We can make a movie out of those words without much trouble.

What's the point? When we *go meta* to a higher logical level of symbolization and use more abstract words (nominalizations, class words, abstractions, etc.), we use a different kind of representational system, a non-sensory based modality. We call this higher-level abstraction *auditory-digital* (A_d) and because we can continue the process of saying more words about words, we can create ever more abstract words and language forms.[4]

Using Language Patterns To Make a Difference
With this introduction about the various forms and "logical levels" of language (the levels of abstracting), we can easily see how language patterns play a

relevant and inescapable role in all areas of life. Whether in the structure or system of families, businesses, churches, schools, political parties, or any social environment, we have to use language. Language influences and effects the "life" of the system: enhancing and/or limiting, creating and/or destroying.

Therefore, *language patterns* truly offer a gold mine of opportunity where we can enrich our lives. Such language patterns provide us more understanding about how we effect the "life" of such systems by the way we talk, the symbols we use, and how we language ourselves and others. These language patterns empower us with more flexibility of behavior necessary to more effectively manage or control a given interaction.

When we know the outcome for our communication, we can utilize various language patterns to move the conversation in the direction we desire as we relate to another person. This enhances our powers of persuasion, influence, clarity, and much more.

In addition, our language both *reflects* and *describes* our model of the world. It arises through the modeling processes of deletion, generalization, and distortion from our deep structure of neurological representations of the thing we have seen, heard, felt, etc.

Is this important in our everyday talk? You bet! It's important because ultimately the secret in how to move a person (ourselves or another) in a particular direction involves languaging. It involves understanding how language works, what language does within us, and how we make sense of language through the movies that are evoked in the theater of our mind. As we language ourselves and others we evoke the creation of movies, see-hear-feel representations along with the words which, in turn, activate the mind-body-emotion system to conjure up the corresponding states.

In the final analysis we *influence* and *persuade* ourselves and others by means of symbols, and particularly, words. Words influence because they evoke us to create representations in our minds at multiple levels. We track over referents and ideas onto the "screen of our mind." We then generalize *about* those representations, classify them, categorize them, etc. as we go meta to our snapshots and movies. This structures our minds, constructs our Matrix of meanings, sends commands to our nervous systems, and creates our felt sense of reality. Pretty powerful, these things called "words," wouldn't you say?

How do we do all of this? *How* can we tell that we have succeeded in influencing a mind? Should we seek to persuade others? To answer such questions, in the next chapter we will jump right into exploring ... *three facets of neuro-linguistic magic.*

Summary

- The *magic* of words lies in how we use them as symbols for representing and conceptualizing, for creating our mental movies and for framing them with various cinematic features ("sub-modalities"), and for setting numerous other multiple frames.

- The *magic* in languaging minds with words and sentences operates according to a structured format that we can learn and use. Language works *magically* in our minds-and-bodies because we are a semantic class of life—neuro-linguistic creatures.

- The *magic* lies in the code. Change the code, and the magic changes.

- There is not only *structure* to the magic, the structure of the sensory systems, and the levels of abstraction, but there are also *secrets* to the magic that puts incantations of growth (and pathology) at our disposal.

End Notes:

1. The Movie Rewind pattern is in the book, *MovieMind* (2003) and *The SourceBook of Magic* (Volume I). In some of the technical jargon of NLP, this is sometimes called the visual-kinesthetic dissociation pattern.

2. In the Meta-Model of Language, a *nominalization* is a verb that's been *nominalized*, that is, turned into a noun. Well, almost turned into a noun. Technically, a *noun* is a person, place, or thing. Technically, you can see, hear, and feel a real live thing like a person, place, or thing. As a thing it occupies space, has mass and form, etc. But a verb-turned-into-a-noun is just an idea and has no empirical reality. You can't put it on a chair, in a wheelbarrow, or in a refrigerator. To *de-nominalize* it we have to recover the verb and pop the illusion that the nominalization is an actual thing.

3. Is the word "languaging" is new to you? Here we use "language" as a verb and do so because we typically use *language* as a nominalization. Yet language is not a thing. Language refers to a set of processes. So by de-nominalizing it, we engage in more accurate mapping and take charge of our languaging. In our "language behavior" we use symbol systems to create or construct our internal "realities." We will talk more about that later.

4. *Meta* is a Greek word that refers to anything "above," "beyond," or "about" something else. To *go meta* refers to moving up to a higher level and thinking *about* the lower level. Awareness *about* our awareness is meta, it is self-awareness. When we apply the state of curiosity to the state of learning, curiosity is *meta* to learning. This creates the meta-state of *curious learning*.

Chapter 2

THREE FACETS OF
NEURO-LINGUISTIC MAGIC

"The most fundamental goal of applying
the verbal patterns of sleight of mouth
is to help people to shift their perspective
1) from a problem frame to an outcome frame,
2) from a failure frame to a feedback frame, and
3) from an impossibility frame to an 'as if' frame."
Robert Dilts (1999, p. 25)

What does it take to become highly skilled with the *Mind-Lines* model? Obviously, we have to develop an understanding of *the magic* that lies within words, language, and the use of symbols. We also have to clearly grasp the structure of *neuro-linguistic magic* regarding how it works and the mechanisms that drive it. Are you up to speed on these facets of neuro-linguistic magic? If not, this chapter will provide you insight to the three kinds of *languaging spells* available to you in everyday language. These three spells give us—

- The Spell of Specificity
- The Spell of Evaluation
- The Spell of Embedded Framing

1) The Language and Spell of Specificity
Use this kind of language to cast spells for precision and clarity or when you want to deframe a limiting or sabotaging frame.

Remember what we did with the sensory-based illustration earlier, the rebuke that I imagined a mother might say to a child?

"Would you turn around (K) and look (V) at the dirt on the carpet? Do you see (V) the dirt that forms the shape of your footprints? Now what do you have to say (A_d)about that?"

How *clearly* did those words communicate to you? If you go with that description for a moment, simply respond to the words as if they were instructions. Begin with the words, "Turn around and look," etc. You may not have carpet under your feet where you are this very moment, so you may have to pretend what a carpet would look, sound, and feel like. You may not be standing, yet you can imagine yourself standing. You may not be standing inside a room, but again, you can pretend, can you not?

To "influence" you with these words to signal your brain to run this particular movie as you have, we only needed to provide you *clear, precise, and specific symbols.* This is the *magic* of communicating with precision. Words of precision work as a director's instruction for making a film or directing a play. The words provide specific instruction about how to conjure the movie that's in his or her mind.

Similarly, for us to invite another person to move their internal representations in a specific direction, we get them to make a movie that corresponds to the one in our head by simply *describing* to our loved one, client, or customer what we see, hear, sense, and say inside our head.

It all sounds very simple, doesn't it? Well, it's not really that simple. And, why, pray tell, not? It's not simple because most people don't know how to talk in sensory-based terms. Instead, we typically do what humans all over the planet do all too well and too quickly. We *go meta* and head to the ozone of the higher levels of abstraction. Then, from those heights of abstraction we talk using lots of evaluative terms. As we do, we end up talking in non-sensory based terms. And while these seem clear to us, they provide no precise sensory instructions to another.

> "You are so rude to come into my clean house and make a filthy mess. I get so angry at your irresponsibility!"

Ah, a different kind of confrontation from the former one, don't you think? By the way, this illustrates an extremely powerful NLP technology. If we need to say something unpleasant or "confrontative" (another nominalization)—*we can say almost anything to anybody if we use sensory-based descriptive language.* Conversely, we can say almost nothing to anybody if we use evaluative, non-sensory based language. Of course, like everything in this book, don't take our word for this, try it out for yourself.

We truly enrich our language and communication skills when we use increasingly more specific visual, auditory, kinesthetic, and sensory-based language components about the movie that we have constructed in our head. Reread the Orwell passage and the biblical referent in Chapter One (page 28). Which makes more sense? Which do you find easier to understand?

NEURO-LINGUISTIC MAGIC

What can you do with *neuro*-linguistic magic?
What are three kinds of *neuro*-linguistic magic?
What spells can you cast with this kind of magic?

1) The Language and Spell of Specificity
   Use this kind of language to cast spells for precision and clarity or when you want to deframe a limiting or sabotaging frame.

2) The Language and Spell of Evaluation
   Use to cast a spell that constructs new realities and that reframes old realities.

3) The Language and Spell of Embedded Framing
   Use to cast higher spells that outframe all meanings to transform things in one fell swoop.[2]

To communicate with more clarity and precision, we have to become highly *descriptive*. The words will flow out of your mouth as you *specifically describe* what you actually experience and represent, and what you wish for the one with whom you communicate. Without the ability to distinguish *descriptive* and *evaluative* language, you will never become truly professional or elegant in your use of language. So begin here. Begin at learning the power and simplicity of see-hear-feel language (sensory-based language). It provides *the magic of clarity, the magic of precision, and the magic that deframes.*

Deframes? Yes, it pulls apart old constructions or frames. It pulls apart abstractions that confuse. More about that in Chapter Five on Deframing.

2) The Language and Spell of Evaluation
   Use to cast a spell that constructs new realities and that reframes old realities.
Given what we've said about the language of precision and specificity, the question may arise, "Should we therefore *never* use abstract or non-sensory based language?" And the answer may surprise you, "Of course not."

Reflecting on our evaluations and evaluating them, and transcending them to draw even higher level abstractions and conclusions represents our uniqueness and glory as human beings. Non-sensory based language and abstracting is not a curse. But we need to do so *mindfully* and thoughtfully, or as Korzybski put it, with "consciousness of abstracting."

Here, too, NLP provides a most wonderful paradigm and tool for guiding our understanding of *what we do with words,* and the effect that our languaging has on ourselves and others.

Many times, instead of getting a person to accurately and specifically represent information with certain sensory signals for specific movies, we need to move them to a higher level. From there we can offer new and different ways of abstracting and conceptualizing. When we do that, it enables the other person to *set a whole new frame of reference* that will transform everything. Using such language enables us to construct new "realities," create new meanings, establish new reference systems, and call new worlds into existence as we build new matrices. Sometimes this moves a person from one position at a meta-level to another level.

For instance, suppose a father sees his teenage son lying on the couch watching TV. At this point, we only have a sensory-based set of representations, right? Or have you already drawn a conclusion and evaluated it? Suppose the father sees his son and immediately jumps a "logical level" to classify that behavior as a member of the class that we call "laziness." In doing that he sets *laziness* as his frame and perceptual filter. He looks at the specific behaviors and no longer sees them as sensory-based pieces of information. He looks and sees *Laziness* with a capital L. Right?

Of course, "laziness" does *not* exist in the world. Yes, we suspect that you might have begun to smile at this statement, but go with us for a moment, it will make more sense in a bit and then your smile will be that of a new and more exciting quality.

What exists in the world is simply the see-hear-feel information: a boy lying on a couch, watching TV. The meanings that we (as meaning-makers) give to that inner movie evoked by those sensory signals depend upon our beliefs, values, understandings, abstractions, and paradigms. It depends on our *frames.* What are we using as references? Some parents may look at the same signals, and using *other* frames may say,

> "I'm so glad John can relax and enjoy the good things of life, unlike my traumatic childhood and I'm so thrilled that I can provide for him all the things I never got."

Isn't that what your parents would say? It could happen. *Meaning* ("semantics") exists only and exclusively in the "mind." It exists and arises as *a form of evaluation and appraisal.* It occurs through bringing other *frames-of-reference* to bear upon the see-hear-feel movie that we represent.

Consider what this suggests. It suggests that *meaning* is a higher "logical level" abstraction *about* the sensory information of the movie. *Meaning* operates as information-about-information at a higher level. It involves meta-level thoughts *about* lower level thoughts. For these higher levels, we will reserve and use the term *neuro-semantic.* We will do this in contradistinction to the term *neuro-linguistic* for the primary level of sensory-based descriptions.[1]

While this is an arbitrary definition we have found it an useful distinction between the associations and meanings that we experience at the primary level when our consciousness *goes out* to recognize and represent the world and when our consciousness *comes back onto itself* to have thoughts about its thoughts. In *reframing,* we essentially do a horizontal shift at the meta-level that basically says,

Figure 2:1

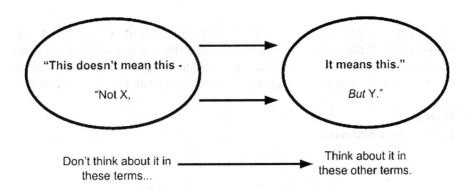

"John isn't being lazy, he simply really knows how to relax and enjoy himself."
"Jill isn't rude, she just forgot to wipe her feet."
"Jerry isn't ugly and hateful, he has just gotten into a very unresourceful state and feels really threatened."
"Terri isn't trying to put you down, she just feels overwhelmed and has become emotionally preoccupied with three little ones and the recent death of her mother."

In the *language patterns* or mind-lines that follow, the NLP model offers numerous ways to reframe meanings using this horizontal shifting pattern. So what?

So what? The primary value in this is that *reframing transforms meaning.* So these linguistic mind-line patterns provide all sorts of resourceful ways *to put the best frame-of-reference on things so that we can operate more effectively.* Doing so empowers us to use the *magic* of our evaluative powers to set frames of references (meta-states) that will bring out our personal resources as well as the personal resources in others. It evokes and creates higher level states or frames.

This allows us to take control of the meanings and meaning-making power at our disposal. It points the way to how we can order and re-order any meaning that does not serve us well, but that creates limiting beliefs and toxic ideas. It gives clues to the secrets of magic that are at our command... if only we notice.

Figure 2:2
Reframing a Statement

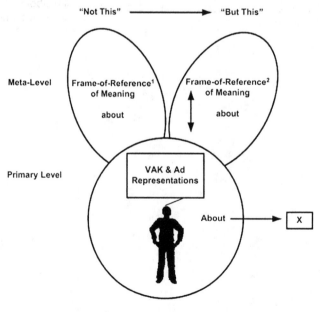

3) The Language and Spell of Embedded Framing
Use to cast higher spells that outframe all meanings to transform things in one fell swoop.[2]

The ultimate form of reframing involves making *a vertical move* (going up the specificity to abstraction scale). When we do this, we leave the frame-of-reference at the first level the same and make changes at a higher level. From the higher level, we can outframe the whole context and create a new context for the context.

Consider the case of a boy who has encoded his brain with memories of severe spankings as a child. He signaled his brain with the see-hear-feel movie along with all of the words and linguistic representations of his evaluations so that today whenever he remembers the abuse he received when he was beaten with a stick, he plays the old movie, steps into that movie and begins to feel in his body as if it were still occurring. Suppose the beating occurred simply because he was only acting and thinking like a kid, being silly, yet his dad was in an angry state already and he flew into a rage, and took out his emotions on him.

Within the cinema of his mental movie, he not only has a few snapshots of the images, sounds, and sensations from that old scenario, he has a full-fledged movie, in living color, and he's *inside* the movie. Then, in that inner sanctum of his mind he plays the movie over and over along with the words of insult, "You stupid brat, you'll never succeed in life with that attitude!"

Got the picture? Not very pretty, ah? Now suppose the kid (let's call him Wayne) grows up and makes several beliefs from those experiences. Suppose he reaches the following conclusions:
> "I'll never amount to anything."
> "Something's wrong with me. I must be defective because I have this attitude that provokes dad so much."
> "I don't feel very loved or loveable, therefore I must not be loveable."

Given these *evaluative meanings,* would it be difficult to guess the kind of neuro-semantic states Wayne would continually create for himself as he moves through life? I don't think so. We wouldn't call them resourceful ones. These states would only reinforce and deepen his sense of distress. They would only provide him "proof" about the validity and accuracy of his limiting beliefs.

As Wayne grows and receives more of the same, he would then draw another and even higher meta-level frame of reference,
> "I'll never change. This is the way life is going to be. No need to get my hopes up that things will turn around. I'm just a loser and always will be."

That neuro-semantic state, as a state-about-a-state (or a *meta-state*), will then *multiply* his psychological pain and create even more of a self-fulfilling prophecy. All of this operates as a form of black magic. It sets a high level frame-of-reference typically *outside* of consciousness that governs perception, behavior, communication, expectation, etc. so that it actually seeks out and invites more of the same.

Figure 2:3

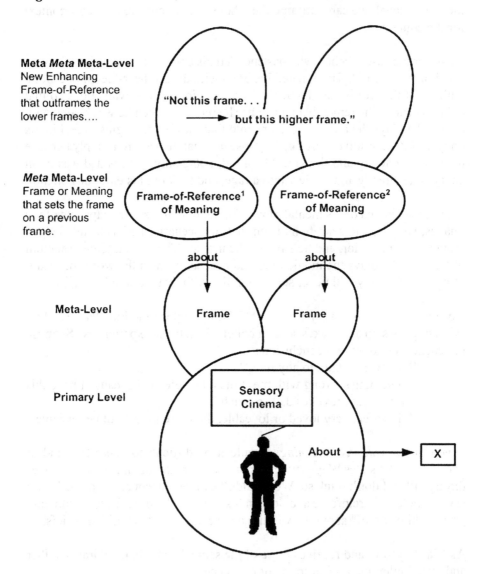

Further, with *that belief* working at an even higher meta-level, reframing Wayne at the first meta-level will not have much effect and almost no long term effect. After all, it doesn't get to the highest or executive frame. Suppose we offer the following powerful reframe,

> "It's not that you won't amount to anything, actually you can decide to become anything that you want, if you just put the past behind you."

Such a reframe probably will not work. At best, it will have little effect because a higher frame will govern his thinking and feeling and will discount the reframe.

> "No kidding, I started with a handicap. And as we all know, 'You can't teach old dogs new tricks.' So don't give me any of your psychobabble crap!"

In this case, we need to *outframe*.[2] We need to move up, find the highest meta-frame, and then go *above* that frame to set a whole new frame of mind. We need to step back and comment *on* the previous frames.
"So those are the ideas and beliefs you built as an eight-year old boy. Then on top of that, at 17, you built that stuck-and-can't change belief."

> "Yeah, so?"

"So now, here you are at 30, living out these old beliefs. How well do you like those beliefs? Do they serve you very well?"

> "No, not at all."

"So the conclusions you drew at 8 and 17 don't work very well. Yet those ideas were probably the best kind of thinking that younger you could do at those times. After all, that does reflect the thinking of a child, not a grown man who can look back on all that and recognize that thinking as mis-beliefs and erroneous conclusions. Because children tend to self-blame rather than recognize that their parents didn't take 'Parenting 101' and never learned how to affirm or validate..."

Neuro-Linguistic Magic as the Framing
that Creates Meaning

In the *Mind-Lines model* we essentially use the process of framing and reframing for the purpose of altering perceived neuro-linguistic "reality." Doing this enables us to transform the external expressions of our emotions, behaviors, speech, skills, relationships, etc. to a trigger. Korzybski described it as changing the *logical fate* within our psycho-logics (or neuro-semantics).[3] This not only speaks about how all beliefs and ideas have consequences, but that when we change an executive frame of reference, it changes our personality, identity, emotions, destiny, and future.

If you believe that you "won't amount to anything," that you "can't do anything right," that you "don't have the right to succeed"—the *logical fate* and the *psycho-logics* within those statements will show up in how you present yourself, talk, walk, act, think, feel, etc. As you digest those words, the ideas metabolize in your neurology.

Via *mind-lines*, we utilize the neuro-linguistic magic in our use of language to play around with frames and to set new frames. We can do so until we find those that result in the "logical fates" that we desire for ourselves and others. *Frames* (as in frames-of-reference) refer to *the references* that we use as we relate to people, things, events, words, etc. Such references may be real and historical, personal or impersonal, conceptual like beliefs, imaginary like expectations, realistic or unrealistic, etc.

Neuro-linguistic and neuro-semantic reality begin with our thoughts *about* the world. Apart from our associations, *nothing means anything.* Apart from our thoughts, events occur and things happen. Sights, sounds, sensations, etc. stimulate our sense receptors. But all of that "means" nothing. It holds no mental or emotional association, it occurs within no mental framework or classification.

Then the magic begins. We see, hear, and feel such and so represent it and connect (or associate) it with other sights, sounds, and sensations. Later, we connect to it even higher level abstractions. In this way we give it "meaning."

Giving or attributing meaning to something (to anything) *first involves an associative process.* First we *link* an external event, person, action, or behavior up with some internal representation (or thought). Sounds simple enough, right? *Not!* This seemingly simple and obvious linkage begins the creation of associative meaning. First we link things together. Our linkage of things may or may not be reasonable, rational, productive, useful, or valid. But once linked, that's what a thing "means."

We ask, "What does anything mean anyway?" To identify the meaning we have to find the associations.

What does "fire" *mean?* It all depends upon what any given individual (or animal) has connected, linked, or associated with it. This sends us back to *experiences,* to our referent experiences.
- Have we seen and experienced fire only as campfires when out on a weekend camping trip?
- Have we associated fire with food, marshmellows, companionship, songs, fun, etc.?

Then the *external behavior* (**E.B.**) of fire *means* (relates to, causes, connects up with, etc.) the *internal state* (**I.S.**) of fun, delight, joy, togetherness, attraction, excitement, etc.

Consider how very, very different this is for the person whose experience of fire relates to getting burned, feeling physical pain, seeing a home destroyed, etc.   What does fire mean to that person? Again, it all depends on what

> *The frame completely and absolutely controls or governs the meaning.*

that person—conceptually and mentally—has connected to, and associated, with fire.   For that person, fire probably *means* hurt, pain, loss, grief, aversion, etc.

Well, what does fire *really* mean? Get ready for a surprise.
It really means nothing.

Fire only exists as a certain event of change in the external world. Alone and unconnected by consciousness, it has no meaning. *Nothing has any "meaning."* Why? Because meaning only and exclusively arises when a consciousness comes along and connects an external thing to an internal state. Doing so creates a frame of reference inside the person *about* the thing. We then see, hear, feel, and language fire from the frame of a campfire or from a home burning down.

In both of these cases,
The frame completely and absolutely controls or governs the meaning.

In fact, we cannot even understand the external behavior (E.B.) or event apart from *the frame*. Apart from the frame, we don't know anything about its meaning to another person. Apart from knowing another person's frame, we typically tend to use our own frames-of-references. In that way we impose our "meanings" upon them.

So when it comes to *the structure of meaning,* what do we have? We have two major factors, one external, the other internal.
*   The external component—the *events of the world.*
*   The internal component—human nervous system/brain taking cognizance of the event and mapping it.

Cognizance or awareness arises as we cognize the event via our sensory-system languages: visual sights (V), auditory sounds (A), kinesthetic sensations (K), olfactory smells (O), and gustatory tastes (G) as well as by our language system of words to create the *movie* in our mind.

These two phenomena occur at different levels and in different dimensions. Yet when we connect them, we suddenly create neuro-linguistic meaning. This is the "magic" of which we speak. When we put this into the format of a formula, we then have the structure or formula of *Figure 2:4*.

Figure 2:4

External Behavior —> Internal State

=

E.B. ———► / = I.S.

This structure of meaning provides us the basic *frame-of-reference* which we all use in attributing meaning to things. It explains not only how we humans make meaning, but how animals can also experience and develop associative learning and understandings. The secret of life's meanings at this level?

Things get connected to things.

Things of the outside world (events, behaviors, people) get associated with internal feelings, moods, states, ideas, understandings, values, etc. That is to say, we connect what's outside with what we experience on the inside. We *frame as we* create a frame of reference about what's out there. This sets a frame around our thought so that we see that external thing in terms of our mental frame. Later, when we set a frame of confirmation about that, we create a meta-level phenomenon more commonly known as a "belief."

Once we have *a frame* (as in the formula: E.B.—>/ =I.S.), we don't stop there. Animals generally do, but not us humans. No way. We have the ability to create much more complexity. With our special kind of consciousness that *reflects back onto itself*, we use our "self-reflexive consciousness" to layer multiple levels of associations. Such reflexivity of the mind creates meta-states. So we begin with a thought:

"I like fire; it makes me feel warm and loved."

Or, "I hate fire. Fire is scary; it makes me shutter just to think about it."

Yet we never leave it there. We complicate matters (wouldn't you know it?).

We then entertain *a thought about that thought* which creates a meta-frame.

"I hate it that I fear fire so much."

"I feel proud of myself for feeling so good about fire, not getting scared of it like some people I know, but enjoying it and appreciating it for its positive values."

Nor do we leave it at that level, we bring even more thoughts to bear on that thought, etc.

"*Why* do I let fire frighten me so much? I *should* get over this thing. *What's wrong* with me anyway that I can't be more reasonable? Well, I guess *I'm stuck* for life. Once you've had a traumatic experience like that, it seals your fate."

Of course, this initiates a *neuro-semantic muddle,*[4] does it not? To the original relations and connections that the person made about fire, the person layers many more ideas onto it. This creates not only beliefs, but belief *systems,* then belief systems about belief systems until we create an entire Matrix of frames. The thoughts that we apply to our earlier thoughts set up a frame-of-reference around a frame, and so on up the levels.

More Neuro-Linguistic Magic
Frames-Of-Frames

Once we have established a basic frame (E.B.—>/=I.S.), we can then set a frame *above* that frame, a meta-frame. Or we could set a frame-of-reference (thoughts) about it *prior* to it. Parents do this for kids regarding experiences (events) yet to come,

"Now don't *fall into the fire*—that would be terrible!"

In the Mind-Lines model, we call this **Pre-Framing**—framing what's going on to happen in the future. In addition to pre-framing, we can frame events and behaviors afterwards, that gives us **Post-Framing**.

"Yep, sonny, if you burned yourself in a fire once, you are likely to do it again and again!"

How do you like that post-frame as a way of thinking? Pretty shoddy and muddled thinking, right? This also will typically operate as a "post hypnotic suggestion."[5]

When we *undermine* or seek to pull apart the E.B.—>/=I.S. formula, we engage in **De-Framing**. Asking specific questions about either the E.B. or the I.S. has a tendency to achieve this. It pulls apart the thought-construction, that is, the belief or meaning equation.

- When did you get burned?
- In what circumstances?

- 　　What did you learn from that?
- 　　Have you used that learning to protect yourself from repeating that experience?

We can even do some fancy kind of mental gymnastics with our equation that summarizes the structure of meaning. For example, we can **Counter-Frame.** That is, we can ask about or suggest experiences that counter the E.B.—>/=I.S. formula.

- 　　Have you ever been around a campfire and enjoyed cooking a hotdog over the fire?
- 　　How fearful and worried do you get when you strike a match and light candles on a birthday cake?

These frames-of-frames provide additional ways to reframe. We not only do **not** have to stay inside our *magical belief/meaning box* (thank God!), we can step outside that box and send our consciousness (or someone else's) in one of seven directions. We can go *way down* deep inside the box and ask specific questions of the qualities of our representations, the cinematic editing and so flush out the "sub-modality" qualities or frames. Doing this **de-frames.**

Figure 2:5

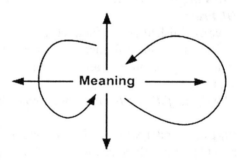

Or, we can **reframe** by going in one of two horizontal directions. We can go over to the left to a time *prior* to the frame-of-reference (the E.B.—>/=I.S. formula) and **pre-frame** the subsequent response. Or, we can go over to the right to a time later to the basic first level meaning, and **postframe** it as meaning or suggesting something new and different.

Or, we can move up and **outframe** as we set up a whole new frame-of-reference with a thought-about-that thought or any other combination. This steps outside of the frame or context and generates a whole new context, a context-of-a-context. With that move, we can embed the idea as a belief into all kinds of higher ideas.

In the chapters to come, you will learn to make these conceptual and magical shifts as you learn to use the mind-lines to alter neuro-linguistic and neuro-semantic realities. As you do, you will expand your sense of choice. You will get more and more of a sense that you have so many options about your meaning attributions. It will develop and expand your sense of flexibility (of mind, emotion, and language). This training in skills of language patterning will enrich your communication skills, making you more effective and professional, more elegant in persuasion, and more influential. (Oh yes, if you didn't notice, this preframes you for this study.)

Mind-Lines — Updating the "Sleight of Mouth" Patterns
The Mind-Lines model makes explicit the ways that we can directionalize and re-directionalize consciousness. It provides us a way to think about sending mind in new and different ways so that we construct new and different meanings, empowering meanings that frame our experiential lives so that it makes us more resourceful, insightful, wise, and thoughtful. This summarizes the neuro-semantic process.

We are now calling this domain *Mind-Lines,* this domain previously known as *the Sleight of Mouth patterns.* Why have we changed the name? Why have we moved away from talking about "sleight of mouth" patterns?

We do this primarily because most people relate and experience *negative connotations* to the phrase "sleight of mouth." All too frequently it raises thoughts of manipulation, control, and pulling something over on someone. So, to avoid that while still exulting in the neuro-linguistic magic, we refer to them as mind-lines.

By mind-lines we refer to the *lines* (the linguistic constructions) that we connect and associate to things that create meaning formulas (E.B.—>/=I.S.). These mental constructs carry tremendous neurological effects. So, as we change the lines that we use in our minds (and those we use on the minds of others), we change, alter, and transform our felt sense of reality. We transform the neuro-semantics of our personal reality and so our lives. By the changing of meaning, our emotions change, as do our behaviors, habits, moods, attitudes, skills, health, etc. and our life.

The following Chart overviews and summarizes the **seven** basic mind-shifting directions and the **twenty-six** different mind-line patterns for reframing reality. This chart represents our latest thinking about this magical neuro-linguistic art.

The Mind-Lines Model
Figure 2:6

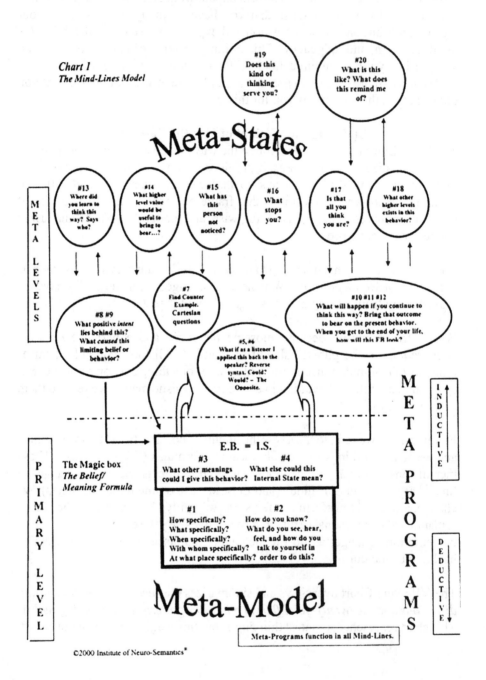

Chart 1
The Mind-Lines Model

©2000 Institute of Neuro-Semantics®

Technology That Drives Mind-Lining
The mental, cognitive, and conceptual shifting of meaning can take seven basic directions. Each direction (backward, forward, down, up, counter, etc.) provides a different way to *directionalize consciousness*. By sending someone's mind-body-emotion system in one of these different directions, we open up space for them (or ourselves) to experience new frames, frames that can empower and facilitate greater resourcefulness, health, joy, love, etc.

The following briefly summarizes *the seven directions*. In the following chapters we will more fully explain each of these dimensions of magic for each offers a domain wherein a certain kind of communication magic prevails. In those chapters we also provide lots of examples of mind-lines that change meaning and personality.

Learning For Competence Frame
As we do this, what frame-of-reference will you, use in reading and exploring this material? A "This is overwhelming!" frame? A "Too many big words!" frame? An "Oh this is complicated!" frame? A "Oh boy, mind-lines to empower me in moving through life!" frame? An "I find this very interesting and wonder about the exciting ways to use this!" frame? The *frame* of mind that you adopt even in your reality orientation will govern the quality and enjoyment of your discovery too. So what will it be?

How about a "One page and pattern at a time and I'll learn this thoroughly" frame? Well, which one of those frames would work best for you? What frame would you like to use?
> [We just used a couple *mind-lines* on you! Later you can come back and check those out to understand their structure.]

Seven Ways to Change a Brain
1. Deframing
We first go down and *deframe*. We move downward into the specific components from which the meaning arises. Moving down allows us to index and fragment the current frame. We chunk-down *the meaning equation* to pull apart the component pieces of the movie (the VAK structure) and the language patterns that make up *the belief*. The chunking-down movement involves deductive thinking and reasoning. Deframing is an *undermining* process. Here we invite a person to "Undermine your mind by thinking like this." This shift helps us to de-think (our belief thoughts) as we analyze the magic and see it evaporate.
> #1. Chunking Down, The Specificity Move
> #2. Detailing the Sequence of the Strategy

2. Content Reframing
We then *reframe*. In the center of the chart where we have the heart and

structure of meaning—inside *the box* (or cube) of meaning. In reframing we do a horizontal switch and use two kinds of statements, Complex Equivalences and Cause—Effect statements (to be explained in the next chapter). These meaning equations and attributions define the heart of neuro-semantic reality and magic. Here we shift the meaning associations by essentially saying, "It doesn't mean this, it means this." In this move, we engage in what's known as *content* reframing. In content reframing, we say, "Don't think that about this thing, event, act, etc. in that old way, here's a new and more empowering way to think about it."

> #3. Reframe E.B.
> #4. Reframe I.S.

3. Counter Reframing

In *counter framing* comes the fancy footwork of offering a reframe that counters the content. Here we let our consciousness *reflect back* onto its own content (i.e., the ideas within the meaning box) and as we do, we *apply* the meaning equation to the other side of the equation. We do this to see if the formula itself coheres or if that breaks it up into a thousand pieces. If it does, it has a deframing effect.

This reframing move involves using *reflexivity* so that mind thinks about its own thoughts. In *counter framing*, we essentially ask, "What happens to your ideas when you apply this way of thinking to yourself?" "What do you think of the belief when you apply it to those cases, times, and events, where it does not fit?"

> #5. Reflexively Apply E.B. to Self/Listener
> #6. Reflexively Apply I.S. to Self/Listener
> #7. Counter-Example

4 and 5. Pre-Framing and Post-Framing

These are the time traveling reframes. In these conceptual moves we reframe by moving to a state prior or post to the idea (in our minds, of course). We view the meaning construction (the formula in the box) from the standpoint of what brought it about or where it will leads.

Actually this is an *Outframing* move. That's because in these responses we are bringing the concept of "time" to our belief. In *pre-framing* we are also applying two other concepts, *causation* and *intention,* to the idea. In *post-framing,* we essentially "run with the logic" to see if the meaning equation will continue to make sense when we view it from a larger time frame. We then ask, "Does the magic still work?" Here we apply *consequential thinking and outcomes* to the original belief.

These reframing moves introduce various *time* concepts into the process and reframes by playing around with the "time" frames that we can put around the *meaning.* Here we apply various "time" conceptualizations (thoughts-and-feelings) to our beliefs in the meaning box.

In *pre-framing,* we essentially say, "When you put this thought in the back of your mind, how does it affect the belief?" In *post-framing,* we say, "When you put this thought in the front of your mind about that belief, how does it play out into your future?" We do this to challenge the magic in the box.

> **Before Time:**
>> #8. Positive Prior Framing (Intention)
>> #9. Positive Prior Cause
>
> **After Time:**
>> #10. First Outcome
>> #11. Outcomes of Outcome
>> #12. Eternity Framing

6. Outframing to meta-levels.

In all of the outframing moves, we step aside from the structure of meaning (as coded in the belief equation) and apply various ideas to it. In other words, we *meta-state* the belief with higher frames and perceptives. By chunking up the meaning construction to higher conceptual levels, we apply many new and different facets to our neuro-semantic construction. These *meta-state* the belief and offer a wide range of choices. These upward moves involve inductive thinking and reasoning.

In *outframing,* we essentially say, "When you wrap your mind around the belief and view it from this perspective, or in terms of this idea, how does it affect things?" These moves not only challenge the old magic, but also apply higher meta-magic to the belief.

> #13. Model of the World Framing
> #14. Criteria and Value Framing
> #15. Allness Framing
> #16. Have-To Framing
> #17. Identity Framing
> #18. All other Abstractions Framing
> #19. Ecology Framing

7. Analogous Framing

In the *analogous reframing* move, we shift from inductive and deductive thinking as well as horizontal and counter thinking as we move to analogous thinking (or "abduction," Bateson, 1972). We do this by shifting to storytelling, metaphor, and narrative. In this abducting type of framing, we essentially say, "Forget all of that, and let me tell you a story..."

> #20. Metaphoring/ Storying and Restorying Framing

Overwhelmed With Magic?
"Wow! That's a lot to remember. How can a person ever learn all of that?"
"Ah, the Overwhelm Frame." Is that the game you want to play? Since our first book we have indeed worked on simplifying the magic. So if you would like a quick and easy way to hurry your learnings, then we offer the following Mind-Line statements and questions. Memorize them. As *semantic environments and prompters*. After you learn them by rote, then you can use them to elicit your own alternative meanings that you can use to reframe a statement or objection.

Detecting and Identifying the "Magic" of the Belief
#1. Chunk Down on E.B. or I.S.:
> What component pieces of VAK comprise this?

#2. Reality Strategy Chunk Down:
> In what order or sequence do these parts occur?

#3. Reframe E.B.:
> What really is E.B. is ...
> What else would qualify as this E.B.?

#4. Reframe I.S.:
> This isn't I.S.^{1}, it is I.S.^{2}.
> What other IS could we just as well attribute to this E.B.?

Immediate Concept about Concept, Reflexive Applying
#5. Reflexively Apply E.B. to Self/Listener:
> What a X statement!

#6. Reflexively Apply I.S. to Self/Listener:
> So you're doing X to me?

Reversal of Reflexive Applying to Self—Not-Applying Concept
#7. Counter-Example:
> Do you remember a time when the opposite occurred?
> When does this Formula **not** apply?
> Run the Reverse of #5 and #6 —*not* apply.

Time — Past
#8. Positive Prior Framing (Intention):
> You did that because of ... (this positive intention).
> Weren't you attempting to accomplish X positive purpose?

#9. Positive Prior Cause:
> You did that to accomplish... (this positive consequence).

Time — Future
#10. First Outcome:
> If you follow this belief, it will lead to...

#11. Outcomes of Outcome:
>   If you experience that outcome — it will then lead to...

#12. Eternity Framing:
>   Ultimately, this belief will lead to ... how do you like that?

Recognition of a Map as a Map

#13. Model of the World Framing: Frame as merely one model of the world, one worldview.
>   Who taught you to think or feel this way?
>   When you think of this as a mental map, how does that change things?

Values, Criteria, Standards

#14. Criteria and Value Framing:
>   What do you find more important than this?
>   How does X (some other value) affect this?

Allness, Universal Quantifier

#15. Allness Framing: Apply an universal quantifier to the belief.
>   Always? To everyone?

Modal Operators of Necessity and Impossibility

#16. Have-To Framing: Apply a Modal Operator of Necessity to the belief.
>   What forces you to think this way?
>   What would happen if you did?
>   Do you have to?
>   What would it be like if you couldn't?

Identity, Self-definition Beliefs

#17. Identity Framing: Apply the Identity question.
>   What does this say about you as a person?
>   What does this mean about you as a person?

All Other Abstractions

#18. Abstracting the E.B. or I.S.: Create an abstract concept about the belief formula.
>   This is actually a case of... X, isn't it?

Ecology, Evaluation of Evaluation

#19. Ecology Framing: Apply an ecology question to the belief.
>   Does this serve you well? Does it enhance your life?
>   In the long run, does this make your life more of a party?

#21 Both / And Framing:
>   To what extent is this absolutely true?
>   What makes it so either/or in structure?

Is there any ground for a middle position?

#22 Pseudo-Word Framing:
>   Is this word just a noise and not real word?
>   What are you actually referring to?

#23 Negation Framing:
>   How real is this thing you're talking about?
>   What if you found it vanishing in your mind?
>   What would it be like if this wasn't so?

#24 Possibility / "As if" Framing:
>   Of all the likely possibilities, what would you want to happen?
>   If you were experiencing that right now, what would you be feeling?

#25 Systemic / Probability Framing:
>   What else plays a significant part in this system?
>   What are the borders and boundaries of this system?

#26 Decision:
>   So what have you decided about this?
>   What would you like to decide?
>   So is this what you have decided to believe?
>   Is that what you want?

Meta-phoring—Transferring over another domain of knowledge
#20. Metaphoring/ Storying and Restorying Framing:
>   Literally, *meta-phrein* which is Greek for "to carry over," it refers to
>   applying one thing (an idea, experience, referent event) to some other
>   referent. This enables us to understand something unknown or new it
>   in terms of something already known.
>   I had a friend who just last month was telling me about...

Simplifying the Simplifications
Having now sorted out the word magic within the *Mind-Lines model* to create
seven directions in which we can "send a brain," and having illustrated this with
the Mind-Lines Chart, we now have a confession to make. The model actually
only consists of *two* levels and *two* kinds of reframing.

"Oh really? So why didn't you tell us that upfront? What are these *two* levels
and directions?" Actually we only have *a primary level* and then *the meta-
levels.* Regarding the two kinds of reframing; we have content and context.

1) Inside: Content Reframing
>   This means that #1, 2, 3, and 4 refer to the mind-lines *inside* the box.
>   These refer to the *content* reframing that more specifically addresses
>   the details of the E.B. and the I.S.

2) Outside: Context Reframing
>   This means that *all* of the other mind-lines actually occur as *a meta-
>   stating* of the belief statement with some other idea or concept. In all
>   of these, we set a higher frame on the belief frame and thereby outframe
>   it with considerations to other concepts:
>
>>   Reflexivity or apply to self (#5, 6)
>>   Reverse of reflexivity or *not*-apply to self (#7)
>>   Time (#8, 9, 10, 11 and 12)
>>   The abstraction process itself (#18)
>>   The modeling process (#13)
>>   Values and criteria (#14)
>>   Allness (#15)
>>   Modal Operators (#16)
>>   Identity and identification (#17)
>>   Ecology (#19)
>>   Metaphor (#20)
>>   Both/And (#21)
>>   Pseudo-Words (#22)
>>   Negation/ Unreality (#23)
>>   Possibility and "As If" (#24)
>>   Systemic and Probability (#25)
>>   Decision (#26)

Understanding that all of these forms of *context reframing* involve an outframing of the belief statement (E.B.—>/ =I.S.) with some other concept, idea, or meaning also offers another insight. In the original edition, we only listed the first twenty. Later we realized that there were more as Denis Bridoux assisted Michael in adding additional conversational reframing patterns (see Chapter 19). Using the theoretical foundations described in the extended Meta-Model (see *Communication Magic,* 2001. It was formerly entitled, *The Secrets of Magic,* 1998) we have added Either/Or—Both/And Framing, Pseudo-words, Multi-ordinal terms, etc.

Beyond the Box
First-level meanings (or primary state meanings) occur *inside* the box. Meanings at this level arise via the formulas and equations that we create neuro-linguistically from associations as we move through life. After that we have second-level "meanings" (meta-state meanings or higher level meanings). These meanings occur *outside* and *above* the box as we move through the world.

We refer to the first meanings as *content* reframing. *W*e refer to the second meanings as *context* reframing. With of *content* reframing, we alter and transform the content. By way of contrast, *context* reframing keeps the content the same and changes the frame. As we put the same content into a different context, that new context qualifies and alters the content.

"Outside of the box" refers to all of *the contexts* in which we use the formula or equation—and to the various contexts and contexts-of-contexts that we can put around the box—which thereby tempers and qualifies the stuff inside the box. (See *Unfolding Mind-Lines*, chapter 12)

Did you get that? How does that work? Remember, what we have called *"the box"* is only as a concept, a conceptual understanding, meaning, or association. This neuro-cognitive process governs how we think, perceive, feel, and respond. Therefore, if it exists and operates as a piece of *conceptual work* when we put it inside of another conceptual framework or box we have a concept of a concept.

Figure 2:7

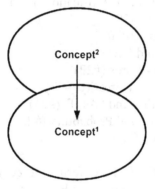

At this point, we now have one magic box inside of another magic box and by this maneuver we can generate magic-of-magic. In linguistics this shows up as language-about-language and ideas-about-ideas. We use our reflexivity to refer to other references. In neuro-linguistic experience, it shows up as states, and then states-about-states (or meta-states).

Telling a Brain Where to Go
Directionalizing and Re-Directionalizing Consciousness
So from *inside* and from *outside* of the magical box of our concepts, by which we construct and formulate meanings, we can now maneuver consciousness in the seven directions. As a result, this provides us the chance to magically reframe meaning in a multiple of ways.

Summary

The key understandings about this realm of human meaning and reframing involve the following insights:

- *He who sets the frame governs the resultant experience* (i.e., emotions, thoughts, and responses).

- *Someone* (or some idea) *always sets a frame.* We can't escape from frames, beliefs, presuppositions, paradigms, etc. Someone will set the frame of the conversation. *Mind-Lines* assists the salesperson, the leader, the parent, etc. in setting the frame.

- *Awareness of the meaning process* (i.e., the meaning placed on a particular belief, statement, objection, etc.) *gives us control over it.* Understanding the structure of Mind-Lines enables us to stay aware of the meaning of objections, questions, perceptions, communication, etc. from a client, customer, partner, or child. By having and understanding this meaning, we are able to manage the flow of the conversation.

End Notes:

1. In Neuro-Semantics we make this distinction between *neuro-linguistics* and *neuro-semantics.* The first term refers to primary state language use and the sensory languages of the mind (the representational systems that comprise the movie in the mind). The second term refers to the meta-levels and meta-states as we move up the "logical" or psycho-logical levels.

2. "Outframe" refers to moving to a place where we can set up a frame-of-reference **over** everything that lies underneath it. Doing this *outframes.*

3. Psycho-logics refers to the fact that our inner logics are *psycho-logical* and do not fit the logics of mathematics or of a syllogism. It is the inner logical that we create as we set states, frames, and meanings *about* things. What we call "logical levels" are actually our psycho-logical levels and come from how we classify and categorize things as we construct meaning. More will be said about this later, also see *The Matrix Model* (2003).

4. The fact that we can and do create all kinds of *neuro-semantic muddles* explains why we need to understand the nature and power of our neuro-semantics, how we meta-state psycho-logical levels to set frames. The meta-muddles usually result in the "dragon states that we experience. To undo this damage and interference, we need the skills of Dragon slaying, taming, and transforming (*Dragon Slaying,* 2000).

5. Oh yes, did I mention that because all "beliefs" or frames are "in the mind," they are all forms of hypnosis? Well, they are. Most of us do not hallucinate cats, elephants, or aliens that are not there. We rather hallucinate *concepts*, beliefs, ideas, memories, imaginations—things like "rudeness," "fairness," "responsibility," "blame," "ownership," etc. Such "thinking" is a higher level of thinking, that is, the thinking that occurs at meta-levels.

Chart of Mind-Lines

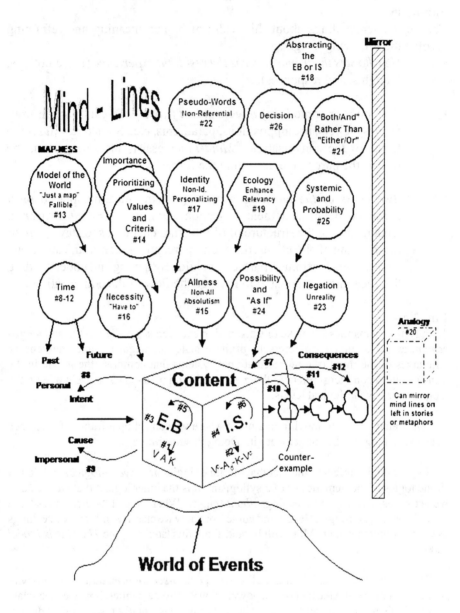

Chapter 3

CONVERSATIONAL REFRAMING PATTERNS

To *Lines* For Changing *Minds*

"The limits of my language are the limits of my world."
Wittgenstein (1922)

"Language is what bewitches,
but language is what we must remain within
in order to cure the bewitchment."
Henry Staten (1984, p. 91)

Mind-lines empower us to conversationally transform
our meanings to enrich the quality of our lives.
L. Michael Hall

The Myth
A long, long time ago (somewhere about 1980), so the story goes, at an NLP training in Washington, D.C. with co-founder Richard Bandler, Robert Dilts recognized some truly new patterns in Richard's interactions with a participant and the group.

Richard was working with a new process that dealt with the theme of "going over threshold" and experiencing "the last straw" in a relationship. He wanted to explore the possibility of reversing the foreground/ background shift in a person's thinking and perceiving. Could a person's perceptual filter of only seeing all the bad, wrong, and ugly things in another person that leads to wanting to end a relationship be suddenly reversed? Could that entire perceptual gird suddenly fade into the background of a person's mind while simultaneously all of the good, right, and beautiful things zoom into the foreground of awareness and change one's moods and emotions?

At a certain point in the training, Richard was working with a young man who was breaking up with a girlfriend who he thought would be willing to reverse things. Yet this young man ended up being "quite creative at thwarting every option, possibility, or reason that Bandler brought up as to why he might reconsider his opinions about his girlfriend and their relationship." (Dilts, 1999, p. 272). It was in this context that Dilts made his discovery.

Though the young man wanted to be cooperative, he found himself getting into a very stubborn state of mind. In response, Richard with "a flare for the outrageous" used the chance occurrence of the stage breaking as a metaphor and played *a frame game* with the young man and the audience. Robert Dilts tells the full story and presents a transcript in *Sleight of Mouth* (1999, pp. 270-296).[1]

Richard adopted the attitude that a participant had intentionally sabotaged the stage in order to hurt and embarrass him and that he would not give him another chance. Then as a psycho-drama, he acted out the young man's dilemma by sitting down and challenging the group to fix it. He as much said, "I have this problem. See if you can fix it." This put the young man in a meta-position to observe his own patterns being acted out by Richard. At the same time the psycho-drama was a *metaphorical* mind-line that analogously mirrored his own thinking in a dramatic way.

As Richard played the client's role, he invited the NLP practitioners at the training to do what they could to alleviate his problem and to fix him. Yet they could not. In spite of all the magic of NLP they knew, nothing they said seemed to touch the stubborn belief system. Bandler was consistently able to respond to their helpfulness in a way to resist their best influence.

Somehow, using some special language patterns Bandler deflected every attempt that otherwise could have enabled him to experience a positive transformation. (Perhaps he had modeled how people generally defeat positive endeavors.)

All of this evoked an *"Ah ha!"* response and experience in Robert Dilts. Suddenly he recognized certain linguistic patterns that corresponded to other patterns of influence which he had been studying. Consequently, he and Todd Epstein formulated the first fourteen patterns which from that day forward became known in NLP as the *"Sleight-of-Mouth"* patterns.

The "Sleight of Mouth" Patterns
The "Sleight of Mouth" patterns utilize patterns and frames-of-references and neuro-semantic meanings which we can use to *persuade* ourselves and others. We can use them to empower ourselves to make enhancing transformations that bring out our best. We can just as equally use them to limit ourselves by

deflecting any and every transformational idea that comes along.

All of us use these patterns anyway every day of our lives (or at least some of them) to maintain our beliefs. They are not new or uncommon to the way we think and frame things. In this, neither Bandler nor Dilts invented these patterns. They are operative in people in every culture. Bandler, Dilts, and Epstein only made them explicit, and in making them explicit we are now able to more effectively work with them, detect them, and use them with more precision and insight. Robert Dilts, in fact, speaks about his own study of the linguistic patterns in Jesus of Nazareth, Karl Marx, Abraham Lincoln, Albert Einstein, Mohandes Gandhi, Martin Luther King and others. With these masters, he discovered that they used common patterns to influence the minds and beliefs of those around them.[2]

In the 1980 training, Richard artfully used these language patterns, to show their power in deflecting and breaking up valued and helpful ideas. He also used them to show how we can use them to put ourselves into conceptual boxes that prevent growth, change, transformation. We can use them to detect such and to open up new space for generative change. Learning these patterns puts us more in control in handling our conceptual world, that is, of our own neuro-semantics and that of others.

Using "Sleight of Mouth" patterns enabled one of the founders of NLP to resist highly trained professionals and defeat their best efforts. This illustrates one way these *powerful language skills* operate in molding our beliefs and creating our realities.

From "Sleight of Mouth" to Mind-Lines
In this work we have made these patterns even more explicit as a facet of training and skill development in neuro-linguistics. Such training results in developing greater competency in our use of language. With *Mind-Lines,* you will be able to break up unwanted belief patterns that hinder and sabotage your best efforts. You will be able to shift the paradigms of your conceptual reality in one fell swoop and really learn to control your own brain.

We begin with the original formatting of the fourteen "Sleight of Mouth" patterns as Dilts and Epstein codified the language patterns they picked up from Richard Bandler. These formats enable us to eloquently reframe almost anything and so they represent the first NLP model of persuasion.

In the first edition of *Mind-Lines* (1997), this work became the first book in the field of NLP on the "Sleight of Mouth" Patterns. Yet there's a difference. *Mind-Lines* reworks the persuasion patterns and provides *a new structure* to the mental and verbal moves. We have sought to make the model more rigorous, methodical, and streamlined as we examined the theoretical foundations of the model. We also used the meta-levels structure inherent in *Meta-States,* the reflexive levels of thought to model the structure of the construction of meaning.

This enables us to recognize the *levels* of meaning. On the primary level, "meaning" arises from, and is, associations and linkages. Reflectively, every higher level of meaning involves the setting of frames or mental contexts. Given that, we can send the brain in seven directions. This gives us seven reframing directions and within these directions, 26 conversational patterns.

The *"Sleight of Hand/Sleight of Mouth"* Metaphor

In a sleight of *hand* move, a magician *distracts* those watching. He or she will do something to capture the attention of the audience. Simultaneously, the magician will be doing something else which contains the source of the perceived magic. A similar thing happens with the "Sleight of *Mouth*" patterns.

Similarly, shifting language patterns involves a distraction so that as we listen, the distraction leads our mind off in one direction, while simultaneously making a conceptual move in another direction. What results when this happens? It evokes us a new and different perception. Suddenly we experience a new idea or belief coming into view, and we really don't know where it came from, or how. That part of it seems almost mystical or magical.

When a card illusionist does sleight of hand movements, he or she performs one set of actions that so captivates the interest of the viewers, that they really don't see what the illusionist actually does that changes things. Consider what happens to the *attention* of those watching. Attention is shifted and captivated. Attention preoccupies itself at a place where the observers think and anticipate the action will occur. Then, on another place, the more significant action occurs.

When this happens, sleight of hand creates for the viewer *an illusion,* and this illusion frequently results in a shock to consciousness.

> "How did he do that?"
> "Hey, I saw her move it over there, so this can't be!"

The process itself then becomes codified in a distorted statement which encourages the illusion even more because the operator will say, "Well, the hand is quicker than the eye." But not really.

The solution does not lie in "seeing faster," it actually lies in *not getting distracted.* No matter how fast or skilled a person's seeing, if the person sends his or her mind to pay attention to irrelevant factors, the illusionist will get them every time. The magic is in the distraction.

A similar process occurs with verbal behavior when we deliver a really good mind-line. This happens all the time in human interactions and communications anyway. Sometimes it occurs in interactions that we engage in just for fun and enjoyment. Sometimes it occurs when we interact and negotiate with someone to create Win/Win situations. Then again, sometimes it occurs when someone intentionally seeks to pull the wool over someone else's eyes in order to take advantage of them.

What corresponds linguistically, or conceptually, in *mind-lines* that distracts a person's mind? *Content.* Yes. Just invite another human being into a discussion about content and you can do all kinds of things (and I'm not kidding about this) in altering, changing, and transforming the context. And best of all, when you do, most people will never notice.

Conscious minds seem to have this thing for *content.* Feed them a little gossip, some details, the specifics of this or that person, in this or that situation, tell them a story, or even better—a secret, and presto ... you can shift the person's frames and contexts without them ever suspecting. (Do you yet feel anxiously impatient for hearing more about content and context.... well, just wait and we'll let you in on it!)

Hey, Is that Ethical?
There you go! We knew you would bring that up. And, yes any talk about *doing things to people's brains* (especially shifting their consciousness) which then influences their feelings, moods, responses, actions, etc. inevitably brings up the question of ethics.

And so it should. We applaud this. Yet the problem doesn't actually pose that much of a problem. Not really. After all, given the nature of communication and relationship, we cannot *not* communicate, we cannot *not* influence, we cannot *not* manipulate. Actually, "manipulation" only refers to *handling* (manual means "by the hands") ourselves, our messages, our intentions, etc.

Of course, in *negative* manipulation we *handle* ourselves in relation to others for a win/lose effect wherein we seek to benefit at another's cost. Conversely, in *positive* manipulation we relate to others for a win/win result so that everybody benefits. Further, while manipulating someone to that person's disadvantage may "work" momentarily, it will not work over the long-term.

NLP actually assumes this ethical position. It does so because it operates from a systemic and long-term perspective, it begins with the presupposition that when people feel resourceful, empowered, and at their best, they will bring out their best, not their worst. This underscores the importance of *the Win/Win perspective* in personal relationships and communicating, does it not? It also eliminates any need to engage in negative manipulations with people. Since NLP grew out of a systemic paradigm that encourages systemic thinking, it disavows any behavior that creates long-term pain for others.

The language patterns of persuasion that have gone under the label, "Sleight of Mouth" patterns, originally arose from the Meta-Model. This very powerful model explains how language works *neuro*-linguistically (rather than linguistically), and how we can work with language effectively. When we translate the Meta-Model into *a conversational model for reframing* to transform meaning, as we have here, we incorporate a lot of powerful verbalizations—which an unethical person *could* misuse. Yet the best defense against this lies in knowing the model. Then we can catch mind-lines that would attempt to "play with our mind."

Mind-Lining "Beliefs"

What do we use *mind-lines* for?

> We use mind-lines primarily to work with, transform, and enhance beliefs.

Beliefs, as such, can involve a wide range of conceptual ideas. Frequently they relate to the semantic *shoulds* that we put upon ourselves as moral imperatives. They relate to our assumptions about causation—what causes or leads to what, and to our assumptions of meaning—what equals ("is") what, what associates with what. These semantic constructions describe mental filters which we rarely question. Yet via these linguistic patterns, we can loosen a belief or semantic structure. We can question whether we really want a particular belief as a part of our mental map.

* Why do we have *beliefs* in the first place?
* Why do we construct such things?
* What are they good for?
* Do we have to have them?

We develop beliefs to *confirm* our maps or models of the world. And we construct maps to make sense of the world. Our mental maps help us to reduce the size and complexity of the territory of the world. This makes us feel less scared and more in control of our world. These two facets of "thinking" and "understanding" allow us to take effective actions.

Maps and beliefs enable us to delete a great deal of the chaotic over-load of the world by *shifting our attention* to an organizing frame-of-reference. Given the complexity of the world, Aldous Huxley (1954) said that our brains function primarily as "reducing valves." So with all of the information that constantly bombards our brain and nervous system, to make sense of things, our brain deletes most information and then constricts its receiving valve. This allows us to only let in so much data. After that, our brain generalizes that data into mental maps and as we validate that data, we create *belief* frames. Of course, doing this obviously distorts things and yet it does so in both useful and unuseful ways.

Suppose every time we encountered a buying or selling situation, we had to learn all over again what these events mean, their purpose, how to handle them, what thoughts and feelings to experience, what criteria to use, etc.? We would always be re-learning the things we already know and we would never develop stability in our learnings. Then we would not be able to use our previous conclusions and understandings as a map for how to now navigate this experience.

Happily for us, however, our brains know how to delete information that's not important to the map that we have generalized about handling buying and/or selling situations. Our mental map provides us understandings about what it means, how its important, what's not important, what to pay attention to, how to make decisions, how to think about money, budgeting, etc. Our first level map about buying and selling as well as our meta-mapping of beliefs about ourselves as buyers and sellers, money, value, relationships, etc. enable us to delete unimportant distinctions as we focus on what's important.

If our first level maps provide us the base line information for what things are and how to function, our beliefs operate as a higher set of frames. They operate as the frameworks of our mind as they establish classifications of meaning. As beliefs do this, they then inform us about how to feel and respond.

Suppose we hold a belief like, "All merchants are out to trick and deceive you." What will that idea do inside of our neurology? Inside of our mind and emotions? As a command to the nervous system, it will classify the situation as threatening and dangerous and it will set us up to feel suspicious and wary. Believing a generalization like that will induce us in numerous negative neuro-semantic states like fear, distrust, dislike, etc. It will control our perceiving, it will govern our thinking, and it will format our feeling. That's what beliefs do.

At the first level, we have thoughts, ideas, and understandings. This establishes the content of our basic mapping. Then we move up a level to confirm and validate that mapping through reason, evidence, history, etc. This creates "beliefs" or confirmed thoughts which then encode our sense of reality—what's real, what things mean, etc. Our beliefs emerge as learned and invented understandings about ourselves, others, the world, etc. They make up our reality strategy. Yet beliefs are not just sequestered ideas, beliefs lead to external manifestations because they operate as a command to the nervous system. We manifest our beliefs in our gestures, talk, emotions, behaviors, thinking, etc. "Beliefs" are not real externally; but they are "real" internally inside of our neuro-semantic system. As our frames-of-references, our beliefs govern the quality of our lives, and how rich or impoverished our experiences.

> **Beliefs are commands to the nervous system telling our body and physiology how to feel and respond.**

Because our mental maps and beliefs are ultimately *information,* other *ideas* can and do influence them. The interface point between beliefs (information about what we consider as real and valid) and mind-lines (information that restructures either the content or structure of those ideas) is that both involve the encoding of data in a processing mind.

For this reason, current beliefs (as lines that encode and invite the construction of meaning in the mind) respond to mind-lines. Using one or more mind-lines gives us the power to shift our limiting paradigms and transform them to enhancing ones. We can use mind-lines to liberate ourselves from our meaning boxes and transcend the current matrices of the mind that imprison us.

It is precisely because these mind-line patterns reframe meaning that they work directly on beliefs. That's why we can use them in a wide range of contexts: personal and interpersonal, business, negotiating, arguments, persuasion, sales, advertising, effective public speaking, writing, etc. If you or another needs or wants a new perspective on life, a new attitude, a new point of view—*mind-lines gives you that vista.*

Learning Mind-Lines
The following chapters presents 26 *Mind-Line* patterns for handling objections, persuading someone of your point of view, motivating yourself, doing therapeutic change, inviting others to consider your viewpoint or proposal, incorporating in your presentations and much more. All to increase your influence.

The reframing patterns that make up the mind-lines especially play a significant and powerful role in therapy. Connirae Andreas supposedly developed her skills in using these patterns by spending an entire year just using these shifts with all of her clients. In this way she became highly skilled.

I have a friend in sales who read the first edition of this book and immediately began writing twenty mind-lines every day to address some thought, idea, or problem. He did this to familiarize himself with the mind-line patterns and to develop elegance in conversational reframing. When I met him in person a few years later, he was highly skilled in being able to quickly use the magic of mind-lines with clients and customers.

Is this Psychotherapy?
While the short answer is *no,* it also depends on what you mean by "psychotherapy." If you mean, are these patterns "therapy" in any traditional sense of searching out *why* people *are* the way they are, working with them to get them to re-feel all of the old emotional business that they are carrying with them so that they can finish it, then *no, this is not therapy.*

In NLP and Neuro-Semantics we do things very differently from traditional psychotherapy, that is, from Freudian and Rogerian therapies. For beginners we do *not* focus on the past, nor do we assume that people are broken, or that they need to understand the origin of their problems. We assume people have just mapped things in unproductive, limiting, and impoverishing ways and that they simply need to re-map things. They have all the resources they need for that re-mapping. If you're interested in that, see *The Structure of Personality: Modeling "Personality" Using NLP and Neuro-Semantics* (2001).

Yet, on the other hand, because mind-lines *open up mental and emotional space* where personal transformations can occur, they do have a therapeutic, or a healing effect. We can use them to feed the mind with ideas that increase our personal resourcefulness, tap into the wisdom of the mind-body system, and provide profoundly new ways to think about things. As psychotherapists, we have used mind-lines to loosen up (deframe) beliefs, reframe ideas, set new frames that open up a solution-orientation to problem solving, and outframe with transformative ideas that generate all kinds of profound changes.

These patterns are for framing and reframing, for defining and establishing meaning and the embedded frames of meaning within our personal matrix. That's why leaders, managers, coaches, consultants, parents, trainers, and anyone involved in persuasive communication need to master *Mind-Lines.*

Conversational Reframing: Overt or Covert?
Typically, in therapeutic reframing we make a person's frame-of-reference conscious and explicitly overt. We do that so that the person can alter his or her frame with choice and awareness. Of course, this takes time and effort.

> "Okay, let's think about what this means to you.... And what does that mean to you? ... And what learning or belief do you attribute to that behavior?"

Conversational reframing avoids the time and effort involved in this conscious work of reorganizing the contents of consciousness. We just get "down and dirty" and do it. None of the overt stuff. No stopping in the middle of a business conversation or negotiation to therapeutically explore a person's beliefs systems, or where he or she learned it.

No. We work more covertly with mind-lines so we deliver them in our everyday talk. We speak the conversational reframe, redirect consciousness, speak the line, and then watch someone suddenly develop a more resourceful frame of reference.

Typically these conversational reframes occur during those times when we find ourselves communicating with a client, customer, friend or even ourselves and need an easy and quick way to *redirect a brain* to a new point of view. In such moments, we don't have the time (or even permission) to go through all the trouble of meta-modeling. So we just reframe the person with one or more mind-lines. If the person buys the reframe, then presto—a new perspective. Doing this provides new enhancing meaning to what otherwise produced an unproductive state.

When we offer a different viewpoint, we frame a piece of behavior, understanding, situation, etc. in such a way that transforms its meaning. We offer some of the following *lines for the mind* to redirect someone to expand perspective. If this increases resourcefulness, then it expands the person's model of the world so that their experience of the world becomes richer.

Conversationally Reframing To Avoid Resistance
Mind-line patterns presuppose a basic communication principle that governs interpersonal relationships.
> *People will fight tooth and nail if they feel attacked.*

Induce someone into a state where they feel attacked, inadequate, or vulnerable, and we can count on their defense mechanisms being activated. Does that sound familiar? When people become defensive, that complicates communicational clarity.

Mind-Lines enable us to do several things. They enable us to track a person back to the experience or experiences from which they constructed impoverishing belief frames. They enable us to invite someone to then view the old maps with new eyes and a sense of choice. They empower us to remap—to create new and better mental maps. As conversational reframing, mind-lines utilize the Meta-Model strategy for using language more creatively, precisely, and hypnotically (see Chapter Ten).

Other mind-lines enable us to align with a person's intentions. This grants them permission to re-map their understandings. Yet other mind-lines challenge and provoke by "putting one's own logic back in one's face." This allows them to see if they can handle that logic when applied to themselves or to their future.

Because most of us become too easily entrenched and enmeshed in our maps, we seem to easily forget that our perspectives, beliefs, understandings, drives, etc. are *just maps*. Forgetting that, we think and feel that they are real. Yet our ideas and beliefs are only maps *of* reality, and not reality. When we forget, we confuse belief maps and territory. Korzybski described this process as *identifying*. We *identify* our maps (thoughts, beliefs, decisions, etc.) with reality. Yet there's a difference between our maps *about* the territory, and the territory. Our maps are always inherently fallible and limited constructions.

With Mind-Lines, we can now engage in some very *elegant map-shifting* with ourselves or others. As you practice them, notice when they shift you. Notice when they create a shift in another. Some will elicit pleasant shifts, some will evoke unpleasant shifts. As a neuro-semantic class of life, whenever our internal representations shift, so does our experience, our neurology, our identity, etc. This describes "the magic," so get out your wand; and let the magic begin!

Finally, because each of us already uses various linguistic patterns to maintain our beliefs, this gives us a route for learning these patterns. First aim to discover the patterns that you already use. Once you identify your favorite and default patterns, notice the ones that you do *not* use at all or very seldom. Then as you explore the reframing patterns, notice and give special attention to the categories that you find unfamiliar or new.

Summary

- Staten (1984) noted the *bewitching* nature of language in the quote we used at the beginning of this chapter. Certainly, language can bewitch. We can and do frequently find ourselves bamboozled by words and caught up in various word prisons. "I am a failure." "He's nothing more than a sexist pig." "You're always sabotaging yourself."

- A new use of language can cure the bewitchment of limiting beliefs. In *Mind-Lines* we adapt the NLP re-languaging model to reframe meanings conversationally.

- Recognizing this power of language now empowers us to take charge of our own neuro-linguistics.

- *Unsanity* results when we use ill-formed structures to map out how to navigate through the territory of reality.

- *Mind-Lines* sorts out the structure of meaning and believing enabling us to more clearly understand and develop our reframing skills.

- And now *the Mind-Lines Model* for Neuro-Semantic Magic for fun and profit, for transformation and health.

End Notes:

1.   Also you can see our analysis of this event on the website, www.neurosemantics.com.

2.   By the way this story illustrates a missing insight about *modeling* that's often missed in NLP. While Robert Dilts modeled one expert (Bandler) in language patterns in a given context, he also had been studying "the literature" of the field of persuasion patterns and modeling what others had written and recorded. Modeling that ignores "the field of literature" of a given field does so to its own detriment. It was Dilts' prepared mind, a mind focused and immersed in a single subject, which was able to suddenly *see* and *recognize* that moment.

Chapter 4

THE FORMULA

The Magical Structure of Meaning

"Every belief is a limit to be examined and transcended."
John C. Lily

"Words and magic were in the beginning one and the same thing,
and even today words retain much of their magical power.
By words one of us can give another the greatest happiness
or bring about utter despair;
by words the teacher imparts his knowledge to his students;
by words the orator sweeps his audience with him
and determines its judgments and decisions.
Words call forth emotions
and are universally the means by which we influence our fellow creature.
Therefore let us not despise the use of words in psychotherapy."
Sigmund Freud (1939, pages 21-22)

"You can't dance until you know the steps."
"You can't restructure until you know the structure."
Suzanne Kennedy and Tommy Belk

When we enter into the wild and wonderful world of neuro-linguistic magic, we enter into a strange and mysterious world, a world that operates by a different set of principles and mechanisms than the outside world. It's a mental world that operates by the *psycho-logics* that we create and that works systemically within our mind-body-emotion system. This means that our thinking-and-emoting will go round in circles, will call meanings and worlds into being, and will be quite messy compared to the linear logic of mathematics.

When you first read about the "magic box" (or cube) that we use to describe the wonder and power of conversational reframing with Mind-Lines, you might be tempted to think about it using a logic that fits mathematics, physics, or syllogisms. Resist that seduction. It will mislead you. Instead, prepare yourself for a strange kind of logic and for the way that seems unpredictable and "magical" in many ways. There's a reason for this and it goes back to the nature of *meaning* itself.

"Meaning"— An Internal Job

In the previous chapters, we described a lot about the nature of meaning and beliefs. The key to truly comprehending these phenomena is to realize that *meaning does not exist in the world*. You have never stumbled over a hunk of belief, value, expectation, decision, understanding, knowledge or any other meta-level phenomenon when walking down the street. These are not "things" and do not exist "out there." You can search as long and hard as you want and you will never find these functions of the mind-body system in empirical reality.

No. Beliefs, meanings, frames, etc. only exist in a human mind. They lurk in the reaches of inner space because we make them up. They are all invented. They are mental constructs about the things of the world. We give birth to them. That's why they rise and fall according to how and when a mind re-constructs or de-constructs them. The matrix of the frames of your mind is the womb and birthplace of your meanings. You are a meaning-maker.

The Structure of Meaning

We invent *beliefs* to sketch out a mental map about ourselves, others, time, the world, what things are and mean, how to respond, etc. In our mental mapping, we map out linkages between things and ideas as we *associate* various things, events, experiences with what we think This describes the primary level structure of meaning: we take our representations of external things and connect them to our internal states. As you will soon discover, this creates our *mental boxes*. We then think inside that box. We feel inside that box. We live inside that box. That box becomes our world. It makes us feel safe, secure, and protected. It defines "reality" for us. It is our Matrix.[1]

By our representational thinking, we construct ideas and invent beliefs to understand things: what things "are," how they work, what they mean, their importance, relationships, etc. Once formulated, our beliefs then shape our everyday realities. Beliefs shape our internal experiences, our self-definitions, resources, hopes, expectations, experiences, accessing of resources, skills, abilities, emotions, etc.

No wonder our beliefs so incredibly important. They are not neutral. They are not mere "thoughts." Beliefs are *meaning structures*. They compose the very frames and frameworks of our mind-and-emotion—of our personality. No wonder they are so influential in the effects they have upon us. They command nervous system functions. They govern perception. And, once installed, beliefs take on *a life of their own*.

The "Thought" / "Belief" Difference
- As we consider beliefs, are they not just thoughts?
- Or is there a difference between a thought and a belief?
- Can we think things without believing them?

Yes, *thoughts* differ from *beliefs*. While beliefs contain thoughts, all thoughts are not beliefs. It is when our thoughts grow up to become fully developed as *beliefs* that they operate as self-fulfilling prophecies. Then, "as we believe—so we are," and so we perceive and receive. If we believe that people will hurt us, we suddenly develop the eyes to see hurt all around us. If we believe that we can't do something, our body and neurology takes this belief as a *command*. It becomes our frame of mind about that ability.

Every belief has at least two levels of thoughts. First, we have *a set of representations* about something, then we have thoughts of *confirmation and validation* about those representations. This differentiates a "thought" from a "belief."

We think at the primary level by representing. We encode the cinema of our mind with sights (images), sounds, sensations, smells, tastes, and words. But mere representation a belief does not make. It takes something more. It takes a higher level thought *about* the representation. It takes a meta-state or meta-level structure of validation, and that thinking at a meta-level creates mental contexts and frames.

Test it. Think about something you believe or do not believe. Here is a menu of some "thoughts" to try on. See if you can *represent* these words on the screen of your mind and create a see-hear-feel movie of them. Notice also if you "believe" them or not, and to what degree.
- Failing at something important to you reflects on who you are as a person.
- There is no failure, there is only feedback and information regarding the attempt; it says nothing about you as a person.
- People have to exercise regularly to stay fit.
- Hitler was actually a good man who was only trying to improve the quality of life for all people.
- Santa Claus flies around the world on Christmas eve in a sled and comes down fireplaces to bring toys to good boys and girls.

How did you do in terms of *representing* these thoughts?
- What sensory-based representations do you use as you *think* such thoughts?
- What language and words do you say to yourself?
- Which statements do you believe and which do you not believe?
- How do you know you believe or don't believe?

•   What's the difference between a thought and a belief?

I can *think* all of the above thoughts. I can *represent* them. I can entertain them as *ideas*. I can even amplify these thoughts so that I see them vividly and dramatically as I create a three-dimensional movie of them and step into them. Yet does that mean I *believe* them? No way! Can you *think* all of those ideas *without* believing in them? Of course you can!

Are there other thoughts that you can 'think' (represent) *without* believing? I hope so.
•   So what actually distinguishes a thought from a belief?
•   What distinguishes an idea that we believe from one that we do not?

Even if you make a movie with the most life-like and reality-like representations of the thoughts you do not believe using all of the modalities and "sub-modalities" of an idea that you strongly believe—that shift, in and of itself, will not turn the idea into a belief. Even if you make your movie brighter, closer, more colorful, if you step into it as a three-dimensional movie, etc., it may seem more believable or more intense, but it will not necessarily transform the thought into a belief.

That's the traditional way NLP attempted to create belief changes. And while it's a nice and fun pattern, the problem is that it doesn't work very often or very well. Why not? Because it failed to deal with the structural difference between a thought and a belief.[2]

So what is a belief? How does it differ from a mere thought?
> *Beliefs exist on a higher "logical level" than thoughts. To transform a thought into a belief we have to set a frame of validation over or around the thought. This meta-level confirmation then transforms the thought into a belief. The confirmation may entail reasons, reasoning, proof, evidence, authority, repetition, etc. The language of the validation typically involves a "Yes!" The "Yes" says, "That's right!" Or "That's real!" Or "That's true." This meta-states the thought with validation and that's what transforms it into a "belief."*

The *"Yes!"* that we speak to the primary level thoughts (our representational movie) *confirms* the ideas. The *"Yes"* validates the thoughts and so establishes the representations as real or true. After all, that's what we're saying. "Yes, that's true. Yes, that's the way it is." The *"Yes"* applied to our thoughts and feelings meta-states the representational-thoughts with a frame of confirmation. This transforms thoughts into beliefs.

When this happens, we not only "think" that a given *External Behavior (E.B.)*

means, leads to, causes, creates, or equals a specific *Internal State* or *Significance,* meaning, value *(IS)*, we also affirm and assert that it does. We make it an item for our list of "true" statements and real things. In this way a belief involves a thought that already has a frame around it. A belief has a *confirmation frame* around some thought. A belief involves a thought embedded inside of a frame-of-reference of validity, a *"Yes!"*

Figure 4:1

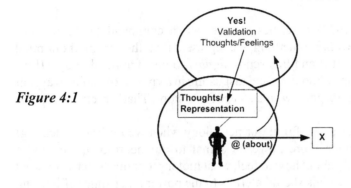

The Neuro-Semantic Power of a Belief

Could this explain why we experience some "thoughts" as if they were "real" and "solid" things? Yes, indeed. In fact, that's the feeling tone of a "belief." When we have a *belief*, we feel sure. We feel convinced about something. We "just know" that something is a certain way and we don't even question it. These meta-feelings are meta-states.

This explains why beliefs also are so difficult to change by a direct assault. As they become part of our understanding frame about some domain of experience, we not only think but we *feel* them as being "true" and "valid." Our higher level *seal of approval* (the meta-*yes* that we utter to the thought) solidifies the belief. That's why we do not even think of our beliefs as thoughts, ideas, representations, or opinions. They *feel* "real." When we *believe* something it becomes part of our inner "fabric of reality" which is why we close our mind to other alternatives. We feel so sure we are totally convinced. That's because in the process of believing, that is, confirming thoughts, we create our felt sense of "reality."

> Richard Bandler (1985) describes a belief as "a command to the nervous system."

This generates what we call our reality strategy—a meta-state structure that we very seldom call into question.

- "What's wrong with you son, it's a fact that boys shouldn't cry!"
- "You need your head examined! Anybody with any sense can see that Bill Clinton is a cheat and a liar!"
- "She's crazy. She thinks that if I raise my voice I'm being abusive."
- "Leave him alone. You can't reason with him. He's got it stuck in his head that all X are stupid."

Richard Bandler (1985) describes a belief as "a command to the nervous system." When we *think* something, we represent it on the screen of our mind and create a movie of it and this sends *signals* to our brain and body. If we think about something obnoxious and disgusting in a vivid and graphic way, our nervous system will respond with a state of aversion. That's pretty powerful!

Yet how much more powerful in our neurology when we *believe* something! Then we send a much more powerful signal to our neurology, we send a *command* to our body about how to feel, what motor programs to activate, what neurology to engage. This should alert us to the power and danger of limiting beliefs as the following.

- "I just can't learn very well."
- "I can't say no and mean it."
- "I can't think well of myself."
- "I can't say I'm sorry."
- "I'm just not the kind of person to smile and think positively."
- "Whenever you use that word, I feel put-down."
- "To make a mistake is just terrible."
- "I'll never forgive because that would let him off the hook."
- "I can't change—that's just the way I am!"
- "People can't control their beliefs."
- "If you feel a certain way, then you have to express it."
- "It's terrible to not achieve your goals in just the way you dream about them coming true."

Such toxic and limiting beliefs do not merely rattle around in our heads as harmless thoughts. They operate as meta-state *energy fields* and set forth a frame-of-reference that governs all of our mental, emotional, and body operations. Pretty scary, huh?

Reframing Meanings/ Beliefs
Centuries ago William Shakespeare wrote these famous words,
"There is nothing either good or bad, but thinking makes it so."

If a *belief* is a set of representations that we confirm linguistically with a *"Yes!"*

then as soon as we begin to say *"Well, maybe..."* (questioning doubt) to it, or *"No, no way!"* (disbelief), or apply other sets of representations or frames to it —we initiate the reframing process. Re-framing means that we have put another and/or a different *frame-of-reference* around a thought. We *frame* it in a different way, with a different thought.

Now we understand the significance and power of this. Now we understand that when we do something as simple as put another frame around a thought—we change "reality." We change neuro-semantic reality, that is. And it is at this point that the magic occurs.

This means that reframing is one of the most profound and incredible powers of mind that we have. Reframing puts into our hands a way to change a mind, send new signals and commands to a nervous system, increase options, expand choices, enhance emotions, enrich life, liberate from imprisoning mental boxes, and turn limitations into resources. It does all of this because our mental-emotional frames determine and govern our internal reality.

The Internal Structure of Meaning

Since *meaning* does not occur in the world, but in the mind of a meaning maker, then *in and of itself, no event, word, or experience means anything.*

Things (events, actions, people, situations, and even words) only *mean* something (have connection with a mental understanding) when *we* make the linkage. Meaning is an inside job. It takes a meaning-maker to create meaning. You've never walked along the sidewalk and stubbed your toe on a meaning that someone discarded. You've never picked up a meaning and smelled it.

Why not? Because meaning doesn't exist "out there." It takes a *performer* to act on the events of the world to construct meaning. In the Meta-Model we have the distinction of "Lost Performative." It would be nice to find some "meaning" that just dropped out of heaven. But no. There's always a human fingerprint (mind-print) on every piece of meaning.

> Re-framing means that we have put another and/or a different *frame-of-reference* around a thought. We have *framed* it in a different way, with a different thought.

To use the box metaphor ("thinking in a box," "thinking outside the box"), we create meaning and call it into existence as we attach and link a thought or feeling to our representations of an external event. There's a formula for how we do this. At first this may seem so simple that you may be tempted to say, "Yes, of course" and rush on without realizing that there's wonder and magic in this.

Figure 4:2

E.B. —>/ = I.S.

External Behavior —>/ = Internal State

This gives us the first level structure of meaning. Our neuro-semantic fabric of reality arises in this way. It arises because we do not operate on the world directly, but only indirectly. We operate upon "reality" via our models *of* the world.

Given our neurological constitution we are not able to see all of the electromagnetic wavelengths. We only see via the *transforms* that our sense receptors (rods, cones, neuro-pathways, visual cortex, etc.) allows us to see. Creatures with different internal constructions of their eyes create different models for seeing and so see differently—ultraviolet light, zooming-in on great distances (hawks), seeing through the surface of the ocean (sea gulls), etc. Ultimately, we all construct models of the world which we call beliefs, learnings, ideas, values, etc. We operate from these models or paradigms as they internally organize us.

Meaning arises from, and operates according to, *the frame* that *we put around any event or situation.* Here the contexts (or frames) that we apply to the information controls our derived and attributed meanings. To "understand" any event we have to *reference* it in terms of something. The context that we bring to the event may be another event, a symbol, word, experience, etc. That operates as our *frame-of-reference.*

Meanings change with every shift of our frames. We call this re-framing. Whenever we change a frame-of-reference, we change the meaning. We see, think, feel, etc. the event according to a different reference. Meaning is plastic and moldable. We can shape and reshape it. It's not rigid or stiff. It slips and slides in our hands and minds. Ultimately, whatever we think and believe about something—so it is to us.

If we think of the planet as flat and as the center of the universe, then we see the sun circling the planet, rising and setting, etc. The old Ptolemaic paradigm can indeed take into account many facts and "make sense" on one level.

If we see a voodoo priest stabbing a pin into a representative doll and we believe this is a true and inescapable hex guaranteeing our death—so it will become to us. Autopsies of the "Voodoo" deaths in Haiti consistently

> Meaning arises from, and operates according to, *the frame* that *we put around any event or situation.*

reveal no "natural" cause of death. Somehow, in some way, the autonomic nervous system of the believer shuts down. The belief in voodoo sends commands to the autonomic nervous system that one will die ... and so the person dies.

If frames control or govern meaning (which then controls the emotions, states, experiences, behaviors, etc.), then framing things in ways that make solutions possible provides a very powerful intervention at the paradigmatic level which lies outside of our consciousness.

Maybe It Means This/ Maybe It Doesn't

Bandler and Grinder introduced the following story in their book on *Reframing* (1985):

> A very old Chinese Taoist story describes a farmer in a poor country village. His neighbors considered him very well-to-do. He owned a horse which he used for plowing and for transportation. One day his horse ran away. All his neighbors exclaimed how terrible this was, but the farmer simply said *"Maybe."*
>
> A few days later the horse returned and brought two wild horses with it. The neighbors all rejoiced at his good fortune, but the farmer just said *"Maybe."*
>
> The next day the farmer's son tried to ride one of the wild horses. The horse threw him and the son broke his leg. The neighbors all offered their sympathy for his misfortune, but the farmer again said *"Maybe."*
>
> The next week conscription officers came to the village to take young men for the army. They rejected the farmer's son because of his broken leg. When the neighbors told him how lucky he was, the farmer replied *"Maybe."* (p. 1).

What a fascinating interplay of meanings and emotions. When the farmer's horse ran away, the neighbors grieved. Framing it as a loss for the farmer, they felt sad. However, when the horse returned with two wild horses, their *grief changed into joy* as their frames shifted from loss to gain.

Later when a wild horse threw his son so that he broke his leg, they framed it as pain and so their *joy turned into sorrow*. What they felt as good news turned into bad news. Yet when the conscription officers came to draft young men the following week, they rejected the boy because of his broken leg. Again, the frame changed to that of gain and so their *sadness turned back into joy*.

The arrival of the conscription officers changed the context of the broken leg so that what they had viewed as a handicap, they now viewed as a blessing. *The change of context kept changing the meanings.* All the while, the old farmer held back from making such quick (and inadequate) evaluations—so his emotions didn't bounce all over the place as did those of his neighbors.

This story helps us to more fully appreciate the importance of *contexts* or *frames.* It facilitates our awareness *that* meaning does not lie in words, actions, stimuli, etc. It lies in the evaluative understanding of a meaning-maker and that every meaning maker constructs meanings using some reference point or frame.

We say that meaning is context dependent. That is, what something means depends upon the context of who said it, when, where, how, why, etc. The villagers too readily assumed their frames whereas the wise old man didn't behave in such a semantically reactive way.

In the story, we experienced a continual rapid shifting between frames so that "the meaning" of the events also quickly kept changing. When the frame of the son's broken leg changed, the meaning changed. *This the magic of reframing: when we change a frame, we transform meaning.* That's why giving an event a different meaning typically leads to different responses and different emotions. It's that simple; it's that profound.

Since meaning isn't a thing in the see-hear-feel world, but mental framing in the mind-body of a meaning-maker, all meaning depends upon context. Meaning depends on the internal context of our thinking, believing, valuing, and deciding. It depends upon the social and cultural contexts in our mind that we apply to things.

Context determines the meaning of everything we say, think, or hear. In the farmer story, the content didn't change, the events remained the same. Yet, the meaning changed as different contexts of significance and value came into play. Precisely because the contexts changed so quickly, it awakens us to the realization that "nothing inherently means anything." Meaning is a function of the conceptual and belief constructions that we bring to the events.

Competency at Identifying the Structure of Meaning
If beliefs offer us such a port of entry into neuro-semantic reality (our own and that of others), then how do we develop competency in identifying operating beliefs? How can we train ourselves to recognize the structure of meaning in

the process of communication?

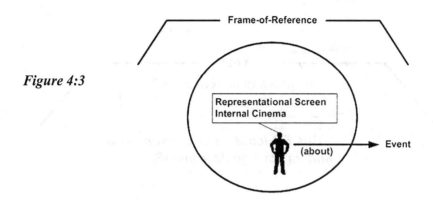

Figure 4:3

The answer lies in the box metaphor. That's why we have put *the magic box or cube* at the very center of the Mind-Lines model. What is this "magic" box or cube?

> The box describes a way of thinking about the linguistic structure of meaning and provides a diagram for representing it visually. It is a formula that summarizes the complexity of how we construct meaning. It is the E.B. leads to (—>) and equals (=) the I.S.

This refers to how we have taken representations about events and connected them in a frame of identity ("is," "equals") and causation or contribution ("causes," "leads to"). These words map out a conceptual reality about how the world works, what things "are," and what leads to what.

When we move beyond mere representation and come to validate the thought, we come to *believe* it. Then, as we say *"Yes!"* to it, we transform it into the very fabric of our reality strategy. Then, this meta-state of confirmation makes the thought a command to our neurology. In a "magical" way, we create an organizing force inside our nervous system. We create a piece of neuro-semantic reality that may enhance our life or severely disturb it. Saying *Yes* puts the thought within a box. We then think about that subject inside that box. The box (or cube) becomes our mental world—the framework of our mind about that content.

Figure 4:4
The Structure of Belief

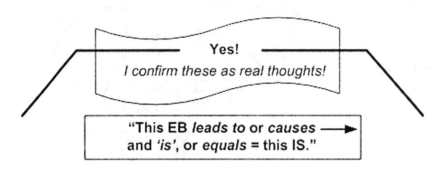

The Meta-Model gives us numerous *linguistic markers* or key words which mark out the mental maps that we call "beliefs." The central ones include: "is, makes, causes, equals, equates to, leads to," etc. This gives us a way to identify *beliefs*. We only need to listen for:

- *Causation statements:* Any statement about "cause" describes how we model the way the world works, functions, relates to itself, etc.
- *Equation statements:* Any statement that equates things describes how we model meaning, what abstractions equate with behaviors.
- *Value words and ideas:* Any word or statement about importance describes ideas, events, experiences, etc. we deem important.
- *Identifications:* Any term that identifies one thing with another describes what things equal we identify as the same as something else.
- *Presuppositions:* Any statement that is an unquestioned assumption indicates what we assume is as true without question.

To develop competency and skill in hearing these linguistic distinctions we mentally move to a meta-position. That is, we go above and beyond the content of the words and consider them in terms of their function. We can then inquire about the kind of words and patterns that we detect:

- What representational signals do these words elicit?
- What "Yes!" affirmation does this presuppose about an idea?
- What frames-of-references do they imply?
- What operational beliefs drive these statements?
- What does the person assume as real for this to make sense?

A Technology of Magic
For several chapters we have dropped some hints about the Meta-Model, now it's time to spill the beans about this technology of magic. The Meta-Model gives us an explanatory model regarding *how* we create our reality models from our experiences.

How? We *model* the world or territory by abstracting from the world to create our conceptual *model of the world*. We model it first in see-hear-feel representations, then we use words. As this shows up in language, we have cause-effect constructions, complex equivalences, identifications, etc. In Appendix B, we have a summary of the Meta-Model itself.

The original *Meta-Model* highlights 12 neuro-linguistic distinctions in language. These indicate that the meaning or structure of our words are not formed very well. As maps, they are ill-formed. This does not make these ill-formed expressions "bad." Not at all. They simply indicate that in our *mental mapping* we have left things out (deletions), generalized to create summations and categories (generalizations), and changed things (distortion). Sometimes deleting, generalizing, and distorting enhances our lives as we generate powerfully enhancing maps. At other times, they create major problems so that we can't tell up from down, reality from imagination. We then have lots of problems adjusting.

Along with the 12 linguistic *distinctions* that highlight potential semantic problems, the Meta-Model *questions* each distinction. These questions enable us to think about our mental maps in a way so that we can re-map and develop well-formed structures. The name, *meta*-model refers to the fact that this is a model *about* our linguistic creation of meaning. The questions in the Meta-Model empower us to build more well-formed paradigms in areas where we have left things out, over-generalized, distorted, or nominalized in non-enhancing ways.

Overall the Meta-Model provides a way to think and talk about how we engage our mental mapping processes. By identifying the innate modeling processes (deletion, generalization, distortion) it gives us some categories for thinking about our mental maps and how to *think about our thinking*. As a model-of-models (a meta-model), it enables us to tune our ears to hear paradigms—our own and others.

Transforming Reality Through Reframing
Everything we say occurs within a frame-of-reference and that frame within yet other frames. We live our mental-emotional lives within multiple layers of embedded frames. These represent the presuppositions and paradigms that govern our lives outside of awareness. At a larger logical level than internal representations of specific visual, auditory, and kinesthetic components we have over-arching frames which govern the representations.

The reframing process entails several things. First we identify the frames we use to process information that create our reality and experience. Then we flexibly shift frames to generate more enhancing meanings. In *reframing* we cognitively restructure our perspective (i.e., points of view, perceptual positions) as we generate new meanings that transform life.

Whenever we put a piece of behavior or perspective in a different frame, we *transform* the *meanings*. Because reframing changes the frame-of-reference from which we perceive, it changes meanings. And when meaning changes, so do our responses, beliefs, and behaviors. Reframing enables us to bring about change which becomes especially useful in transforming behaviors, habits, emotions, and even physical symptoms that we don't like.

How important are frames? Frames govern experience and hence the quality of our lives. Because frames run our perceptions, understandings, values, emotions, behaviors, etc. whoever sets a frame assumes psychological control of a situation or set of relations. *Whoever sets the frame, runs the show.*[3]

If meaning does not exist in the world, but in our minds, it inevitably arises from our thinking, evaluating, explaining, attributing, believing, interpreting, etc. What exists in the world are the brute facts of empirical reality—stimuli, actions, events.

It's the frames we put around the brute facts that determine our meanings. By reframing we attach new frames which evoke new meanings to the same sensory stimuli. We can leave the world alone and still invent new ways of responding. Isn't that incredible? Without changing external events, people, situations, etc. we can still change how we think, feel, and respond to things. Talk about power! Talk about taking charge of how we move through the world! Talk about running your own brain!

When should we reframe our perspective*?* That's simple: *Whenever we want to change our response.* Sure we could (and sometimes should) change the world. Frequently, that's not possible. Yet we can always change one thing, we can change our attitude and frame-of-reference. Human history has long demonstrated that we can attribute a great number of meanings (some enhancing, some disempowering) to any given stimuli of actions or events. And whatever meaning we attach to the event will become "real" to us—on our insides, in our nervous system.

Identifying Frames-of-Reference

Given that we process information through various *frames,* the problem in finding these frames rests in that most of them lie *outside* awareness. Once we formulate our thoughts as meaning structures, put them into our "reality" boxes, and say *"Yes"* to them, we then live inside those frames. As we then get used to them as our models of reality, we stop noticing them. They become a canopy of consciousness through which we perceive the world. They define our felt sense of "reality." Comprising our beliefs, learnings, and decisions, these frames also establish our identity.

> While we can't always change the outside world, we can always change one thing—we can always change our attitude and frame-of-reference and when we do, the world changes.

Identify frames by stepping back from your processing. When you have that perspective, you can then ask some questions and reflect on your thinking.

- What am I referencing? What events, ideas, contexts?
- What perspective governs this way of thinking?
- What assumptions and presuppositions drive this?
- From whose eyes do I see this?
- What has to be true for this to make sense?
- What thoughts and ideas am I assuming as real?

While the frames we adopt and utilize extend as far as human understanding, valuing, and believing, common frames-of-reference include the following.

- *Comparison frame:* "She does this so much better and quicker than I do!"
- *Self-esteem frame:* "I would feel like a nobody if I got fired from this job."
- *Self-identity frame:* "I'm not that kind of person."
- *Historical frame:* "That's the way I have always been."
- *Relational frame:* "I'm a mother first and foremost."
- *Success/failure frame:* "Could I succeed if I tried to write a book?"
- *Masculinity/ femininity frame:* "I won't say that, it wouldn't seem manly."
- *Right/wrong frame:* "You shouldn't talk that way; it's wrong."
- *Emotional/intellectual frame:* "He's a guy who lives out of his head."
- *Pleasure/pain frame:* "Will this be fun?"
- *Relevance frame:* "How is this relevant to what I'm doing?" Etc.

Kinds of Reframing
Because changed meanings lead to new responses, when we change the meaning of something, we alter the way that we respond to it.

In **content reframing,** we operate inside *the formula box* and simply shift the frame from one frame-of-reference to another. "It doesn't mean this, it means this other thing." We can discover more useful meanings if we ask such questions as:

- *How can I view this event as valuable?*
- *What is the positive intention that initiated this behavior?*

Nelson Zink suggests a most useful process for developing reframing flexibility. "Try giving every event at least three different meanings and see how this changes your world." Use this as a way to challenge yourself to get out of your current mental boxes:

- How else can I view this?
- What other perspectives could I use?
- What are some of the other viewpoints that others use?

In **context reframing**, we move outside of the formula box. We then explore the context that surrounds the box, the contexts of contexts, and what shifts of contexts would make a greater difference.

- *In what context would this behavior or response function usefully?*
- *Where would I want to produce this response?*

From Meta-Model to Mind-Line Patterns

The Meta-Model provides overt and explicit understanding of how we create our mental maps using language. *Mind-Lines*, by contrast, provide a model for *conversational reframing*. Here we do things covertly. To do this we start with two Meta-Model distinctions that deal with meanings that relate to cause, association, identity, intention, etc. In them, we will find the heart and center of most neuro-semantic magic.

> 1) Complex equivalences (CEq) and
> 2) Cause-effect (C-E).

Reframing also involves making a distinction between *behavior and intention*, behavior and person. We distinguish what a person *does* (the behavior, E.B.) and what a person *seeks to achieve* by those actions (the person's internal representations, intentions, and meanings). Again, this encodes the *inside* and the *outside* worlds. So, this step-by-step process goes:

Step 1: Notice the Meta-Model distinctions.

> As you engage in conversation with people, listen for *causation beliefs* (C-E). Pay attention to causative words ("because, if, when, in order to, so that" and all present tense verbs). Listen for *meaning beliefs* (CEq) by paying attention to equation words ("equals, is, equates to," etc.) and universal quantifiers (all, always, never). As you listen, constantly inquire about specifics (i.e., see, hear, feel behaviors) and what the person thinks, believes, or means about such.

Step 2: Create an E.B. = I.S. equation.

Either do this on paper or in your head (which you will find easy enough after you get some practice writing it on paper). Formulate how the statement links up two sets of representations—some **external behavior** and some **internal state** (thought, understanding, state, emotion, etc.). The formal structure of this equation will show up as:

$$E.B. \longrightarrow/ \; = I.S.$$

"She's angry or upset (I.S.) with me because she didn't smile (E.B.) at me as she usually does."

Step 3: Representationally test the statement.

Do this by noticing the see, hear, feel referents, that is, *video-think* about the statement. If you had a video-camera, what would flash across the screen of that camera? Use this as an empirical test for the E.B. in the statements. By *representationally testing* we track directly from only the words offered to some sensory-based representation on the inner theater of our mind.

Step 4: Formalize the structure of meaning.

Next, identify the *meaning* (or I.S.) that the external behavior stands for (or equates to, or causes, etc.) in the mental map. This gives us enough to create the formula.
"Didn't Smile = Angry or Upset with Me"

Suppose someone says, "You made me forget the answer when you asked in that tone of voice." What is the formula? What equation do you hear in that statement? How about: "Your tone of voice = my inability to remember."

Suppose someone says to you, "I can't believe that you're late again." Here we have a see, hear, feel E.B. of "late," but we have no meaning. The "I can't believe..." doesn't specify any meaning. So we meta-model to get the specifics. "Really? What does that mean to you?" "It means you don't care about me." Now we have a meaning and can generate an E.B.=I.S. formula: "Being late = not caring."

Step 5: Playfully offer new frames as you seek to reframe the statement.

When we get the belief to this stage and form, the time has come for us to use the Mind-Line patterns. With this, the fun and magic begins! From here, we can play around with 26 shifts for conversationally reframing.

Do I Have to Think in this Formulaic Way?

No, you don't have to do anything. Yet doing this will tremendously help. Avoiding the clinician or technician stage of developing competence makes it really hard on yourself when you want to move to the ultimate expert stage of unconscious competence.

This step-by-step process enables us more to efficiently and effectively train our intuitions to hear higher level mental constructions involving causation, meaning, intentionality, and identity. Further, since the center of reframing begins with some human meaning-maker attributing, and associating some *meaning* (I.S.) to some external stimuli (E.B.), the more quickly and automatically we train our consciousness to sort and separate between the sensory-based level (E.B.) and the higher evaluative level (I.S.), the more quickly and automatically, we will know where to begin. To develop the greatest effectiveness with these language patterns, tune your ears to hear two kinds of linguistic structures.

1) Cause-Effect Statements (C-E)

When a person speaks in such a way as to imply that one thing *causes* another, they present a *causation* model of the world.

> "When you say mean things to me, it causes me to wonder about the stability of our relationship."

Here, "saying mean things" (E.B., a tangible, empirical see-hear-feel reality) *causes* "me to wonder about the stability of our relationship" (I.S., an internal subjective meaning, state, feeling, etc.).

2) Complex Equivalent Statements (CEq)

When we link two such statements together so that we use them interchangeably, we have created a complex equivalence. Why *complex*? Because one item belongs to one level of reality, and the other to another level. So what looks simple (X=Y) actually involves a very complex set of relationships.

> "When you say mean things to me, it means that our relationship is on the line."
> "When you show up late for these meetings, it means you don't care about me."
> "His tone of voice (E.B.) means that he does not like me (I.S.) and that he will reject me (E.B.) since it is a form of verbal abuse (I.S.)."

Creating a mental equivalent which equates two items existing in different worlds (or levels), creates in our mind-neurology a belief. We then experience it in our nervous system as a *"semantic reaction."* Korzybski described such complex equivalences as "identifications." He described it as *identifying* things that exist on different levels (see Appendix B).

E.B.—>/ =I.S. Thinking

Obviously, we don't always go around presenting our beliefs and surface statements in direct and overt C-E or CEq formats. Nor do other people. More often than not, we talk using only half of the formula. It shows up in everyday language like this:

"I'm depressed."

Here, however, we don't have enough information to even start reframing. We only have an internal state (I.S.), "depressed." We don't have any information from the person's model regarding what *caused* this internal state (C-E) or what the internal state *means* (CEq). This illustrates the value of using the indexing processes of the Meta-Model for information gathering:

- What do you feel depressed about?
- What lets you know that this is depression?
- When did you first begin to feel this way?
- When do you not feel this way?
- How do you know to call this "depression?"

Index by meta-modeling statements of problems, feelings, beliefs, and other abstract concepts to gather high quality information about another person's model of the world. What does he or she think brought this about (C-E)? Or what meaning does it have (CEq)? What other significance does he or she give to it?

Use the following five simple questions to elicit *causational maps (*C-E) and *meaning attributions (*CEq).

C-E	How does this create a problem for you?
C-E	What makes it so?
C-E	How much of a problem does this create?
CEq	What does this mean to you?
CEq	What other meanings do you give to this?

Since we want to make sure that we actually have a problem on our hands (a limiting, non-enhancing map) before we fix it, these questions effectively assist us in converting the sentences and statements that we hear into a C-E or CEq.

Suppose someone says, "You are staring at me." We begin with "staring" as an obvious E.B. (Can you video-think about that? *See* a person *staring.*) We now have half of the formula. So we ask for the person's meaning.

- Is that a problem for you?
- How does that create a problem for you?
- What does it mean when you see him staring?

These questions invite the person to specify the meanings that govern that statement.

"Your staring at me causes me to feel uncomfortable."

The I.S. ("uncomfortable") results from the E.B. ("staring"). We could now run some of the Mind-Line patterns on this. Or we could continue to meta-model the I.S.

*   How specifically does my staring at you cause you to feel uncomfortable?
*   What do you mean by "uncomfortable?"

Another question helpful in translating statements into a complex equivalence for Mind-Line patterning involves *asking the meaning question over and over: What does that mean to you?*

This question directly inquires about a person's neuro-semantics and rarely do people feel it as threatening. Typically, people will give their belief that drives the problem: "Joe is so uncaring."

Now we have a fully blown *identification.* When someone offers the belief itself, simply inquire about the evidence for such.

*   How do you know that Joe is uncaring?
*   What does Joe do that makes you think that?

After you find the evidence and put it into E.B. form, you can construct the complex equivalence.

Thinking and Speaking Like A Magician
When using *Mind-Lines to work semantic magic,* you need to keep a few things in mind.

First, and foremost, keep your outcomes positive and respectful.
These reframing patterns can be used destructively. These patterns have much potential to make a smart ass out of us if we don't keep focused and oriented in a positive and caring way toward the person. Used wrongly, these patterns can alienate people.

Conversely, when we establish a strong, positive, and caring outcome in mind for our communications, that outcome will direct our reframing so that we interact with others respectfully. People will pick up on this. Operating out of a positive and respectful outcome also builds rapport.

Second, stay aware of how the patterns affect your own internal representations.
A great deal of the power within these paradigm shifting patterns

occurs in how they effect how we have coded our representations at the level of the qualities and features of our internal mental cinema.

NLP has traditionally called this the "sub-modality" level. And indeed, much of the magic will occur in terms of the changes that result from editing our internal movies. Actually "sub-modalities" refer to the qualities of our visual, auditory, and kinesthetic representations, the cinematic frames of our movies.

Third, recognize that the plasticity of meaning will make this whole process an art, not a science.

As a semantic magician, refuse to expect every pattern of word magic to work equally well with every belief. It will not work like that. Neuro-semantic magic depends upon many facets and frames that any given person brings to the table. Some patterns will work more effectively with some beliefs than others. Frequently, we need to "keep firing off" different magical lines one after the other until we find one that makes the desired change.

Fourth, keep your eyes and ears open to see what's happening.

Keep your eyes open while you perform your magic. In NLP we call the state of keeping our eyes, ears, and senses open sensory acuity. This uptime state gives us a way to read and use feedback with regard to the effect of our reframing.

Bob says that sometimes a *mind-line* pattern will "scramble a person's eggs" as it creates major shifts and alterations in experiences at the level of the cinematic frames that govern the editing of our movies. Internally the person is experiencing a new or different movie. The internal pictures, sounds, and sensations are recoded so that the experience seems different. Sometimes it radically transforms a person. If that happens, it's a good idea to have your eyes and ears open!

As you meta-model toxic and limiting beliefs and formulate them into *the formula,* continually check out how they effect your own cinematic frames or "sub-modalities." Then, as you later formulate and deliver mind-lines with people, you will have a well developed intuitive sense of how the mind-lines create new and different movies and make editorial shifts in cinematic features. Once you reach that level, you can become truly elegant in delivering mind-lines.

Fifth, layer "one for the road."

Aim to *layer* the reframing patterns. You will make your mind-lining powerfully transformative when you deliver not just one, but several mind-lines in a row. Do this one after another. So feel free to pack them as tightly as you can if you want to pack in magic upon magic. [For more theoretical understanding and depth about Mind-Lines, see Chapter Nine, the summary of the Meta-Model in Appendix B, *The Structure of Magic* (1975), and *Communication Magic (2000)* formerly *The Secrets of Magic* (1998) .]

Summary

- Okay, wake up! Thus endth the theoretical section. Yes we have traveled into the ozone of abstraction in this chapter and given you *Everything You Always Wanted to Know About the Neuro-Semantic Structure of Meaning and Belief and How to Formulate a Meaning Equation.*

- Why in the world did we indulge in that? We did that to satisfy the theoretically minded who want to explore the neuro-semantic structure of meaning. Why is that important? Because knowing the structure enables them to model and remodel experiential states.

- The good news is that you do *not* have to fully understand this chapter to become elegant in conversational reframing. The only thing you really need to get from this chapter boils down to the formula.

- *The formula within the magic box, the neuro-semantic magic formula.*

$$\textbf{E.B.} \longrightarrow / = \textbf{I.S.}$$

- The first reframing move that we have in store for you (Chapter Five) involves a kind of naughty thing. So before returning to this text, get yourself into a state where you feel like you'd really like to mess up some "realities," then meet us back here for.... *deframing.*

End Notes:

1. The word *matrix* literally means "womb." It speaks about the place where something is given birth. As meaning-makers we give birth to belief frames embedded within belief frames. It is beliefs all the way up. And this makes up our Matrix. See *The Matrix Model* (2003).

2. Why doesn't the "sub-modality" belief change pattern work consistently or dependable to change beliefs? This was the question that we asked when we first began to suspect that there was something wrong with the pattern. We didn't find a single person who successful used the pattern with themselves to change beliefs. So what's wrong? No cinematic feature of a "sub-modality" (not even close, in color, bright, loud, etc.) consistently *means* confirmation. This is the critical distinction. A cinematic feature like 3-dimensional and in color is only a distinction about how we have edited our movie, in itself it *means* nothing. What it means and what it stands for as a symbol depends on the meaning-constructions of a given person. All of this is discussed in detail in *Sub-Modalities Going Meta* (2005).

3. For a fuller description of this meta-level principle about the critical role of frames see *Meta-States, Sub-Modalities Going Meta, Frame Games,* and *The Matrix Model.*

PART II:

THE 7 DIRECTIONS

FOR REFRAMING

**"Magic
is hidden
in the language we speak.
The webs that you can tie and untie
are at your command
if only you pay attention
to what you already have (language)
and the structure
of the incantations for growth."**

Bandler and Grinder
The Structure of Magic, 1975

Chapter 5

DEFRAMING

A De-Constructionist's Manifesto
For Overthrowing Regimes of Limiting Beliefs

The Art of Getting Your Grubby Little Linguistic Hands
on Belief Formulas
to Tear Them to Smithereens

- Are you ready for some real fun?
- How about waving your magic wand and making something *vanish into thin air?*
- How about using a magical mind-line and seeing an old limiting belief blown to smithereens?

Sometimes when I go to the beach and watch people having fun, I see them build castles in the sand. I have enjoyed that many times and I still do. And sometimes a big part of that fun comes when we watch the ocean waves rush in and wipe out a pitiful little sand castle. Sometimes, when we feel kind of naughty, we might even have fun running through someone's sand castle with our big giant feet. Have you ever done that? Have you ever thought that you would?

Say, come to think of it, how about letting us start by using the reframing models which specialize in *that* kind of fun?

Well, ready or not—here comes the reframing patterns that we call *deframing*. With these we can really tear things up! With these, neuro-semantic constructions of meaning don't stand a chance. With these, we can ruin a perfectly good *Meaning Cube* any time we so desire. With these, *the formula* crumbles, dis-integrates, collapses, pulverizes, decomposes just as the sand does before the returning ocean waves.

Or to change the metaphor, running these mind-lines feels like flushing the toilet on a belief system that really smells. Say, would you like to run amuck for awhile and learn how to trash belief systems?   And sabotage precious superstitious magic boxes? Or wipe out a belief system with just a word?

```
╔══════════════════════════════════════════╗
║                                          ║
║        Mind-Lines in Chapter Five        ║
║                                          ║
║  #1. Specificity: Chunking Down          ║
║  #2. Detailing a Strategy's Sequence     ║
║                                          ║
╚══════════════════════════════════════════╝
```

De-Constructionism at its Best
These deframing patterns hark back to *the Meta-Model* which we have used in theorizing about all this stuff in the first place.   Actually, the Meta-Model operates as a reductionist tool *par excellence*. It does so because, as a neuro-linguistic tool, it enables us to tear apart linguistic and semantic constructions.

By asking for specificity, precision, and clarity, the *questions* of the Meta-Model enable us to coach a speaker to go back to the experience out of which he or she created the mental map in the first place.   This frequently has the effect of *tearing apart* the map, or imploding the old construction.

Yet we must offer *a caveat* about this as we start. If we don't handle the Meta-Model *questions* with care and respect, we can get so caught up in the process of tearing a piece of meaning apart that we end up drilling a person like a district attorney.   This can lead to becoming a meta-monster.   In fact, this apparently happened when John Grinder first began teaching the Meta-Model at the University of Southern California in Santa Cruz.   His students returned after the first weekend complaining that they had lost all of their friends. So be gentle. It can feel abrasive to people not used to too much clarity or reality.

As a technology of de-construction, the Meta-Model empowers us to untie the knots of our abstractions. With it, we can de-nominalize nominalizations.   So in *deframing* we will primarily use the twelve sets of questions in the Meta-Model to pull apart meaning constructions (and with the expanded Meta-Model, 21 sets of questions).

Conceptually, think about *the meaning formula* that we illustrate with the meaning cube. Now imagine floating down deep inside that three-dimensional box and getting to the bottom of things in there. Imagine floating down deep within it and all the way down until you reach the very conceptual foundations of the belief that you or another constructed. As you do that, access a state of feeling "picky" or analytical. Access a state where you became very critical and analyze something to pieces. As you do, feel yourself putting on your white laboratory coat and, like a good analytic scientist, come with us to discover the component pieces that make up the formula so that you can sabotage it for good.

Playground Equipment for our Explorations

We begin with *the meaning formula* well planted in our minds. You do have it well planted in your mind, do you not? If so, then we can easily stay focused on translating any and every conversation and "problem" expressed or heard into **the E.B.—>/ =I.S. formula.**[1]

This formula plays the crucial role in all conversational reframing patterns. So we first formulate the language and talk that we hear in the things that people say that we call statements, beliefs, values, problems, issues, and put it into the **X—>/=Y** structure.

If you have done that, then *Let the Reframing begin!* To give some content to these patterns, we want to play around with the following belief statements. Think about these as *playground equipment* in training your intuitions.   The first four of these come from long forgotten worksheets that various NLP developers as created and used.

   A) Saying mean things makes you a bad person.
   B) Cancer causes death.
   C) Showing up late means that you don't care about me.
   D) Stress causes me to eat chocolate.
   E) I can't really make a difference because management doesn't walk their talk.
   F) I can't buy your product because it costs too much.

We begin mind-lining by working *inside* of the magical cube. We failed to do that in the first edition but quickly corrected that in the first revision. Why? Because before we can really work with meaning as a constructed map or frame, we have to understand how it works and its component parts. We have to explore and understand the speaker's construction.   That's why we first *deframe*. We first *ask lots of questions* about what the person means, how the person knows what he or she knows, what goes on in the cinematic movie of the mind that cues the person to think this way. So, with that in mind, on to *Deframing*.

#1: Specificity: Chunking Down

Mind-lines are not only statements, they are also *questions*. In fact, as you will discover, they are mostly *questions*. Why? Because we can do a lot more by asking questions than we can by making statements. When we assert things, declare things, and announce things—it is very easy for people to counter with their own assertions, declarations, and announcements. Don't you find that true?

But ask a question and notice what happens. *Questions engage consciousness, do they not?* Questions pull us into a thought, emotion, or experience. And don't you want to become more resourceful and elegant in your communications? Wouldn't it be nice to double or triple your skills at persuasion? If you do, I wonder how much more effective you'd become, or how much more money you could make, or how much more charming you could become?

So while it may, at first, seem strange that we will begin by asking lots of indexing questions, this is what enables us to pace or match a person's model of the world and come to understand the meanings that drive his or her experiences.

Indexing the specifics has traditionally been called "chunking down" in NLP. We listen for abstractions as we listen to people talking and we then begin asking questions that invite them to be more specific and precise about the details. This "chunks down" the generalizations and thereby gives us the structure of the meaning formula, namely, the E.B. and the I.S.

As we do this we essentially engage in a meta-modeling or indexing process. This *tests the reality* of the belief (or meaning). As it employs the meta-modeling process, we come to more fully understand *what* the person is representing on the screen of the mind, *how* the representations are encoded (the cinematic features of the movie), and the higher frames that provide the mental *whys and wherefores*. This gives us the strategy of the cube.

A single term gives us an excellent way to remember the Meta-Model and how it operates. Just remember the term *specifically:*
-      *Specifically* when does this happen?
-      *Specifically* where does it occur?
-      How *specifically* does this work?
-      Who *specifically* do you do this with?
-      In what way *specifically*?

With this focus, you can easily meta-model the language of any belief or meaning statement. Aim simply to *index the referents* of the belief to the person, place, time, event, etc. This will give you *the referential index,* that is, the time-space-person, etc. co-ordinates of the referent idea or experience.

Reducing (or chunking down) the component pieces of a belief system that link the external world (the E.B.) and our internal states of thought, feeling, and experience (I.S.), means that we have stepped into the role of a modeler. We have begun to model the structure of meaning. *Modeling* refers to discovering and specifying the sequential pieces that make up the structure of how a person attributes meaning to his or her experience which creates mind-body states.

What will this do? First and foremost, it will enable us to pull the meaning apart in terms of modalities (the sensory representations and words that make up the movie) and "sub-modalities" (the cinematic qualities, properties, and distinctions of the movie). In other words we will be able to see the internal movie that the person experiences on the inside.

*   *What* is the person seeing, hearing, feeling, smelling, tasting, etc. on the screen of his or her mind?
*   Is the person *inside* the movie or watching it as an observer?
*   What sound track is playing?
*   How close or far is the movie?
*   How is the movie edited in terms of color, clarity, etc.?

As we discover the person's internal cinema, we discover the higher frames that establish the internal *contexts* of the movie. We call these the meta-programs and the meta-states.

*   What are the *perceptual filters* that the person is using as he or she watches the movie?
*   What feelings is he or she experiencing *about* the movie?
*   What intentions, decisions, understandings, thinking patterns, etc. is the person using and how are these influencing things?

All of this questioning comes together to give us insight into the *syntax* (structure and order) of the meaning and how a person has ordered his or her awareness. It flushes out other influencing criteria as meta-level frames so we can specify the very strategy that governs the belief's magic formula. Whether you know it or not, doing this brings us to the heart of NLP and Neuro-Semantics, namely, the art and science of modeling excellence.

We "chunk down" the size of the information coded in the belief inside the magic cube because *beliefs* as generalizations typically involve a lot of fluff (i.e., over-generalizations and vague expressions). In other words, by their very nature, beliefs lack specificity. And no wonder. We create them by *generalizing,* to say nothing of deleting and distorting. This explains why toxic and limiting beliefs depend on vagueness and this creates the destructive "black magic."

"Boys shouldn't cry." Pretty vague, wouldn't you say? No specifics about who, when, where, in what circumstances, says who, for what purpose, etc.
"You can't change beliefs."
- Who specifically came up with that idea?
- When and where did they come up with that?
- Under what circumstances did they draw that conclusion?
- And why? How did that serve them?
- What specifically was that belief in regard to?

Here is the magic. When we chunk down abstractions and over-generalizations to the small pieces of information that construct these limiting ideas, they typically dissolve. They just vanish. *The specificity questions* expose the faulty logic and the sickening consequences of the belief. The specificity questions cause the non-sense to simply melt away.

Think about the Wicked Witch of the West in the movie *The Wizard of Oz* melting into the floor when Dorothy threw clean sparkling water on her in the presence of her monkey-guards. And as you do, hear her shrieks,
    "I'm melting... melting..." What did I ever do to deserve a fate like this?!"

That's what happens to sick, morbid, and limiting beliefs through using the specificity questions. Doesn't that sound like fun? And all you have to do is chunk down abstractions by asking *questions of specificity*. Frequently doing this gives us the feeling that we have thrown magic fairy-dust into the air and uttered something like, "Begone you vague fluffy bugger!"

A) Saying mean things makes you a bad person.
    Saying what 'mean' things specifically? What makes a thing said 'mean?' What specifically do you mean by the term 'mean'? How does the mere saying of words to convey ideas and symbols correlate with the negative emotional state that we refer to as 'meanness'?

B) Cancer causes death.
    Which cancer specifically causes death? How specifically does cancer cause death? Over what period of time? Depending on what other contributing factors? So how does remission play into this understanding?

If you have Meta-Model training these de-framing patterns will be a cinch. Or, if you have studied critical thinking skills. If not, then just keep in mind the specificity question, *"How specifically?"*

Do you find the phrases, "chunking down," or "chunk size" new or odd? The term "chunk" comes from the field of information processing and refers to *the size* of information that we process. George Miller (1956) spoke about the limits of conscious awareness to hold 7 plus-or-minus 2 "chunks" of information at a time. So we speak about a "chunk" of information. How big or small is that chunk? Are we dealing with a large global chunk ("You can't change beliefs!") or a tiny little chunk ("Jill believed that chocolate was the greatest pleasure on the planet when she was six years old.'). As a verb, "chunking" also refers to whether we are moving up to larger chuck of information or down to smaller pieces of ideas. It can refer to the direction that we mentally move as we can go up or down the scale from specific details to large abstractions.

When we *chunk down* we move down the abstraction scale into more and more specific details. When we move up to the heights of abstracting, we engage in outframing. This enables us to directionalize consciousness to move or chunk up the scale from specificity to more global awareness. Doing so describes hypnosis and the meta-stating process. Generally we use *the Meta-Model* to chunk down and *the Milton Model* (after Milton Erickson, MD., the medical hypnotist) to chunk up. The operationalizing questions of the Meta-Model take us down while the hypnotic language of the Milton Model takes us up.

Figure 5:1

Consider the sentence, *"Mind-Lines describes a model of how we frame and reframe meaning."* That's pretty global. It's pretty abstract. To understand it and make sense of it, we need to be more specific. So we "chunk down" on the general terms.

What do you mean by "Mind-Lines?"
>   I mean the seven categories of direction in which we can send our awareness: down, up, before, after, reverse, inverse, and metaphorical. I mean the 26 classifications of language patterns that fit into those directions.

Okay, well, what do you mean by "model?"

> I mean a structured way of thinking about these directions. It is based on how we link events which include actions, experiences, words, and behaviors (E.B.) with what happens inside of us (I.S.). Recognizing this gives us a form or pattern that we can detect in language and that we can use for thinking about the construction of meaning.

And what do you mean by that term, "meaning?"

> The word *meaning* literally refers to what we "hold in mind." Meaning refers to the mental ideas that we entertain and hold in our awareness as our knowledge base and reference system (frame of reference) that governs our perceiving, feeling, and responding.

What does "frame" and "reframe" mean?

> These terms describe the process of organizing our representations of events and ideas. We create a frame of reference by using an event as a prototype for our thoughts. If we were burned badly by fire, we might think of "fire" in terms of that event. The event becomes our frame of reference. From that we construct our frame of meaning, "fire means pain."

How do you represent the idea that "Mind-Lines describes a model of how we frame and reframe meaning"?

> I see the diagram of the cube that has the formula in it, E.B. —> and = I.S. Then I think about the ways I can turn the cube and manipulate it, and I use that as a metaphor for how I can turn an idea around and look at it *from inside the box* and from *outside the box.*

If I were to peak into the cinema of your mind, what would I see?

> You would see the cube about the size of a large box, big enough for a person to step into. It is bright red ... and the letters E.B. and I.S. are on different faces of the cube. On the corner between them in bright yellow there is the arrow (—>) and in bright blue is the equation size (=). I see a magician standing to the side of the box. Why its me! I'm in a black robe, I have a cape and a magic wand ... and I'm saying words that can alter the box...[2]

Okay, okay, I get the idea! Enough chunking down. In communication, chunking up and chunking down the levels of abstraction crucially determines understanding. It alerts us to inquire about the degree of abstraction in any given word or concept. So we learn to ask:

- At what level of abstraction or specificity are you speaking and thinking?
- At what level of detail am I thinking and speaking?

Failing to take one's level of *specificity—abstraction* into consideration invites misunderstandings. We can speak at different levels using similar words and yet hear and make sense of the words differently. Typically, when we fail to recognize the unspecified nature of noun, verbs, adjectives, etc., we *fill in* the details with our own referents. This process describes the very mechanism that makes hypnosis possible.

Even when we use the very same term (i.e., love, science, state, learning, etc.) we can easily misunderstand each other if we use the term *on different levels*. Then we can't level with each other because we're not operating *on the same level*. Korzybski described words that have different meanings on different levels as *multi-ordinal terms* (*Communication Magic*, 2001).[3]

The difference of chunk size, and this process of moving up and down the abstraction scale, describes one of our most basic meta-programs—global - specific. Some people think more *globally* (at a higher chunk level) than others who think more specifically in *details* (or at a much lower chunk level). As such these styles of processing information and levels operate as a neurological and attentional filter and creates different styles of perception. (see *Figuring Out People*).

This distinction identifies rather profound opportunities in moving up and down the scale of abstraction and specificity so that we can tune into the same channel as the person with whom we talk. If we detect that the person speaks globally and with a gestalt picture of the whole, we create rapport if we use those kinds of words. Then we can invite him or her to chunk down by indexing the generalizations.

C) Your being late means you don't care about me.

How specifically does my being late carry all of that meaning? How does it mean that I don't care about you? How late do I have to arrive for it to mean this—30 seconds, 1 minute, 5 minutes, 1 hour? How many minutes suddenly translates into the meaning that I don't care about you? How do you know that at twelve minutes I care, but that at thirteen I don't? If I arrived late by nine and a half minutes, then you will know that I still care about you?

D) Stress causes me to eat chocolate.

How much stress do you need to experience to begin eating chocolate? If you feel pressured to get up and get to work does that do it? If someone says, 'Let's go out on the town!' does that do it?" "Does *eu*-stress as well as *dis*tress cause you to eat chocolate? How specifically does feeling stressed cause you to eat chocolate? If you ate one small piece of chocolate, would that indicate that you must be feeling stressed?

E) I can't really make a difference because management doesn't walk their talk.
> Do you think management never does anything it says? Incredible. ... How much of its talk does it carry out? How do you know how much of its non-walking to use to feel down and depressed? What specifically does management need to do in order for you to believe that you can make a difference?

F) I can't buy your product because it costs too much.
> How much makes up this evaluation of 'too much?'" (It costs five dollars too much.) "So if it only cost four dollars, would that be too much? What about four dollars and one penny? Would that be too much? By lowering the price, I then can count on your purchasing the product?

Pattern Summary
To elicit this conversational reframing pattern, use elicitation questions that move a person down the scale of abstraction to specificity:
- How specifically?
- What specifically?
- When specifically?
- With whom specifically?
- At what place specifically?

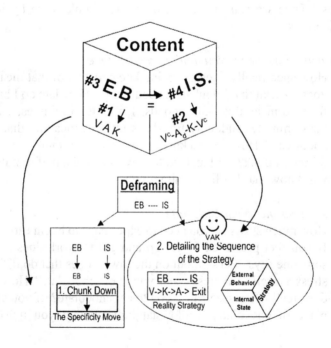

#2: *Detailing the Strategy's Sequence*

In the process of "chunking down" from the belief systems which encode the magic that runs meaning cubes, we not only discover the pieces and components that make up and formulate their subjective experience, we also find their *strategy*.

The term *strategy* refers to how we sequence our internal representations (the visual, auditory, kinesthetic, and words in our movie). We sequence the code so that when we put all of the ingredients together, it creates a formula for cooking up a particular soup of human subjectivity. A strategy describes the process by which we generate an experience.

Consider the strategy *within* the following statement:

> *"When she looks at me and narrows her eyes, I feel judged and put down."*

Now let's suppose that a guy uses this induction as his way to feel depressed.[4] Many people do. The meaning formula goes:

> "Eyes narrowing —> **and =**   feeling judged and put down."
>   the E.B.   leads to and equals   the I.S.

$$\textbf{E.B.} \longrightarrow / = \textbf{I.S.}$$

We could verbally describe the strategy that creates this experience in the following way and then diagram it accordingly.

> External visual awareness (V^e) of her facial expression with special focus on her eyes, represented image in color, close, three-dimensional, then a rehearsing of the words (A_d), "She's judging me and criticizing me," then more words (A_d^m), now words of self-evaluation, "I don't measure up to her expectations," then feeling tension in stomach (K^-), an ache in back of the neck and head, remembering other times of criticism, etc.

$$V^e \quad \longrightarrow \quad A_d — \quad A_d^m \quad \longrightarrow \quad K^-$$

external visual awareness of facial expression, especially her eyes Image in color close, 3-D	"She's judging me & criticizing"	"I don't measure up to her expectations,"	Tension in stomach ache in back of neck

Of course, strategies occur at lightning fast speed. That's why we do not experience them consciously. We only notice the final kinesthetic feeling and emotion, the "depression," in response to the stimulus. As strategies streamline, this process becomes so quick, so automatic, so immediate, that she only has to do one thing to evoke the entire gestalt: narrow her eyes (E.B.) and his *meaning equation* fires off.

Suddenly he feels depressed. He even says so, "She *made* me feel this way!" And because he almost immediately feels depressed, he "knows" that her look "causes" this. Consciously or unconsciously, this becomes his belief. It's a limiting one. It induces him into the state of feeling like a victim. And yet, he really believes it.

Here we have a neuro-semantic "program" in fine working order. It may not improve the quality of life. It does not reflect human excellence or offer a person a very pleasant experience. Yet in terms of *an operational program*, it works and it works regularly, consistently, and predictably. Sure the "magic" here leads to some really rotten experiences like feeling down, discouraged, powerless, controlled, etc. The magic here turns princes into frogs and sends them to the swamp. Yet the structure, the neurology, and the process work perfectly.

Finding this strategy for a given person's reality (reality strategy) offers us a conversational reframing pattern whereby we can pull off some elegant Mind-Lines. It enables us to both identify *the pattern* of the meaning formula and *the strategy* that runs the thinking. Here we will essentially use some mind-lines that question or challenge the data of the program.

•   How did you arrive at this understanding and conclusion?
•   How do you know that you feel "depressed?"
•   What lets you know that it is depression, and not fear?

Process questions like these invite us to access our strategy, to run it from a more objective point-of-view and to develop awareness of it as we notice how it operates. Simultaneously, this interrupts the strategy, introduces a distinction between stimulus (E.B.) and response (I.S.), and plants a question of doubt about how useful or real it is.

A) Saying mean things makes you a bad person.
> Let me get this straight, when you think about this belief you represent *"mean" things* as a harsh tone of voice, and then you recall a memory of a teacher you had in the third grade who seemed really mean and hurtful to you. Then you feel stupid and bad, and as this harsh tonality increases, you hear your own nine-year-old voice say that only a bad person would talk that way. You can also run this belief about certain

cuss words. When you hear those, you recall a school bully from the eighth grade and you say, "Only a bad person can say mean things like that." Is that right?

How do you know to use these black and white categories for "nice" and "mean" and "good" and "bad" today? How would you know if it was not true? What would falsify this understanding?

B) Cancer causes death.

So when you hear the word "cancer," you immediately see a diagram of cancer cells, black consuming cells that expand through an organ or the entire body to end a person's life? You see this as if it's only twelve inches away, in color, and the voice speaks with a tonality of dread and terror. You remember Fred who died of cancer and you hear the terrified voice of his wife talking about "cancer killing him."

So you believe that the human immune system in all humans never has, and never will, respond effectively to cancer cells? And since carcinogenic substances occur in almost everything and in all of us, I wonder how do some immune systems protect so many people against cancer?

In *detailing the strategy's sequence,* we ask for both the evidence and the process that comprises the strategy. In doing this, we discover *how* a person constructs the limiting belief. As a planter of doubt and skepticism, this mind-lining of *Detailing the Strategy's Sequence* deframes by the very process of inviting a person to pull the program apart and examine its logic and structure.

And, as any good constructionist knows, when you start playing around with the "reality" by asking questions, making suggestions, offering advice, linking it up conceptually with other understandings, if the logic doesn't hold, it messes up the psycho-logics of the program. This reality testing enables us to explore the validity of the thinking and to bring more clear and rational thinking to bear upon the programs that we find operating our experiences.

By the way, this explains how we humans can get so messed up. We are not born deficient; we just learn so quickly and associate things in our consciousness with so many other things, that when people talk to us, especially when they don't feel good, when they come out of a grumpy and grouchy state—we can easily get all kinds of toxic and stupid ideas linked up. So people "walk with their dirty shoes in our minds" bringing with them poisonous and irrational crazinesses and, lo and behold, we link it up to some E.B. and presto, a *meaning formula* that will do us great harm.

C) Your being late means you don't care about me.

Really? So when I'm ten minutes late, you begin to make pictures of me and seeing me as someone with a non-caring expression on his face. You see me doing things at the office or talking with someone and you feel an immediate anxiety in your stomach as you recall other memories of someone acting in a non-caring way.

And you do this without any consideration that being late may be a matter of traffic, phone calls, incompetence in scheduling on my part, my weak ability to say "No," or any of a dozen other things that could influence this?

Since the voice you hear about my lack of care sounds so definitive, I guess you never hear it using a questioning tonality, and asking, "I wonder if this really does mean he doesn't care or if it could be something else?"

D) Stress causes me to eat chocolate.

How fascinating that stress "causes" you to eat chocolate. How specifically does this process work? How do you represent stress? You feel tension and discomfort in your body, where specifically? Your stomach. So then you see a box of chocolates and you start telling yourself that you would really like to have some. What tone of voice do you use to say that? And then you taste the chocolate in your mouth? Then what happens? Oh, you tell yourself that the stress causes this, that if you didn't have so much stress you wouldn't be doing this?

So you really believe that your motor programs which activate your feet go looking for chocolate and make your hands rip off wrappings and cram the chocolate down your throat has to carry out this process once you feel "stress?"

E) I can't really make a difference because management doesn't walk their talk.

Wow! Management must really have a powerful hold over your neurology. What they do prevents you from being true to yourself? How does management *not* walking their talk "cause" you to make this choice of believing that you can't make a difference? Oh, you represent "management" as giant people who force you to feel yourself as a little dwarf in comparison? Do you see any particular persons when you see these giant people? No? Just big, vague giants.

Then what? How do you know that they prevent you from walking your talk? You just feel overwhelmed? How? In what way? You feel anxious? How do you know that the tight feelings in your stomach and your restricted breathing means anxiety? It reminds you of a time when you were eleven and playing baseball with some big boys?

Does it always work this way? So you have a black-and-white photo of these giants and you're sure you don't have a color picture of Fred or Bob or Mary Ellen? If you did, would it still feel overwhelming?

[Here *we* have walked in the mind of the speaker and have begun messing around with the old strategy. How fun to tear things apart! Oops, there goes your sand castle! Sorry about that!]

F) I can't buy your product because it costs too much.

I'm interested in how you think about "the price." You said you make a picture of it, what does that picture look like? You know, if I could peak into the theater of your mind, what would it look like? And you said that you tell yourself that "It's just too much." In what tone does that voice speak those words? Oh, it's a panoramic and definitive voice? Kind of like the voice of God, huh? Not like, say, Elmer Fudd? Now do you feel sure you don't hear that in a questioning voice? Or better still, a lustful voice? ...

Pattern Summary

To elicit this reframing pattern, use the strategy elicitation questions:
- How do you represent that belief?
- How will you know if and when it does not hold true?
- What comes first? What comes next? How do you have each piece coded representationally?
- And you're absolutely sure you don't have that in this other format?

The Passion for De-programming

Growing up I (MH) loved pulling things apart to see how they worked. I usually couldn't get them back together—you know, clocks, toys, lawnmowers, car transmissions, but I had such skill (marvelously skilled) at tearing them apart. My younger brother Steve could put them back together. He had that aptitude. But not me. Perhaps that explains why I grew up to play around with neuro-linguistic and neuro-semantic de-programming.

Did you have fun de-framing in this chapter? Well, take some time and practice long and hard (or playfully if you just have to) deframing every piece of neuro-semantic non-sense that you can get your grubby little linguistic hands on. But don't worry about running out of content to play with. Just listen to any talk show on radio or television, any sit-com, most movies, conversations among friends ... and you can find neuro-semantic non-sense everywhere. Ever listen to a politician? A preacher?

Oh yes, do take care with this one. It might alienate friends and loved ones if you do it without their permission, or if you get on a roll and do it for hours on end. Do it here. Do it there. Set up a private practice so that you can privately practice on people! As Richard Bandler says, "Why do you think they call it 'private practice?'"

Summary

- Unsane, unproductive, toxic, and limiting neuro-semantic constructions just can't stand up to the deframing power of using *the indexing questions* of the Meta-Model. When you simply explore what a person means by using unspecific terms (nouns, verbs, nominalizations, etc.), it tears apart the old structures and de-programs the old strategy.

- Conversely, when we do the same with sane, productive, and empowering beliefs, it strengthens the program by *refreshing the frame*.

- The meta-modeling kind of mind-lining unglues toxic dragon states. You will find this very process used in the meta-stating process of slaying and taming dragons in *Dragon Slaying: Dragons to Princes* (2000).

- Mind-Lines that chunk down to specifics tap into the specificity move and so elicit clarity and precision.

- In detailing a strategy's sequence, we mind-line by using the component pieces that we chunked down to to identify the program that runs the magic.

End Notes:

1. The meaning equation refers to the linking of something *external* (E.B.) and something *internal* (I.S.). We take an event, behavior, stimulus, or trigger and equate it to an internal significance or state. We can even create meaning using the structure of I.S.=I.S. When we do, we first have to find an external event or behavior for one of the *internal states.* So with "feeling guilty makes me feel bad" we can ask, "What triggers the guilt feeling?"

2. In Mind-Line trainings we actually use a three-dimensional box that looks like this. You can see this in the video-tapes of various trainings. See Tom Welch's website, www.nlp-video.com.

3. A multi-ordinal term is any term (mostly nominalizations) that can be used at different levels of abstraction. At the primary level *love* refers to attraction and affection. Can we apply this term to itself? Can we *love* love? Yes. We call that infatuation. Can we love our love of our love (that is, can we love infatuation)? Yes, we might call that romanticism. Can we love romanticism? And so it goes. At each level the term *love* means something different.

4. We use the word *induction* because any words that *induces* us to think-and-feel in a certain way operates as an induction, a hypnotic induction.

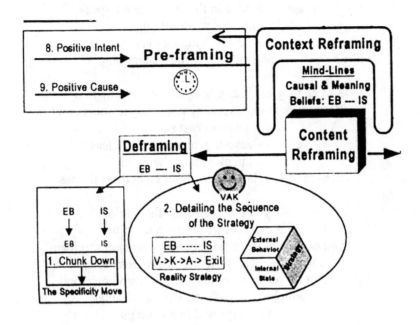

Magic is hidden in the language we speak.
In a process world of ongoing
and ever-changing events
nothing inherently means anything.

Yet, magically, anything can mean something.
Because with words and symbols at your command,
you can cast spells
as you weave together a web of ideas
for the movies of the mind
and all the higher levels of our embedded frames.

As you move through the world,
and meet *events* on the road of life,
you can associate the most enhancing states to them
and thereby call forth *neuro-semantic magic.*
Then for good measure, you can wrap your spell
with higher level contexts and frames,
meanings within meanings
and those meanings embedded
in yet higher meanings for a new robust Matrix.

The spells you cast are at your command
if only you pay attention
to your magic wand of symbolism
and its secrets about the structure of magic
as you speak enchantment throughout your world.

L. Michael Hall

Chapter 6

CONTENT REFRAMING

REFRAMING THE MEANING
WITHIN THE BOX

The Magic of Changing "Reality"

"Those who control language control people's minds.
Sloppy language invites sloppy thought."
George Orwell

"I could have had a moment of
restructuring my neuro-semantics!"
L. Michael Hall

- Would you love to be able to shift meanings to thereby transform
  reality as you know it?
- Are you ready to do some basic reframing?

While we went on and on about lots of theoretical stuff in the first three chapters
(and if you have an addiction for theory, check out Chapter Ten), you actually
don't need to know all of that stuff to *reframe*. The art of reframing itself is
simple and, by the way, you've been doing it all your life anyway.

Oh, really? We do? Actually, all you really need to know with crystal clarity
concerns *the formula*. You do remember the formula, do you not? The
formula lies *inside the three-dimensional box* (or cube) that we represent in the
Mind-Lines Chart. This highlights the most central facet of this whole neuro-
linguistic and neuro-semantic approach.

If you look at *Chart 2:6* (page 48) for a moment, you will notice that at the very heart of meaning there is *a semantic equation*. This equation codes three forms of meaning-making that come directly from the Meta-Model, namely:

- Meanings of *causation* (C-E)
- Meanings of *equation* (CEq)
- Meanings of *identity* (Id.).

The equation, X=Y, or E.B.=I.S., summarizes succinctly that as we move through life, we experience **events** (E.B., External Behaviors, events, empirical see-hear-feel stimuli) and we attach **meaning** to those events (*meaning* or I.S., Internal States or Significance). We do this in a variety of ways that we summarize as causation, linkage or association, and identity:

- *Cause:* A trigger that leads to and creates effects (C-E)
- *Linkage:* We associate a meaning (thought-emotion) with an event (CEq)
- *Identity:* We identify with a person, thing, or ideas to create an *identity* or *identification* (personal and impersonal, Id.)

All of this describes how we enter into the wild and wonderful world of *meaning* (associative meaning and contextual or conceptual meaning). By the way, we often use the term "semantics" to refer to language or words, rather than meanings as when we say, "Oh that's just semantics." Typically, we do that to complain about the term or phrase rather than the "meaning."

In this, we first produce a mind-body-emotion neuro-linguistic construct of meaning and then we experience it. In doing this we connect, associate, relate, and equate something of the world of forces, physics, and energy—the E.B. or the world of *Plethora* (to use Bateson's terms, 1972) with something of the world of ideas, information, communication, organization—the I.S. or the world of *Creatura*. Bateson used these terms, *Plethora* and *Creatura* to distinguish two very different realities. We more commonly label these "objective" and "subjective" realities (Figure 6:1).

The neuro-semantic constructions as our maps of the world are our personal and professional paradigms, our frames-of-reference, and our beliefs. They create the contexts and frames within which we work, live, move, breathe, feel, and have our being. Yet sometimes they do not serve us well. Sometimes they make life a living hell. Sometimes they box us in and create all kinds of personal limitations. That's when they really suck.

Figure 6:1
The Inside and Outside Worlds

Creatura   **Plethora**

The living person   The Everything else
Ideas, Information   Energy Manifestations
Communication   Behavior, Actions
Organization   Physics
Mind   Non-Mind

It's when our meaning creations suck that we need to reframe. At that point we need a paradigm shift to transform our limiting beliefs into enhancing beliefs. Whenever I (MH) say that, I think about the V-8 Juice commercials where someone slaps their forehead with the palm of the hand and sighs in an expression of sudden insight, "I could have had a V-8!" Except, when I do it in this context, I see-and-hear, *"I could have had a paradigm-shift!"* When we suffer from toxic ideas and beliefs we need a cognitive restructuring:

"I could have had a cognitive restructuring of my neuro-semantics!"
"I could have experienced the world through an enhancing belief!"

Well, that's what this chapter is about. Here you will find *four ways to reframe your realities.* Do you remember Paul Simon's song, *"Fifty Ways To Leave Your Lover"*? Well, this book offers you *26 Ways To Change Your Neuro-Semantics.*

Mind-Lines in Chapter Six

#3. *Reframe E.B.* by redefining it.
#4. *Reframe I.S.* by redefining it.
#5. *Reflexively apply E.B.* to self or other.
#6. *Reflexively apply I.S.* to self or other.

Back to the Playground

With the meaning formula in mind, we can translate any and every conversation into the *E.B.—>/ =I.S. format* so that we can then run the conversational reframing patterns. And again, we will use the following as the playground in which to train our intuitions.

> A) Saying mean things makes you a bad person.
> B) Cancer causes death.
> C) Showing up late means that you don't care about me!
> D) Stress causes me to eat chocolate.
> E) I can't really make a difference because management doesn't walk their talk.
> F) I can't buy your product because it costs too much.

#3:   *Content Reframing:*
Reframe the E.B. by Redefining It

In content reframing we create new frame meanings about a behavior by *re-defining* or *re-labeling* the external behavior part of the equation. In other words, we call it by a different name. We give it a new and different label which frames it with a different meaning. And, as we call it by another name or classify it in another frame, this re-defines the external behavior. It links it up with a new frame of reference, and sometimes—just sometimes —it creates magic for our minds and emotions.

A) Saying mean things makes you a bad person.
> True enough at times, although in this instance I am actually not uttering *mean* things, Actually I'm just expressing some of my understandings in an attempt to let you know where I stand. Is that mean? I hope you can see that this isn't really mean talk, just talk that may be a little too expressive and assertive for you.

B) Cancer causes death.
> Well, yes, in a way. Actually, I think it's more accurate to say that cancer causes a weakened immune system, not death, wouldn't you?

In reframing by *re-defining* an external behavior, we are asserting something about the meaning frame. We are saying, *"X doesn't mean Y, it means Z."* The Z offers a different attribution or label for the behavior. And when we change the meaning of a behavior or event, we reformulate the neuro-linguistic system out of which comes the responses that generate the first behavior.

C) Your being late means you don't care about me.
> Really? Actually I didn't think that being late meant I don't care about you, not at all. Do you know that I simply viewed it means that I had

a lot of things to do at the office, that's all?

It doesn't mean that I don't care; it actually means I care about the quality time we have together and I wanted to get my work done and over with so that I could focus on being with you. Did you know that?

In these cases, we have structurally left the E.B. behavior the same ("coming late..."). Yet what does that behavior mean? Here we have only reframed the I.S. side of the formula. We have shifted it from, "You don't care about me" to "I got busy with other things." In this case, it alters *the meaning of the actions* and reduces the significance which the other person has given to it. It also implies a change of meaning about caring. It as much says,

Please don't measure my caring about you in terms of when I arrive for an appointment. Measure my caring for you by how frequently we get together and the quality of those experiences.

Now try your hand at reframing the E.B. To do that, put a sheet of paper or three-by-five inch card on the book so that you see only one line at a time —after all, we don't want your to cheat yourself from your own discoveries and creativity, now do we?

D) Stress causes me to eat chocolate.

[What's the E.B.? When you have that, then you are ready to reframe.] Stress doesn't cause you to eat chocolate, it only leads to certain feelings which you then want to distract yourself from. So, presto! you eat chocolate. Haven't you simply developed a habit of using chocolate to distract you from those feelings?

E) I can't really make a difference because management doesn't walk their talk.

Do you really think that just because management doesn't walk their talk, it means you can't make a difference? What if it actually means that you simply have to invest more effort into making a difference, and as you do, you will make an even bigger difference?

F) I can't buy your product because it costs too much.

Is price really the most critical issue? What about the quality of service that your money purchases? May I show you how our price will actually save you money in the long term?

Pattern Summary

To elicit this pattern and to bring out this conversational reframing pattern so that you can shift the old E.B. as equaling I.S. to other meanings, ask yourself the following questions. Let these operate in your mind as *flexibility expansion questions*:

• What other meanings could I give to this behavior?

- What other meanings have others given to it that transform it into a much more positive meaning?
- What significance does this behavior hold in other cultures?
- If you did see it this way—what would you see (or have) instead?
- In what situatoins do I apply these meanings?
- In what contexts does this content make sense?
- What are other terms and labels that could reduce, alter, or transform the meaning of the E.B.?

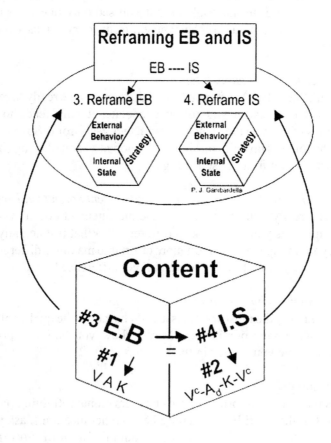

#4: Content Reframing: Reframe the I.S. by Redefining It

Not only can we give different meanings to external behavior, we can do the same for any given *internal state of significance* (I.S.). We can specify other behaviors that would more appropriately fit as the I.S. description. In doing this, we redefine or reframe the I.S. of the equation that governs the meaning of the belief.

A) *Saying mean things makes you a bad person.*

> Bad, huh? If you want to know what really makes a person a bad person, think about the kind of things Hitler did. Executing people, don't you think, that is what makes one a truly bad person, not uttering mere words?

B) *Cancer causes death.*

> If you want to know what really causes death—consider a firing squad or an electric chair! There's no question about what causes death in those instances, is there?

C) *Your being late means you don't care about me.*

> Actually being late only means I had a lot to do at the office. If I really didn't care for you I would not call or come home at all or give you the finger when I pass by! But I took the time to finish the stuff at the office so that I could spend the day with you tomorrow, isn't that truly caring?

In this last one, we doubled up and reframed both sides, the E.B. and the I.S. If you have exceptionally good rapport with someone, you may even bluntly express a direct disagreement. Of course, doing that means that there's nothing "sleight" in your hand or mouth and will probably initiate an argument rather than a new insight or way of looking at things.

> No! For me, arriving late doesn't mean not caring, it means I want to get other business done and over with so that I can focus on you.

D) *Stress causes me to eat chocolate.*

> Actually, don't you think that what really causes stress is eating chocolate because it adds to your body weight and fills your body with sugar? Eating chocolate won't reduce stress. What really reduces stress effectively is learning good relaxation techniques.

E) *I can't really make a difference because management doesn't walk their talk.*

> If you really want a picture of management *not* walking their talk, think about something like the Watergate cover-up or Enron; now isn't that

really not walking your talk? And shouldn't we be glad that there were
people who worked with and against that to make a difference?
Does the fact that management is not walking the talk dis-empowering
you? It sounds to me that it has actually fueled up your grievances
against them!
What really happens when management doesn't walk its talk? It
undermines its ability to lead effectively, does it not?

F) I can't buy your product because it costs too much.

What really costs too much would be to try to operate without this
product because then you would not have an effective operation,
wouldn't you?

Pattern Summary
In re-defining the I.S. we have repeatedly used two linguistic environments.
These facilitate us in thinking about the I.S. and in connecting it to some other
behavior. We have used:

What the internal state (IS) really *means* is ...
What the internal state (IS) really *causes* is ...

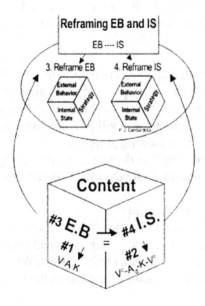

#5 & #6: *Reflexive Reframing*
Reflexively Apply E.B. to Self or Listener
Reflexively Apply I.S. to Self or Listener

In the Meta-Model, we call the person or thing doing or receiving the action of the verb the *referential index*. [Don't you love the terminology bequeathed us by linguists?] The referential index answers the question, "What are you referring to?"

    Larry's dog bit him and took out a hunk of flesh.
Whom did the dog bite?
    The dog bit Tim.

A *referential index* is a term that indicates either the actor ("Larry's dog") or the recipient of the action ("Tim"). So when we *switch* the referential index, we apply the statement (the action of the verb) from one object to another one.

As you make a mental movie of that statement, you have an *actor* (the dog) and the object of the the action (Tim). He receives the action of the past tense verb ("bit"). That makes Tim the referential index of the verb. The speaker refers to Tim as the object when he says, "the dog bit Tim." We *switch the referential index* dramatically when we turn it around,

    Tim bit the dog.

Now that's a very different movie in our mind, wouldn't you say? Here we have given the action of the verb "bit" a new reference. With this switch, the dog now gets a taste of his own medicine. I wonder how well he likes that?

To prepare yourself to make this conceptual move so that you can then deliver a *mind-line* conversationally, you need only to ask yourself one of the following questions:
-     What if, as a listener, I *applied this back* to the speaker?
-     What if, as the speaker, I *apply it back* to myself?
-     Who else could this statement or belief refer to?
-     To whom or what could I apply this?
-     How else can I switch the referential index?

What happens with a *referential index switch*? When we apply the action of the verb to another person or object, we invite the listener to *check out his or her* belief *map* to see if it has more universal applications or not. This can interrupt double-standards in beliefs that we apply too generally. Typically, poor or limited beliefs involve precisely that—someone has made a specific incident or group of incidents too general.

A) Saying mean things makes you a bad person.
    Mercy! That's really a mean thing to say to me!

B) Cancer causes death.

> You know, that belief is spreading like cancer. Personally, it would be more interesting to me if the belief died out. I wonder what would then happen?

C) Your being late means you don't care about me.

> It's kind of late to tell me know, don't you think? That must mean you don't care for you, right? So I can also take it that any and every time you run late for an appointment with me it really means that you don't care about me, is that what you're saying?

Pretty powerful mind-lines, huh? By applying a belief statement to the person saying it, or to the person listening to it, *we essentially test the applicability of the belief to other contexts and references.* Is the belief frame robust enough to work both ways?

In doing this we frequently find that the person's statement won't hold up. Consequently, the formula of meaning that informed and drove the other person's reality breaks apart and fragments. As a frame, it does not hold up and so the switch de-frames the old belief. Also, it is usually useful to notice the features of the mental cinema in our mind (the "sub-modalities") that change when we shift the referential index. Simply contrast the movie representations in the two statements.

In switching the referential index, we *apply the statement* to someone else. I love these next ones. They address the limiting belief that someone might hold who wants to go on a diet (well, those who kind of want to do diet and simultaneously kind of does not want to), yet who suffers from a limiting belief that frames the whole experience in a very unpleasant way. They think, "Losing weight means suffering." That's their frame of reference and frame of meaning. Now notice the effect of these replies:

- 1) That's funny thinking that losing weight implies suffering, that wasn't the story that Dolly Parton tells when she lost some weight.
- 2) To you losing weight has always meant suffering, yet when Oprah lost a lot of weight, she presented her new look on international TV and used it as a sign of personal success and empowerment.

Here we have not only switched the referent, but we also provide a Counter-Example (#7). In these two examples, Dolly Parton and Oprah provide *Counter-Examples* to the belief map presented. By the way, this illustrates how we can multiply our influence when we nest or embed Mind-Line patterns one within another. It increases our leverage in changing beliefs.

D) Stress causes me to eat chocolate.

> So stress causes you to eat chocolate? Does *eating chocolate* ever overwhelm and stress you out? Have you ever eaten chocolate in response to anything other than stress?

E) I can't really make a difference because management doesn't walk their talk.

> You know, whenever I notice any area in your life where you don't seem to be perfectly walking your talk, I feel helpless and impotent in attempting to make any difference with you. I wonder why that is? Have you ever not walked your talk and someone compassionately pointed it out to you *and* you listened, made some changes, and began living more congruently? Has that ever happened to you?

F) I can't buy your product because it costs too much.

> You know, I have recently been feeling the same about buying your products also. Don't you think that the services your company offers is just too high?

Pattern Summary
To elicit this pattern, explore the possibility of applying it to yourself, or to the other, or to others, in some way:
- How would this belief system fit if I applied it back to this speaker or to myself as the listener?
- In what way can I switch the referent around to see if it equally applies?

In applying a behavior (E.B.) or a state (I.S.) to oneself or to a listener, take the formula of the belief (or some criteria in the belief) and simply *apply it back* to whoever created that model (if the speaker said it or if someone said it to him or her). Switch the referential index by going meta to the statement to see if the other person wants or will receive their formula applied to them.

This conversational reframing pattern works because of our need for congruency. As Leon Festinger (1957) discovered from his studies of cognitive dissonance, when beliefs and behaviors conflict, something has to give.

> "The need for consistency will arouse a tension-like state of dissonance in an individual when there is a *discrepancy* between two or more cognitions that are in a *relevant* relation to each other and of *importance* to him ... When consistency does not exist naturally, it must be created by restructuring of the ill-fitting elements. Dissonant cognitions must be changed or consonant ones added." (Ruch and Zimbardo, 1971, p. 412)

When we reflexively *Apply to Self/Listener*, the reframe directly challenges the possible incongruencies of limiting beliefs that can then completely deframe a belief system.

A story goes that someone once complained to a well-known trainer asserting, "You are not communicating." The trainer responded to this by retorting, "You know (pause) ... that statement seems to really cut off communication, doesn't it?" As such, the response went meta to the communication exchange and communicated a meta-comment. The reflection offered a counter-example while simultaneously pointing out how the first statement functions as a communication stopper.

A) Saying mean things makes you a bad person.
> Only a bad person could say a mean thing like that!

B) Cancer causes death.
> That's a pretty deadly belief to hold onto. It can only lead to a dead-end street, don't you think?

C) Your being late means you don't care.
> It seems a little late to tell me, don't you think?

In the last example we apply the criterion of *lateness* to the communication of lateness itself. This switches the referential index from us back to the speaker. To give more leverage we could include something about the I.S. side of the statement, "Lately, I have been wondering if you cared." Now we can combine the two:
> It is a little late to tell me, isn't it? Lately, I have been wondering if you cared.

Here we apply late to late and caring to caring. In both cases we have gone meta from being late and caring to the overall concept of lateness and caring. We have thereby switched the referential index from self back to the speaker. When we use Apply to Self/Listener, we take the criteria within the statement and *loop them back onto itself.* For this reason we describe these patterns as reflexive. If we do this with a little spite in our attitude, we could respond to "Your being late means you don't care about our relationship," in this way:
> What relationship? Better late than never, right? Wouldn't a truly caring person be able to overlook a little tardiness now and then for the sake of a loving relationship?

D) Stress causes me to eat chocolate.
> Holding on to that belief must create even more stress for you, doesn't it?
>
> Quick! Hand me some chocolate. These stressful ideas of yours is making my mouth water for chocolate. I wish you'd stop doing this to

me! It makes me eat chocolate.

E) I can't really make a difference because management doesn't walk their talk.
So what? If you think that's tough, I can't make any difference in listening or responding to you because I can find places in your life where you don't walk your talk.

F) I can't buy your product because it costs too much.
That sounds like a pretty expensive idea to buy. After all, since you can't purchase products that you desire that must feel impoverishing.

Pattern Summary
To elicit this pattern, keep asking the application question:
*   What would happen if I applied the criterion or meaning to its source (to the speaker)?
*   How can I change the reference to reality test the validity of this idea or belief?
*   Would the speaker like to have this same idea applied to him or her?

Summary

- Our sense of reality is just that—*a sense* of what we have mapped as real for our reality strategy. Yet all of our constructions are just that—*constructs* that we mapped and thereby called into existence. As framers, we frame things into being.

- *Reframing alters frames.* We take the constructs and de-construct them so that we can then re-construct them in new and more enhancing ways. In reframing we find and shift the frames-of-references that we have set around the happenings and events of everyday life. We set up new frames.

- "Out there" in the world *things happen* (the external behaviors, actions, events, conversations, etc.) to which we *attach meaning* (the internal states and experiences). As we do this we create neuro-semantic reality.

- We attach meaning primarily by attributing causation, association, and identification. This gives us several forms of meaning-making:
  1) Causation: Cause-Effect (C-E), what causes what, consequences, past—present—future.
  2) Equation: Complex Equivalence (Ceq), what have we associated with what?, linkages, X=Y, E.B.=I.S.
  3) Identifications: identity, what do we identify with what? sameness, classifications.

- While these three forms do not account for every facets of meaning-construction, they do identify the central and most crucial meanings governing our lives. These meanings determine our neuro-linguistic and neuro-semantic *states* from which we live our everyday lives.

- We all move into the world with *beliefs* frames that we use to make sense of things. Yet often they do not always serve us well. That's when and why we need to re-frame. And now we have *five more ways to reframe a belief.* And yet the fun of *this semantic magic* has only begun.

Chapter 7

COUNTER-FRAMING

*"Beliefs can become surprisingly simple and easy to change
if we respect and pace the natural process of belief change."*
Robert Dilts (1999,p.176)

*"You see things and you say Why;
but I dream of things that never were and I say, Why Not?"*
George Bernard Shaw

This chapter is about *turning things inside out.* Clothes turn inside out very easily, but turning a car inside out isn't so easy. Then there are lots of things that we can't turn inside out at all. But the *mind* isn't one of them. Not only can you get a mind to go backwards as when we imagine stepping into a memory and feeling it rewind very quickly, but we can even turn a mind inside out. We can enter *opposite* thoughts and feelings. We can imagine *reversing* things and countering our way of reasoning. And these powers of mind gives us yet another way to *frame* things—we can turn ideas inside out.

Reversing Presuppositions
Connirae Andreas developed the following twist on the *Apply to Self/Listener pattern.* She calls it, *Reversing Presuppositions.* In doing this, she added some nice qualities to it. She noticed that as she used this pattern, it seemed to differ from the other patterns. So though this *mind-line* has some similarity to Counter-Exampling (#7), it also differs from it. In Counter-Exampling, we look for one example where the limiting belief does not hold up. In Reversing Presuppositions we ask ourselves a very different question.

> *How is the whole thing actually the opposite of what you thought it was?*

As an example, Connirae provides this story:

> I knew this woman who had some illnesses and who really needed to rest, and yet she was not resting . . . she had a very serious illness, it was potentially life threatening. And yet she wasn't resting, but living as a work-a-holic. She said, "I need to rest, but if I rest I will be lazy. You know, I should work hard, I shouldn't be lazy."

In this model of the world, the behavior of *rest* (E.B.) equaled the internal state of *laziness* (I.S.). Connirae responded with a reversing presuppositions question:

> In what way is your resting actually *harder work* than if you were just to do what you have always done?

To that the lady said, "What? That doesn't make any sense? What are you saying?"

> Well, you know how to work and to work really hard. That comes natural to you. You don't have to work at working, do you? But if you rested, how could that actually be harder work than working? Because at least you are familiar with working all the time. It describes your pattern. And therefore, in some ways, you find it a much easier thing to do. So conversely, to learn to rest would actually be more of a stretch for you, and harder work than if you were to do what you have always done.

In this statement she so completely reversed presuppositions that it turned the previous belief inside-out. Our normal paradigm goes, "E.B. causes I.S." And when someone conversationally asks a mind-line question which reverses the basic presuppositions in our model of the world, it invites us to entirely shift our perspective as we seek to process their statement or question.

> In what way does (can, might, could, would, will) E.B. actually mean or cause the opposite of E.B.?

What happens when we do this? What happens to our belief that we have built and all the conclusions that go along with that belief?

> We *reverse* things in the cinema of our mind. We turn things upside down and so adopt a very different perspective.

Suppose that early in life nobody paid much attention to Jill. Suppose Jill did not get much love or affection. It would make sense that Jill would draw some unenhancing and erroneous conclusions from that experience and map herself of low self-value. "I have no personal worth." With a belief frame about self like that she would undoubtedly go into the world looking for evidence to prove her map. And, she would probably find support for it in her history of experiences.

When a belief becomes a *frame of reference*, we move through life searching for and finding evidence for it. That's how a self-fulfilling prophecy works. In everyday life, our self-fulfilling prophecies (or belief frames) gather up evidence that keeps the beliefs alive as our reality strategy. It puts us in such an orientation that we do not challenge or question the belief. In this, the belief state protects itself. It does this by altering the way we perceive, think, feel, and relate. So no wonder our beliefs as frames organize and govern our perceptual filters or meta-programs. And because we can (and do) constantly find evidence for our beliefs, we continually reinforce them. This is how they stay so strong and vigorous. They may be toxic, but at least they are *vigorously* toxic!

Suppose we start from an opposite presupposition. Suppose we take the opposite belief, and, as a *mind-line,* offer it as a suggestion to someone. If we did, we could ask the person to simply step into the new frame for a moment, and look at the world in terms of that new belief frame. What then? If we use the *as if* frame to turn a frame matrix upside down, then what will we see, what will we feel, hear, experience? I wonder. Let's just suppose ... what would fit that model of the world?

This is what we're doing with these mind-lines. Suddenly we will discover that we can find lots of experiences that can equally well fit that frame of reference. If that's so, then let's invite Jill to go through life for awhile and sort for things that will give her evidence of her value and worth. Let's invite her to step into the self-esteem frame, "I am worthwhile. I have personal worth and dignity"

What will happen? You know what will happen. Using that frame-of-reference, she will find all kinds of things in her personal history that will give evidence and make sense as evidence to that frame. Approaching the raw data of life's events *using that frame* will enable her to see things in those terms. That frame will also function in a self-fulfilling way and will "magically" transform the way Jill experiences life.

This *mind-line* pattern ingeniously demonstrates the presupposition that we have all the resources we need to solve our problems. So if we create a resourceful and enhancing map and "try it on" using the pretend frame, we will begin to imagine what tomorrow will look like, sound like, and feel like with that perspective. In this it uses a future pacing process which will enable us to actually begin to construct and experience a whole new world.

Imagine that! Isn't that fantastic? What does this mean? It means the ability to succeed in a particular way in the world primarily depends on having or developing the right map, having an empowering meaning frame that self-organizes to that enhancing map. It indicates that we have enough plasticity in our neuro-linguistics so that if we begin with a good resourceful map for navigating the world, then that map will not only orient us to our resources, but it will enable us to create those resources.

Mind-Lines in Chapter 7:

#5 Reflexively Apply E.B. to Self/Listener
#6 Reflexively Apply I.S. to Self/Listener
#7 Counter-Example Framing

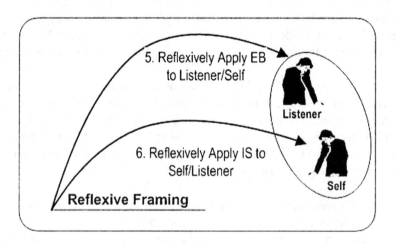

#5 Reflexively Apply E.B.
#6 Reflexively Apply I.S.

A) Saying mean things makes you a bad person.

Well, that's a really mean thing to say to me. I can't believe that you say such mean things to me. I didn't know you were such a bad person.

C) Your being late means you don't care about me.

In what way does (can, might, could, would, will) my being late actually means that I do care for you?

So every time you are even a minute late, I now know what that *really* means?

D) Stress causes me to eat chocolate.

How could stress actually cause you *not* to eat chocolate?

So when you see me eating chocolate, you know that I am under stress?

E) I can't really make a difference because management doesn't walk their talk.

How can their incongruence actually lead you to increase your effectiveness in making a tremendous difference there? Could it not stand in contrast to your congruence and give you even more influence?

Well, I can't make a difference in getting you to see this differently because there you are not perfectly congruent in every single aspect of your life.

F) I can't buy your product because it costs too much.

How might the cost of not having this product actually cause you to believe that you cannot afford not to buy it? How could the expensiveness of this item actually get you to buy it?

Well, you know I can't buy this idea from you because it would cost too much to my style of living and way of life. And, as you well know, if it's too expensive, then it's out of the question, right?

One more example for our mental play. Try on this toxic belief and then come up with a mind-line using the reversing presuppositions format.

The fact that I have personal flaws will always cause any relationship with a man to fail.

How about this?

In what way, now that you think about it, will the fact that you have personal flaws, and you know it, actually support you in developing a better relationship than if you had no personal flaws at all?

Reversing Presuppositions — A Meta-State Move
There's another way to think about *reversing presuppositions*. We can correlate it to the *meta-stating* process and see it as a way of framing or establishing higher level meta-states about the original idea. Doing that will provide yet another way to understand and perceive how the *reverse presuppositions* work.

If we start with a belief and make a move to a meta-level and *apply* the very reverse of that belief, then we frame (or outframe) the belief with its opposite. In terms of Meta-States, we are meta-stating one thought, feeling, or state with its opposite.

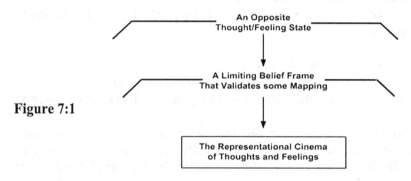

Figure 7:1

In terms of the *interfacing* effect of state upon another state, when we set a frame of an *opposite or reversal* we typically reduce the first state, nullify that state, or create a paradoxical situation. These are but a few of the many ways that states interface with each other.

For example, suppose you start with anger at the primary level. Then you outframe it with calmness and presence of mind. Those are a couple of states that we typically experience as the opposite of anger. What happens? The *presuppositions* within calmness and mindfulness (as higher states or frames) transform the lower level presuppositions in the state of anger. This leaves us with a new and more complex state: *calm* anger, *mindful and thoughtful* anger. We could even generate *respectful* anger, *seeing win/win relationships* anger, etc. Then we will have an anger that's very different from *freaked-out* anger or *out-of-control* anger.[1]

Pattern Summary
To elicit this pattern from conversations, use the reversing presuppositions questions:
- In what way does this behavior (E.B.) actually mean or cause the opposite of the internal state (I.S.)?
- When I think about this E.B.—suppose I imagine that it actually means

and leads to the complete reverse of what I have always thought?

Reversing Presuppositions

Not long ago, I (BB) had a client who "just couldn't relax." Fred felt that he just had to be in an intense uptime state in business meetings. He wanted to be alert, totally present. He wanted that because, as he said,

> "I'm a serious person, but I've been too serious lately."

I said, "You have become very serious lately, but have you been serious enough about relaxing as you stay alert?"

That did it. By the time we ended the session, Fred walked out singing a different tune. He took as his theme the phrase, "Totally and completely serious about relaxing..."

> So imagine moving to a place where you feel serious enough about your relaxing so that you can more fully relax, because, after all, you can, can you not? And when you do, into what kind of state does that put you in?

How does this work? It works by pacing and validating Fred's experience and then taking the presenting problem in the form of a cause-effect statement:

$$A \longrightarrow B$$

Seriousness leads to stress and inability to relax

It then reverses the syntax:

$$-A \longrightarrow B$$

Not serious enough to fully relax

In terms of Fred's maps about work and business, his beliefs about "being serious" and about "not being able to relax," were switched around and reversed. He had thought that the problem was being serious. Bob shifted him to wondering, perhaps he was *not* serious enough. He valued relaxing, but had not become *serious enough* about that.

Bob outframed his old belief state with a higher level state and he did so with the very state that Fred thought was the problem (seriousness). But when Bob brought *serious enough* to bear upon the lower state (relaxing) in this way, it transformed the psycho-logics of his frame. This pattern of reversing the C > E statement provides a very simple way to construct an Apply to Self frame.

Meta-Stating Mind-Lines with Nancy

Another person that Bob worked with came into his office with a list of things that she wanted to "fix" in her personality. At the top of her list was the fear of water. So Bob inquired, "How does *water* pose a problem to you, Nancy?

What's the problem with water?" She talked for awhile about various past experiences with water that she didn't like. Finally she commented,

I will drown and die.

"So, Nancy, you feel afraid of water because you fear you will drown and die...?" I repeated to make more overt the cause-effect structure of her subjective strategy.

Yes, that's right.

Bob then said, "What would happen if you *died to the belief* that you are afraid you are going to drown and die?" Upon saying this, her face reddened and I'm sure that smoke oozed out of her ears [metaphorically speaking] ... after awhile a smile spread across her face and she said with a laugh.

Why, I could enjoy water! ... Well, that blew that one out of the water!

In this, mind-lines do not have to make sense to work. In terms of Aristotelian logic, they often do not make sense. What needs to happen is that *we* make sense of them within the inner psycho-logics of our mind and how we put things together. If we *make sense* of them, then change will occur. And if they work there, then they will work as signals and commands to our nervous system changing our feelings, our physiology, perhaps our skills, etc. When they work there, they change and even transform our neuro-semantic reality.

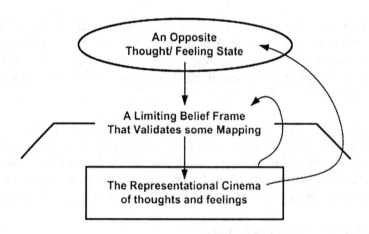

#7 *Counter Example Framing*

In counter-exampling, we do several very powerful things. For one thing, we run a reality testing function:
* How real is this?
* Is this realistic? To what extent?
* Does this ever *not* occur?
* What accounts for these counter-examples to the principle?

We also bring against the belief undeniable evidence to the contrary. To engage the counter-exampling strategy, we can identify current exceptions or we can track a person backward in time to the original experience out of which the learning arose. Behind counter-examples also lies the presupposition that people almost always demonstrate in their behavior the very thing or things they claim they cannot do.

A) Saying mean things makes you a bad person.
    So you've never said a mean thing to anybody in your life without having that statement turn you into a bad person?
    So when you said X to me last week, that made you a really bad person?

B) Cancer causes death.
    Have you ever heard of anyone who had cancer and lived?
    So no one ever experiences remission?

Once an extremely over-weight woman visited Milton Erickson for help. She had a difficult time even making an appointment because she saw herself as so objectionable. She complained to Dr. Erickson, "I am so ugly that no man will ever have me." Obviously, a belief like that in her model of the world would be very limiting and restricting, it would stop her from taking so many actions that could change things for her. Yet at the same time she also desired to get married and have children.

How did Erickson handle her? He asked her to go to the library and pick up a stack of the *National Geographic* magazines. He then requested that she look through the magazines to find all the weird looking women that men found attractive and had married. In the process of doing this, these multiple counter-examples to her thinking reframed her belief.

When we *counter-example,* we identify the specifics (e.g., when, where, and with whom) concerning how a belief does *not* hold up. To counter frame, we only need to find an example that functions as an exception to the assertion, a time, place, person, etc. that doesn't fit the mold of the limiting belief.

Frequently in counter-exampling we will switch perceptual positions. When we find an example counter to a belief, the person will often associate into the first position of the example. That is, they will step into the person and see, hear, and feel the world through the person's eyes. Sometimes the person may even go to second position and look out on the world from the perspective of the recipient. Minimally, they will have to go to a meta position to process the significance of the counter example.

Behind *Counter-Examples* is the presupposition that—

People frequently or always *demonstrate* in their behavior the very thing they claim they cannot do.

By the way, *perceptual positions* refer to three or four basic positions that we can take as we perceive things.

- *First perceptual position:* first person, viewing things from out of our own eyes, ears, and skin as if we are in an experience.
- *Second perceptual position:* second person, imagining the events of a situation from the person to whom we speak, empathizing with the other person. Conceptually stepping into the other person's body to see the world through his or her eyes, ears, and skin.
- *Third perceptual position:* the meta position, taking a spectator's point of view to see ourselves and the other.
- *Fourth position*: the system position, the "we" point of view, seeing an entire system.
- *Fifth position:* the universe, God, or spiritual perspective.

C) Your being late means you don't care.
>　Have you ever been late and still cared?
>　Isn't it possible for a person to arrive late and still care? Isn't it possible to be uncaring and punctual?
>　My son showed up thirty-minutes late for dinner last night and I know that he loves us deeply.

In making these counter-example conceptual moves, the four questions from Cartesian Logic can provide an additional excellent means for assisting us in producing counter examples.

D) Stress causes me to eat chocolate.
>　Have you ever experienced a time when you felt stressed and yet you

did not eat chocolate?"
The Non-Mirror Image Reverse:
Stress is not reduced by not not eating chocolate.

Figure 7:2
Cartesian Logic Questions:
> *Theorem:* What will happen if you do?
> *Inverse:* What won't happen if you do?
> *Converse:* What will happen if you don't?
> *Non-Mirror Image Reverse:* What won't happen if you don't?

Examples:
> Has there ever a time when someone was late and cared?
> Has someone ever not been late and cared?
> Has someone ever been late and did not care?
> Has someone not been late and yet did not care?

E) I can't really make a difference because management doesn't walk their talk.
> Who do you know at your company who does make a difference in spite of management's hypocrisy?
> Could you make a difference if they walked their talk? How would you do that?
> Have you ever made a difference when they didn't walk their talk?

F) I can't buy your product because it costs too much.
> Joe bought my product just yesterday. He said he felt convinced that in spite of its price, it was a great buy.
> Have you ever not bought something even when the price was very low?

Pattern Summary:
To elicit this pattern in conversations, use one of the following four choices. We've played with the belief, "I can't handle criticism."

1) Invert the belief:
> So criticism can't handle you, right?

2) Make it into a universal statement or question.
> So you can *never* handle criticism under any circumstance or situation, because you *always* have to feel bad, right?

3) Explore exceptions:
> Has there ever been a time when you did not experience criticism as equal to feeling bad and crumbling on the inside?

4) Explore other reverses:

Have you ever felt bad or crumbled on the inside when you expected criticism but did not receive it?

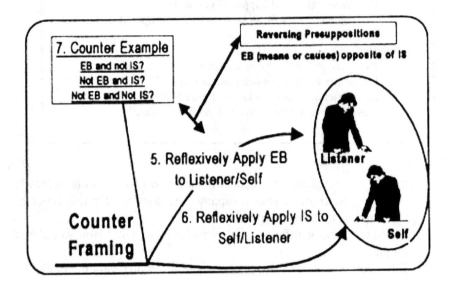

Figure 7:3

Cartesian Quadrants

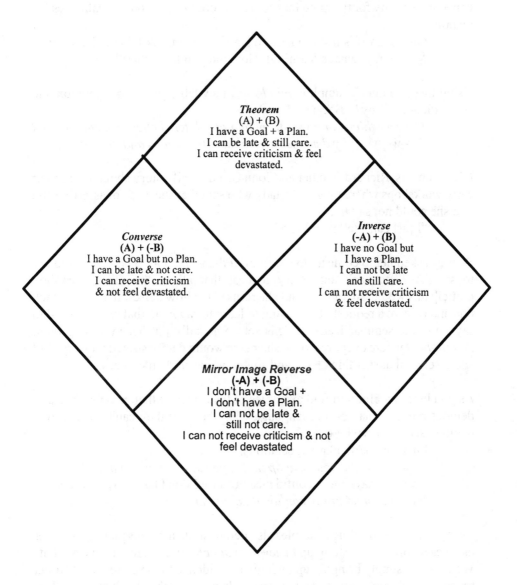

Theorem
(A) + (B)
I have a Goal + a Plan.
I can be late & still care.
I can receive criticism & feel
devastated.

Converse
(A) + (-B)
I have a Goal but no Plan.
I can be late & not care.
I can receive criticism
& not feel devastated.

Inverse
(-A) + (B)
I have no Goal but
I have a Plan.
I can not be late
and still care.
I can not receive criticism
& feel devastated.

Mirror Image Reverse
(-A) + (-B)
I don't have a Goal +
I don't have a Plan.
I can not be late &
still not care.
I can not receive criticism & not
feel devastated

Using Counter-Example Mind-Lines
The mind-lines that arise from counter-exampling offer some truly powerful and profound ways to run the language patterns of persuasion. They *redirect* a brain (even your own) and *swish* it in an entirely new direction and to new referents. Using the counter-exampling process we deframe the old generalizations that created the limiting beliefs while simultaneously constructing a new piece of conceptual reality for the mind that somehow does *not* fit and so challenges the mapping.

> Oh this stuff is just too hard to learn, I don't think I'll ever learn this!
> My, oh my, what a learning! How did you learn that!?

Using these counter-exampling *mind-lines* inevitably plays on a paradox and contradiction. Why? Because

> *The very things that we affirm and absolutely believe we can or can't do—we typically demonstrate in our affirmations and denials.*

NLP founders, Richard Bandler and John Grinder, tell a story about one of their early workshops where they met a lady who said that she was not assertive and that she could not say *no*.

> "I just can't tell people no."

So they asked her to come up to the front of the workshop. There they told her to say *"No!"* to each and every request that all of the other workshop participants would ask of her. But she refused to allow herself to go up to each one and receive a request. In refusing to learn to say *no* in that way, she had to say *no* to the seminar leaders. This set up actually put her in *a benevolent double-bind* where every response she made would demonstrated the very skill she asserted that she didn't have and so get her desired outcome.

As you listen carefully to find examples of the principle that people generally demonstrate in behavior and language what they say they can't do, you will begin to see it everywhere.

> I have no particular expectations...
> *Wow! How did you develop that expectation about yourself?*
> I want to have more confidence because I don't have any confidence.
> *My, you sound pretty confident about that!*

These counter-exampling examples also demonstrate how this pattern provides us an easy format for setting up *benevolent double-binds*. How do we do that? We do so by simply bringing up undeniable evidence to the contrary. At other times, we ask a person to do the very behavior which will then deny their generalization. In a sense, in counter-exampling, we track the person backwards to experiences which prevent them from (or make it hard to) maintaining the old generalizations. Counter-exampling questions also provide a standard of comparison.

I can't learn things like this!
> Do you mean that you learn language patterns more slowly than others?
> Could it be that you simply take a more methodical approach to the things that you want to learn thoroughly?

This *reframe* invites a person to *step out* of his or her current behavior while at the same time it validates him or herself as a person and simultaneously invites the speaker to *step into* a new state.

Do you believe all learning has to occur in a fast way? Can a person learn slowly and yet still *learn*?
> I believe that there is no change.

Have you had that belief since birth?
> No?

Then you mean that you began life without this understanding and then later, somewhere along the line, something changed so that now you have this understanding?

When we use these kinds of *mind-lines* with people, we should always remember that *if* we attack someone's belief (or if they *think* that we have attacked their belief), they typically will fight us tooth and nail. We have all had interactions like that, have we not? So we want to aim to avoid a push-shove scenario. Instead, we want to first track with the person back to either the experience out of which the old learning came, or to new experiences that will allow for an expansion his or her maps.
> How do you know that? [Deframing by asking for specifics and detailing down to more precision.]
> What does believing that do for you? [Searching out the positive intention behind the belief.]

We can also use temporal presuppositions to conceptually take a problem away from a person. We do that by coding the "time" element as in the past.
> "Now what *was* it that you *thought* at that time *created* what you *felt* was a problem?"

In this response, we offer four temporal presuppositions as *mind-line phrases* and have conceptually created layer upon layer of distance from the problem. Simultaneously, we have subtly presupposed that some change has already occurred. If you imagine yourself the listener, you can feel the effect of this kind of response as very powerful.

"Picking your nose in public means you're inconsiderate."
"I can think of a situation when, if a person didn't pick his nose, there might occur some consequences that would score as worse than merely being inconsiderate; can't you?"

Or, putting it into metaphor or story form (#20):
"We were out on this camping trip and this mosquito got up my nose..."
"Sniffling your way through life, and never giving it a good robust blowing represents an even greater act of inconsideration."

Hiding the Meaning Equation in Identity Statements
We have all heard or uttered statements like the following. Consider the structure of this statement, and the *magic formula* in this very succinct statement: *I am depressed!* (see page 88 for an earlier description of this.)

What mind-lines can reframe that? In fact, what do we have in this expression as the meaning equation? On the surface, it seems that we *only* have the statement of an internal state (I.S.), namely, depression. What is the external behavior here?

This streamlined statement lacks a map of the triggering event. Perhaps it is, *"I am depressed because I lost my job."* If so, then perhaps the situation has continued for quite some time. In that case, then the original trigger may have faded into the background of the person's awareness especially if it has operated as a self-fulfilling prophecy and has become a frame for everyday life. We often forget originating events as other events arise reinforcing a belief frame. Then all we might be aware of, think about, and experience would be the state itself, "depression." This leaves the map even more global, over-generalized, and an even larger level frame.
     "I am depressed."

The only verb we have in this statement lurks in the passive "is" verb. In the *"am"* we have a state-of-being verb that the person now maps as his identity. Now, using this *"is "of identity* verb to summarize *everything* about his whole self, he maps out that his whole being, essence, and existential self is depressed. As the belief takes the form of an *identity complex equivalence*, we can now describe the belief structurally in this way:

Person/Self/ I —>/ = Depressed
External Object   Internal Experience

As a complex equivalence, *identification* statements are especially dangerous and insidious. Why? Because we usually frame our *identity* (as a belief that conceptually constructs the self) at a higher logical level than most of our other beliefs. This commissions it to operate as a belief about a concept—the concept of "self."

So first, we need to do a little meta-modeling and deframing.
- How do you know this?
- Do you have these feelings all the time?
- What specific experiences, actions, circumstances has led you to conclude that "you" as a person can be summarized in the emotional term "depressed?"

Whenever we make an *"I am..."* statement, we encode and represent ourselves using a *nominalization.* We nominalize ourselves. Gregory Bateson (1972) commented about the problem with small words such as "I" and "ego," saying that "ego" was the biggest nominalization of them all. This is true also of "I," "self," and the "am" verb of identification.

When we use a nominalization to describe ourselves, we create a frame-of-reference about self that has no movement or action. We represent ourselves in a static and unmoving form. This is the problem with all of the *"to be" verbs* (i.e., "is, am, are, be, being, been, was, were," etc.), when we use them as an "is of identity." We thereby limit ourselves, put ourselves in a box, and fail to map our "self" in terms of growth, development, change, etc. This is an insidious form of linguistic mapping that we need to de-nominalize (see Appendix C).
- How do you currently, at this moment in time, experience this emotion of depressing?
- How and in what ways *are* you more than this emotion? What else *are* you? How else can you define yourself?

When we start with a global generalization that someone has condensed into *"I am..." form*, I typically like to first explore for the person's *evidence* for the belief.
- How do you know that?
- What lets you know that it represents depression and not patience?

If the person gives another vague generalization (which we can generally expect and count on), "It feels that way," I just explore that one as well.
> How do you know that *that* feeling means you *are* depressed? It might mean that you feel calm.

And again, we can expect more vague fluff,
> Because I lack energy.

So we continue to ask about specifics to get the movement back into the mapping, "Energy to do what? At what times? According to what standards?"

Meta-modeling questioning enables us to look for evidence and to help the person index his or her thinking. This questions the generalizing. In this way, we invite the person to step back into the experience out of which the original mapping occurred.

Once we have deframed sufficiently, they can re-map from that experience and create a more enhancing map. This process facilitates a new kind of mental mapping—one where we put the process back into a form that represents "process" and movement, and so frees us from the static and permanent nature of nominalizations. The word "I" helps us to re-associate to the kinesthetics. And, getting ourselves back to the experience and the evidence lies at the very heart of the NLP method.

> Being in control always gets results.

To invite greater clarity and specificity, we might inquire:
* What behaviors would I see if I saw you "in control?"
* What kind of results do you here speak about?
* Results in business, in personal life, etc.?
* Does not being-in-control not always get results?
* How do you control being-in-control?
* Do you have awareness that being in control, in the way you have described, won't always get you the results you want?
* Being knowledgeable means you won't be loved.
* Say, since you use very knowledgeable words to tell me this, does that mean people can't love you? Have you ever spent time with someone you thought as knowledgeable and yet also lovable at the same time?

Summary
* In *Counter*-framing we reverse the meaning attachments we make to things. We turn the fabric of the reality inside out and see how things play out from there.
* Mind not only goes forward and backward, up and down, but also *inside-out*. Mentally we can perform the mental magic of reversing things.

End Notes
1. The system dynamics that occur and guide the interface of one state upon another is a key facet of the Meta-States model. We now have identified sixteen of the most common interfaces. See *Meta-States* (2000) and *Frame Games* (2000) for more about meta-levels, interfacing relationships, transformation possibilities, etc.

Chapter 8

PRE-FRAMING
AND
POST- FRAMING

Reframing in Time to Make a Positive Difference

Behind every behavior is a positive intention.
This means that every behavior seeks to accomplish something useful
or positive in some context.
NLP Presupposition

"Words are the most powerful drug
used by mankind."
Rudyard Kipling

We have deframed, we have reframed, and we have counter-framed. Now we are ready to *outframe*. In this chapter we will distinguish the particular kind of outframing that we will do with "time" as *Pre-framing* and *Post-framing*. This will give us five more conceptual and linguistic moves with mind-lines that we can use in shifting beliefs in ourselves or others.

In the previous chapters, we began by working *within* the box. We worked *inside* the conceptual framework of our central formula of magic: **E.B.—>/ =I.S.** First we deframed to pull apart the magic formula and to identify the critical components. This enabled us to model the form and structure of the experience. Then we explored two ways to reframe the *content* inside of a belief. Then we engaged in three kinds of *reflexive reframing*. In this chapter we will now broaden our horizons in reframing skills to become much more graceful and elegant in our everyday conversations. This will build up our skills and artistry in conversational reframing.

Throughout the moves in this chapter we will essentially "run with the logic" of the central meaning formula. We do this in order to see if the logic will continue to make sense when we shift *the context* and/or apply other contexts to it. This explains why we call this kind of reframing, *Context* Reframing.

We will move conceptually backwards in "time" to explore *the reasons why* a person constructed his or her formula in the first place.
-         What were your *positive intentions* in doing that?
-         What value did you seek to achieve when you mapped it in this way?

We will also move the context back in "time" to check out and transform a person's attributions of causation.
-         The factors that brought this about were what?
-         What were some of the contributing influences that influenced you to develop this particular map?

We have designated these as the *Positive Prior Intention and the Positive Prior Causation Frames.* In this construction, we will make the first reframe *personal* and the second *impersonal* for reasons that we will shortly make clear. After the three reframes using *past time*, we will go into *future time* and there "run with the logic" once again. First we will go to the immediate consequences, and then into more distant and future consequences. We will explore the consequences that arise from the semantic formula. How well will this idea serve you in the long run?

In doing this, we apply good old "consequential thinking" to our mental constructs. Or, as we say in NLP, we will "run an ecology check" on our model of the world. In that way we can check out if it truly offers us a well-balanced experience.

Mind-Lines in Chapter 8

Before — **Pre-Framing**
    #8 Positive Prior Intention Framing
    #9 Positive Prior Causation Framing

After — **Post-Framing**
    #10 First Outcome
    #11 Outcomes of Outcome
    #12 Eternity Framing

#8 Positive Prior Intention Framing

This conceptual move utilizes the basic assumption within all of the reframing models. It is namely the idea that—

> *Behind (or within) every behavior (E.B.) is a positive intention (I.S.). Therefore if we search long and hard enough, and high enough, we can find or create a positive intention.*

Utilizing this presupposition, we assume that all people produce behaviors to accomplish significant things, that they do things that hold importance to them. Yes, we also recognize that sometimes people get into some pretty nasty states and from those states do some pretty horrible things. Sometimes we feel hurt, wounded, violated, and unresourceful. Sometimes, *out* of those kinds of states, we produce some pretty obnoxious and ugly behaviors. We can even get vicious and vindictive.

And yet ... when we do so, inevitably, we do so in order to accomplish something of value and importance, do we not? Does that not hold true for you? It does for me. Our obnoxious and ugly behaviors might accomplish nothing other than to express an uninformed and ignorant expression that we hurt and want to get back at another in revenge. It might express some form of protection. It might communicate that we don't want to live as we have been living any longer. In this we make a very important distinctions between the following factors or areas:
- *intent* and *behavior*
- *person* and *action*
- *internal intent* and *external expression.*

Even behind *bad* and *hurtful* behavior we can find (or create) positive intentions. Usually when we produce hurtful behavior, we do so by accident, ignorance, confusion, or unresourcefulness. And when at the conscious level we get into a really nasty state and actually seek to hurt someone, get back at someone, rage about life's injustices, etc., we do so for some positive value—we want to live in a more equitable and fair world.

We do not always produce good, useful, productive, or resourceful behavior. That much is obvious. Yet at the same time we attempt, via our behavior, to accomplish something of value and importance. What we do, whether it succeeds or fails, creates more problems or exasperates others, it has some *meaning* and *significance* of *value* in some way to us.

So if we set about to discover and/or set *a Positive Prior Intention,* we tap into the innate and inescapable human drive for meaning. This drive causes us to *not* endure life without meaning. That which is meaningless in human neuro-semantics disrupts our entire mind-body system, typically leading to suicide or self-destructive life-styles. In the long run, it does not work. Meaning makes up a significant part of our daily bread for psychological health.

In this reframing pattern, we use the meaning drive. Here we look for, explore into, or even construct *positive intentions and values* in the behaviors offered us. Many will want to call this approach a positive thinking approach, yet it is so much more than that, and so different from that. In this mind-line we are *not* denying or repressing evil or hurtful actions, we are rather moving to a higher level of mind. Nor are we just moving up one or two levels, sometimes the first levels of intention are not positive or positive enough. We will therefore move to whatever level is high enough to give us a new and enhancing frame of mind. Let's now see how finding and setting *a Positive Prior Intention* with our first two playground pieces shows up in mind-lines.

A) Saying mean things makes you a bad person.
> I appreciate you saying that because I know that you're trying to help me avoid relating to you in mean ways. What other positive intentions do you have in expressing this?

B) Cancer causes death.
> I wonder if this is your way to prevent creating a false hope? That's good. We should not fill our minds with false hopes. I wonder what other ways you have for avoiding being seduced by false hopes and for distinguishing valid hopes?

This finding positive intention pattern describes what we try to accomplish with a particular belief, model of the world, or behavior. By shifting our focus from the negative statement or behavior to the positive intention behind it and within it, we *open up a space* so that we can explore with the person other more effective statements and behaviors. As you can see, this form of mind-lining *paces* or matches another's model of the world as it searches for the heart and spirit within and above the behavior. And treating people in this way brings out their best. It facilitates and coaches new resources into being.

To do this, start with the question, "What is the positive intention behind, within, or above this behavior?" You can find it or you can invent it. Then you can attribute it to the person's response as a frame that establishes the purpose and drive of the other person's beliefs and actions. This then invites the person to search for more effective ways to accomplish the positive intention.

With this, we assume that while people do things purposefully to their benefit, they do not always do so consciously. We are simply assuming that every behavior and belief, no matter how obnoxious its external presentation derives from a positive intent, that somewhere in the background a higher intentional frame is driving it. If we find an external behavior in which we can't find a *positive* intent at all, we simply move up one more level and ask the question again. If we go above that intent to *the intent of that intent,* we will always eventually get to a positive intent.

Using this Mind-Line pattern empowers us to discover or establish a positive intent for a presenting behavior. In doing this, our mind-line *pre-frames* the external behavior as "seeking to accomplish something positive and of value." This meta-states the behavior with some unarticulated or forgotten positive value. Then we set about to explore the specific positive intention.

* What positive intention motivates this person to say or do this?
* What could a person seek to accomplish of value here?
* What secondary gain may one seek to obtain or not lose?

Now we must warn you. Once this Mind-Line pattern because habitual in your way of perceiving people, it will do something magical inside you. It will create a new orientation for the way you move through the world. You will begin to orient yourself to *guessing in the direction of positive intentions* of people. You will begin to habitually formulate positive intentions about things and put the best spin on things with your loved ones, friends, associates, customers, etc. And, of course, that will change you.

Consider the positive effect this will also have on your own attitude. By shifting attention from the negative behaviors to the positive intent behind it, we open up *a new space* for ourselves as well as for them. Into this new and more *solution oriented* space we will then invite others. Doing this will set a more positive direction for relating. Doing this will facilitate communication as it taps into a respect and appreciation for others. All of this, in turn, will build up hope. Ultimately, this appreciation attitude will create the basis for even new and more positive behaviors. Such reframing can actually turn around a negative cycle and create a positive one.

C) When you arrive late that means you don't care.
> I can see how being late means to you that I don't care. I'm touched by the fact that you really do want to know and feel assured that I truly care for you. That's more valuable to you than I realized. And when you experience that in the way that counts fully for you, what does that give you?

In this statement we assume that their behavior (E.B.) of "criticism" intends to find out if we really care and to get us to show our care. So, instead of taking offense and arguing with the person about the behavior that's disliked (showing up late), we validate the implied intention and empathically affirm our care.

How much nicer, don't you think? Setting this positive frame about criticism enables us to talk about solutions rather than blame about the problem. We shift from the Blame Game to the Solution Game.[1]

D) Stress causes me to eat chocolate.

So does that mean that what you really want to do is to reduce your stress? That's truly a most admirable choice, and yet you are now in the habit of seeking to reduce stress by eating chocolate? Does that work? Does eating chocolate really reduce your stress? It's a positive goal, but does it work? If not, perhaps we could explore other ways you could fulfill your objective of de-stressing.

E) I can't really make a difference because management doesn't walk their talk.

Listening to you, it strikes me that you really do want to make a difference and perhaps even help management walk their talk. Is that fair to say? I bet this strong desire to make a positive difference will cause you to persevere until you can find a way to make a difference. What do you think?

If your true desire in saying this is to motivate yourself to hold back so that you don't get your hopes up and then feel crushed if things don't change, I wonder what other ways you could reach that goal without pouring so much cold water on your motivation?

F) I can't buy your product because it costs too much.

Thanks. I'm glad you brought that up because it seems that you really do care about getting the proper value out of your purchases, so I'm wondering how much value do you want from that item?

Pattern Summary

As mentioned, the eliciting questions for this pattern involve exploring intentions, the "why" question which drives a person's motivation, secondary gains, etc.

- Why is this valuable to you?
- How is this important to you?
- What's your positive intention?
- What does this mean to you?
- What happens when you get this?

#9   Positive Prior Cause Framing

Just as we can conceptually move backwards in "time" to identify the positive intentions that drive a behavior and a person's *meaning formula* that creates his or her semantic reality, we can also go back in "time" to identify *a Positive Prior Cause.*

Why in the world would we want to do that? For the same reason that we want to attribute *positive* intentions to any and all behaviors, we want to frame behaviors, experience, emotions, etc. Doing so allows a person to move on in life in a resourceful way, rather than get stuck in a corner with nowhere to go.

Actually this may be a more difficult Mind-Line pattern to learn because we more commonly attribute *negative* prior cause reasons and explanations for things. Most of us are far more skilled in identifying *negative* things that "cause" us to do what we do. We're more used to blaming and excusing ourselves from being responsible. We are more likely to say,

> "That's just an excuse! Cut it out! Face up to reality. Quit justifying yourself. It doesn't get you off the hook!"

When did you last try that one? Personally I never have found that it worked very well, have you? In fact, as I think about it, I don't like people using that *mind-line* on me. Do you? That one typically evokes defensiveness more than anything else. If you don't believe me, do your own research. Go out tomorrow and tell people that the reason they do what they do involves making excuses and self-justification for things!

Positive Prior Cause involves attributing to someone a reason, explanation, cause, etc. for some behavior (E.B.) that we or another do not like and that creates some kind of difficulty. We do so in such a way that it allows us or them to develop a new perspective. We frame a new way to see so that we can operate out of a much better place—a place that gives them room for change, better aims, more resourcefulness. It lets a person "off the hook." As we identify *non-personal contributing influences* for the action, it creates new opportunities for change.

Can people misuse this approach? You bet. Should we? Ah, the ethics question again. It's also an ecology question. Well, why don't we just decide to *not* do that while at the same time using it to assist people in overcoming negative behavior. After all, we could spend time accusing, blaming, and pointing the finger. Or we could set a frame that gives a person a new way to look at the behavior—a way that allows them to rise above it.

Begin with a negative behavior (i.e., showing up late for a meeting, missing an appointment, or forgetting to take out the garbage). Now run this behavior through the frame of a *positive prior cause,* and apply it to yourself. You show up late or do something else that someone does not like. They feel angry. They are huffing and puffing about it. Now deliver the mind-line, making sure, of course, that you have sufficient rapport to at least have the other's ear.

> "I'm sorry that I'm late, with all the traffic on the road, an accident occurred and wouldn't you know it—right in my lane."

Yet we may have a problem with that. It may sound far too much like *an excuse.* Does it strike you as "an excuse?" If so, then we don't have much of a reframe yet. So far we just have the mere relating of facts. So lets spice it up—with some *magic,* with some words that set a positive frame.

> "I'm sorry that I'm late. I was looking forward to this meeting with you all week and really wanted to meet with you. Repeatedly throughout the day I have thought about the possibilities of working together with you. So I do apologize for getting here late. I should have considered the traffic at this hour and the possibility of an accident—which of course happened. I guess I was thinking more of you then those details."

In this expression, we here attribute a *Positive Prior Cause* to our unpleasant behavior, an impersonal cause—something that has nothing to do with our heart. We counterbalance that cause, with the intent of our heart, namely, wanting to see and be with this person, wanting to experience a positive relationship. We have also tossed in and, downplayed another factor, our recognition that "traffic happens!"

The positive prior cause is positive in that it puts the *cause* on something outside of ourselves and on something that is *non-personal.* This conversational reframe puts the emphasis on these contributing influences as the thing that actually *causes* the problem. This sets a non-personal frame. It swishes the recipient's mind to realizing that beyond the *positive intentions* there are other factors, accidental and beyond our control, that we also have to factor in.

Typically, most people do *not* do this. We don't do it either for ourselves or for others. Instead, we seem to lean toward attributing *negative* intentions and *negative* causation to things. We blame and accuse. We seek to find fault with something or someone. Somehow we have a sense that if only we could find someone to blame, then things would be better. So we play the Blame Game. Yet it seldom works out. When we *negatively* frame the influences in our world, we then elicit the thoughts, emotions, conversation, and behavior that correspond to that frame. So then we get negative and seek to find fault.

With this Mind-Line we can change all of that. Now we can re-directionalize our brains (and the brains of others) and send them in an entirely different direction. If we hear a limiting belief about the "reasons" people, mates, children, bosses, companies, the government, God, etc. do things—we can *set a positive frame of causation*. This allows us to neutralize blame and accusation by setting a non-personal frame.

When we choose to establish *a Prior Cause* with our language we offer constructive justifications and explanations as to why we did something. We do this to create a more enhancing map about the response. This undoes the damage that occurs when we attribute *negative* explanations and reasons to actions. This also differs from when we try to *positively* validate or justify an ugly behavior. To do that only increases the sense of grievance and so reinforces the sense of being a victim. Doing that increases the making of excuses.

When we bring *a Positive Prior Cause* to the limiting belief and/or the behavior, we invite the other person to broaden his or her understanding of the contributing causes and influencing factors. Simultaneously we can invite that person to catch a vision of living by a more positive image. This re-directionalizing of thought can give a person permission to stop blaming and to move into a more solution oriented direction.

A) *Saying mean things makes you a bad person.*
> If being hateful or ugly [I.S.] caused me to say those things you consider mean, then I would agree with you and immediately change. But I cut you short [E.B.] because I had a terrible day at work [E.B.], was feeling very unresourceful [I.S.], and just didn't think about your feelings [I.S.] as I usually do, and as I want to. So I apologize for that.

Using a *Positive Prior Cause* appeals to socially acceptable reasons for a behavior while simultaneously disconnecting the behavior from mere excuse making and focusing on negative causes that we personalize. This reframe asserts that the behavior does not arise from a personal negative cause, but that *other* reasons, causes, and factors play a role. When offered on behalf of someone else, we use this to set a positive prior cause that invites the other to step into a more responsible position and live out of that causation frame.

B) *Cancer causes death.*
> I can appreciate this perspective on cancer especially given what you experienced with your uncle John. Given his experiences, it only makes sense that you would draw a conclusion like that. How about we visit the Hospice program? I think that your sharp and intelligent mind will draw some different conclusions when we see some of the very different experiences there. What do you say?

D) Stress causes me to eat chocolate.
> Yes, obviously stress effects people in different ways. And people de-stress in different ways, by running, exercising, creating something, smoking, etc. How did eating chocolate come to be connected with de-stressing for you? With your inquisitive mind you have identified a possible cause of your habit of eating chocolate. I wonder what other reasons could prompt this eating of chocolate?

E) I can't really make a difference because management doesn't walk their talk.
> Maybe you can't make a difference because you feel burned out and need an extended vacation. You only say that because you find it much easier than applying your creative powers to making a change there as you have at other times and can do so again at any time you choose ... but haven't yet because you operate best when you have their congruency.
> You must really want to make a difference! And yet how strange. *That very ability will enable you to find a way to make a difference, won't it?*

F) I can't buy your product because it costs too much.
> I'm glad that you take a position like that to make good decisions about purchases because I would like to give you some other facts about this product that you will appreciate for that very reason.

Pattern Summary
To elicit this pattern, simply explore other possible *Positive Prior Causes* that cause or contribute to the response or belief statement.
- What could be a possible cause for this limiting belief or hurtful behavior?
- What else could explain this that opens up space for change?
- What behaviors or actions of others, or of neutral events could also explain how a person draw a particular conclusion?

#10 *First Outcome Framing*

In the previous move, we shifted back to previous "times" to develop a new perspective on the nature of things. We stepped *outside* the magic belief box to explore *why* we act as we do. We went to previous times to see things through the lens of a *positive intention* and a *positive cause*. When we take either of those points of view we gain new insights with regard to what could have given birth to the belief formula.

Positive Intentionality enabled us to pace the person and *Positive Cause* empowered us to bring in and attribute non-personal causational factors. These two moves pre-frame a person so that he or she can step into a place (a mind-body-emotion state) that allows them to become resourceful enough to look at the belief without defensive feelings.

As we continue to operate *outside* the box, let's now move in the other time direction. Let's move into the future, to the times in the person's life when *the formula* will give birth to various outcomes and consequences. As we directionalize our brains to go in this direction, we will adopt a very different perspective. We will begin to think about the belief from the point of view of outcome and consequence.

*   Where will this idea take us?
*   What will it produce?
*   What planned and unplanned consequences will emerge?

Conversationally, we convey these ideas of consequences with the following kind of mind-lines:

*   What do you think as you consider how this idea might play out into the future? Is this what you want?
*   Would you find this particular consequence desirable, useful, productive, enhancing, etc.?
*   When you think about that belief leading first to this outcome, and then that outcome of outcome, etc., do you want to give the belief the power to operate in these ways?

These mind-lines allow us to inquire about the consequences which a belief or behavior will (might or could) elicit if we follow it out to its logical conclusion and let it run its course. Here we state the cause-effect (C-E) prediction as to where the belief or behavior will take us or another. These mind-lines radically differ from the previous ones in that they generally feel much more confrontational and challenging. Whereas with the two previous ones we operated from compassion and seeking to understand the source and to validate the person, here we take the *consequences* and put it in the person's face to see if we can provoke a reaction. So, if you feel ready for this, get out your magic wand, and… on to the playground!

A) *Saying mean things makes you a bad person.*
> You know, in the long run that belief will prevent people from speaking the truth to each other. Is that what you want? Is that really acceptable for yourself and your relationships?

B) *Cancer causes death.*
> What a belief! Of course, since beliefs are "commands to the nervous system" and operate as self-fulfilling prophecies, is that what you really want to be programming in? That belief sounds so definitive; I bet if you really believed that you would stop exploring your options. Is that what you really want?

First Outcome Framing shifts our frame-of-reference toward future results to enable us to engage in some *consequential thinking*. It invites us into a future perspective, to consider the influence of present behavior. Projecting a person (a client or customer, friend, child, etc.) to the future consequences of a particular behavior can make something currently perceived as positive look negative, or vice versa. As we use these mind-lines, we engage in some guessing about the future or prophesying about the future.

These mind-lines enable us to confront more than to pace. They aim to hold a person responsible for a course already set out rather than put a positive spin on where the belief or meaning came from. You will need to be in more of a confrontational state to deliver these effectively. Of course, be sure to temper that confrontation with love, compassion, and playfulness. With sufficient love and respect, then feel free to tease the daylights out of them!

C) *When you show up late, it means you don't care about me.*
> When you keep telling me that being late means I don't care about you it seems that you don't listen to how I do care about you, I feel frustrated and put off. I then wonder if we should even stay together. Is that the response you want—for me to back off from you or to break off our relationship?

First Outcome Framing can also intensify an already perceived positive or negative perception.

C) *When you show up late, it means you don't care about me.*
> Sweetheart, I've noticed a pattern. Every time you start our evening with accusation that when I'm late I don't care about you, we then spend our evening arguing over who's right or wrong about this? Is that what you really want to do?
>
> Honey, I'm confused. Given that half of the people in the world are *In-*

Time regarding their style of relating to time and so easily get lost in time, do you really want to argue about this? I've tried to let you know that when I arrive 30 minutes or even an hour late, it really has nothing to do with you. I could use your help with a reminder because you do know that I get lost in time.

D) Stress causes me to eat chocolate.

It sounds like you are prepared to gain weight and take the chance of getting diabetes because you are justifying your chocolate eating as a de-stressor. Is that right? Is that what you really want? Wouldn't you prefer to lose weight and experience greater health?

E) I can't really make a difference because management doesn't walk their talk.

What a belief! Apparently management doesn't have a chance in changing when people talk and believe that way. It does give you a good out from even trying. Is that what you want? Is that your highest path?

F) I can't buy your product because it costs too much.

Thanks for bringing this up because it seems that you really do care about getting value from the purchases that you make. Yet is this way of thinking actually helping you achieve that objective? What do you think? With that attitude, what do you usually experience?

Pattern Summary

To elicit this conversational reframing pattern in your dialogues with people, ask the consequential question:

- What will happen if you continue to think this way?
- Do you like this outcome as it plays out into the future?
- What does this way of thinking lead to?
- Is this your highest path?

#11 *Outcome of Outcome Framing*

Since conceptually shifting a person into the future works so well (and it did, did it not?), then let's do it again! This conversational reframing pattern simply and magically sends a person even *further* into the future. This time it does the time-shift to get the person to not only consider the immediate outcomes and consequences of the belief package, but to consider *the outcome-of-the-outcome*. We invite the person into a frame-of-reference when he or she considers how the logic of the belief will play out when we take even more time into consideration.

If a belief is limiting or worse, toxic, then it will not lead to a good result. Sometimes this is not immediately recognized especially when there are some secondary gains or when the consequences takes time to realize their full negative potential. Sometimes the first results are not all that bad, but the results of those results are. That's what these mind-lines goes after.

We here linguistically directionalize a mind as we invite a person to engage in consequential thinking over the long-term. We do that to gain an even greater perspective over time about effects and effects-of-effects. This allows us to explore and set a frame around additional outcomes that will (or could) result from the person's reality construct.

A) *Saying mean things makes you a bad person.*
> Since, in the long run this belief will prevent people from speaking the truth to one another, this idea of moralizing on how people express themselves verbally will most likely only lead to an argument. And if we keep moralizing in this way, won't that make us more and more judgmental and ugly to each other? Is that what you really want? Is that why we got together?

B) *Cancer causes death.*
> Isn't this thinking about cancer as only and exclusively death producing a very negative perspective? What will that kind of death thinking get you but more depression and resignation as it signals your brain to go into even more gloomy and sick states?

What does something mean? What does a piece of behavior (E.B.) mean? We hope that by now you fully appreciate just how much it depends upon contexts and frames. When we worked *inside* the conceptual box, as we did in the previous chapters to deframe, reframe, and counter-frame, we offered numerous ways to transform meaning. As we now move out *beyond* that mind-box of belief and meaning into future "times" to look at consequences we extend the frame-of-reference. And, because changing frame alters meaning, the original formula of meaning changes. In this mind-line move, we essentially say,

>That particular external behavior doesn't mean the internal state or significance that you have given it because as you look at its long-term effects and the effects of those effects, just consider what it now means! Is that what you want?

Using the metaphor of *a time-line* we have been framing things from a linear point-of-view. When you look at it from the past intention or causation, its meanings shift in this way. When you look at it from the future consequences, it takes on this look. Yet in doing this we have actually simply *outframed* the belief with its meaning formula. We have applied other thoughts-and-feelings to the magic box. We have meta-stated the belief with a frame-of-reference about consequences.

Meta-stating refers to simply bringing one state to another state and putting one at a higher "logical level" to the second.[2] Here we bring the conceptual states of mind and feeling regarding "consequences," "the future," outcomes, etc. and apply them to the belief.

In this *outcome-of-an-outcome* move, we aim not only to expand the meaning in terms of consequences, but also to find other consequential results that can arise in a wide range of contexts and dimensions of life. Obviously, a new outcome will change the meaning even though our focus here doesn't particularly lie on what the E.B. equals, means, or causes, but what it will or could *cause* over time. When we send our consciousness to future consequences and bring that awareness back to the belief, we *feed forward* information into the ongoing development of the belief (like feedback except the results haven't actually occurred yet).

Doing this allows us to use *the wisdom* that we can develop by taking a future perspective and bringing those insights back to the present. This reframing move can prevent a lot of later exclamations on the order of, 'If I had only known that it would have led to *that!"*

C) *Your being late means you don't care about me.*
>While the first effects of what you are saying only seems to undermine your feelings of being loved by me, in the years to come they seem to invite you to call into question the validity of my love. And I wonder what will happen over time if you feel less and less loved and I feel my love more and more invalidated? It doesn't seem to really build anything solid between us, does it?

D) *Stress causes me to eat chocolate.*
>So you say that stress causes you to eat chocolate, so over time as you eat more and more chocolate to relieve stress, won't that create even

more stress as you gain unwanted weight, and then feel bad about yourself, out-of-control, and from that additional stress you will then eat even more until ... what will any of that really get you?

> **"Vice is after all a dull business**
> **whether it be physical or intellectual,**
> **and an effective cure can sometimes be achieved**
> **by indulgence to the point at which the patient realizes this.**
> **It is a way of proving**
> **that a given line of thought or conduct**
> **will not do,**
> **by extrapolating it to infinity,**
> **when its absurdities become evident."**
> (Bateson, 1972, *Steps to an Ecology of Mind*, p. 83)

E) I can't really make a difference because management doesn't walk their talk.
   Is the real issue truly about whether or not management walks their talk or whether you want to live with the consequences of thinking that way? If you keep using that as an excuse for not acting with responsibility or walking your talk, where will that lead you? Will that get you the promotions you want? Will that demonstrate self-management, leadership, vision, or even congruency to your own values? Won't that encourage you to behave as irresponsibly as the management you are complaining about? Is that want you want? Do you want to live with all these outcomes of that limiting belief?

F) I can't buy your product because it costs too much.
   The price certainly seems to cost too much now, but I wonder if by putting off the purchase now, and seeing the price go up next year, and the year after, until it gets so high that you'll never have the opportunity that you now have. I wonder how you feel about the missed opportunities your fear of price caused?

Pattern Summary
To elicit this conversational reframing pattern use the elicitation question:
•   What consequence will occur after this first outcome?
•   What results will or could arise from the first results?
•   Yes, the issue may seem to be this internal state at this point in time, yet what will it result in later on?
•   When you expand your vision to the years to come and the accumulating consequences, is that what you really want?

#12 Eternity Framing

"Hit me one more time, Charlie!" Since these time-line mind-lines work so well, let's play it out one more time. These pseudo-orientation in time mind-lines in this reframing move continue to conceptually shift our mind until it expands our sense of "time," outcomes, consequences, effects, and outcomes of outcomes. In this final move into the future, we go to the ultimate time-frame possible. We bring thoughts of life and death, eternity, human destiny, etc. to bear upon the belief. Now we think about things from the point of view of *eternity*.

This linguistic reframing utilizes what Covey (1987) popularized as "starting with the end in mind." If we start from the perspective of designing the epitaph on our grave stone, what do we want it to say? If we start from the perspective of what our closest friend, our mate, our parents, our children, our associates will say at our funeral, what do we want them to have said about us? And do remember that *fun*eral begins with the word "fun," so aim to live a fun life for yourself and others. Make it a party.

Milton Erickson frequently played with people's consciousness about "time" in the context of therapy to help them develop better and more enhancing *meanings*. He would move a person conceptually to places of the past and places of the future to thereby create new and different frames-of-reference. Today we speak about these shifts as creating a *pseudo-orientation in time*. This describes what we have been doing with all of these "time" reframes. Here we do it again, except we just do it in even more exaggerated terms, using an end of life frame.

The mind-lines within these three future shifting reframes enable us to post-frame a belief or a behavior. Starting with the end in mind enables us to look upon any response, (i.e., a behavior, belief, conversation, idea, etc.) with hindsight. And since, throughout history, people of every time and culture have praised the wisdom of hindsight, *pseudo-orienting ourselves* (and others) *in time, conversationally,* to gain such hindsight up-front offers us a truly marvelous neuro-semantic tool, don't you think? No? Well, maybe one of these days, you'll look back on this skill and fully realize how much you appreciate this mind-line or could have appreciated it. How will you view things in that light when you look back upon your experience in life from the perspective of eternity?

A) Saying mean things makes you a bad person.
>   It may seem mean to you now, but when you come to the end of your
>   life and look back on how our relationship developed to the point where
>   we could truly handle the storms that life threw at us and we didn't have

to walk on egg-shells with each other, don't you think you'll appreciate the feedback, especially if, in the long run, it helped you to become effective over such verbal static?

B) Cancer causes death.

Is that what you want people to remember about you—that you became a victim of cancer who just gave up? Surely, because all of us mortals will die, wouldn't you like to be remembered for something other than cancer? When you think about the legacy you'll leave—how would you like others to remember you?

C) Your being late means you don't care about me.

This seems really important and big now, doesn't it? I wonder when you get to the end of your life and look back on this experience— and take in the overall meaning of your life and our relationship —what will this experience mean in the light of that?

D) Stress causes me to eat chocolate.

Travel with me in your mind, for just a moment, to the end of your journey in this world ... experience a kind of trip that Ebenezer Scrooge took one night when he took the hand of "the Angel of Christmas to come" and went into his future. There he saw his own funeral and his own grave stone, and from there he looked back on his life ... as you can now on your experiences of stress that caused you to eat chocolate, and tell me just how significant you see those experiences from that perspective. And with that in mind, do you really want to make "eating chocolate" as your way of relieving stress?

E) I can't really make a difference because management doesn't walk their talk.

Because their incongruent behavior has such a powerful influence on you today ... zoom forward to the day when you will retire from work altogether, and turn around and look back from that point of view to this day and these complaints you have... and tell me what they look like when you take that adventuresome step.

F) I can't buy your product because it costs too much.

It really seems like a big deal today ... and maybe that's the problem. Just for the fun of it, imagine yourself having come to the end of your sojourn, and ready to leave this world, and look back to this day when you had this opportunity to make this purchase ... and how expensive does it seem when you view it from that larger point of view?

Pattern Summary

To elicit this pattern, use the elicitation question of eternity:

- When I get to the end of my life, how will this external behavior look from that perspective?
- If I take the perspective of eternity, how would that change the way I am looking at this?
- How will this look say 50 or 100 years from now?

Designing Alternative Futures

I (MH) first discovered the conversational reframing patterns from Chris Hall in my Master Practitioner course. During her presentation, she described a point in her life when she had come to "a point of indecision." I wrote about this in *The Spirit of NLP* (1996):

> In my mind I went out to my future, and then to the end of my time-line. From there I then looked back on *the decision point* of this day when I was attempting to make a decision. When I did this, the process brought about a dissociation for me. The effect of that was that *some new criteria* came into play thus providing me the needed information and frame from which to make a good decision. Now I could play each scenario out and more fully notice the values of risk, fear, hesitation, etc. (p. 134)

When we change *the time frame* of an event and recast it into a much larger perspective, it often has the effect of bringing or creating other perspectives, ideas, and values into play that then impact the original thinking.

We can often gain an empowering sense of the small size of our fear when we step back and see it in a larger perspective. We can ask, "What do I fear?" "Do I need this state of fear?" Such questions invite us to step into a larger time frame and context and so it changes our thinking and feeling. We can use this reframing pattern on ourselves to replace repeating and looping worries when we get caught up in the state of indecision and just go round and round the same information of pictures, words, and feelings.

These "time" frames track us forward in "time" as we future pace a belief. If we utilize *the consequence frame* in this way and also use exaggeration, the reframing can become even more powerful. Here we can even suggest and install some fearful consequences that a person ought to put his or her mind around.

One man had the habit of "straightening out" the woman with whom he was living. It may seem strange, but there are people who actually do such things. He didn't think anything of it until it started creating problems for their relationship. She didn't like it. From his perspective it seemed strange that she didn't appreciate it. After all, he was just trying to straighten her out and it was obvious to him that she needed it. So he wanted to know, "What was her problem?"

What drove this behavior? He operated from the frame, "You're wrong about what you're saying, wanting, doing, so I'll straighten you out and then things will be fine." That was the magic that drove his behaviors. When he showed up for counseling, he had a clearly thought out *outcome,* "I want to be calm so I can be more effective in setting her right."

And what has your intention of trying to straighten her out gotten you so far?
> Well, she gets into some pretty negative moods.

And what does that lead to?
> Well, arguments and fights.

And what results from that?
>> I don't know. I guess we both feel bad and then withdraw from each other. I tell her not to do that, but she does it anyway.

Suppose you keep doing this for years, and you get more distance, and the bad feelings increase. What will that get you?
>> A rotten relationship. It wouldn't last if that happens.

So when you think about the outcome of trying to straighten her out and the outcomes of those outcomes, is this what you really want from a relationship?
>> [Pause] ... Well, no ... but how can I change things?

Ah, great question. You want to change things?
> Sure.

How would you like to be with her in a way that would be loving and supportive?

Back to the Future... a Few More Times
As an alternative way to handle future pacing, consequential outframing, and the mind-lines of outcome thinking, let's respond to this request by asking the four questions from Cartesian logic:
> #1: What would happen if you do?
> #2: What would happen if you don't?
> #3: What would *not* happen if you do?
> #4: What would *not* happen if you don't?

What effect do these four questions have on you? Apply them to some future activity that you are planning to initiate. Now entertain each question and step into the thoughts and feelings that emerge.

Do they not create a set of internal representations that generate a *push and pull dynamic*? They first whisk us off into the future consequences (#1). They then pull us back to the present to choose *not* to take the action and then back out into a new future (#2). They then whisk us back off into yet another alternative future as we think about what things will *not* play out as we take the actions

(#3). Then we're pulled back to the second choice, to *not* engage, and then to speed out into the altered universe of things that *don't* occur when that emerges (#4).

"Would you want that future **now** so that it could become your present reality?"

Summary

- We have moved backwards and forwards in "time" in the *five reframing patterns* of this chapter. As conversational *time-travelers,* we have cued brains (ours and others) repeatedly to use our neuro-semantic powers to zoom up and down their time-lines.

- You now more fully realize that the magic formula does *not* occur in a vacuum. How we use various *"time" frames* in our referencing influences and shapes the *meanings* that then govern our emotional states.

- The "time" reframing here can empower us to stop using "the past" to torment ourselves and others. It's never too late to set up frames in our past that create a better future for us. We can return to the past to set up positive frames that will allow us to live more fully today.

- Use these "time" mind-lines also to exchange worrying and fretting yourself about the future to tapping into the power and wisdom of good consequential thinking. You can access the wisdom of the future today if you start with the end in mind and embed your perspective in that frame-of-reference.[3]

- Did you notice that many of the future consequences Mind-Lines involve accessing strong aversion states? Not only can we think of the "future" in terms of the *attractions of desired outcomes* that pull us into a bright future, we can also think of the things that we definitely do not want to have in our futures. Awareness of the goals that we do *not* want creates aversion values in a human propulsion system. And such aversion power gives us the energy to *move away from* such unacceptable consequences.

End Notes

1. The *games* that we play in life via our actions, responses, and behaviors are, in truth, *frame games.* For more about this, see *Frame Games* (2000) and the series of frame game books: *Games for Mastering Fear, Games Business Experts Play, Games Great Lovers Play, Games Slim and Fit People Play.*

2. We have put "logical levels" in quotes here because there is no such thing as a "logical level." This phrase does not refer to a *thing* in the real world, but to a complex idea in the mind. As a phrase made up of two nominalizations there are some hidden verbs within it. What are those verbs? It is "to layer" and "to reason" and that describes the meta-stating process itself. See the Neuro-Semantic website, www.neurosemantics.com for several articles on "Logical Levels," as well as *Meta-States* (2000) and *NLP Going Meta* (2001).

3. If you like playing with the conceptual "time" frameworks, then check out *Time-Lining: Patterns For Adventuring in "Time* (1997).

Chapter 9

OUTFRAMING

Beaming Up To Get a Heavenly Perspective

"What about the deeper magic?
Yes, what about the deeper magic?"
C.S. Lewis
(The Lion, The Witch & the Wardrobe)

"Each level synthesizes, organizes, and directs
a particular class of activity on the level below it.
Changing something on an upper level
would necessarily 'radiate' downward,
precipitating change on the lower levels."
Robert Dilts (1999, p. 246)

Did you enjoy all of that de-framing and de-constructing of reality in the chapter on *Deframing?* We did. How about the switcheroos that we pulled in the chapter on *Reframing?* Did you like the time-traveling shifts in the chapter on *Pre-Framing* and *Post-Framing?*

What we did in the last chapter with *the time frame reference shifts* actually involved a meta-level shift. Did you noticed that? We put those reframing moves as if they involved moving a person laterally, hence the use of the spatial language, *before* and *after* the three dimensional box. Yet "time" is only a *concept.* So in that, we actually jumped up a "logical level" and applied the concepts of "past" and "future" to our belief frame.

So we actually up-framed, or as we will describe it here, we *out-framed.* We challenged the content within the Belief Box by running with the logic (the neuro-semantic logic) within the meaning construction in the cube and applied some conceptual frames-of-references about outcomes and consequences (Mind-Lines #8—#12).

If you liked that, then you'll enjoy the many more that's yet to come. In fact, that's all we will do in this chapter. We will come out of the closet about the outframing as we do it overtly. So how about it? Are you ready to spend some time moving up the specificity/abstraction scale to *induce* and *generalize* to new principles and constructions? Making such meta-moves sets up entirely new frames-of-references and so this frames these new ideas *over* the previous ones. It establishes ever-higher contexts within which we think, emote, respond, and behave.

You can also think about these outframing mind-line moves as *conversational meta-stating*. After all, when we take a meta-position to a belief, we move to yet another higher meta-state level. From there we set up a meta-relationship between the meaning frame using some thought, emotion, or other conceptual construction. This reveals a secret about all of the mind-lines—a secret that we did not realize when we wrote the first edition.

What is the secret behind or within the Mind-Lines model?
> *When we create a mind-line, we actually meta-state. We meta-state a conceptual state that we call a "belief" as we apply other frames to it. What we have in the actual line or question is the language or linguistic expression of the meta-state.*

Context Reframing is Meta-Stating
In the reframing moves of this chapter, we engage in *context* reframing. At this level, we are operating *outside* the cube of meaning and the foundational formula for linking things up. Traditionally *context* reframing has referred to asking context questions:
•   When and where would this behavior be a resource?
•   Where would I want to keep this response?

We will continue this process of finding, or creating, new contexts, but now with a twist. Now instead of just finding other physical and environmental places where we can use the magic, we will intentionally apply some higher magic to the lower magic. Then we will stand back to watch the fireworks.

This means that we will apply *conceptual contexts* to the limiting belief. We will go beyond just finding a new or different context, we will beam up to numerous higher levels and create contexts about the belief formula (i.e., the magic cube), and even contexts for those contexts-of-contexts.

In the quote at the beginning of this chapter C.S. Lewis' stories for children about Narnia, the black magic of the Queen had brought perpetual winter to the land of Narnia. But when the children met the Lion, they discovered that he had *a higher magic* much more powerful than the magic of the cruel queen. Here we want to do a similar thing, we want to find and create *higher magic* for the highest levels of our mind.

In the Meta-States model, this outframing process of *going meta* enables us, *in one fell swoop,* to change a whole system.   By moving up and above the formula of belief in the box, we put all of that magic within a larger frame-work of magic and thereby embed it in new and higher magical contexts. Doing this changes everything. Why?

> *Because higher "logical levels" drive, modulate, organize, and govern lower levels.*[1]

By moving up and beyond the belief and outframing it with other frames-of-references, we *wrap* these thoughts *around* the belief. Why? To increase our options. We do this to see if the belief will cohere and maintain itself. What thoughts can we move up to and access to set these larger frames? As the following summarizes these mind-line patterns, they indicate belief *tests* and mind-lines for working with and reframing beliefs.

Mind-Lines in Chapter 9

#13 Model of the World Framing
#14 Criteria and Value Framing
#15 Allness Framing
#16 Have-To Framing (Necessity)
#17 Identity Framing (Personalizing)
#18 Framing with Other Abstractions
#19 Ecology Framing

The Up-framing Moves

The meta-stating *mind-line* moves (Mind-Lines #13—#19)   include the following meta-moves and responses. These seven mind-lines were in the original model. Later we discover additional ones (Mind-Lines #21 —#26).

#13: Moving up to the person's *Model of the World* itself enables us to question and examine the limiting belief *as a map* and a mental construct and to bring that understanding to the belief.
*   Who made this map anyway?
*   Do you want someone else's map in your head? After all, you never know where that map has been!
*   How did this model of the world frame arise in the first place?
*   Is it still relevant or useful?

#14: Moving up to the person's *Criteria and Values* of importance enables us to question and examine the belief in light of these values or others. By applying the person's values to the belief gives everybody a chance to see if the belief coheres and remains consistent with other values. When it doesn't it begins to rattle apart from incongruency and cognitive dissonance.

- Is this important or valuable to you? How important?
- Is being right and making your point more important than having a loving relationship?
- Are there any other values that haven't been integrated into this belief?

#15: Moving up to *Allness* enables us to test and question the generalization of the belief using universal quantifiers terms (i.e., "all, everyone, everywhere, none," etc.).

- What if *everybody* believed that?
- Does this always occur? When doesn't it?
- Has it never been otherwise?

#16: Moving up to *the modal operators* within the belief empower us to question and test some of the assumption of the belief. *Modal operators* is a fancy abstract phrase that refers to our style or *modus operandi* (our M.O.) that we use in moving through the world. In this there are several *modes of operation* that can describe how we move through life:

- The mode of *necessity* (have to, must, ought, should): Do you *have to* do this? What if you didn't?
- The mode of *impossibility* (can't): Is this a psychological *can't*? What stops you?
- The mode of *possibility* (able, may, can): Does being able to do necessitate it? What else is possible?
- The mode of *desire* (get to, want to, desire to, etc.): How much do you want to do that? Can you want it and not act on it?

#17: Moving up to *Identity* enables us to question and examine the belief in terms of what it says and/or does to our identity, our identifications, and our self-definitions. This empowers us to challenge and explore the person's mapping of his or her self matrix.

- What self-definition enables you to believe that belief?
- Who does this belief make you?
- What have you identified with or personalized in order to use this idea?
- Who would you have to become to not be limited by this belief?
- Is this who you want to become?

#18: Moving up to *Other Abstractions* enables us to question and explore a whole range of other concepts about the belief. By moving up to higher abstract conceptions *about* the belief or its specific terms (the E.B. or the I.S.), we can meta-state it from a wide range of concepts and perceptions. Originally we created this mind-line as a catch-all classification. After that, wouldn't you know it, we began discovering and adding many additional outframes. In this edition, you will find these in Chapter 17.

#19: Moving up to the idea of *Ecology* enables us to question and expolore the idea of how the belief frame works over time for our health, balance, wholeness, relationships, congruency, etc. We call this running an ecology check. It's checking to see if the meta-frame of the belief really works to our welfare.
*   Does this enhance your life or empower you as a person?
*   Does this enrich the various dimensions of your life?

We noted earlier that when we take a whole of something and then go down to its parts, we create a reduction of the old magical formula. Conversely, if we take a part and move up to some larger whole, and then use that new higher category at a meta-level, we bring new resources and choices of that category or frame to the belief. By moving up, inductively, we access thoughts that we can then apply to the belief. This outframes as it puts a frame around the belief.

When we create a mind-line, we actually meta-state. We meta-state a conceptual state that we call a "belief" as we apply other frames to it. What we have in the actual line or question is the language or linguistic expression of the meta-state.

#13 *Model of the World Framing*

In the conversational reframing pattern called *Model of the World* we move to a level *meta* to the magical box where we have the construction of a belief. We chunk up to this level to identify the person's overall mental map for negotiating the particular territory that the belief corresponds to. In doing this, the presupposition is that we recognize and consider the limiting belief as *a map*. By using the map/territory distinction, we apply that awareness to the belief. Doing so essentially communicates the relativity and fallibility of our maps.

> Hey, it's just one way of mentally mapping the territory, that's all! It's not real. It's just a map.

As in all of these *outframing* meta-moves, this shift involves stepping back from our maps and even from our mapping functions. This initiates several delightful consequences. One most delightful and freeing results involves the ability to hold our map more tentatively and less rigidly. That consequence (ah, an outcome-of-an-outcome frame), in turn, enables us to avoid confusing our map with the territory. Then we can examine our maps with a greater objectivity.

In the Meta-Model, we describe *free-floating maps* of belief statements as *Lost Performatives*. These linguistic statements seemingly appear out of the blue or as commands that drop down from heaven. And yet, because no map-maker appears with the map, and no Wizard of Oz peers from behind the curtains to reveal him or herself, typically we are more likely to assume that the unowned maps as "real." This leads to an unquestioning acceptance of the lost performative. We just assume it to be true.

However, when we use the *Model of the World mind-line,* we begin to question both the map and the map-maker:
- Says who? Who specifically said that?
- Do you realize this is *just a map* about the territory?
- *When* did someone create this idea? In what context?
- Is this belief still relevant or useful?

Yes, this mind-line probably seems quite provocative, challenging, and even irreligious, but someone's got to do it! Challenging a *lost performative* in this way assists us in recovering the person, group, culture, etc. who originally came up with the mental map. When we understand who, when, where, and why the map was created, we are in a better position to make a clear-minded decision.

A) Saying mean things makes you a bad person.
> Where did you learn to think and judge statements in terms of "meanness?" Does that belief about meanness come from your experiences or someone else's? No? Then who created that rule? At

what time did they come up with this idea?

B) Cancer causes death.
> Yes, I've heard that before. Of course, not all medical experts hold that belief. Where did you first learn to view cancer in that way?

Connirae Andreas once commented about her frequent use of the *Model of the World* pattern. This indicates the power and practical usefulness of this pattern. When we directionalize a mind upward to the *Model of the World* level, it typically loosens "reality" or our strategy of reality. It brings into awareness the fact that we operate in the world using our mental maps. In doing this, we embed the belief inside the higher frame that all of our thoughts exist, at best, *only as maps.*

Accordingly, when we find a limiting belief in ourselves or another, we can move up to *the Model of the World* to invite the other person to momentarily step aside from his or her entire frame-of-reference. This will refresh the other's awareness that the belief is only a mental construct anyway. When a person does this, it empowers him or her to shake off old confusions that have accumulated over the years from the cultural and family assumptions the person grew up with. This conversational reframing pattern empowers us to remind ourselves that our beliefs are just maps.

> These are just my thoughts, my maps, about things. They are *not* real! They have no more external reality than I give them with my mind. There's no need for me to confuse this mapping with the territory.

"Sub-modality" Codings—Mere Facets of Mapping

To appreciate how this linguistic pattern works on our internal representations, notice what happens to the cinematic features of your mental movies as you process the following information. Notice the see-hear-feel modalities that you use to encode the information and the qualities of your representations.

> 1) What do you consider of significant value in your life? What's truly important to you? Anything of value will work. You could choose to think about an object like an automobile, a person like a friend or loved one, a book, a valued experience like reading a book, swimming in the ocean, etc. Do you have it?

> 2) Now pay attention to how you now encode your awareness. What movie is playing? What are the qualities in your visual, auditory, and kinesthetic representations of that movie? How close is your picture, how far away? How loud is the volume? Etc.

> 3) When you have noticed the movie, next look at your cinematic frames and noticing them, notice what happens when you say, "This *seems* like my car" (friend, child, book, etc.).

4) What happens? What shifts or changes occur to the snapshot or movie when you utter those words?

Many people report that the location of their image changes. For some, the picture may suddenly seem further back in the distance. What about the focus of your picture? In processing the word, "This *seems* like my car," you may find that the visual qualities of the movie lose focus, move into a less prominent position, fade out, or shift in some other way. What happens to the sound track (the auditory system)?

> 5) Think of your automobile noticing the qualities of your pictures and sounds and as you do, consider the following question: *How long* have you thought that this car belonged to you?

Once again, notice how this statement affects the features and qualities of your visual and auditory movie. The question of this form of the *Model of the World* mind-line pattern typically takes us back to a previous point in time when we did not think of the car as our car. In doing this, it also brings to our awareness, that our "thoughts" come and go, change, and transform.

How did it affect you? Bob said that he typically locates his present day pictures directly in front of him.

> "When I get a picture of my car and consider the question, 'How long have you thought that this car belonged to you?' the image of my car swishes far out in front of me and disappears. I think that's because a year ago I didn't even own this car. As I process the statement, it causes the image to disappear in my immediate past."

> When I use these *Model of the World* questions, my visual pictures suddenly become much less colorful. The color representations fade out as if bleached by the sun and so have much less kinesthetic intensity. With the second question, I step out of the movie and take a second position to it as I observe it running back to the date of the purchase, and then a little before that.

What does all of this mean? It demonstrates how these words and questions facilitate the awareness that our internal representations *of* things differ from the things themselves. It refreshes our experience that they are only a map of the valued object or person. Now try your hand with this statement.

> *When you raise your voice and yell at me, it causes me to shut down emotionally and I feel a distance between us.*

Use the *Model of the World* response to conversationally respond to this. What would you say?

> How long has yelling caused you to shut down?
> How much does it seem to you that you shut down emotionally when I raise my voice?

These questions use a presupposition term ("how") and thereby set a frame by implication. Because we have used a temporal phrase ("how long") the phrase establishes a presupposition frame that there was a time when either I did not yell at you and a time when you did not shut down to that experience. To answer the "how long" question, we process the temporal element. This sends us inwardly in some time travel. As we do, the way we think about the experience exercises certain effects upon the qualities of our internal representations.

What effect does it create for you? Does it not loosen up your belief statement by triggering some shifts in the way you actually represent the information?

Watching the Cinema Change
We use *mind-lines* in conversation all the time. We have to. It's the way language works with our mind-body-emotion system. With the Mind-Lines model, we simply pay more attention to it so that we can utilize the magic of language. As a neuro-linguistic magician it serves us very well to use our acuity skills (both sensory acuity and mental acuity) to pay special attention to shifts and transformations that occur in how the qualities and features of our internal movies change in response to such questions.

For example, using the previous example, notice *where* in physical space the person puts his or her *past, present,* and *future.* How does this change when you use temporal shifts? If you speak with someone who has confused map and territory, pay attention to his or her eye accessing cues, language patterns, gestures, etc. Remember to watch for changes when you apply a *Model of the World Mind-Line* to the limiting belief and the person's frames begin to weaken. He or she will begin to recognize, "I always thought that X was real, but it was only *my* map!"

It's a high skill to be able to *see* these patterns and processes. It describes the advanced skills in Master Practitioner training, that of learning to read "sub-modalities" and Meta-Programs on the outside.[2]

When you find that a particular Mind-Line pattern weakens a person's beliefs by means of shifting the internal movie in its cinematic features and frames (meta-programs and meta-states), follow up your comment with another *mind-line* pattern. This will help to solidify the person's internal framing so that it becomes a more enhancing belief. In fact, count on getting more mileage with such conversational reframing patterns if you deliver several of them sequentially, one after the other.

When a *mind-line* loosens a person's belief by triggering various cinematic feature changes, we have at that moment a window of opportunity for extending the change. Dive right in. Layer on another one. By the way, the content of what we say in these interactions usually have less effect than *the structure and strategy* of applying this *Model of the World* context to the belief. These structural facets of information work directly on the structure of a limiting belief.

D) Stress causes me to eat chocolate.
> So, stress *seems* to cause you to eat chocolate? Does it really *seem* that way to you? Have you always believed that or did you come to think that way after some particular experience? How would you feel if you discovered that it wasn't true, but just an old way of thinking about it?

E) I can't really make a difference because management doesn't walk their talk.
> So, it *seems* that you can't make a difference because management doesn't walk their talk? Does it seem this way to everybody at your work as well? Do they all think this way? How did you come to think this way?

F) I can't buy your product because it costs too much.
> I know that you presently do not believe you can afford this product or at least it seems that way. If everybody thought this way, it would put me out of business entirely. Yet as you can see, I'm in business and doing very well. I'm genuinely glad that many see the importance of adding quality to their lives through purchasing this product.

Pattern Summary
To elicit the Model of the World frame as a conversational reframing pattern, use these elicitation questions:
- Does this belief hold true for everybody?
- Where did you learn to think this way?
- Who taught you to think or feel this way?

#14 *Criteria and Values Framing*

What is a *criteria*? What are *values*? Obviously, they are certain kinds of thoughts that we have about things. And because they also involve feeling states that affect our neurology, they are mind-body-emotion states. Yet because they are not representational thoughts that we can see, hear, or sense in our movies, they are not primary states. So *criteria* and *values* are meta-states—thinking-feeling states *about* other experiences.

At higher mental states, the experiences that we view as significant or valuable are our values and what we think about the conditions and rules that determine these make up our criteria. These terms refer to the frames that we use to encode our standards and rules which, in turn, govern our meanings regarding what's important. While these terms sound static and permanent, *values* and *criteria* are not *things*. These nominalizations only leave that impression which creates difficulty as we attempt to think clearly about our "values."

So what are "values" and how do we *value* something as important? We value and set criteria for what we *care* about as significant in enhancing our lives. We first represent some event, experiences, people, state, or idea and then we frame it as valuable to our well-being or value as a means of reaching some end-value.

As a mind-line, to reframe something as valuable, significant, meaningful, etc. allows us to organize and re-organize ourselves *in terms of* value and importance. It empowers us to *hold and frame* something as having lots of value or meaning. When we do this with activities, experiences, feelings, things, and ideas, we apply the category of value to them. This elevates these items in our estimate. We appraise them as of more significance.

As we deem something as important, we value it. In terms of meta-stating, we apply the *value* state to whatever movies and beliefs we have about that person, event, idea, or thing. This accomplishes several things. It invests more of our neuro-semantic energies into it. The object of our *valuing* becomes more meaningful to us. It reclassifies it as a highly valued item in our mental world and sends commands to our nervous system to *invest* more and more of ourselves into it. This investment shows up as the time, energy, thought, emotion, care, etc. that we put into the valued item.

All of this describes the power and magic of *meta-stating* a representation or a belief with a sense of importance. By doing this we *qualify* our belief with a sense of significance. It transforms the belief to a *valued* belief. This gives us more motives and motivation, more desires and passion. As a higher frame, our *value* frames establish what's meaningful in our world.

Consider, for example, the belief in speaking and relating assertively. When we embed that belief within a value frame, we then care about and desire to speak up assertively to make our voice heard. When we embed that inside of the value of kindness, it becomes *kind* assertiveness. We enrich it further by applying the value of *respect* to create *respectfully* kind assertiveness. At a meta-level the qualifying *adjective* (whether *kind* or *respectful*) add new qualities to the belief.

This gives us another perspective on how to think about outframing. In outframing we are meta-stating. *We are accessing and applying one state of mind-emotion to another state.* Doing this allows us to build up more complex states like respectful assertiveness, resilience, proactivity, etc. It enables us to *layer* thoughts-and-emotions *upon* thoughts-and-emotions.

We all do this anyway. This is simply the way our reflexive minds work. We feel afraid of something, then we feel guilty for feeling afraid. Or, we feel afraid and then feel angry about our fear. We feel upset, then angry at our upsetness, then guilty about our anger, then afraid of our guilt. Does any of that sound familiar? In this *mind-line pattern,* we meta-state in a much more positive and resourceful way as we apply princely states (full of rich values) to states that we want to enhance.

Here's something else about reflexivity. We can not only do this once or twice, we can do it multiple times. In fact, there's no limit to the amount of valuing that we can bring to another primary or meta-state. This is the secret in neuro-semantics for engaging in high level anger control. We not only bring calmness and thoughtfulness to anger, we bring respect, compassion, empathy, care, spirituality, honor, being noble, etc. In the end, we so texture the state of "anger" that it becomes something valuable and useful, and never something to fear.[3]

Not only that, but we can also appeal to our hierarchy of values. Doing so brings a discernment to our beliefs, a discernment which allows us to gauge what to value as *most important* or important to a certain degree. Then we can make sure that our beliefs accord with what we truly deem valuable. When doing this conversationally, we inquire about what a person considers important. When we discover that, we can then simply invite the person to apply that value to their primary level thinking and feeling. This performs neuro-semantic magic. It tempers the belief making it fitting and ecological.

A) Saying mean things makes you a bad person.
> Help me to understand this, which matters most to you, how someone speaks or what they actually do? Do you think it more important to have honest feedback from others or would you prefer to receive patronizing responses that preserves peace at all costs?

B) Cancer causes death.

> Which is more important to you, having a sense of peace by giving in to fate and giving up or standing up for yourself, your health, and fighting for options? Would you prefer to spend your energy hunting for options or to use this to feel sorry for yourself?

This pattern of framing with values empowers us to be more direct with the personal and professional values of those with whom we deal, and to gently hold them accountable to those values.

> [Did you notice that sentence? Check out the mind-line within it. Do you now see it? There is the recommendation that we deal directly with people and hold them accountable. Then there is the embedded value of doing so from the higher frame of *gentleness*. That gives us the richer response of gently holding someone accountable.]

As with beliefs, we code our values at the level of the movies that we play in our mind as we *represent* the object of our valuing and how we *edit those movies* with various cinematic frames ("sub-modalities"). So when we think about something that we give *importance* to, we create internal mental movies and edit them with certain qualities and features to convey the idea of "value." Accordingly, as we outframe by applying values to beliefs, we can expect that our movies and their editorial features to change. The features at the higher frames will sometimes radically influence the "sub-modalities" at a lower level. Typically the "sub-modalities" will become richer, more life-like, closer, brighter, etc. Sometimes valuing at one level will transform how we encode the belief about the representation.

There's something else to notice when you use this particular *mind-line* pattern. Notice how *Value and Criteria Framing* comes with a built-in ecology. This works because higher levels of the *valuing* inevitably modulate lower levels and so apply the ecology of our values to our thinking. So when we move up to what a person deems most important (the person's *values*) and invite the person to apply that *value* to another idea, experience, or event, the higher level *value* will drive, modulate, organize, and govern the belief. Neat, don't you think?

To develop your skill and train your intuitions to do this, you only need to do two things:
1) Access a higher level value or criterion.

> What do you highly value? What really significant to you?
> What touches your heart with a sense of the sacred?
> What do you know without a doubt is ultimately significant?

2) Apply the higher value or criterion to the limiting belief.

> Does this belief allow you to act with love, kindness, assertiveness,

respect, etc.?

How much do you feel respectful or playful when doing X?

Now we're ready to check out how this works in our playground of some limiting beliefs and ideas.

C) Your being late means you don't care about me.

Actually, arriving late, while an important issue, isn't nearly as important as respecting you and our relationship and planning to spend quality time with you when we do get together, don't you think? I am guessing that you are saying this because of how important you feel it is to know whether or not I truly care for you, is that right? So would you say caring holds a higher value than does timeliness?

D) Stress causes me to eat chocolate.

Avoiding stress seems pretty important to you? I wonder what would happen if you applied your other values like taking good care of your physical health and staying fit and slim to handling stress and used that rather than eating chocolate? Would you prefer to do that? Would that be valuable to you?

E) I can't really make a difference because management doesn't walk their talk.

It must be pretty important to you that management walks their talk and acts in congruent ways. You must like people living with integrity and congruity. Do you also value management enabling employees to become productive through innovative thinking? [Yes.] Good, which do you feel you should concentrate most on to be true to yourself?

F) I can't buy your product because it costs too much.

I can see that your value of appropriate cost means a lot. So I have a question, Will this concern help make you money? If you knew you could make a return on your investment with this particular product, a return of five dollars for every dollar that you invested, would you buy this in an instant? So shouldn't we focus on increased value rather than risk of spending?

Pattern Summary

To elicit this conversational reframing pattern, use elicitation questions about values and application of values:

- What are some of the higher criteria or values of this person?
- What would happen if I invited this person to apply his or her higher values and principles to X?
- What value would prove useful to apply on this limiting belief?
- What values would qualify X in such a way as to reframe it in a more positive way so that it is no longer limiting?

#15 *Allness or Universality Framing*

Do you feel ready for another meta-move and mind-line? Good, then let's go *all out* and apply this next one to *everybody* and do so *all* the time *everywhere* we go. In *Allness framing* we make a meta-move that allows us to shift the size of the frame which governs the magic inside the belief formula. Doing so allows us to totally exaggerate things. We do this by simply sticking in some well-placed universal quantifiers.

Universal quantifiers? Oh, excuse us, we slipped into talking the linguistic distinctions of the Meta-Model again. Just use *allness* words: "all, always, everybody, nobody, all the time, never, none," etc. Just apply the idea of *universality* to the belief.

Transactional Analysis or T.A. labeled these as "parent words." That's because these are the kind of words that parents typically use and over-use. Technically, a universal quantifier refers to the set of words that make *a universal generalization* and leave off qualifiers (or indexes) of time, place, condition, etc. These terms imply and/or state an absolute condition.

This move shifts our consciousness as we step into a frame-of-reference that applies the formula to everybody on the planet. Will the belief cohere when we do that? This shift involves a large conceptual one and aims to get the person to temporarily step outside his or her frame altogether to check it out. This involves, as do many of these patterns, *a referential index switch*. What seems so real and reasonable when *I* apply it in my life or to you, suddenly seems ridiculous when we apply it to *everybody* else on the planet. This mind-line pattern asks,

• 	How would you like it if we applied this to *all* others at *all* other times and places?

• 	How would this belief sound if we made it universal?

In this outframing move, we apply *allness* to the belief. Why would we do such a thing? Because we typically express beliefs in absolute terms. They sound universal. So we test it. *If* the belief is absolute and does represent a good, ecological, and balanced generalization, it should apply universally, it should have application across the board at all times and places. *If* not, then we need to qualify, contextualize, and index it to keep it contained.

As we move to a meta-level to frame the belief with *allness*, we can now begin to exaggerate it and push it to its limits. We take it to its threshold to see if it will still work, if it will still cohere as a reasonable belief. Or do we need to limit it? Will we discover that it falls apart? If it doesn't cohere, then the shift will *deframe* the belief to some degree or all the way. It will fall apart as an inadequate generalization that doesn't hold universally.

Because *allness* words do not make room for any exception, they express a limited mindset. Similarly, in Rational-Emotive Behavioral Therapy (REBT), *all-or-nothing thinking* is one of the key cognitive distortions that enable us to make ourselves miserable.

A) Saying mean things makes you a bad person.
> Since everyone has at sometime said something mean, the only kind of people that we have on the planet are bad people!   How enhancing does that make this idea that mean words create bad people for the human race? Would this encourage honesty, authenticity, genuineness, and the like?"

B) Cancer causes death.
> If all of the doctors and researchers working on cancer believed that, would we ever have any hope of finding a cure for cancer? Would you recommend that everybody who gets any form of cancer immediately think that it will cause them to die?   Would you recommend that everybody who gets any form of cancer immediately think that it will cause them to die?

When you put the universality frame over and around a belief, pay attention to the effect that it has on the cinematic features and the sensory-based representations within the magical formula that structures the belief. As it embeds the belief, what happens to the movie qualities of belief? Do the visual, auditory, and kinesthetic modalities and their qualities change? Precisely because ever higher frame adds and encodes information into the primary state pictures, sounds, and sensations, the higher qualities and properties will temper our representational movies.

C) Your being late means you don't care about me.
> So I show up late once, and that means I don't care at all about you? Since everybody arrives late at some time or another in their life, then the only kind of people on the planet are those who don't care about anybody? Yes, that makes total sense and is the only way anyone could think about time schedules!

This conversational line changes the frame.   The line invites us to shift from focusing on a specific behavior that occurred (showing up late) to a larger generalization (you do not truly care or love me).   In this we are essentially asking, "Once means always and/or forever!?"

It is interesting that even though the loved one showed up (even though late), the speaker continues to focus on the hurtful meaning. That's all that seems to be in the person's awareness. The hurt one is living in a state of discounting, complaining, griping, fussing, badmouthing, feeling bad, feeling unloved, etc. How productive is that? Yet, when considered from the frame that the person care enough to show up, will the person focus on the person showing up or not showing up precisely on time? Will the person use the interpretation that the other doesn't care to totally overwhelm the experience of being with someone who did show up?

In all *context* reframing, we leave the content the same and only alter the frame around it. We do that because when a frame changes, so do the meanings embedded within it
- Do *all* people who show up late not care?
- Would you consider *everybody* who shows up late as suffering from a lack of care regardless of circumstances?

It is by going meta to higher level awarenesses, values, understandings, etc. that enables us to establish a more expansive frame. To think in terms of meta-levels we only need to ask ourselves questions like:
- What has this person not yet noticed?
- What results if we apply a universal quantifier to the statement?

When we move up and apply it to the entire human race, the exaggeration frequently elicits humor. The humor that arises in such cases indicates that the belief no longer fits and that it seems ridiculous when viewed *from that perspective.*

D) Stress causes me to eat chocolate.
>If *everyone* believed that, do you think the government would make chocolate a controlled substance?
>Yes, of course. It *always* makes *everybody* all over the planet eat chocolate—this explains why, in the more stressful places on the planet, the chocolate companies grow and expand. This explains why the chocolate companies want wars, famines, earthquakes, traffic jams, etc. —it increases sales, does it not?

E) I can't really make a difference because management doesn't walk their talk.
>Yes, making a difference describes what life is all about, nothing else at all counts. So if you can't, you might as well end it all!
>This explains why we still have to deal with the Roman Empire. As a terrible management system, a pure bureaucracy which really didn't walk its talk, it continues to maintain its power and authority over the entire civilized world and so, no wonder, we're all doomed!

F) I can't buy your product because it costs too much.

My God, if everyone held on to that belief, the entire economy around this product would entirely collapse.

Well, of course, you can't. Nor could anybody else anywhere on the planet. Nobody ever buys anything that costs too much according to your standards. Life just doesn't work that way.

Pattern Summary

To elicit this pattern for conversational reframing, use the elicitation questions:

- What has this person not noticed?
- How can I use an universal quantifier to exaggerate this belief by pushing it beyond its limits?
- Suppose we apply it universally as a frame to all humans, would the idea still make sense? Would it still cohere as a legitimate belief?
- Everybody? Always? Never?

#16 Necessity Framing

In the development of the beliefs that formulate the maps we use to navigate the territory, we often use linguistic structures which prescribe *a mode of operation* (i.e., our *modus operandi).* In the Meta-Model, we classify such words under the category called modal operators. These refer to our *modus operandi* or style of moving through the world and dealing with life. In so conceptualizing the world, we imply various ideas about the nature of the world that we live in. There are several kinds of modal operators.

1) *The modal operators of necessity* are terms that imply necessity: "have to, must, should, ought, got to," etc. When we talk this way, we map out a world of force, pressure, law, obligation, etc. We then develop an M.O. involving the feeling of necessity.
*   I *have to* go to work.
*   I *must* clean the house.
*   I *ought to* write her a note.

2) *The modal operators of possibility or desire* are terms of desire. When we uses these words and language ourselves with these terms, we construct and/or express a reality that's characterized by opportunities, possibilities, desires, passions, etc. This gives us an entirely different M.O. for moving through the world.
*   I *get to* do this task.
*   I *want to* clean the house.
*   I *desire to* write the letter.

3) *The model operators of impossibility* are terms that indicate the lack of possibility, limitations, and constraints: *can't, won't,* and *it's impossible.* These words set a frame of lack whether of possibility or of options. They present inability, helplessness, prohibition, etc.
*   I *can't* do this job.
*   I *can't* stand criticism.
*   You *can't* say those kinds of things to people, they'll think you're nuts!

In the Meta-Model we have numerous questions that enable us to challenge modal operators. These questions invite us to step outside our model of the world as expressed by the modal operator to take a new look at the territory beyond and to explore it using a different *modal operator.*
*   What would happen if you did?
*   What would it feel like (look like, sound like) if you did?
*   What stops you?

A) Saying mean things makes you a bad person.

What would happen if a person could say a "mean" thing without becoming a bad person? Does a person *have to* turn into a "bad" person because they utter some words that someone considers "mean?" It that the rule?

B) Cancer causes death.

What kind of indicators would you expect to see or hear if cancer did not always and only cause death? How would you know if you saw evidence that questioned this?

C) Coming in late means that you don't care about me!

Does being late to a schedule always and only carry this meaning of being uncaring? Does it have to? What if it didn't? What would you see or hear or feel if you realized that I could care very much and very deeply for you and sometimes arrive late?

D) Stress causes me to eat chocolate.

Does stress have to make you eat chocolate? Could stress lead you to other behaviors? What stops you from experiencing stress as leading you to exercising or deep breathing rather than eating?

E) I can't really make a difference because management doesn't walk their talk.

What stops you from going ahead and making a big difference at work in spite of the incongruency of management? What would it feel like for you to not feel compelled to let the incongruency of management control how you respond?

F) I can't buy your product because it costs too much.

What stops you from going ahead and investing the money to buy this product even if you think the cost may run a little high compared to what you would prefer to spend so that you could begin to enjoy its benefits now?

Pattern Summary

To elicit the pattern for these mind-lines, use the Meta-Model questions to the *modal operators* that you hear people use.

*   What stops you from doing this?
*   Do you *have to* do this? Who says?
*   What would happen if you did this? What's the worst case scenario? Do you have any resources for handling that?
*   Is that a true and legitimate fear or is that just a vague apprehension that you use to avoid taking action?

#17 Identity Framing

When it comes to beliefs, and to the neuro-linguistic realities that our beliefs create and which we live in—we easily, naturally, and unthinkingly use our reality structures to define ourselves. It seems the most natural thing to use them for identification. You can hear it in our language, "I *am...*" "He *is...*" "They *are...*" "That's the way it *is.*"

Korzybski (1933/1994) warned against this saying that *identification* on all levels is a form of primitive Aristotelian thinking which does not serve us well. Starting from the General Semantic principle that distinguishes map and territory ("The map is not the territory"), he noted that there really is no such thing as *sameness*, that it does not exist. Nothing is the same as something else. "Sameness" between any two things, or even "sameness" of a singular thing with itself differs over time. Things may be similar, but are never exactly the "same."

The key reason why there is no sameness is that we live in a world of processes. And in the process world, everything changes and is continually changing. Nothing remains the same. Not even the mountains and rocks stay the same. When we look at the world at the microscopic level and at the sub-microscopic level, we discover that reality exists as "a dance of electrons."

This explains why whenever we describe anything as static or the same on the primary level, we engage in false-to-fact mapping. "Sameness" at best only exists at a meta-level of the mind as a high level abstraction. Yet even then, when we access what we consider to be the "same" thought, it is not the "same" thought. It may be a very similar thought, but not the same thought because our brain has changed. The process of our thinking does not occur at the same time, in precisely the same way, within the same neurology, etc.

When we talk about "beliefs" we have already moved one level up from mere "thought." A belief also involves a level of *identification* to the extent that we have *equated* or made "the same" some behavior (E.B.) with some state (I.S.). Already we have treated some external behavior as "always the same," or some internal state as "always the same." Frequently, we don't leave it there. We then engage in another level of *identification* as we *identify ourselves* with some belief, emotion, behavior, context, etc.

By making a meta-move up to the concept and idea of *identification,* we test the belief's reality and validity in terms of whether it really serves us well to create such an identification.

A) Saying mean things makes you a bad person.

Ah, so whatever kind of language comes out of my mouth, that makes me, or transforms me, into a certain kind of person? So if I now say a nice thing, I suddenly become a nice person? If I say something about physics, that makes me a physicist?

B) Cancer causes death.
I really didn't know that death and cancer were one and the same thing. Let's tell the Cancer Research People so that they can close shop and use their money for something more productive.

C) Coming in late means that you don't care about me!
So how I handle time and schedules turns me into a caring or an uncaring person? So truly caring people have got time-management down to an art? Truly caring people always use Day Timers.

D) Stress causes me to eat chocolate.
Wow. Stress makes me into an eating-chocolate kind of person? Silly me, I always thought it was my genetics!

E) I can't really make a difference because management doesn't walk their talk.
So your identity as someone who gets things done, makes a difference, and contributes significantly in the world depends on the inner congruity of management? Their integrity, or lack of it, forces you to become this kind of person?

F) I can't buy your product because it costs too much.
A cheapskate, huh? Does that belief endow you with a cheapskate identity? Or has it led others to think of you in that way? And do you really want your purchasing habits to so label you?

If *identity* occurs, not in the world, but only in human minds, and if *identification* without conscious mindfulness represents a form of *unsanity*, then it becomes useful to learn to *dis-identify* ourselves from limiting self-definitions, does it not?

What can we do about identification? We can notice all of the "to be" verbs that we use in our everyday language and learn how to *E-Prime* our language of those *is* verbs. E-prime refers to eliminating the "to be" verbs (i.e., is, am, are, be, being, been, etc.) from our talk and writing. For years in both private consultations and trainings, we have asked people to *describe* themselves *without* using the "to be" verbs.

"Tell me about yourself, what you like, value, feel, think, experience, etc., but don't use any of the 'is' verbs—'is, am, are,' etc."

It's an interesting experiment that most people find extremely difficult at first. Yet in doing so, it raises our consciousness about how much we *identify* and use the *is* the verbs.   This technique has been around for years in General Semanticists and journalism classes have used it by asking students to write a biography without using the "to be" verbs. And while most people find this extremely challenging, the process typically empowers people to begin to overcome the limitations of *identification*.[4]

The problem with *identification* is not that it's bad or unhealthy. The problem is that by *identifying with* something and using it as part of our self-definition *without awareness* of doing this invests whatever we identify with (whether a person, event, experience, idea, concept, memory, emotion, etc.) with incredible neuro-semantic meaning and power. We load it up semantically so that it has incredible power over our neurology. This explains why the "logical level" of identity (or identifying) so powerfully affects our thinking, emoting, behaving, speaking, and relating. Whatever we *identify with* sets a self-organizing frame that then forms us into its likeness and image. So be careful what you identify with. By careful how you identify yourself. When you do identify with something, recognize what you are doing and how, and do so with a degree of tentativeness.

Pattern Summary
To elicit the pattern for this mind-line, inquire about what a person has identified with and how.
- Who *are* you? How do you identify yourself?
- What have you identified with?
- How have you identified with this?
- To what extent is this identification?
- How much awareness do you have that you have done this?
- How much control do you have over the identification?
- Does it serve you well?
- Does it empower you as a person?
- Does it give you sufficient flexibility so that you are *more than* the identification?

#18 *Framing All Other Abstractions*

In the process of *going meta,* we conceptually move up to higher level principles, understandings, and meanings to the belief system which contains the magic meaning formula (E.B.—>/=I.S.). In this way all of the *outframing meta-moves* (the Mind-Lines #8-12 and #13-17) work as meta-stating processes. We move up one or more "logical levels" from the belief system and toss a magical black silk over the construct. With each move, we rise up in our mind to set a new frame-of-reference that then governs the belief. As such, this meta-stating function qualifies and tempers the belief in numerous ways.

Doing this has numerous effects. For example, outframing allows us to test the strength and ecology of the belief. We can make it stronger and more robust or we can reduce it to a more appropriate strength. We can set a higher, larger, or more expansive frame to transform it and give it an entirely new texture. We can completely alter a belief, transforming a toxic dragon belief into a glorious princely belief.

Yet even this does *not* exhaust the possibilities. Regarding how many ways we can outframe a belief, there are many more ways. We have many other concepts, ideas, beliefs, understandings, etc. that we can apply to the belief. We have actually only scratched the surface of the possibilities. In Meta-States we recognize this seeming infinity of choices because for whatever thought-emotion we experience, we can always generate a thought-emotion *about* it.

We can bring many other *ideas, principles and abstractions* to outframe a person and a belief. How do we generate more choices? We can ask ourselves:
•   What principle would possibly empower this person?
•   What idea will make this belief more empowering?

With so many choices before us, the following are but a few of the ones that we have found useful and which we included in the first edition. In Chapter 11 we will add additional ones to round out the mind-lines to 26 in number.

The Unreality Frame
Suppose we mapped out "un-reality" and represented the idea of something being "unreal" and then applied it to a belief? What would happen? Would it make the real but limiting belief seem less real? If we use some "unreality" predicates (words we use to make assertions) in our talk, then we "bring *unreality* to bear upon the person's belief statement." Here we will use words that question the person's "reality" or truth. *Unreality* predicates include: "seems, appears, thinks, looks like," etc. These all imply some question, some doubt.

So, it *seems* to you that when I am late, even a little bit late, that that somehow means that I don't care about you? It *seems* that way even when you can identify a hundred other things I do that confirms my love for you?

The Self and Other Frame

Imagine that we spoke in such a way that we put emphasis on *you* in contradistinction to *me*. If we did this, then we could (by implication) suggest that *your* model of the world may differ from *my* model of the world, and that the ideas, opinions, feelings, experiences, etc. which may hold true for one person, may not hold true for another. This idea would undermine a rigid sense of sameness and allness about models of the world.

So for *you*, the idea of being late means that I don't care?

The Tonal Emphasis Frame

What we communicate does not only occur in *what* we say (the content), but *how* we say it. This is where voice inflection, tone, volume, and dozens of other facets of our expressions and gestures influence what we say. From the NLP modeling of the structure of hypnosis, Bandler and Grinder discovered that Erickson often marked out certain words and ideas using tonal variations, shifts and different inflections. This allowed him to embed questions, statements, and commands *inside* the content of his talk. Typically, doing this will direct a listener to create alternative internal representations and to "hear" other messages outside of conscious awareness.

So if we use this on the *Unreality Frame* just mentioned, we could use our voice to add power to the emphasis:

So, you *think* [implication, you do not know] that my being late means I don't care.
You think that my being late means I don't care.

We could even embed a different message inside of saying words.

So you think that in being late *I* don't *really care for you* and yet I wonder if you can *know with confidence that I do care for you.*

Applying an embedded message or messages to a person's belief statement can create higher level messages or frames *outside* that person's conscious awareness that set up a higher frame.

The Time Zones Frame

In *Pre- and Post- Framing* we played with some of the ways that we can do "time" reframing. As an abstract idea or principle, we can apply the "time" distinction in yet another way. We can distinguish a current situation that is now occurring and a situation as it did occur or will occur at some other time.

How long have you thought this way about the feelings of love and caring and the way we measure time? So, if I understand you, *at this moment in time* you *have been* thinking that lateness and caring are intricately related to each other? Have you always thought about it that way?

The framing that we put in this classification of *All Other Abstractions,* as a mind-line, serves as a kind of catch-all category for any and all other concepts, principles, and beliefs that we might use to outframe a limiting belief.

A) Saying mean things makes you a bad person.
> So the way I talk to you totally and completely determines my moral character? Does the character of one statement always have this kind of effect on one's identity and being? [Abstracting using Identity, #17, and Morality.]

B) Cancer causes death.
> So one single mutation of a small part of a system will automatically cause destruction to ensue to the entire system? Does this describe how parts of systems inevitably work? [A concept about how systems operate.]

As we noted in the *specificity* pattern, a person who thinks in specific details, and does so most of the time, will rarely think globally. With that person we will need to reframe their statements by chunking up to more general statements. Doing this will present them with new choices that make sense to them.

C) Your being late means you don't care about me.
> Certainly I can agree that my general and typical behavior towards you says something about how I feel toward you. But how have you decided that one, or several, actions around time management have this level of global meaning that I don't care about you?

This reply reframes both sides of the equation, the E.B. and I.S. In using the word "behavior" we chunk up the action coded in the verb phrase, "being late." Similarly, how I "feel toward you" chunks up to a higher level of abstraction from the term "caring." We would also chunk up if we said,
> So, if for whatever reason, I showed up very late (extending the idea of lateness), that would mean that I care even less? So if I arrive a few minutes early, does that show I love you even more? Does this relationship of time and care always hold?

D) Stress causes me to eat chocolate.
> It sounds like unpleasant and negative emotions [an abstraction from

'stress'] cause you to do things you don't want to do [an abstracted meaning from 'eating chocolate']. So experiencing negative emotions really makes you a victim to your emotions? [An even higher abstract concept on the entire statement.] How do you feel about chocolate when you think of it in these terms?

E) I can't really make a difference because management doesn't walk their talk.
So what management does, management's congruency or incongruency, plays the determinative role in how you think, feel, and act as you move through the world? I did not realize that management had that much power over your responses. Sorry to hear that you have given your power away.

F) I can't buy your product because it costs too much.
Well, we do often get what we pay for. And, if you really don't want the best product available, I can understand how you would let the price tag totally control your decisions.

The Realization Frame
This mind-line frame comes from Denis Bridoux who originally wrote it into the chapter, *Unfolding the Mind-Lines.* We have put it here as another great outframing frame. Denis happened upon this from noticing the experience that therapy or coaching clients will often simply fail to notice the changes that they have made. That is, a person can change, and even change in significant ways, without noticing. They fail to *realize* something critically important. Suppose that a therapist or coach asks, "How have things been since the last session?" and the first response is, "Well, I have had a hard time."

Oh really? So, tell me how have things gone since last time about X?
Well, after X happened, there was Y and Z ... and now when I think about it all, it hasn't been so bad. Actually, considering how it was before, it went rather well. In fact, when I think about it now, things have actually been remarkably easy."
So it not only was it *not* a bad week, but you actually achieved A and B, and you're working on C, and then D occurred.
When you put it all together like that in a summary statement and compare it with where I started , I realize that I have not noticed all the changes. How could I not see all of that?

This all too common exchange highlights that we can get so busy with things that we can fail to notice, or fail to take time to ratify, the changes that we make. Without a little reflection to count even the small steps in the right direction, we can fail to realize the difference our efforts make.

In other words, we can change without taking notice of the change. This failure of noticing and realizing can then leave us with the feeling that we have not changed, that nothing much is happening, or worse, that we're not progressing. Then, remaining unconscious of the changes that we have made, we unknowingly *discount* what has changed and fail to celebrate our achievements. Sadly, this can undermine our motivation so that we slide back into feeling and acting unresourceful.

All of this highlights the importance of *realizing* our achievements and changes, acknowledging, ratifying and validating them and using them to both avoid sliding backwards and as stepping stones to move forward. In a similar way, after we lead a client up the levels of intentions and intention of intention in identifying the client's highest positive intention governing a behavior, we can ask the ecology question to get a confirmation about the validity of a change.
- Is this intention your highest intention?
- Is this what you are truly after and actually want to achieve?
- Are you willing to apply this highest intention to your everyday activity and attention?

Typically this deepens a person's realization and awareness of the contrast between presenting behavior and the highest preferred intentions. Actually, the first level behavior is frequently *a negative mirror image* that contrasts to the positive intention. For example,
> "I snap at people for bothering me when I get interrupted and yet I'm doing this work to be a more loving person and to contribute."

Upon eliciting this new realization, we can then use a direct *realization question*, a question that presupposes and implies a translation from idea into a feeling in the body:
> And how does it feel to realize this?

Within this question is a presupposition, namely, *you now realize this, don't you?* The question however focuses on the person's body and emotions, "How does it *feel* to realize this?" In this way, the question is truly a powerful mind-to-muscle question. Denis says that "the question enables the resource to become operational." How does that work? It invites the person to translate the *realization* into a *feeling*. In this way, "it opens up a gateway for new resources to emerge."

By simultaneously sending the person's mind *down* to the level of what they see-hear-and feel in the primary state and *up* to *the realization level,* the question operates as a three-second Mind-to-Muscle elicitation. And, now that you know this, how does it feel to realize this? We can use variations of this to lead people in slightly different directions.
- *What do you think* when you become aware of this?

- What will you do now that you know?
- How will your life be different now that you have noticed this?
- Who will you be now that you have realized this?
- I wonder how you will interact with others now that you have become aware of this resource and what it can do for you.

We can directly and indirectly ask the question recurrently with each answer to lead the mind simultaneously up levels of intentionality and down into resourceful emotionality.

I have now asked this type of question of perhaps hundreds of people, with clients and with participants at trainings, and having incorporated it into all of the NLP and Neuro-Semantic patterns I know. In doing so I have found that it turbo-charges remedial or generative change processes. Try it for yourself. And as you apply it to yourself and others, how does it feel to realize that such a resource is yours to make use of wherever and whenever you see fit?

Pattern Summary
To elicit this pattern, question what and how you can move up from the specific E.B. or I.S. in a belief statement to other abstractions and concepts. Think of a classification at a higher level to the terms that you could use to add some particular texturing or coloring to the belief.

- What higher abstractions summarize the facets in the belief?
- When you think about your belief in terms of these larger abstractions, does it still make sense?
- What principle or idea could I use to outframe this belief?

#19 Ecology Framing

In outframing we move up from the belief statement where the original and conceptual magic begins. With this meta-move to *ecology,* we can wrap other *ecology testing* ideas around the first belief frame. Doing this enables us to generate even higher constructs of magic. We can do this not only for the belief formula (E.B.—>/=I.S.), but also for all of the other ideas (*Mind-Lines #5—#18*) that we use to encompass the belief. This means that with the *Ecology Check Frame*, we will not only make a meta-move, but that we can make two or more meta-moves. Let's go up and up and away to the overall meta-frame level where we can then evaluate all of these evaluations.

We call "running an ecology check" taking a meta-position in NLP and when we do that we evaluate our evaluations. That's how Korzybski described this process. As a "second level abstraction" he spoke about the reflexivity that allows us to evaluate our evaluations. Whatever we call this process, it's all about checking out the productivity, value, usefulness, congruence, etc. of a belief, behavior, or emotion. To do that, simply move up, in your mind, to a meta-position and ask,

- When we construct this reality in this way and wrap our minds around it in this or that way, does it serve us well?
- Does it limit us or enhance us?
- Does it keep our whole system in balance and well-ordered, or does it throw things out of balance and endanger our overall well-being?
- Does it make life a party?

A) Saying mean things makes you a bad person.
        As a belief, does the idea that saying mean things makes you a bad person make communicating and relating with others richer or does it seduce you into thinking of people in good and bad terms depending on how you evaluate their communications in terms of meanness or niceness? Does this enhance your relationships?

B) Cancer causes death.
        How well does this way of thinking serve you? Does it empower you to look for things that will help? Does it enable you to feel more positive and hopeful about life—two attitudes that always influence health and well-being?

C) Coming in late means that you don't care about me!
        While that's an interesting idea I wonder if this idea is all that useful. How often do you argue with people, especially loved ones, about time schedules and being late? How often do you spend your time with them arguing, rather than enjoying their presence?

D) Stress causes me to eat chocolate.

Since this is the way that you have come to handle stress in your life, how well does it really work for you? Does it work for you in the long-run? Does it contribute to your health, energy, weight, etc.?

E) I can't really make a difference because management doesn't walk their talk.

How well does that way of thinking about management empower you as a person? If it shuts down your creativity, perseverance, and interferes with your good judgment, how ecological are these negative effects on your mind and body?

F) I can't buy your product because it costs too much.

Thinking about purchasing solely in terms of cost probably gives you eyes that sort exclusively for price tags. Does this enable you to purchase or enjoy the things that you want to in life without money grubbing about everything?

Summary

- In *Outframing* we move to a conceptual position in our mind, to a positive above our beliefs and belief frames, and over the magic box that contains our meaning formula. It means setting up new frames to provide new structures for more enhanced meanings.

- *Outframing* is valuable for establishing higher level ideas, emotions, beliefs, values, states, attitudes, etc. It brings new resources to bear on the magical formula and creates transformations in beliefs.

- Outframing actually involves a meta-stating process as we access mind-body conceptual states and apply these to a limiting belief or matrix.

- With *one fell swoop* of our magic meaning wand, we can set up our frame as an umbrella over-arching everything underneath it. We can embed old beliefs inside of conversational mind-lines that transform reality.

- With this mind-line move we can now leave a belief alone, stop fooling with it directly, and temper it from a meta-level where few will ever suspect.

- *If* we take these reframing forms and think about them as *a dance,* rather than a war, we may just feel a lot freer in using these movements and rhythms of thought and speech with elegance and grace. Doing this will endow our conversational reframing with a more gentleness. Of course, this was an outframe with a metaphor, in case you didn't notice.

- You now know many of the dance moves that we can make with people to help maneuver them into a more solution-focus orientation. And now for the last dance....

End Notes:

1. To explore more about Meta-States and "logical levels" and how the higher levels govern the lower levels see *Meta-States* (2000), *Dragon Slaying* (2000), *NLP: Going Meta* (2004), *Meta-States Journal* (1997, 1998) which are now incorporated in *Meta-State Magic (2003), Sub-Modalities Going Meta* (2005), *Secrets of Personal Mastery* (2000), and *Frame Games* (2000).

2. For reading "sub-modalities" on the outside see *The Spirit of NLP,* chapter 7, and *Sub-Modalities Going Meta* (2005, chapter 15). For reading meta-programs on the outside, see *Figuring Out People,* chapter 11.

3. For more about the Neuro-Semantic approach to anger management, see our training manuals on Defusing Hotheads and other Cranky People.

4. For more about the *Dis-Identification* pattern, see *The Sourcebook of Magic,* Volume I (1998).

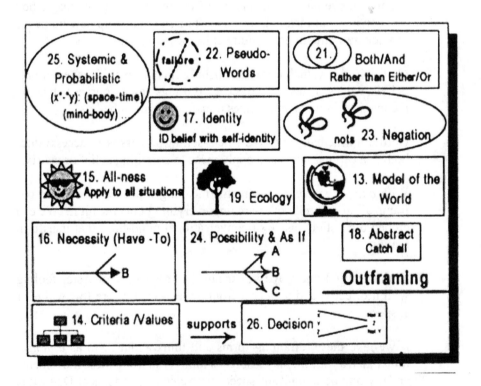

Chapter 10

ANALOGOUS FRAMING

REFRAMING USING
STORIES AND METAPHORS

A man wanted to know about mind,
not in nature, but in his computer.
He asked it (no doubt in his best Fortran),
'Do you compute that you will ever think like a human being?"
The machine then set to work
to analyze its own computational habits.
Finally, the machine printed its answer on a piece of paper,
as such machines do.
The man ran to get the answer and found,
neatly typed, the words:
"That reminds me of a Story..."
Gregory Bateson

Human reasoning and thinking not only goes up and down the scale of specificity and abstraction, it also makes lateral moves. When we chunk up and chunk down we move from smaller to larger "chunks" of information. We *induce* upward from specific details to draw general conclusions. This gives us *inductive thinking and reasoning.* We also *deduce* downward from general principles, ideas, abstractions, proverbs, etc. to specific applications and details. This gives us *deductive thinking and reasoning.*

In a general way these processes reflect *the scientific attitude* (induction) that technicians, clinicians, and statisticians use to work efficiently in their fields. They also reflect *the philosophical attitude* (deduction) that gives philosophers, theologians, managers, planners, etc. their edge.

Is there any other way to think? Yes, another form of thinking and reasoning beckons us, *abduction* (Bateson, 1972, 1979). Abduction refers to thinking *on the side or laterally,* so to speak. In abduction, we think of one thing by indirectly using another thing as a symbol. Here story, metaphor, analogy, proverb, poem, koans, riddles, jokes, etc. give us formats for thinking, reasoning, and talking in this way. Let me give you a taste of Bateson (1979) on this.

> "This lateral extension of abstract components of description is called *abduction*, and I hope the reader may see it with a fresh eye. The very possibility of abduction is a little uncanny, and the phenomenon is enormously more widespread than he or she might, at first thought, have supposed.
>
> Metaphor, dream, parable, allegory, the whole of art, the whole of science, the whole of religion, the whole of poetry, totemism, the organization of facts in comparative anatomy—all these are instances or aggregates of instances of abduction, within the human mental sphere." (p. 153)
>
> Every abduction may be seen as a double or multiple description of some object or event or sequence. If I examine the social organization of an Australian tribe and the sketch of natural relations upon which the totemism is based, I can see these two bodies of knowledge as related abductively, as both falling under the same rules." (p. 154)

Dilts has noted the same thing. First in *Modeling With NLP* (1998) and then in *Sleight of Mouth* (1999):

> "Abductive Transformations" that map between one deep structure and another, or between one surface structure and another." (p. 25)
>
> "Abductive reasoning involves looking for the similarities between objects and phenomena—i.e., 'chunking laterally'." (p. 69)

While we may think deductively intuitively and without being conscious of what we're doing, more typically we first take a meta-position, see the similarities of the referent object and some other event, story, or referent. So to think abductively, we more often than not first think inductively as we "chunk up."

Mind-Lines in Chapter 10
#20 Metaphoring Framing
Storying & Re-storying

#20 Metaphoring Framing
Or, Storying and Re-storying Framing

In this conversational reframing, we make a conversational move that may at first seem "beside the point," or a complete distraction. We simply *tell a story* using a different referent content and/or context. When we do this we tell a story that is structurally *isomorphic* (*iso*, same, *morph*, form), that is, it shares a similar form to the problem or context. We can then use it as a vehicle for implicitly communicating a meaning that we wish to offer. In this way, we can use the format of a story or metaphor to communicate any of the previous reframing or mind-line patterns.

In so creating and designing a story, we again directionalize the brain of the listener to an entirely different subject. And yet, at a higher and more unconscious level, we speak to the formula of the old belief.

A) Saying mean things makes you a bad person.
> When the fire broke out in the apartment building, Sam worked fast and furiously to get everybody out in time. But one kid thought he would be selfish if he rushed out, so he waited. He wanted to be the last one out. When Sam saw him holding back, he yelled at him. He yelled at him in a harsh tone of voice, "Kid, don't be stupid, give me your hand, come on, get out of there!"

What's a Meta-Phor?
The word *metaphor* comes from ancient Greek. *Meta* means "over" "above," "about" and *pherein* literally means "to carry." When we use a metaphor, we "carry or bear over" (transfer) a message to another person's mind *in terms of something else* (i.e, a story, other referent, myth, etc.). The listener then takes the framework or structure of the metaphor and interprets it in the framework of his or her own experience. In this way, the listener *uses other terms* to think about something.

Dilts (1976) has defined a metaphor as—
> "... a figure of speech in which something is spoken of as if it were another." (p. 74)

A metaphor can be anything (i.e., story, narrative, joke, drama, movie, personal referent, mythology, quote, etc.) that enables us to *think about one thing in terms of another thing.* As such, metaphoring represents a meta-stating process. We frame one thing in terms of another. We "carry" *up and above* (meta), and then *apply to* (*pherein*) the previous thought, idea, representation, etc. some other idea, concept, representation, etc. (the basic meta-stating process). In a metaphor, we *apply one idea to upon another idea,* usually something well known and more tangible to something less known and more abstract.

Yet because we put the message *in the frame of* an unrelated story, that unrelated story or terms typically bypasses conscious awareness. In doing so, it allows the unconscious parts of the mind to receive and process it. This is what makes metaphors implicit rather than explicit, covert rather than overt, and so more hypnotic in nature rather than propositional.

In order to create a well-designed metaphor as a set of mind-lines that conversationally changes beliefs, we must design it so that it has *a similar structure* to the person's thinking or experience. This similarity at the structural level explains how it invites the unconscious facets of mind to interpret it in relation to one's own needs. We use the term *isomorphic* to describe this correspondence of form.

The nice thing about metaphors as a device for communicating is that we seldom experience *stories* and *narratives* as threatening as we do with direct instructions, statements, and/or advice. This enables us to use stories, narratives, case studies, jokes, and metaphors more covertly. We can then communicate subtly, veiling the reframes that we offers for changing a limiting belief within the metaphor.

In addition to this, as a multi-level device, we can also use *story* to communicate on numerous levels simultaneously. This was Milton Erickson's genius. Via metaphors he would communicate, at the same time, with both the conscious and unconscious facets of mind. While he was providing the conscious mind a fun and entertaining message and thereby distracting the person with some fascinating or boring content, he would simultaneously speak to higher and deeper concerns (frames) via the structure of the story. In this, the surface story primarily keeps the conscious mind occupied while the deeper (or higher) message involving *frames by implication* "carries over" to the levels outside of conscious awareness of the story's similarities. For these and other reasons, we use lots of stories and metaphors in hypnosis.[1]

The Meta-Model explains all of this using the theoretical foundations of Transformational Grammar. In Chomsky's model, he set forth a "logical level" model making a distinction between surface and deep structures. The driving metaphor in this theory was the depth metaphor, hence the words *deep, going down, plunging below a surface,* etc. Since his original models (1956, 1965), Chomsky renounced that *Deep-Structure* model (D-Structure) as he searched for other ways to explain the transformation of meaning (See *Communication Magic,* 2001).

In *Meta-States,* we use the height metaphor and picture the "deep" issues and structures as meta-level frames. In this the metaphor turns things upside down so that we speak about *higher frames, ascending, transcending, going meta, high, up,* etc. In the following paragraphs I have made this translation from the depth metaphor.

Metaphors work by presenting a surface structure of meaning that engages and captivates the mind's attention. These surface statements at the primary level comprise the story's *content*. At this level, we *just hear a story*.

At the same time, the "deep structure" of meaning operates as higher levels and frames which activates us to engage in what's called a trans-derivational search to our referential index. This means that consciously and unconsciously the story activates us to make sense of things by finding inner references (actual or vicarious). This search connects us to the story at deeper (or higher) levels that are unconscious or outside of consciousness. For the most part we experience the *connecting* at other levels as occurring outside of conscious awareness. We make connections between the levels without knowing how we do it or even that we are doing so. We only have an intuitive sense of the connection. It "feels" right or meaningful.

When this *connecting* at other levels occurs, it sometimes brings healing at these out-of-consciousness levels. As this happens, the story performs its magic on us. The theory is that the metaphor operates isomorphically on us. In Neuro-Semantics we say that the metaphor enables us to set higher *frameworks* and it is the setting of a new frame that governs the experience.

And there is more. When a story or metaphor performs its magic and creates healing on this order, we can expect that simultaneously there will be within our problematic movie a mapping across across from the cinematic frames from the story or metaphor. Of course, we don't do this consciously. It happens entirely outside of our conscious awareness. With the new frames in place, the higher levels bring a tempering and texturing influence that alters the representations at the primary level. *The story or metaphor,* operating at a meta-level, even governs our autonomic nervous system processing.

So, as the other mind-line reframing patterns function directly on our mental internal representations, metaphors work on us more covertly and indirectly. Yet they also work on us. Metaphorical mind-lines can introduce new strategies, references, memories, imaginations, goals, meanings, states, ideas, etc. Metaphorical mind-lines can outframe beliefs with all kinds of new resources.

What's the difference then between all of the previous Mind-Lines patterns and this one? The *metaphorical mind-line* operates "on the side" in an isomorphic way and so apart from direct conscious intervention. As an additional benefit, story and narrative provide an ideal environment for running *as if* formats that allow us to try on new meanings.

Did you have any idea that story, metaphor, narrative, poetry, etc. involved such depth or complexity? On the surface, stories seem so simple. Yet the transformative power of a story does not lie on the surface, but *under,* or more accurately, *above,* the surface. Three mechanisms empower a story to operate as a *mind-line:*
• Activating trans-derivational searches (TDS).
• Shifting of referential indices.
• Structuring isomorphic similarities.

Activating Trans-Derivational Searches
Don't you love the technical jargon of transformational grammar? How about this one—*Trans-Derivational Searches?* Give me a break. We threw this mouthful of a term at you earlier. Remember? Generally NLP-ers use the acronym TDS (Trans-Derivational Search) to describe this neuro-linguistic process whereby we make meaning of symbols (i.e., words, language, mathematics, diagrams, etc.). This refers to the inward journey, of *going in* and accessing our memory banks (i.e., our library of references or internal references) and then relating those references (associations/ meanings) to the surface level terms. So TDS means that we search inside our heads and bodies to find or create referent frames. Accordingly, TDS can just as easily stand for *Traveling Down inSide.*

Whenever we describe an experience, we move from the actual experience to *a description of the experience.* We have to. Describing any experience moves us from the territory to our *map* of the territory. Language, as a description or symbolic representation of the experience, moves us into the realm of neuro-semantic reality. At this level, the experience *only* exists as an internal mental representation. As it is several levels moved away from external reality, it does not have that kind of "reality." It only exists as an internal map or model of the world. What's the significance of this?
> *This highlights how language, always and inevitably, stands in a meta relationship to experience.*

Language operates at a higher level of abstraction to the internal representation to which it refers, which exists meta to the experience. For language to work, it must *elicit* or evoke sensory-based representations for the movies of our mind. Language becomes meaningful to us and we experience its "magic" when the words work symbolically, that is, as symbols that trigger us to see, hear, feel, smell, taste, touch, etc. the referents on the inner screen or theater of our mind.
What does the word "car" evoke in terms of sensory-based

representations for you? Does it evoke a black Pontiac as it does for Bob? Probably not. That reference arose from his TDS. Where did your TDS take you? It's definitely a blue Toyota for me!

What does the word "dog" evoke? Where does the travels of your TDS take you? Bob has an internal representation of a black Cocker Spaniel named Buddy. What kind of dog did you find in your library of references?

In this way we *make sense* of language. We understand things by searching through our internalized and stored experiences for visual, auditory, kinesthetic, olfactory and/or gustatory sensations that correspond to the language symbols we use and hear. This explains how language operates metaphorically.

This process of associating the language we hear with our own internal representations is what we mean by *a trans-derivational search*. When we go from the surface structure (or primary state) language of a metaphor to the deep structure or the higher frame-of-reference (meta-state), we make an internal search. We search for our *references*, metaphorically we visit our personal "library of references."

So when we listen to a story or metaphor, our brain and nervous system makes *an internal trip* to connect the metaphor with our reference model. Count on metaphors triggering this automatic process. Count on every story activating us to search our reference frames or "memory banks" to make sense of things.

Shifting Referential Indices
When we work with story, narrative, and metaphor, we work with *symbolism*. A symbol refers to any object, situation, or character that becomes an anchor for certain responses. Many everyday metaphors take the form of, *"I once knew a person who..."* What's the symbolic link here? The open-ended induction word "person." And with that, further links will arise from whatever similarities the story has with the hearer's life.

Symbolic links like this exemplify what we mean by the displacement of referential indices. This refers to talking about a personal experience with sufficient vagueness so a listener has to hear the story *in terms of his or her own* experiences. (Come on, you know you do this also!) We all do. And when we do, we shift or displace the reference (the referential index). (Don't worry. The mind police won't arrest you for this.) Doing this causes us to listen sympathetically and experientially to the story and that empowers the story to deeply effect us, to even speak to us.

Making referential index shifts like this occurs all the time. Everyday we all do it many times. It also occurs at both conscious and unconscious levels. We distort our sensory representations, we switch the referential index, *we enter into the story, and the story casts its spell.* This activates its magic. No wonder that in olden days, they talked about stories as *"spells."*

Storying, narrating, metaphoring, etc. encourages the switching of referential indices. This invites *the as if quality* of stories which then begins to work its wonders in our minds and bodies. When it does, suddenly we feel transported to another time, another place, in another body, etc. The spell *entrances* us. We lose track of time, place, self, environment, etc. as we go zooming off into new and different worlds and realities.

Once inside the story, an animal, another person, even inanimate objects transform and take on special meanings. They frequently take on powerful symbolic representations for us. In the process of hearing the story, we are *storied.* Themes, plots, sub-plots, dramas, comedies, tragedies, victories, heroic journies, etc. define, describe, limit, and/or free us. These facets of the story become frames, frames-of-references for our thinking and feeling.

In the field of psychotherapy, White and Epston (1990) have developed an entirely new therapy model based upon these marvelous phenomena. Two people trained in NLP, Freedman and Combs (1990, 1996) have further contributed to Narrative Therapy using NLP distinctions. In the field of Linguistics, Mark Johnson and George Lakoff (1980, 1987) have individually, and together, also contributed to the pervasive nature of metaphors.

Structuring Isomorphic Similarities
What component drives the power of story and metaphor to transform meaning and change the magic formula? The component is that the story has a similar structure to the life and experience of the recipient. This similarity of structure makes it *isomorphic.* Characters, events, emotions, dramas, etc. in the story relate and correspond to similar formats in life. This mechanism makes the story meaningful.

Isomorphic structure explains how and why we can so easily, even without conscious awareness, use a story to shift our referential index. Dilts offered this explanation:

> "Isomorphism involves the formal similarities between representations of different responses ... Individuals can learn much about the possibilities of their own behavior by considering the operation of other systems. Imagining that you are a bird in a certain situation, as opposed to a lion, will open up and abolish many different avenues of response ... In general, symbols will identify the structural aspects of the metaphor, while isomorphisms will deal with the relational or syntactic

components.
The neural networks of the brain constantly generalizes information making learning possible. Isomorphisms describes the brain's ability to incorporate information about behavior from one class to another similar class. This is cross class learning."

Transforming Meaning Using Metaphor
Using the language of metaphor, analogy, story, etc. enables us to conversationally reframe, and hence gives us yet another *Mind-Line* pattern. Because this language form reframes laterally (on the side), instead of in the up and down directions like the ones previously explored, we can use story and narrative to package any of the other reframing patterns.

C) Your being late means you don't care about me.
> A friend of mine always complained about her husband being late. But then after he died, she often thought about him and wished that he would just be late rather than dead.
> If a surgeon is late for dinner because he's saving someone's life, does that mean he doesn't care?

D) Stress causes me to eat chocolate.
> I have a really uptight friend, John, who really enjoys eating carrots because he said, and I know this sounds really crazy, but whenever he feels stressed, he pulls out a carrot and takes a break so that he can think ... and the sound of the crunching makes him feel like Bugs Bunny coming up with some zany way to elude Elmer Fudd or Daffy Duck. Or, have you ever noticed that a wound up rubber band gets loose in hot water?

E) I can't really make a difference because management doesn't walk their talk.
> And the water held captive behind a dam yearns for the sea, not really caring about the dam, but only about feeling true to itself to flow ... ever flow, graciously, gently, yet inevitably down, down, down ... toward the sea ... And it does so, regardless of what the dam wants.

F) I can't buy your product because it costs too much.
> When Mary poured the expensive ointment on Jesus' head and feet, it was Judas who got upset saying that she wasted it. He felt that she spent far too much."
> I once had a friend who always complained about the high cost of clothes for his teenage daughter. He complained bitterly. Then, one day his daughter died in an auto accident. Now when he thinks about spending money on clothes for her—he wishes he had that opportunity.

To *story* someone with a narrative or metaphor, think about what a particular problem, issue, concern reminds you of. *What is this like?* More frequently than not, we do our best *lateral thinking* when we *stop thinking* about a problem as we shift to think about something else (especially when relaxing, kicking back, and enjoying ourselves). Then all of a sudden, presto, an idea pops into consciousness that we can then relate to the problem.

Narrative Therapy uses *externalization* as a central eliciting process. We do this by externalizing a problem as if it were a person and then metaphorically responding to it we would to a person trying to undermine our success. By *externalizing* a problem, situation, theme, idea, emotion, etc. we separate person from behavior (and all other functions involved in *behavior,* thoughts, emotions, coping patterns, etc.). This underscores a central theme in Narrative Therapy that we have highlighted in *Frame Games,* namely,

The person is not the problem;
The problem is the problem.
The frame is always the problem.

As we externalize, we change our thinking and emoting about our life story, our thoughts and emotions, etc. This invites another story—*a Preferred Story* that we can build out of "unique outcomes" and "sparkling moments."

How has Anger sabotaged your success this week?

When did the Rages invite you to enter back into that story?

So Sneaky Pee pulled one on you when you went to stay at your best friend's house, huh? And I bet you'd really like to get back at Sneaky Pee so he doesn't embarrass you like that again.

What tactics have you found that Wimping-Out uses to trick you into giving up? How have you stood up to Wimping-Out?

Summary

- You now have *twenty* ways to shift a frame of mind, twenty ways to reframe a limiting belief. This gives us lots of control over the *meanings* that govern our lives that we give to something, our skills, and our emotions.

- In *content reframing* we made shifts inside the formula that governs meaning. In *context reframing* we alter meaning by applying other ideas and frames to the formula.

- These mind-line moves highlight how our conceptual reality effects and transforms our experiences. When we bring *mind* to bear upon *mind*, neuro-semantic reality arises, that inner dimension of meaning. This puts us into a neuro-semantic state.

- Mind-Lines offer us elegant and professional ways to communicate meaning. By them we can manage our states, enhance our mental and emotional experiences, improve our health, etc. Neuro-linguistically all of these things work together as an interactive system and give birth to the "magic" of ideas that govern consciousness and neurology.

End Notes:

1. For more about this see *Therapeutic Stories* by David Gordon and *The Patterns of Milton H. Erickson* by Bandler and Grinder. For *frames by implication*, see *The Matrix Model.*

"Language

is what bewitches,

but language

is what we must remain within

in order to cure

the bewitchment."

Henry Staten (1984)

Chapter 11

LET THERE BE
MORE MAGIC!

Additional Outframing Magic

The *Mind-Lines model* has allowed us to dance with meaning in seven directions to create many patterns for conversational reframing. In the process of learning new steps and moves with the very structure of meaning, we have developed some new flexibility and rhythm.

We begin the mind-line dances by using the two deframing steps which enable us to tear a piece of "meaning" apart. What a dance! It is a wild and furious dance. Clothes are taken off and flung out (similar to a strip tease). We swing Meaning this way and that. As we test the stability of the structure of the magic we elicit more data from *the meaning* that we're dancing with. This gives us more steps for the other reframing moves.

Next we moved to the dance of *content* reframing. When we engage in this dance we declare that an event, experience, person, or idea is not one thing, but another. *"Not X, but Y!"* In these steps, we call things by new names. We redefine things. We substitute one term for another. After all, even individual words frame things. So we take to ourselves *words* and play with the word magic of using different categories to create entirely new frames of reference.

After that straight-on reframing, we engage in three dance moves using *counter-*framing. These are the dance moves that really get our heads spinning. We dip our partners, we toss them in the air, we spin them around, we reverse our direction, we even go head-over-heels in our jumps. In these moves, we apply the magic of the meaning back onto the person and watch to see how well the countering or reversing meaning does in creating fresh meanings.

We don't stop there. After that we can play in the Matrix of Time and reframed from several temporal perspectives. With the two *pre*-framing moves and three *post*-framing moves, we learned to dance with the concept of "time." This empowers us to dance with grace and gentleness as we pace a person's positive intentions and direct causation to impersonal sources. It allows us also to get tough and get in the face of the person with the magic of confrontation and consequences to dance with the "logical fate" of ideas and meanings. We usually work up a good sweat with those moves.

We also soar upward. We float way up above the structure of meaning itself and identified seven meta-framing dance patterns—more expressions of outframing. It's like dancing in the air. We feel as light as a feather as we transcend to some of the higher levels of the mind. We then dance with a wide range of over-arching concepts.

Finally, we ended by dancing on the side as we made some covert lateral moves. That's when we were whispering some stories and using metaphors in what we called the analogous framing move. When we do this, the other isn't always sure if we are dancing or not. It kind of seems like it, but we don't know ... not for sure.

And then there were 26
The original list of 20 Mind-Lines was by no means an exhaustive list, it was just the beginning. Since we designated *Mind-Line #18, All Other Abstractions*, as a catch-all for other conceptual frames, the model has continued to grow. Actually, this extending of the model began just a few months after the second edition. It was at that time that we found numerous other *Mind-Line patterns* emerging.

This occurred primarily from the *Merging of the Models* training that I did in London, now titled, *Advanced Flexibility Training*. It was through returning to the source of Alfred Korzybski and seeking to mine more of his treasures from the field of *General Semantics* that Neuro-Semantics developed. Some of the first expressions of this was the extension of the Meta-Model (*Communication Magic,* 2001) and, of course, its practical application in terms of the *Mind-Lines model*. This arose, in part, from the rich and creative mind of Denis Bridoux and has led to the new mind-line patterns in this chapter. And inasmuch as these are all meta-level structures, we have put them here in a chapter that extends and adds to the outframing patterns.

> **Mind-Lines in Chapter 11:**
>
> #21. Both/And Framing
> #22. Pseudo-Words Framing
> #23. Negation Framing
> #24. Possibility and "As If" Framing
> #25. Systemic and Probability Framing
> #26. Decision Framing

#21. Both/And Framing

Most of us learn very early in life to frame things in terms of *Either/Or.*
Thinking in either/or terms manifests what we call *black-or-white* thinking.
This dichotomous kind of thinking sorts the world into two categories, "Either
this or that." Typically it arises as a form of Aristotelian logic, reasoning, and
language—that logicians refer to as *the excluded middle.*

*   Either you love me *or* I will die.
*   Either cancer means I'm going to die *or* it doesn't mean that at all.
*   If you're late, it means either that you don't love me at all *or* that you
    do love me.

Of course, in a world where we can imagine and make distinctions *between* the
two poles and distinctions that include *both* poles at the same time, the Either/Or
way of thinking creates limitations in our view of the world and how we
navigate through it.   *Both/And framing* allows us to generate reframes by
including the excluded middle and by identifying a context or idea that includes
both poles. This allows us to take the grays into account, to embrace both sides
of a polarity (Both/And), and to consider degrees of how much we experience
something.

A) Saying mean things makes you a bad person.
    So the utterance of something that you consider "mean" is black-or-
    white? Either I speak with kindness or meanness? There's nothing in-
    between? There is no degree of kindness or degree of meanness?
    Either I become a bad person or I am a good person?

B) Cancer causes death.
    While I'm sure that sometimes some cancers may cause or at least
    contribute to death, while at other times they do not. I wonder to what

degree you will respond in life enhancing ways to this challenge to your immune system?

C) Showing up late means that you don't care about me!

Certainly a person could show up late due to the lack of really caring, but I wonder if there are some other reasons that could cause that? Could it be that when I'm late it means neither that I love or don't love you, but something else entirely—that my schedule has gotten out of control?

D) Stress causes me to eat chocolate.

So you have learned to respond to stress with eating chocolate. That's certainly one way to de-stress. I wonder how many other ways there are? Are you interested in learning other ways to de-stress that might be more enhancing? To what extent are you?

E) I can't really make a difference because management doesn't walk their talk.

I'm sorry that you seem so stuck in your black-or-white choices. Is that your only choice? What they do *totally* prevents you from making *any* difference at all? You can't make even a little bit of a difference? Couldn't you make some difference while frustrated by their incongruency?

F) I can't buy your product because it costs too much.

Does the price of this product *totally* control your decision? I'm surprised about that. I would have thought your need and your desire, or perhaps the values that you can derive from this product might also influence your decision.

Pattern Summary

To elicit this pattern, listen for *either-or* words, terms, or structure, and then question in a wondering way if it is really that black-or-white.

- Could there be a middle ground?
- Could the issue or problem involve *a degree of* something or perhaps even a *both/and* perspective?
- To what extent is this absolutely true?
- What makes it a completely either/or choice?
- Is there any ground for a middle position?
- Could the solution involve a both/and perspective?

#22. *Pseudo-Word Framing*

Korzybski (1933/1994) pointed out that just because some sounds (*noises*) and some *spell-marks* look like, sound like, and feel like a word, that in itself does not make them real words. *Noises* that rattle sound waves may sound like actual words and *spell-marks* on paper may mimic a word without necessarily endowing it with the qualities and properties of a functional word. There is such a thing as a *pseudo*-word.

What makes any given word a *real* word? A *real* word has to function as a *symbol of something else.* That is, it has to "stand for" a referent that you truly accept, recognize, and desire. Now the reference may be *actual* (an actual person, place, or thing), *conceptual* (an idea, principle, understanding, etc.), or *remembered or imaginary,* yet it has to refer to something physically or conceptually real.

This is what *pseudo*-words failed to do. Though they sound like words that we can speak, and look like words that we can write, they do not point to or reference anything. They are truly *non-referencing.* It is not that they suffer the ill-formedness of a non-specific referent like an unspecified verb or noun. It is that they fail to function as a *symbol* which stands for something else. That's what makes them false or pseudo through and through.

In light of this concept, we consider the word "failure" is a pseudo-word. This pseudo-word derives from the *un*specific verb, "to fail." This at least represents a class of verbs that conveys the overall idea of not succeeding to reach some goal or objective in some specific way at a specific time. But when we nominalize that verb, treat it like a thing, and bring the word "failure" into existence, to what are we actually referring? What is this state of "failure?" What does that mean? As it becomes a concept and refers to some conceptual reality, do you have something in mind as a concept that this term references or do we use the term simply as a paranoid term of some vague thing to avoid?

Personally I sliced that term out from my mental library of references more than a dozen years ago. I refused to allow it any reference. It stands for no actual experience. For me, and for many other people (and their numbers are growing), the term "failure" represents a meaningless noise. When someone speaks it or writes it as a spell-mark, I go, "Meaningless." "Doesn't compute." I can "fail," but I cannot experience or become the nominalized entity, "failure." How about you? Would that enhance your mental mapping?

Unicorn is non-referencing in the domain of zoology, although, in the domain of mythology, it does have an actual referent. This identifies how some words may have a *domain of reference* within which they can operate meaningfully as a symbol while at the same time functioning as a pseudo- and non-referencing word in other domains.

In this, you may choose to have the term "failure" operate within a given domain, and then when it comes to the domain of reference of your self-definitions and associations for identifying your "self," you can frame "failure" as a poor and vague frame, and as a toxic one and so position it as a pseudo-term.

In reframing and/or challenging non-referencing terms, we engage in a deframing process.
*   If I were to get my hands on this thing that you call "failure," what would I actually be handling?
*   What would it look like or sound like?
*   Are you just referring to the emotional experience of feeling discouraged or frustrated about not reaching a goal and so "failing" to reach a goal? Or is there something else that you mean?
*   What do you mean by the term "failure?" What does this term add to what you're saying?

In the contexts of the statements that we have been using as our playground, only the first statement contains a pseudo-word.

A) Saying mean things makes you a bad person.
What are you referring to when you use the term saying "mean" things? I really don't understand, how could a word be "mean?" Undesired and non-appreciated, I can understand, but "mean?"

Pattern Summary
To elicit this pattern, notice the words that people say and write and question them, sit back and really question *the referent experience* for which they stand.
*   Is there really such a thing? If you can't see, hear, or feel it, if you cannot make a video-tape of it, then it is not a real thing.
*   Yet perhaps it is a thing of the mind (a nominalization). Is the mental thing a legitimate concept that you want in your mental world?
*   Is this just an auditory *noise* and/or a visual *spell-mark*?
*   What is the actual referent of this term or phrase?
*   Could this be a pseudo-word rather than a real symbol standing for something actual or conceptual?

#23. Negation Framing

Negation, what is that? And how do we *negate* something so that we make it *not* exist or *not* relevant to our thinking or framing? The very idea of *not*, of *negation* is a very special one. Typically, we negate by first representing something and then making it go away, nullifying it, discounting it, refusing it, and so on.

On this subject Gregory Bateson (1972) wrote an extensive description of how animals, specifically dogs negate. How does a dog communicate to another dog, "Let's just play like we are fight, but not really fight."? Bateson described that dogs say "this is *not* really a fight" by initiating the beginning behaviors of growling and biting, but *not* following through. This communicates, "This is play, *not* a fight."

The negation most of us are most fully aware of is the *command negation*. "Do not X." *Command* negation demands that we represent what we want to go away prior to making it go away. And that's both the paradox and the problem with it, by commanding the negation we first represent and that then makes the negating twice as difficult. "Don't think of blue." "Don't touch the wet paint." "Don't think about bright yellow monkeys dancing around me."

In spite of what's typically taught in NLP, the problem here isn't the *negation* as the *command*. Actually, there are many other ways to negate something and effectively make it go away. The art in doing so lies in being able to distinguish different forms of negation and knowing how to negate without relying upon command negation.[1]

Previously, we played around with one form of negation, with framing things with *unreality* which allowed us to negate things (Mind-Line #18). Of course, do you also know how to frame things to make them real, legitimate, valid, existing, etc.? Of course you do. This describes how you call all kinds of understandings into mental existence. When you set *a reality frame* you can turn ideas into "beliefs," as you confirm and validate them.

If we can do that, we can also do the opposite. To reverse a reality frame, we can frame a thing as unreal, invisible, not-existing, as merely seeming, etc. In this way that we can create and set a *negation frame*. Of course, when we treat things as *not* there, *not* real, *not* visible, etc., we're setting a very special and unique kind of frame.

Bob loves to do this with problems to deframe mental worlds that are limiting and toxic. It really does loosen up a belief. Notice how he does it:

I want you to take that old limiting belief and go out into the void of the

> eternity before you were born ... when you were just a thought in God's mind and when you had no reality of your own. ... That's right .... Are you there, now? Okay, good. So when you open your eyes and look into your as yet unformed future, what do you see?

To this question a person inevitably has to say, "Nothing." The elicitation is framed in such a way as to elicit that response. It is so framed by implication. And with that way of thinking, it cannot but help to induce a very altered state of mind. Nor does Bob leave the mind-line there. Not Bob. He continues to solidify the state.

> And when you fully feel all of that vast potentiality, that pure potentiality which is yet unborn ... all of that wonderful Void ... that nothingness ... Are you there inside that Void? ... How does that feel? ... and just be there with that unformed potentiality.

A) Saying mean things makes you a bad person.

> I used to think that too, but then I found that thought just evaporated from my mind as I realized that speaking is just speaking and that if I evaluate it morally in terms of being "kind" or "mean," that would make me self-righteous and moralistic, which is something I don't want. That's when it just began to fade away, if you can imagine that.

B) Cancer causes death.

> After Lance Armstrong fought his battle against cancer and won the Tour de France I tried to keep thinking about cancer as causing death, but found that I just couldn't think of it that way any longer. Then when he repeated that incredible feat not only one more time, but four more times, that idea totally vanished as it gave way to thinking about cancer as just a challenge to the healing forces of the body.

C) Showing up late means that you don't care about me!

> Do you remember when I showed up that time that we went out and walked on the beach at sunset and got all caught up in the beauty of that moment and ended up really talking and getting close ... Yes? ... and wasn't that a really special time? ... I think of that often when I think about us ... and when I do it seems like some of the details of everyday life just become irrelevant, if you know what I mean.

D) Stress causes me to eat chocolate.

> Yes stress *has* invited you to eat chocolate and *up until now* that has always *been* the story of your life, yet when you think about all the potential choices you have in life and your right and power to make those choices, wouldn't it be great if you know fully that the old pattern *was* just a choice to make no more?

E) I can't really make a difference because management doesn't walk their talk.
Would you want to make a difference at work in spite of what management does? You would? That's great! Then suppose you found your internal voice of *"No!"* so that you could stubbornly refuse to be stopped from operating at your best by someone else's incompetence?

F) I can't buy your product because it costs too much.
As you consider the values and benefits of this product, I wonder just how much it would really enrich your life and make your life a lot easier? It would? Good, so there's really no question about the value of this product? Good. It's just the cost, right? And it is just 8% higher than you wanted ... will you let 8% stop you?

Pattern Summary
To elicit this pattern, consider the *existence* and/or *reality* of something, then frame it as unreal and non-existing. Consider ways of inviting negation that makes something go away, become nothing, disappears, etc.
*   How real is this thing? How real do you want it to be?
*   Does it have external reality or does it only exist in the mind?
*   Do you want to give it this much reality in your life?

#24. Possibility and "As If" Framing

Suppose we step back and apply a frame of *possibility* thoughts and feelings over an old limiting belief? That's possible, don't you think? No? Well, what if it were possible, would you like that? And if it were possible, how would it change things for you? How much would it improve the quality of your life?

In language and thought the idea of possibility, like that of necessity, is fundamental. Linguistically these terms are *modal operators*. These terms describe a basic operational style of moving through the world, a basic *modus operandi*. We noticed this with *necessity* in *Necessity Framing* (#16). Here we cover another operational mode that we can use for framing purposes, namely *possibility*.

Outframing with thoughts of possibility enable us to expand a frame from within. It is as if we're inside a very flexible bubble, a bubble with plastic-like walls so that as we push on it from within, the walls expand and grow and enable us to create more space and more options—an expanded consciousness.

> I'm sorry that I was late, and I plan to use my concern for your feelings to pay more attention to my scheduling so that I won't leave you waiting. I know that's important to you. [Pace, Pace.] And as I do, I wonder if it would be possible for you to feel secure and loved even more deeply so that lateness will not call my love for you into question. Is that possible? Would you like to feel *that* loved?

The *As If* frame has been around for a long time. NLP adapted it as a way to step out of any limiting box to expand our map of the world. Conversationally we can reframe with possibility by using such expressions as *possible, can, what if, as if, imagine what it would be like, suppose, etc.* These expressions enable us to invite a state of possibilities and to set that as a frame over limiting beliefs.

How much richer would your life be if you outframed problems, issues, and challenges with possibilities? What that expand your options and your sense of new opportunities? How many possibilities can you imagine that might arise if you began using this *Mind-Line pattern*? And when you have fully imagined all of those rich possibilities, what would it be like if you realized that you have not even begun to dream but have only touched the hem of the garment about what's possible? How would you then feel?

A) Saying mean things makes you a bad person.

> I know this may sound crazy, but what if it were possible for a person to say something that you may think is "mean" at first and the person still be a good person?

B) Cancer causes death.

How do you suppose that so many thousands of people now get cancer and do not die, not for decades? Some even become stronger as did Lance Armstrong and go on to do new things, make a difference in the world, and even set new world records.

C) Showing up late means that you don't care about me!

What's the possibility that a person could care while being late for an appointment? Is that a human possibility at all? If it were, could it also be possible to realize that someone is late and to feel loved and valued.

D) Stress causes me to eat chocolate.

Really? Stresses causes that? And you believe that? I'm wondering about the possibility that there could be other causes for eating chocolate than stress. Is that even a remote possibility? Could you possibly feel stress and not eat chocolate? Is that possible?

E) I can't really make a difference because management doesn't walk their talk.

So it's not possible at all for you to take any effective action if management doesn't walk its talk? Really? That's not even a remote possibility? That means that what they do *makes* you so that you *have to* feel bad, incompetent, and helpless? There's no other possibility? What if it were possible?

F) I can't buy your product because it costs too much.

It's not even possible for you to choose to go with this higher valued product because of the price tag? So you can't even imagine what it would be like to buy at this level or possible to conceive of the difference it would make in your life?

Pattern Summary

To elicit this pattern, notice the linguistic distinction of *modal operators*. Does the person frame things so that a choice is even possible in his or her world? Invite the person to at least try on the idea using a what if, suppose, or some possibility statement.

- What would it be like if ... ?
- Suppose you could have this desired outcome, what would that be like for you?
- I know it is not possible, and that this is just a thought experiment, but indulge me, if it were possible, what would you be thinking, feeling, or imagining?

#25. *Systemic and Probability Framing*

Another way that we can classifying thinking is in terms of linear and non-linear thinking. When we speak about *linear thinking*, we speak framing processes as if a they moved or followed a straight line. It is linear thinking that says, "The shortest distance between two points is a straight line." And this works great in certain domains and fields, especially for gross or macro-level analysis. Linear thinking allows us to set out step-by-step procedures for manufacturing things or for creating a recipe, formula, doing some forms of mathematics, some computer programming, building an assembly line, etc.

In fact, in the hard sciences, linear thinking enables us to sort and separate, sequence and program so that we can systematically create models and provide step-by-step procedures that allow us to replicate it. This even plays a significant role in learning a model like NLP or how to learn the original modeling process using the representational steps of a strategy. Linear thinking certainly offers one way to frame things. And in a great many areas, it has proved very productive.

Yet linear thinking has its limitations and this is where non-linear thinking comes in. This is especially true for living and even mechanical systems, for processes that involve complex processes with multiple variables and indeterminancy. In those domains it is usually best to shift to systemic and probability thinking.

Systemic thinking is non-linear and involves more holistic and synergistic ways of framing things. Rather than attempting to reduce things to its most simple form, systemic thinking welcomes the chaos, ambiguity, and complexity of a system and seeks to first gain a larger level "sense," intuition, or feel for how all of the interactive parts interact together.

Systemic thinking is not only more holistic, it allows for the simultaneality of events within the system as well as for the "time" that it takes for information or energy to move through the communication loops of a system, Systemic thinking seeks to take the whole system into account. It identifies the embedded systems within systems in order to reckon with the layers. It recognizes that while in a system, lots of things occur simultaneously and that there is a structural sequence to the events. So in systemic thinking, we seek to tease out the layers of embeddedness.

Thinking systemically means looking to connects things. It adds hyphens to things that we have separated into elements. We separate our neuro-linguistic experiences into "mind" and "body" as if these are separate elements. They are not. So as *elementalism* conveys a false-to-fact mapping, *hyphenating* reconnects a fragmented and broken dichotomy of things. Einstein put "time" and "space" back together in his theorizing and discovered the larger gestalt of *the time-space continuum* and that led to his famous formula on the conversion between matter and energy. Korzybski insisted that we reconnect mind-body neuro-linguistic, neuro-semantic, organism-as-a-whole-in-an-environment, etc.

This way of framing things offers a much larger and holistic way of looking at things. It renews and heals fragmented dichotomies and provides new insights and understandings about complex systems.

A) Saying mean things makes you a bad person.
> So that's all there is to communicating? Either a person says "mean" words or "kind" words, and there's no relationship context that plays into this at all? There is no accounting for moods, for negative emotions, for feeling grumpy or out of sorts, or for needing to express a conviction, teasing, or anything else?

B) Cancer causes death.
> Do you really think that cancer is a single thing or that life and death is a single thing? Are these not *processes*? So isn't the real question, "What mind-body-emotion processes could we activate that would begin to strengthen the immune system and counteract the cancering?"

C) Showing up late means that you don't care about me!
> I'm amazed. You mean that in our relationship involving all of the ways that we interact at different times for a variety of purposes, that all of the things that we do and all that we feel toward each other, love and care comes down to time schedules and promptness? That's the only thing that proves or dis-proves whether we really care for each other? We should not take into consideration other factors like travel, friends, associates, energy level, work, etc.?

D) Stress causes me to eat chocolate.
> Yes, I'm sure that one of the factors which plays a significant role for you in eating chocolate is stress. Yet are you saying that how it tastes, your memories of being rewarded with chocolate, the sweetness, and perhaps other factors do not also play a role in eating chocolate?

E) I can't really make a difference because management doesn't walk their talk.
> The incongruency of management does seem to be a key factor in all of the facets of your work, yet I wonder if your personal goals, plans, values, congruency, associates, and many others don't temper this for you so that you don't let one unpleasant factor weigh all of the influence to that one side. Wouldn't these factors also play a role?

F) I can't buy your product because it costs too much.

>Certainly the price plays a role in your decision, yet are you saying that your need for this item, your realization that this will cut down on time and trouble, that this investment will make your home more valuable, and that it will free up some more time plays no role at all? If these other factors play into your decision making, how do they? How much influence do they carry in deciding to purchase this product?

Pattern Summary

To elicit this pattern, step back to a meta-position to the whole system and inquire about the many different facets and factors that play a role.

- Is the subject linear or non-linear?
- Is there a system of interactive parts involved?
- Does linear thinking adequately address this subject?
- What else plays a significant part in this system?
- What are the borders and boundaries of the system?
- What is the probability that the subject can be framed in this way and this way only?
- What is the probability that non-linear thinking or systemic thinking would more accurately or usefully frame this subject?

#26. *Decision Framing*

Frequently (perhaps even most of the time) we frame things in terms of ideas, insights, curiosities, shoulds, musts, etc., all the while never getting around to actually making a *real decision* about actually *doing* something about it. We talk and talk and talk. We theorize, explain, analyze, diagnose, talk some more, and then cycle through yet one more time. Yet in the end, we never take any action. We never *decide* in a decisive way to do something. Yet, we have not made a *real* decision until we do take action.

What frame drives that? Numerous frames contribute. A perfectionistic frame that "it's not good enough." A fear frame could hold one back from actually acting and wanting more assurance. A reflective frame that believes in getting second opinions again and again. An incongruent frame that one isn't really clear about what to choose. A hesitation frame driven by the need to get outside confirmation.

So what's involved in a decision? *De-ciding* most literally refers to "cutting" (cision) one thing away from another. In a decision, we *choose* one thing, idea, feeling, activity, person, task, etc. in distinction to another. As we say *Yes* to one thing, we simultaneously say *No* to another. The comparing, weighing, evaluating, representing, etc. operates as the cognitive part of a decision. As we do, we *cut away* what's really important from what's less important or not important at all. Then finally, we send a message to our motor cortex that says, *"Make it so!"*

Introducing the decision frame on various ideas, understandings, beliefs, values, identities, etc. empowers us to put our ideas into action. It empowers us to *implement* the knowledge that we have attained so that we can put it to the test to see how solid and complete it is. As such, decision helps to create personal *power,* that is, the ability to take effective and intelligent action.

We can use this framing in several ways. Sometimes we can frame an enhancing belief or value that we know "intellectually" with a clear cut decision to empower us to act more congruently on our insights. At other times, we might step back and explore what decision frame by implication has been covertly driving our behavior.

A) *Saying mean things makes you a bad person.*
> Is this what you have decided to think for anything anyone says that you interpret as "mean?" You really want to moralize people in terms of their words? You've made a decision to cut off other possibilities?

B) *Cancer causes death.*

I'm sure many people think that, have you actually made this your decision for how to respond to any news about cancer? Is this your decision for how to think about cancer in yourself or others? Is this the best decision that you can make about this?

C) Showing up late means that you don't care about me!

Yes, I'm sure that at this moment it feels like I must not care since I came later than expected. And I'm sorry for being late and will be more prompt next time. So where do we go from here? Are you going to use this feeling as your decision about how to spend the rest of the evening?

D) Stress causes me to eat chocolate.

Is this just your thinking about the cause of your eating chocolate or is this a decision for how to de-stress? I can understand the urge to stuff something in your mouth when stressed, but certainly you're not going to make this your decision for stress reduction, are you?

E) I can't really make a difference because management doesn't walk their talk.

It must be frustrating to have to put up with management who says one way and does another; but I hope this isn't your decision about how we can take effective action at work. You're not going to decide to give all of your power away to their incongruency are you?

F) I can't buy your product because it costs too much.

I can see that you don't want to spend the extra 8% that it would cost to invest in this, but as we know, sometimes the best decisions we can make for our long-term value isn't based upon our immediate feelings, but upon our more thoughtful decisions.

Pattern Summary

To elicit this pattern, look at the issues or problems from the standpoint of a decision and contrast it to a thought, feeling, desire, urge, etc. As a mind-line pattern, we express the decision frame as:

- What have you decided?
- When do we get started?
- What one thing are you going to do today that will support and give feet to this new understanding?
- What one thing can I begin to do today so that I will be more able to arrive on time in the future?
- Is this the best decision given this event or belief?
- Does this decision limit or enhance your life?

Summary

- In regard to "How I love to Reframe Thee, let me count the ways," we have a great many ways to set new frames. The amount of frames we can set extends endlessly.

- To become a true master of conversational reframing, you only need to recognize the structure of meaning as first involving associations or linkages (this X leads to that Y) and as second involving the embedment of frame upon frame (idea X is embedded inside of idea Y).

- *Meta-States* articulates the layering of idea upon idea, feeling upon feeling, thought upon thought, etc. So in learning the meta-stating process, we train our intuitions to become highly tuned to the process of meaning making and reframing.

End Notes:

1. For ten forms of negation, see *Sub-Modalities Going Meta* (2005). There's an entire chapter on negation.

PART III:

THEORETICAL

FRAMEWORKS

FOR MIND-LINES

Developing a Neuro-Semantic Mind

Chapter 12

UNFOLDING MIND-LINES

By Denis Bridoux[1]

I first encountered the Mind-Lines model at a training in the UK. *Post-Graduate Profession Education,* along with *Frank Daniels Associates* invited Dr. Michael Hall to provide training in Meta-States, the Merging of the Models (NLP and General Semantics), and the Mind-Lines model. Upon numerous occasions, Michael and I talked about the linguistic distinctions of the Mind-Lines model and I began to recognize that there was an even deeper structure (or higher framework) hinted at within the model. As I began working on making that structure manifest, we discovered additional patterns. Some of these were included in the third edition of *Mind-Lines* (2000).

There's a common feature of many scientific discoveries in how they occurred from a shift in the way that we perceive things. This was true of the Copernician and Newtonian revolutions where the discovery of the outer planets transformed astronomy. It was true of chemistry at the end of the 19th century, where Mendeleyev's Periodic Table enabled physicists to deduce the existence of new elements, including some surprisingly common ones. It was true of particle physics where, in order to identify the underlying simpler structure of particles in nature, physicists had to posit the existence of many unknown particles.

It was through becoming aware of these underlying symmetries that the discoveries were made. When I applied this principle to the Mind-Lines model, I found that it vindicated the model and made it more robust than ever. As I made these symmetries explicit, many new patterns have been identified that have given the model even more elegance, simplicity, flexibility, and versatility. Several things resulted from this. For one thing, I found that Mind-Lines explains the operating features of many therapeutic disciplines other than NLP and Neuro-Semantics. By a further integration with the Meta-Model, Mind-Lines provides a comprehensive understanding of *the structure of communication.* When I first became aware of this, I began to think that the model could lie at the core of any Counseling course. Now I realize that we can revise it and make it the core of English or even Communication. This is no mean feat for a model that's only five years old.

To gain a sense of the underlying (or over-arching) symmetries, I want to go back to the various representations of the Mind-Lines model. In doing this, I will offer a recapitulation which will put the whole model in its historical context.

In the Beginning
NLP began with the Meta-Model. This language model offered an elegant use for enabling us to identify how an experienced problem relates to the way we express a "problem" and how it directs our attention in a particularly unresourceful direction. In so doing, we learn the underlying linguistic structure of the problem and how to find more resourceful ways for operating in the world. We do this through the building of a better map.

Early on, Bandler and Grinder identified the exquisite languaging abilities of three therapeutic wizards whom they modeled. Yet they did not limit themselves solely to the Meta and Milton models. The wizardry of these experts also displayed itself in *the way* they applied the patterns. *How* they spoke affected the manner that their clients thought, felt, and consequently operated in the world. Yet this happened without the clients needing to understand the process itself. Indeed, this was part of why Bandler and Grinder found those communication experts worth modeling in the first place.

They called the change patterns *Reframing* and directed them to both *the content* of the information and to *the context* in which the information applied. In reframing, two things can change. Because every picture has *an inside* and *an outside,* every mental image has both an internal *content* and format and an external environment or *context.* For sake of description, Bandler and Grinder called the internal content and format of a picture (or information) its meaning, and hence *content reframing.* They called the external environment which provides the context, *context reframing.*

If a picture does not fit in a given environment and yet you like the picture (or information), you can change its environment. You could perhaps redecorate the room, change the lighting or move the picture about. On the other hand, if you like the room, you could change the picture altogether. We call these two change processes *content framing* and *context reframing.* The meaning of any experience results from the interaction between the content of the experience, or what actually happened, and its format, or how we re-present it in our memory in sensory-specific terms and linguistic terms.

In language terms, *content reframing* changes the meaning of an experience while retaining its context. This re-casts the experience in different words. Conversely, *context reframing* changes the context of the experience and so changes the perception of the problem, the meaning remains while the context changes.

Does any given process involve content reframing or context re-framing?

Ultimately, the two inextricably interact so that one will change the other. For any *inside* to exist requires an *outside,* and vice-versa.

In the 1980s, Robert Dilts mapped out the reframing model with greater precision and moved beyond the simple division of context and meaning reframing. He charted key reframing patterns in the languaging of Richard Bandler who had become far better at conversational reframes than those whom he had originally modeled. Richard also modeled Frank Farrelly who created *Provocative Therapy*. He realized the value of the power of Farrelly's polarity responding and so incorporated it into his language patterns.

Dilts used the analogy of a stage magician who conjures rabbits out of hats and coins out of on-looker's ears to the amazement of their audience using "sleight-of-hand" processes. Dilts gave the 18 patterns he identified the overall title of *the "Sleight-of-Mouth" patterns.*

While providing useful patterns, these patterns suffered from a lack of sortedness. So, apart from the initial Context/Meaning reframing distinction, learning and practicing "the sleight of mouth" patterns was arduous. For one thing, they extended far beyond the $7^{+/-2}$ chunks of information for conscious awareness (George Miller, 1956). This was similar to the original Meta-Model patterns which had confused a generation of trainers because they were not sorted into categories of deletions, generalizations, distortions and presuppositions.

In 1994 L. Michael Hall formulated the Meta-States model, based in part on Alfred Korzybski's levels of abstraction (the Structural Differential) and Bateson's work in meta-levels. This model of *the levels of mind* enabled him to distinguish mental-and-emotional states into *primary states* (states wherein we respond to events in the world mediated by our senses) and *meta-states* (states wherein we respond to our responses, mediated by our language). This enabled him, working with Bobby Bodenhamer, to initially sort out Dilt's patterns according to the primary state / meta-state distinction. They then identified an over-arching structure in these patterns and elegantly sorted them out into the seven categories of the Mind-Lines model. This has made them easy to learn and remember as it has set up the seven directions that we can send our minds.

One of the early diagrams of the Mind-Lines model occurs in the figure on the next page (p. 232). That diagram provides us an understanding of the evolution of the visual representation of the Mind-Lines model. I want to use it to assist us in understanding the effectiveness and pervasiveness of the model. Here we see the sorting out of the levels, from the primary level to the meta-levels. From there Michael and Bob created the chart in Chapter 2 (page 47).

Later, Pascal Gambardela turned the model into the diagrams that you find on chapter 19 of this edition. In 1997 and 1998, Michael used the original model in his trainings and it was from that model that I drew upon to suggest one of the first "cube" representations.

From that I sketched some diagrams during that training and later reformatted them. After that Michael integrated these drawings into the Mind-Lines model. You can see them on pages 47 and 57. Early in the Mind-Lines training I became interested by the metaphorical language that's involved in the "Magic Box" at the heart of the Mind-Lines model.

External Behavior = Internal State

Thinking in pictures, we turned it into a three dimensional box or cube. Upon doing this, I realized that we could use the very shape of the box to present the layering of *External Behavior* and *Internal State* with the E.B. (External Behavior) operating as our "front window" and I.S. (Internal State) as our "backstage." These relate to our public powers of *speaking* and *behaving* and our private powers of *thinking* and *feeling*.[2]

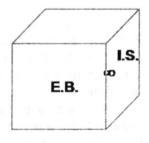

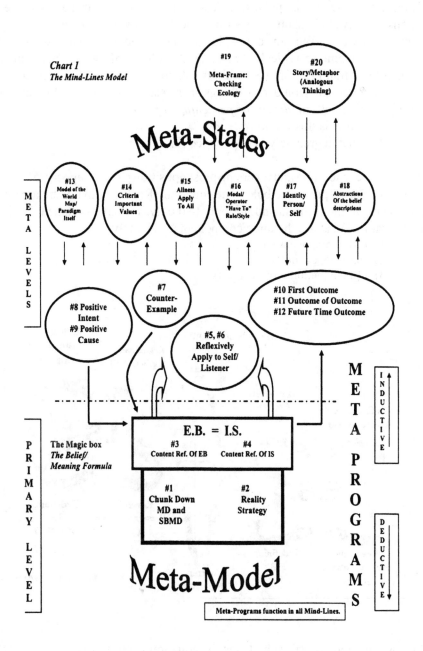

Chart 1
The Mind-Lines Model

The Discovery of the Over-Arching Symmetries

One of the first symmetries I became aware of during the training related to the *Allness/Counter-Example* polarities. These are two questions that we make in response to universal quantifiers (words indicating universality, i.e., all, always, never, everybody). We can "chunk down" toward identifying an exception to a statement. Doing so typically breaks up the allness of the statement and so reframes by deframing. Or, we could "chunk up" towards universality to see if an allness statement would map things in a resourceful way. We can also identify another pattern, *degree or percentage of allness*.

- How true is this for you?
- To what degree do you experience X?

Also, because redefining and reversing presupposition patterns appear to "chunk down," they are represented below the equation. Realizing that there are three components in the formula and not only two only, we have sketched that into the diagram. What are the three components? Namely,

         1) E.B. (component A)
         2) I.S. (component B)
         3) = (the Equation formula itself).

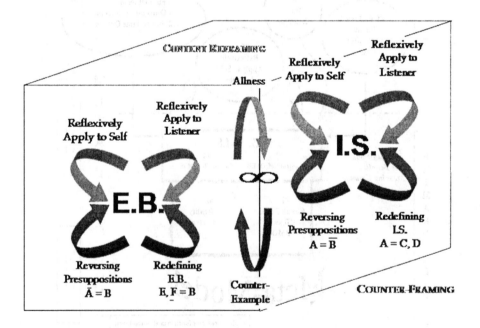

Many Mind-Lines actually challenge the equation itself, thus:
         A =/ (or does not equal) **B**, instead A=C, D, etc. or E, F (=B), etc.
         A = Non B
         Non A = / Non B
         Non A = B (where A means Non-A, anti-A or the opposite of A)

Note how the Reversing Presupposition reframe now includes the Negation reframing (#23). Counter Reframing remains inside the box.

Accordingly, the whole Counter Reframing Mind-Lines remains inside the box.

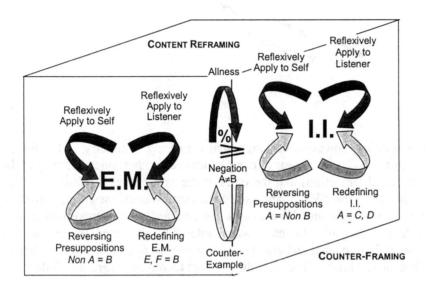

The next symmetries that unfolded already appear in the model. Yet teasing them out occurred in several phases. These symmetries relate to the Pre-framing and Post-framing patterns. In Pre-Framing for Positive Intention, the mind-lines are based on the identification of *positive intentions*. This is a key facet in Meta-State training as well as in the agreement frame, visual squash, and core transformation patterns. Our intentions hardly ever appear only on their own. They are always involved in a chain of intentionalities, that is, intentions of intentions.

In the Pre-Framing for Positive Cause, we return to the origin or some contributing causation. This explains why we go back to the cause of the cause, and even the primordial cause, to enable a person to resolve an issue. We do this in numerous NLP patterns such as numerous Time-Lines processes, and specifically the Change Personal History, and Re-imprinting patterns. This allows the model to evolve as shown below.

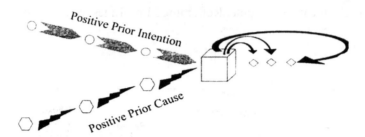

This unfolding, however, has suggested a missing symmetry in the future. *Intentions* and *Causes* appear to complement each other, one occurring at the internal level (Intention) and the other at the external level (Cause).[3]   This corresponds to the SWOT analysis: Strengths, Weaknesses, Opportunities, Threats.   Strengths and Weaknesses are *internal* while Opportunities and Threats are *external*.   In many ways, internally generated Intentions, and Outcomes focus on self and effect or Consequences operate as the counterpart of Cause in the future. The unfolding should therefore progress as follows.

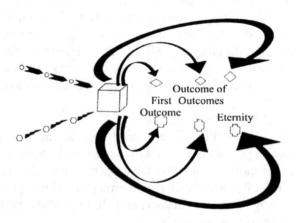

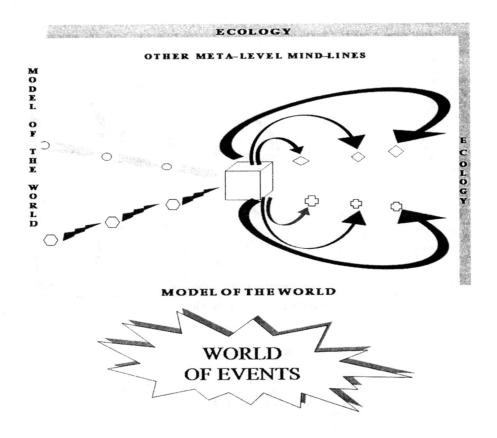

As this unfolding occurred, I realized that this future domain of Ultimate Outcomes and Ultimate Consequences relates closely to the Ecology Frame. From a time perspective, Ecology not only incorporates self-related outcomes and other-related consequences, it also enfolds our higher domains of understanding at a meta-level. Likewise the domain of origins, Intentions and Causes relates to the way we generate our model of the world. How many people for example, still blame the way we live on this world as "Eve's fault?"

The world of physics and cosmology, as well as that of religion and cosmogony seek to explain how the universe exists, from a primordial beginning or genesis to an ineluctable end or eschatology. Indeed, it affects our very filters with which we view the world, our model of the world. The model now attains the following format.

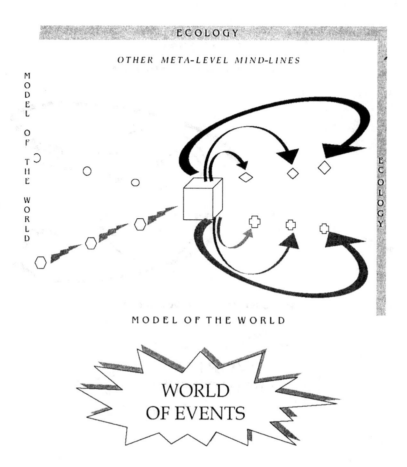

MODEL OF THE WORLD

WORLD
OF EVENTS

Outframing A Hyper-Cube

Imagine the following. Imagine a cube made of cubes wherein all the cubes are nested inside each other, *a hyper-cube.* This metaphor gives us a way to think about these patterns. They all seem to nest inside each other and yet we cannot determine which cube forms the inner shell and which the outer shell because it varies according to the way we experience it. This hyper-cube describes the environmental context of our lives in terms of *space, time,* and *relationships* (or perceptual positions) and the structure of each of these mirrors that of the other two.

The previous patterns have considered a person and his or her perspective on a problem. This means we have been directing questions to them in the *self position.* We have asked questions as a client thinks about himself. In content reframing, we looked at how reframing occurs in a coach/client interaction where *Applying to Self* relates to the way the coach would respond if she applied the interaction to herself and *Apply to Listener* reflects the statement back to the client.

However, we can apply the reframing patterns and multiply them across all of the other perceptual positions. Doing so multiplies the reframe into the *other* position. Here we inquire how the *other* perceives the equation.

> So that's what you think. I wonder how the person you're describing would see that?
> I wonder whether Joe Brown would respond to this in that way?
> How do you think he would go about it?
> Do you think somebody starving in the Sahel would think like that?
> (Applying to an Observer out there)

By asking such questions, we invite the person into a meta position to think about the way others think, feel, and respond. This sends their brain into the direction of *self about other, self about observer*. We can also reverse the order. In the next question we apply the perspective *self about other about self*, as the client puts himself in another's shoes to become aware of the other person's perspective on him.

> Will the person still reject you after the initial shock has subsided?

Or, we can apply the reframe *self about other about other*.

> When Andrew agrees that it might be fun to do this, what does Peter do?

The next one applies the reframe *self about other about self about self*. Notice how you could repeat this ad infinitum, sending the person into a trance.

> So, when Andrew and Peter look horrified, what do you do then?

This reframe relates to identifying another person's Model of the World.

> Who do you think it was who came up with that idea about the unhealthiness of such behavior and when was that?

This reframe relates to the value system of society, here perceived as an *observer*. The perceptual positions form the first cube of the hyper-cube, wherein we can explore each and every previously studied reframing pattern.

> What do you think society is seeking to uphold by doing this?

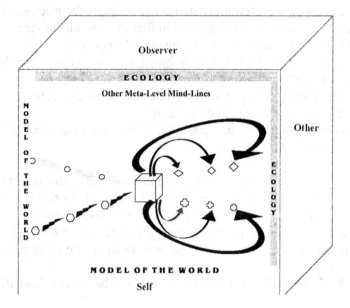

THE SPACE CUBE

In the previous interactions, coach and client share a common space that we call *here*. The *here* position refers to an extended first position, where all the people in *here* can refer to themselves as *we* and which others can recognize as fourth position.

By opposition *there* forms an extended second position and when we refer to people in *there*, we say *you,* which can be singular or plural.

The equivalent of the extended third position in *space* is *elsewhere.* We refer to people in *elsewhere* as he, she, it, they. In the following, we invite the client to perceive the issue from *elsewhere.*
    What is an alternative view?

We apply the reframe *here about there* when we ask:
    What was it about that situation that made you feel sad?

We apply the reframe *here about elsewhere, here about there.*
    How do you think ideas about this type of behavior are going to change over the next 10 years in society, in your school of therapy?

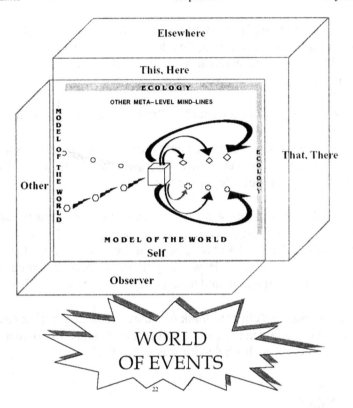

THE TIME CUBE

If we think of space we also think of time. For every *here, there and elsewhere,* we also have a *now, then and else-when* (some other time). Developmental psychologists say that our awareness of space precedes our awareness of time. Indeed we perceive and refer to time in terms of space. Until the advent of digital technology in the twentieth century, we identified the passing of time through progression across space. We did that in terms of the sun, moon, or stars moving across the sky, a shadow moving across a sundial, a hand moving across the clock, water flowing down a waterclock, sand falling down an hourglass, and a candle dwindling. Only bells marking time could represent time digitally to distant listeners, but even bellringers required a space-based device to know the time in order to mark it in the first place.

"Time" functions as meta-space, *now* as an extension of *here* and *then* as an extension of *there.* Notice the lack of specificity of the word *then.* Without a time referent we do not know whether it refers to a past or future situation. Notice also how the unspecificity of *then* may explain why we do not have an equivalent of *elsewhere* in the time dimension, although we could call it *else-when.*

This now allows us to multiply every pattern into time as we did with space. Although it relates to similar terrains, this domain is not the same as that of Pre-and Post Framing. These relate to conceptual or subjective time, as explored within an interaction between a coach and client.

We can ask a question and using a *cause* (a Pre-Framing pattern) let it unfold into *then* (future):

> What do you think will cause the necessary change of mind in society? And what will be the cause of that? Maybe by then they will have evolved new values of tolerance and respect.

Similarly we could say the following where *Consequence* (a Post-Framing pattern) unfolds into *then* (past):

> If something like this had taken place in the past it would have had terrifying consequences. How do you think people would have rationalized it then that would have enabled them to live with it?

In the following we ask the client to think of Values occurring in *then* (past):

> What was important in our culture before the war and how could it have led them to think such a behavior was unhealthy?

WHERE TO NEXT

The outer shell of space/time/relationship is a particular Mind-Line category equation at an earlier time, another at *somebody else's* Model of the World in relation to the issue, another at *someone else's* Values, another at a *distant observer's* Model of the World in the future, etc. This means that we continuously operate within an environment made of space/time and relationship as a meta-environment.

The Time Cube

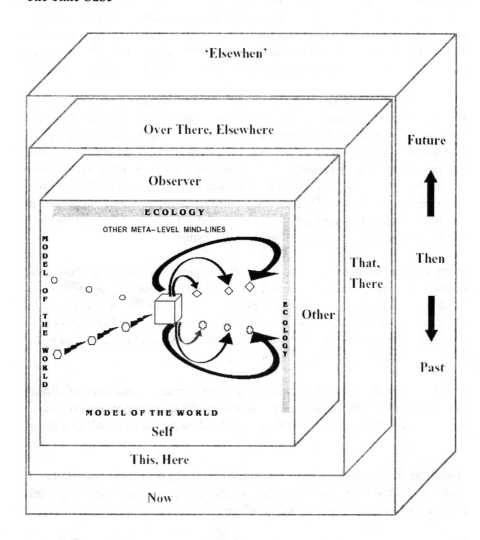

Mind-Lines as Communication #101

It is no surprise that other psychotherapeutic questioning styles easily fit in the Mind-Lines structure. If this was not the case, the Mind-Lines model would not be as robust as we have discovered it to be. As I have compared it with other approaches, it has withstood the test of comparison. The Mind-Lines model has now reached a stage where we can share its effectiveness with other disciplines to our mutual enrichment. NLP originated through such comparison and interaction. Ideally, Mind-Lines should form part of any 101 foundation course on Counseling or Psychotherapy.

All communication has two components, *pacing and leading.* Since the days of Socrates and Aristotle, most of the study of communication has emphasized *leading* the mind into avenues that one sees as desirable. Rogerian therapy redressed this balance by putting emphasis on *pacing,* synchronizing ourselves to another person's style and then leading. However, even this benign approach mismatches the client because paraphrasing distorts what the other means.

The advent of the Meta-Model has enabled us to devise questioning styles which minimize such leading. Much of the emphasis of the Meta-Model charts the structure of pacing. Realizing the necessity of pacing *and* leading as part of effective therapy, communication, and change makes it inevitable that we revisit *leading* to elicit its structure. In declarative mode we utter provocative statements such as the "Sleight of Mouth" patterns to install cognitive dissonance in the listener. We do that to shift a person from a problem state to a solution state. In interrogative mode, this shifting occurs by questioning. Then a person seeks to find an answer to a question.

Many have wondered why some Meta-Model questions and some Mind-Line distinctions, such as universal quantifiers and allness, appear to chart the same territory. They do so from different perspectives and different intentions. In universal quantifiers we respond to an expression of universality that a client has made. We match it and then pace to enable the person to evaluate its truth.
> "Always? Every single time?"

In Allness, we deliberately mismatch the client, initiate an utterance of allness to make the client challenge it and to re-evaluate their own perspective.
> "You always think that everyone who shows up late doesn't care about you."

Notice the role reversal in these two interactions. In universal quantifiers we issue the Meta-Model question while in the latter, the client challenges the utterance to redress the perceived imbalance.

We can now re-evaluate the structure of effective communication. Effective communication requires a balance of the two processes of pacing and leading just as the most profound linguistic mismatch requires a matching, either non-verbal or/and at a higher level of value or outcome mind-lines.

COMMUNICATION	RAPPORT
Pacing	Leading
Similarity	Difference
Matching	Mismatching
Meta-Model Questioning	Mind-Line Utterances
	Declarative/Interrogative Modes
The Practitioner Challenges	The Client Challenges
Elicits the structure of an existing cognitive dissonance to generate a shift	Installs cognitive dissonance in a person to generate shift

SOCIAL CONSTRUCTIONISM SYSTEMIC QUESTIONING

Who is most affected by your behavior and in what ways?	Effect; Ecology; Other; Reality Strategy Now about now; here about there; self about other
When Andrew and Peter look shocked, what do you do then?	Effect; Modality—Sub-modality; Model of World Self about other about self; Outcome; There about there; Now about then (unspecified)
When you tell them to buzz off and get a life, how do Andrew and Peter respond?	Outcome of Outcome; Self about Others; There about There; Now about then (unspecified)
When Andrew agrees that it A=C; might be fun to do this, what does Peter do?	Possibility; Effect; Other about Other; There about there; Now about then (unspecified)
How do you cope with the tension when Andrew and Peter row?	Reality Strategy; Cause; Outcome; Self about Others; There about There; Now about Now
If, one day, you found that all those places had been closed down, what would you do? How would you cope?	Possibility; Allness; Outcome; Strategy; Self about Elsewhere; Here about Elsewhere; Now about Then; Then about Then
If this behavior was declared an acceptable activity by politicians of all parties, would it change your practices in any way?	Possibility; Allness; Ultimate Outcome; A=C; Possibility about Possibility; Allness; Self about Observers; Here about Elsewhere; Now about Then (unspecified) about Then (unspecified)
Are there any circumstances	Allness about Allness; Possibility; Self

in the entire world in which you might do this together?	about Self+Other; Here about Elsewhere; Now about Then (unspecified)
When did you first think of your behavior as "out of control?" When did A first equal B?	Cause of A=B; Value; Self about Self; Here; Now about Then (past)
How did that expression come to mind?	Strategy; Sub-modalities about A=B; Realization; Self about Self; Here; Now about Then (past)
How come you hadn't thought of that expression about that behavior before?	Prior Cause about A=B; Value; Self about Self; Here; Now about Then (past)
How had you thought of this behavior before?	Prior Equation; Value; Self about Self; Here; Now about Then (past)
What is it that you fear you might be "out of control" of — or whom?	Reality Strategy; Value; Outcome; Possibility; Cause; Identity; Self about Other; Here; Now about Now
How do you think your training to be a psychotherapist has influenced your idea that you are "out of control," if at all?	Reality Strategy; Identity; Value; Prior Cause; Quantification of Equation; Allness; D=B; Self about Self; Here; Now about Then (past)
Who do you think might be more alarmed by your behavior —you or your course tutor?	Identity; Possibility; Comparison of Quantification of Equation; Self about Self and Other; Here about There; Now about Then (unspecified)
What does your particular school of psychotherapy say about this type of behavior?	Observer Model of World; Self about Observer; Here about Elsewhere about Here; Now about Now
Who do you think it was who came up with that idea about the unhealthiness of such behavior and when was that?	Identity; Original Cause of A=B; Observer Model of World; Value; Self about Observer; Here about There; Now about Then (past)
How do you think ideas about this type of behavior are going to change over the next 10 years— in society, in your school of therapy?	A=C, D, E, etc.; Then (future) Model of World; Self about extended Observer; Self about extended Self; Here about Elsewhere; Here about There; Now about Then

COGNITIVE-BEHAVIORAL THERAPY
EXAMPLES OF SOCRATIC QUESTIONING

What was it about that situation that made you feel sad?	Reality Strategy; Cause and Effect; Self about Self; Then(past) about Then (past); Here about There
What does it mean to be attracted to someone like this?	Complex Equivalence; What B is this A? What is this B?; Self about Other; Now; Here
What are the advantages or disadvantages and limitations of this?	Outcome; Consequences; Ecology; Now about Then (Future); Self; Here
What are the "truths" about such people's lives and their relationships?	Model of the World; Self about Other; Now; Here
Where did that information come from?	Model of the World of Model of the World?; Model of World somewhere else; Self ; Now about Then (Past); Here
How long have you held this belief?	Reality Strategy; Cause of Cause; Self about Self; Now about Then (Past); Here
Who are the "good" people in your mind and what do you or don't you accept about this?	Identity; Model of World ; Criteria; Self about Other; Now; Here
What is the evidence for and against this?	Reality Strategy; How does A equal and/or not equal B?; Self; Now; Here
What thought distortions are present in your thinking?	Reality Strategy about Reality Strategy; Self about Self; Now; Here
What is the effect of thinking like this?	Effect; Ecology; Self; Now; Then; Here; Elsewhere
What is an alternative view? What else could A be?	Another Model of World, Self; There
Is it better that they know this information now or in several years' time?	Double Bind (Either-Or); Consequences; Ecology; Other; Self about Other about Self; Now about Then (Future); Here about Elsewhere
Is it better to realize that you can never be friends now or	Double Bind (Neither-Nor); Allness about Equation; Reality Strategy;

later?	Realization; Consequence; Evaluation; Possibility; Self about Other; Now about Now; Now about Then (future); Now about Else-when
Will the person still reject you after the initial shock has subsided?	Consequence of Consequence; Possibility; Other; Other about Self; Then (future) about Then (Anterior Future); Here about There about There
What is the worst that can happen if they reject you?	Ultimate Consequence; Possibility; Self; Other about Self; Now about Then (Future); Here about There
How will you cope with this?	Reality Strategy; Self; Now about Then (Future); Here about There

Summary

* It's surprising and delightful to see *the unfolding of the richness of the Mind-Lines model.* I hope that this unfolding provides a similar delight as you see the structural symmetries of the Mind-Lines model. And yet as we know that there is much more within the model that has not yet been charted in relation to the meta-levels, the adventure continues.

* The elegance of the Mind-Lines model enables us to include the questions of other therapeutic approaches into our questions. This comparison contributes to our understanding of the Mind-Lines structure as it clarifies similarities and differences.

* Doing this further clarifies the structure of pacing and leading to build rapport. This clarifies communication itself, at least in English. That's why it may one day form part of the syllabus of Counseling #101 and Communication #101.

End Notes

1. **Author:** Denis Bridoux is the director of Post-Graduate Professional Education in England, an NLP and NS Trainer.

2. This refers to the "Power Zone" pattern in Meta-States, see *The Secrets of Personal Mastery* or *Meta-States Magic.*

3. For more about the SWOT analysis, see *Seven Steps to Emotional Intelligence* by Denis Bridoux.

Chapter 13

MIND-LINES:
THE THEORETICAL FOUNDATION

Mind-Lines and the Meta-Model

As languaged beings, we move through the world using *symbols* to "make sense" of things. Without language, we would experience the consciousness of an animal. We would not live or process the conceptual dimensions that uniquely set us humans apart and that represent the meta-levels of our mind: self, time, space, purpose, destiny, morality, relationship, etc.

Animals obviously think and feel. They do so at a primary level of consciousness. They know things and even experience the meaning level via primary associations. By way of contrast, our consciousness has *a reflexive quality*. It is this reflexivity that ushers us into ever higher levels of awareness which allow us to become *aware of our awareness,* and then aware of that awareness of awareness, etc.

As a semantic class of life, we use symbols as *symbols that stand for something else,* and not as mere "signs" (Korzybski) or mood signals (Bateson). We even develop language systems with a reflexiveness that enable us to meta-communicate about our meta-communications (meta-cognition skills).

Consequently, we move through the world not only using language, but sometimes we forget the true nature of language *as symbolic*. When we do, we *confuse* external and internal realities and then we inescapably live a dilemma. Actually we only operate upon the world indirectly, and only through our language paradigms, and yet our paradigms arise from how we have constructed our perceptions.

These paradigms (e.g., our presuppositions, models, beliefs, values, understandings, decisions, etc.) comprise our *mental constructions or frames of meaning*. Eventually they come to function as unconscious structural elements of our world, which inescapably drive our perceptions, emotions, and behaviors. Or, at least, they do until we develop awareness of them.

Given the nature of human reflexivity, when we become aware of our mental maps as just that—as *mental maps,* we develop mindfulness and "consciousness of abstracting." This enables us to truly experience *choice.* So via our consciousness of abstracting (that is, map or frame awareness), we come to recognize how we have created our own paradigms or beliefs of the world. This opens us up to the *choice* dimension.

A Metalogue

Daughter: So beliefs are not really real; right daddy?
Father: Yes! You have it, daughter. At least they are not real *externally.* Internally, however, they operate as very real. Internally they entirely define and determine things.

So which is it? I wish you'd make up your mind.
Both. Real and unreal. It depends entirely upon your perspective.

What do you mean "perspective?"
From the external point of view, *beliefs* have no reality. They do not exist. That's why you've never stubbed your toe on a *belief* that someone dropped on the sidewalk. Yet from the internal point of view, your *beliefs* create your reality!

So I'm stuck with my beliefs.
No, never.

So while I'm not stuck with my beliefs—I can change them to whatever I want to believe.
Well, kind of ... within certain restraints.

'Restraints?' What do you mean by that, daddy? I have to believe some things?
No daughter, you don't *have to* believe anything. But whatever you do believe —that will become your perceived and felt reality.

That makes it sound as if beliefs are pretty powerful things, like they will determine what I see and feel.
Yes, you have that right.

So it sounds like the key is in learning how to find and change beliefs that don't serve me well.
Very good. You do have an NLP mind after all!

What, you had some doubt ... that have you yet noticed just how gracefully and quickly it vanishes away?
Ah, a mind-line used on your dear ole dad!

Well, did you expect me to read about mind-lines and not apply them?
Another one! Yes *mind-lines* certainly do give us the ability to change beliefs, especially limiting ones, and to relanguage our very neuro-linguistic reality, and to shift our paradigms.

Shift paradigms? Why do you keep using these big words?
To impress you, of course. Do you feel impressed yet?

Oh, go on, what do you mean about these pair of dimes?
Paradigms—you know, *models of the world.* By *mind-lining* someone's belief, you can alter and transform the operational paradigms that guide his or her everyday actions. Doing so also reframes perspectives and meanings and creates new mental maps that will take your plans where you would truly like to go.

Well, I'd prefer to go out for a pizza for supper tonight, wouldn't you?
Not smooth enough. I caught that.

So you're saying that you don't have to remain stuck in any attitude, viewpoint, interpretation, meaning, emotion, reality, or interpretation?
Precisely.

So dad, you can get unstuck from your attitude of avoiding taking me out for a pizza before you allow yourself to relax all the way into the excitement of wondering, really wondering just how much more skilled I'll become with these mind-lines, can you not?
That was good, daughter. What kind of a pizza do you want?

Paradigm Frames
—Models that Reflect and Create "Reality"

A paradigm refers to a model or pattern. In his classic book, *The Structure of Scientific Revolutions,* Thomas S. Kuhn (1962) used the word paradigm as the model that "normal science" operates from containing rules, hypothesis, etc. Later Stephen Covey (1987) and Peter M. Senge (1990) popularized the term *paradigm* for the domains of business and management.

A paradigm, as *a mental model of the world,* refers not only to those ideas, understandings, and beliefs that present themselves in consciousness, but also to our deeply ingrained assumptions, generalizations, and presuppositions. We use such frames to understand, perceive data, and take action in the world.

What happens when one of our paradigm changes? Kuhn (1962) showed that it changes our world. In the history of science as people created new paradigms about the world, the new paradigm led scientists to adopt new instruments and to look in new places enabling them to see new and different things.

"It is *as if* the professional community had been suddenly *transported to another planet* where familiar objects are seen in a different light and are joined by unfamiliar ones as well." (p.111)

In this, a paradigm both *reflects* a worldview or reality and *creates* such. This explains why, when we shift our paradigms, we shift our very world, our neuro-semantic experiences which govern our perceptions and personality. It completely and radically transforms subjective reality which then effects the way we interface with the external world.

Illustrations of paradigm shifts pervade almost every age. This includes such things as the Copernicus revolution which changed the way people thought about the heavens, the earth, and the universe itself. The evolution paradigm radically shifted the creation paradigm—each defining a very different experiential world where the people lived.

The Swiss first began developing digital technology when it first appeared, but the Swiss developers just couldn't "see" that people would prefer digital watches over the high quality Swiss watches. That belief caused them to miss the digital watch revolution.

Edwards Deming tried to get Americans to become aware of the importance of quality control after the Second World War. But they didn't get it. So Deming went to Japan where they welcomed his paradigm shift about business management of empowering and entrusting employees to take ownership of quality.

And what shall we say of the shift from Newtonian physics to Einsteinian physics at the beginning of the twentieth century? Or what of the difference between the psychology of pathology paradigm (based on the medical model, a remedial orientation, and a focus on problems) to the wholeness paradigm in Cognitive-Behavioral Psychology and the Human Potential Movement in the 1960s with a new focus on mental-and-emotional health and solutions?

As frames of reference and meaning, paradigms shift.

When paradigms shift, those embedded within enter into new worlds, live within new frames, and experience a whole new range of solutions, opportunities, and even problems. The changes frequently seem utterly magical because our frames-of-reference create and reflect meanings. Our *meanings* operate as functions of our frames.

How do we discover what something means to someone? We look first to the person's talk and behavior to see the frames lurking in the background. Functionally, paradigm frames offer an unified world-view, a way of organizing perceptions, and a way to make sense of data.

Because "The map is not the territory" no paradigm perfectly describes or models the territory. A model is only and always an abstraction *from* the territory and a map *of* the territory. If our scientific and personal paradigms never express a perfect correlation with reality, we must forever keep open the question about their degree of correspondence and their usefulness or productivity of so mapping. At best maps are only adequate for navigating some experience, and never "the truth."

Viewing things in this way enables us to avoid becoming too wedded to our paradigms; they empower us to remember that our thinking is only a particular way of mapping things. Mindful that we neuro-semantically abstract from the world and operate in life through our frames saves us from mis-believing that our perceptions *are* real.

We experience the shifting of frames or paradigms in the reframing patterns as powerful, and sometimes incredibly profound, because changing a mental frame transforms our subjective sense of reality. Frames of mind govern emotions and neurology. The level of paradigm shifting that we do in mind-lining gives us a place for creating pervasive and lasting change.   Changing our operational frames in that way can completely transform our world. And from that, an entirely new reality can emerge and that gives birth to new possibilities, opportunities, creations, and experiences.

> Changing a mental frame transforms our subjective sense of reality because our frames of mind govern our emotions, skills, health, and neurology.

When Reality Changes
*   How do we change neuro-semantic reality?
*   What are the mechanisms which govern the change process?

Our personal experience of reality forms and changes because we do not and cannot operate on the territory directly. We can only do that indirectly. We only operate upon "reality" via our models of the world.

This is our neurological constitution. We do not see all of the electromagnetic wavelength. We only see via the *transforms* that our sensory receptors (rods, cones, neuro-pathways, visual cortex, etc.) allow us to see. Creatures with different internal constructions to their eyes create different models for seeing. We all construct models of the world as our frames. As we operate from these models as our paradigm frames, they internally organize our psycho-neuro functioning.

> *Meaning emerges from, and operates according to, the frames that we put around events, situations , and ideas.*

Here *the contexts* and concepts that we apply to the information that we hold in mind controls our derived and attributed meanings. Here our meanings change with the ever shifting of our frames or paradigms. So when we change a frame, our meanings change. This explanatory model provides the theoretical basis of reframing and explains the plasticity of *meaning.* Ultimately, whatever we think/believe about something—so it "is" to us.

If we accept the Ptolemaic paradigm and conceive the earth as flat, the center of the universe, and the sun as circling this planet, etc., then we *experience* life as on a flat earth. *As we frame it, so it is.* As we believe so, amazingly we find evidence for it. We develop "eyes" for seeing and inventing supporting facts. The frame attracts events, experiences, ideas, etc. to us that support it. This describes the double-bind of a frame. Once we accept a frame, it becomes increasingly difficult to step outside and to remember that it is just a frame.

This explains in part why so many different kinds of therapy procedures, theories, techniques, etc. work. In different contexts with different people every school of psychology *works* to some extent. Research shows that every school of therapy succeeds to some degree. Even "no therapy" works and creates a therapeutic effect! Given enough time and ongoing life experiences, most people recover from upsets, set-backs, depressions, and other emotional distresses.

How can we explain this wide variation of techniques, interventions, and theories? In human experiences *our psycho-logics* do not work mechanically as if they were mere stimulus/response circuits. The world of mind and communication is a very different world from the external world of physics. The internal world of thoughts, ideas, emotions, meanings, etc. differ radically from the realm of the "hard" sciences. When it comes to subjective experiences (i.e., the world of communication, meaning, and information), we have to consider the role and place of *meaning*, the role of paradigms and frames. In this reality, *cognitive plasticity* dominates.

> *As we frame it, so it is.* At least to us. And as we believe in such, we amazingly find evidence for it. We develop "eyes" for seeing and inventing supporting facts.

So, if the frame controls the meaning and subsequently influences emotions, states, experiences, behaviors, etc., then when we frame things in ways that make solution possible this intervenes at the paradigmatic level and one that we typically experience as outside of consciousness.

Identifying Paradigm Frames
- If paradigms and frames offer us such an incredible port of entry into the internal subjective world (our own and that of others), *how* do we identify "an operating paradigm?"
- How can we become more skilled in spotting frames?

As a model about mental models, the *Meta-Model* provides an excellent tool for this. This model offers insight and practicality in identifying and working with our mental mapping. Bandler and Grinder (1975) originally developed this model using Chomsky's (1956) Transformational Grammar (TG) to understand how language works in the transformation of meaning and how to enrich a person's model of the world. [All of the following runs with *the depth* metaphor so prominent in TG and in NLP.][1]

To do this, the Meta-Model distinguishes surface sentences and the deep structures. In every sentence we hear or utter gives us *levels of representation*. Within and below our everyday surface sentence statements we can discover a fuller set of representations. The "deep" structure contains a fuller representation of our meanings than does the surface structure. What we say "on the surface" reflects a higher level abstraction and so suffers from the modeling processes of deletion, generalization, distortion, and nominalization.

Deletions:
    We impoverish our maps by simply leaving things out. We omit, overlook, or forget.
Generalizations:
    We impoverish our maps to the extent that we lose detail and richness about the original experience. We generalize crucial distinctions as we try to standardize things and detect patterns for similarity.
Distortions:
    We impoverish our maps by turning processes into things (nominalizations). We freeze the world and make it static, inflexible, and not subject to change. We then feel stuck and victimized.

The linguistic distinctions of the Meta-Model gives us sets of *questions* for moving between levels, from the surface sentences to the deep structures [from the movie to the higher governing frames]. By recognizing the fuller representation we can examine the meanings attributed and created in our map-making. The questioning experience also sends the listener back to the experiences out of which the person made his or her maps allowing one to re-map or reframe.

There were other sources in the development of the Meta-Model. Bandler and Grinder developed the communication model by studying gifted therapists who effected powerful and effective therapeutic changes. Through modeling Fritz Perls, Virginia Satir, and Milton Erickson, they discovered how these world renown therapeutic wizards did their word "magic." In explanation, they wrote:

> "...the magic as *introducing changes in their clients' models* which allow their clients more options in their behavior... each has a map or model for changing their clients' model of the world—i.e. a Meta-Model—which allows them to effectively expand and enrich their clients' models..." (1975, p. 18)

In the first Meta-Model 12 *linguistic distinctions* were used to discover the structure of a person's frames. Via the linguistic cues in the model, by listening to a person's ongoing statements we can develop an intuitive sense of the supporting structures or frames. This enables us to recognize the person's way of mapping as well as where and how the person's mapping suffer limitations.

Upon detecting and identifying a person's mental model, we can meta-model the framing to clear up the parts that lack clarity or precision. We can also use the model for ourselves to fill in missing or deleted pieces, to clear up distortions, and to specify generalizations more precisely.

Because we do not operate directly on the world, but move through the world *with* and *through* our frames, our mapping guides our everyday thinking, perceiving, speaking, and behaving. The heart of mapping involves making distinctions which creates our perceptions and elicits our behaviors. Any behavior that does not make sense comes from a map that differs from our own. Conversely, by acquainting ourselves with another's map, we recognize how that person's experiences make sense on the inside.

The Meta-Model distinctions give us the ability to step back and evaluate the degree that the *form* of the map is well-formed or ill-formed. That's why the model focuses on *structure or form,* not content. The *questions* in the model allow us to explore the impoverished parts of maps that are not well-formed in order to enrich them.

Why is this important? Because we know that the words in our linguistic maps only work to our benefit if they *trigger* clear and precise sensory representations or cue us to use enhancing ideas. Whenever we lose or distort important information during the process of codifying experience into language, we end up with impoverished frames. To enrich our lives the Meta-Model enables us to decode the old formations, get back to the experience, and create a fuller and more productive mapping.

Does the Meta-Model Depend on TG?
What follows is an important aside to this description and history of the Meta-

Model. In the years since Chomsky's revolutionary formulations of language, which became *Transformational Grammar* (TG, 1956, 1965), and which brought about the demise of Behaviorism, a great many changes occurred in the field of Linguistics.

The biggest change occurred at about the same time that Bandler and Grinder generated their Meta-Model, namely, Transformational Grammar died. This came about due to the intense intellectual work of Chomsky and his associates as they took his model and pushed it to its logical conclusions. As a result Chomsky (1976) rejected the Deep Structure (D-Structure) and then pursued other formulations such as EST (Extended Standard Theory). Lakoff, McCawley, Ross, and others created *Generative Semantics* (mentioned, in fact, by Bandler and Grinder, 1975, p. 109), but that model also "died" within a few years. Harris (1993) details the controversies, the rise and falls of models, and other developments in Linguistics in his *The Linguistic Wars*.

Currently, various forms of *Cognitive Linguistics* (Lakoff, Johnson, Langacker, and others) have taken the field by storm. Actually these newly formulated models offers a better correlation with the NLP and Neuro-Semantics models. They start from many of the same philosophical assumptions as they have explored *how* the brain represents words and referents in "mental space."

This raises an important question with regard to the validity of NLP, the process of reframing, and the Mind-Lines model.
- Does the Meta-Model *depend on* Transformational Grammar?
- If it does, then to what extent does it depend on TG?

The good news is that it does not. In fact, it surprises many to discover that except for some linguistic jargon (i.e., nominalization, modal operators, etc.), the Meta-Model *only* uses one thing from TG—the idea of *levels* (surface and deep). It doesn't need any of the transformational rules or other facets of TG. *Levels* is really the only thing that the Meta-Model took from TG. Yet for this distinction we do not need the surface and deep structures of TG because we have the idea of levels in Korzybski's *Levels of Abstraction model*. From that set of levels, in fact, the Meta-States model evolved.[2]

The Meta-Model Strategy
Since we all communicate our mental models by means of our surface statements, *language* provides a pathway to our mapping and framing. Here the *Meta-Model questions* work powerfully in assisting us in both detecting and transforming our frames. These questions facilitate our ability to recover missing pieces, straighten out distorted information, reconnect to referent experience, and re-map more effectively. By the process of *meta-modeling* we can bring clarity out of chaos, de-energize the limiting rules in our mental maps,

and transform our mental frames.

Using the Meta-Model directs us to listen for specific words indicating the linguistic distinctions. From the words, we then *construct a representation* in our mind based *solely* on those words. In other words, we representationally track from the words directly to our mental movie. Then we ask:
- Do I have a complete set of representations?
- What have I not been able to representationally track?
- What is missing?
- Are there any limitations in this representation?

The process of *meta-modeling* means listening for the linguistic distinctions that indicate a limitation in representationally tracking from words and sentences to our movie. If the language is ill-formed in terms of representing, then we ask questions to get a fuller description. From there we can look for problematic frames that creates any mapping problems. If it does, we question the mapping which typically invites and provokes the person to expand his or her map.

The attitude we assume in this questioning is one of ***not knowing*** the other's mental world. Assuming nothing frees us to curiously explore whatever the person says and to do so until we gather high quality information.

> "All the techniques of every form of therapy are techniques which affect the processes of representation, or the creation and organization of a clients' model of the world. To the degree that techniques induce change in a clients' modeling of the world is the degree to which they will be effective in assisting a client to change. As a client's model of the world changes, his perceptions change and so, too, does his behavior." (II, page 195)

The Meta-Model gives us numerous linguistic markers that we can use as we search for the problems in mapping and framing. These provide an avenue to understanding a person's frames or beliefs. These linguistic markers include:
- *Causation statements:* How we model the way the world works, functions, relates to itself, etc.
- *Equation statements:* How we create models about what things mean, what abstractions equate with behaviors, and the paradigms of significance about things.
- *Value words and ideas:* The model of ideas about what we think important and significant.
- *Identifications:* The paradigm that we use for self-identification.
- *Presuppositions*: Unquestioned assumptions that we assume as true.
- *Nominalizations:* Verbs we turn into nouns so that we talk about processes as if things.
- *Modal operators:* Terms designating our style (*modus operandi)* in the

world: necessity, desire, possibility impossibility, choice, etc.

As we simply learn how to pay attention to these facets of the linguistic maps that occur in our everyday language, we learn to hear frames, the structural organization of a person's subjective world.

The Structural Format of the Meta-Model
Since we create our neuro-linguistic reality via map-making and representing (neurological and linguistic abstracting) and encode this at various levels, we can now explore with someone *how that person does it.* In other words, we model the person's *modeling* of the territory. Knowing that we all have abstracted, we track the style and nature of our abstracting.

Korzybski said that abstracting is what "flesh" does. Our protoplasm and senses organize *experience* the world in the form of various energy manifestations knocking on the doors of our senses (our eyes, ears, skin, nose, tongue, etc.). From this, our sense organs *abstract*, that is, summarize, conclude, reduce. We begin with neurological abstracts and eventually create linguistic abstractions (i.e., constructions of cause-effect, meaning equations, identifications, etc.).

By using the linguistic distinctions of the *Meta-Model* we explore with a person his or her language to discover what and how that person has framed things. These distinctions give clue regarding the extent to which our map may suffer from conceptual limitations. They may also indicate significant places in our mental mapping where we have left out significant information (deletions), over-generalized into vague categories (generalizations), nominalized processes (nominalizations), and altered things (distortion). Sometimes these deletions, generalizations, and distortions enhance life, sometimes they impoverish.

From these linguistic distinctions, sets of questions emerge that enable us to map and represent things more fully. In this way, the Meta-Model gives us a way to think and talk about how we engage our mapping and framing processes. Identifying the innate modeling processes gives us some categories for thinking about our mental maps, or *thinking about our thinking*.

Deep and Surface Structures
Wedded as it was to Transformational Grammar, the original Meta-Model assumed that every sentence has *levels*. Deep structure doesn't mean "deep" as in "more profound," it rather describes *prior* abstractions *before* the surface level abstractions. The deep structure consists of "what a complete representation of the sentences' meaning or logical semantic relation would be." It represents a linguistic or verbal description from our mental model.

Inasmuch as we "think" via internal representations of sights, sounds, sensations, and words (the movie we create), frequently moving from sensory based referents to the deep structure leads us to experience a fuller description of the world in less abstract words. Someone says, "I'm really depressed!" What do we represent with that? Not much at all. So we meta-model, "How specifically do you know that you feel depressed?" Typically, the person will access a reference experience that thereby recovers the movies that the person is playing from which he or she draws that conclusion. This recovers the pre-generalization data and gives us a peek into the person's style of mapping.

As we "go back to the experience" out of which we mapped something, Meta-Model questions trigger trans-derivational searches (TDS). We "go inside" to find and re-experience the fuller structure—the original experience that we have encoded. The person who engages in a trans-derivational search on depression will have identified his or her reference structures.

Did your brain go somewhere when you read the nominalization, "depression" a moment ago? Or did you stay present, recognizing that there was not enough information for representing? Did you stay here in this time and place or did the word send you inward on some time-traveling? We make sense of things in our mind linguistically and in our body neurologically precisely because we have this marvelous ability to use symbols in this experiential way. The symbol can evoke a time-traveling search on the inside as we go to our own internal "library of references."

Bandler and Grinder (1975) wrote,
> "Transformational grammar is based on the study of *how meaning is transformed into words.* We call the words the surface structure. The actual meaning, or experience, underlying the words is the deep structure. The Meta-Model is built to help you get at the underlying deep structure by clarifying information given in the surface structure." (pp. 96-97)

The design of using the Meta-Model in this way is first of all to *recover the deep structure,* that is, a fuller representation and framing. We can then question the map that we have made of that experience and transform it into a more enhancing map. The principle is that people experience pain, not because the world lacks the richness for them to satisfy their needs, but because *they operate with impoverished representations.*
> "One way in which our models of the world will necessarily differ from the world itself is that our nervous system systematically distorts and deletes whole portions of the real world. This has the effect of introducing differences between what is actually going on in the world and our experiences of it. Our nervous system, then, initially

determined genetically, constitutes the first set of filters which distinguish the world— the territory—from our representation of the world—the map." (1975, p. 9)

The strategy is to re-connect with the experience and to create a richer set of representations and meanings. As we do this, we develop more mindfulness and choices. So as impoverished representations lead to pain, limitation, and fewer choices, expanding and enriching our representations creates less pain, more pleasure, and more choices. Of course, even the deep structure derives from a fuller and richer source which also "is" not the world, but only an earlier abstraction. And beyond the deep structure lies the sum total of all of our experiences of the world, the sensations originating in the world (1975, p.159).

The Frame Games Model
Since we now know that every statement, idea, belief, etc. comes packaged in some *frame-of-reference,* our frames and frames-within-frames give form to our mental mapping which we use as we orient ourselves for various tasks, experiences, and people. So above our internal representations of specific visual, auditory, and kinesthetic components (the movie), we have higher level frames that *drive* those movie representations.

In *reframing,* we first detect and identify the operational frames that we use as we process information which creates our experiences. From there we can shift those frames to generate new and different meanings. Reframing shifts our perspective and so restructures our cognitions and meanings.

Reframing changes meanings by changing *reference frames.* Subsequently this has a rippling down effect so that with the transformation of meaning comes changes in responses and behaviors. All reframing models change responses through altering the governing frame.

This exemplifies the Meta-State principle, *Whoever sets the frame governs the experience.* Because frames govern perceptions, understandings, values, emotions, behaviors, etc. *whoever* (or whatever) establishes a frame of reference thereby has control of the resultant neuro-linguistic reality and experience. This is both scary and exciting, isn't it?

Scary because people and cultures can establish frames outside of our awareness. This partly explains the power of the mind-lines. Language doesn't just work at one level, it operates at many levels. When someone sets a frame at a higher level by implication, presupposition, or outframing, and we buy it or unconsciously step into it, they can *conceptually box us in* without us realizing it.

Exciting because once we learn how to assume ownership over this process, and learn how to play *Frame Games* (2000), we can choose our inner game of frames. We can design the frames and commission them to *take charge* of our mental and emotional responses which make up our outer game. This also protects us from those who might otherwise "set the frame" inducing us into feeling "manipulated" by their "mind control."

Mind-lines occur all around us. They come at us from every media (e.g., newspapers, television, books, speeches, everyday conversations, sale pitches, etc.). Now we can *catch them*. Now we can choose which ones to welcome in and which ones to buy into.

This again, highlights one of the most fundamental principles in Neuro-Semantics: *meaning does not exist in the world.* Meaning only, and exclusively, exists in and by a human mind as it abstracts (i.e., thinking, evaluating, explaining, attributing, believing, interpreting, etc.).

What exists in the world at large are events—*events which provide stimuli for our representing, abstracting, and framing.* The frame-of-reference we put around a stimulus completely determines the meaning it has for us in how we experience it. By reframing, we attach new meaning to the same sensory stimuli to generate new responses in us. In reframing then, we do not change the world, we change the meanings *we* attribute to the world.

> **In reframing, we do not change the world,**
> **we change the meanings we attribute to the world.**

The Inevitability of Framing

James Coyne (1985) says that Bateson is generally given credit for invoking the term "frame" to indicate the organization of interaction which then creates the predisposition that makes us more likely to see and interpret certain events in a particular way.

> "Ascription of a particular frame to an interaction is a statement about what is happening and the experience of participants or observers. Acceptance of a frame allows its users to perceive, identify, and label the events that are occurring, but it may also involve taking a particular attitude toward them." (p. 338)

Creating or imposing a frame on anything involves a meta-communication and so creates *the context* and *set of perceptual filters* by which we then think and feel. This was at the heart of Bateson's argument, any meta-communication may be construed as a frame. Coyne also notes how numerous philosophers have noted the complexities that arise from the hierarchical, nested quality of frames.

> "More recently, experimental social psychologists have begun to explore the determinants of the level at which an activity is framed, and how this may be altered." Why? "Preliminary experiments suggest that when an action can be framed at both a higher ('having a boring life') and a lower level ('watching television all afternoon'), there will be a tendency for the higher level framing to become prepotent, with the lower level framing ignored." (p. 339-340)

The embedded nature of frames nested in a hierarchy of frames gives us a way of thinking about *the levels of mind* and why going meta to the highest frames has a pervasive and profound power in changing everyday expressions. Yet in our everyday experiences, we typically do not give much attention or consideration to our frames. Rather, when we think about the details of our lives or our actions (the story), we seem particularly impressionable about *the overall meaning* of what we are doing. We notice the *gestalt* and don't analyze its levels or structure.

Concepts organize our reality and govern our emotions, perceptions, and behaviors. Benjamin Whorf (1954) noted the *organizing power* of the mind a long time ago:

> "The categories and types that we isolate from the world of phenomena we do not find there because they stare every observer in the face; on the contrary, the world is presented in a kaleidoscopic flux of impressions which has to be organized in our minds." (p. 213)

We organize, construct, and frame things using concepts to form and constrain our experience. As we so frame things, our *experienced reality* arises as the interaction of our minds with the world. Bring a different mind to the world, and our experience of the world changes. This secret of magic is the heart of reframing.

Summary

• The magic that surrounds us, creates our neuro-semantic reality, and orders our sense of reality is the magic of symbols, words, and language. It is this magic that can transform life into a living hell, full of monstrous fears, dreads, hates, etc. or into a living paradise of delight, love, wonder, growth, appreciation, and never-ending learning. The choice lies with us—with our frames.

• The Meta-Model is the foundation of the *Mind-Lines* model. What the Meta-Model does overtly and explicitly as a questioning model, Mind-Lines does covertly. Mind-Lines gives us the ability to *conversationally reframe* ourselves and others for fun and profit.

• May you thoroughly enjoy the process of becoming *a wise magician* so that you can use your words to bring pieces of heaven into your world and all of the worlds of those you touch!

End Notes:

1. In Neuro-Semantics, we turn the metaphor upside down and think of language representations in terms of the *representational level* where we record a video track and a sound track along with a smell and taste track. The kinesthetic track occurs when we step into the *movie* that we play in our mind. From there words and sentence gives us a whole range of frames that influence and govern the movie: comparison, universality, degrees, rules, sources, vague abstractions, causation, equations, identifications, stories, and assumptions.

2. All of this background is detailed in *Communication Magic* (2001) which contains a 25 year update on the Meta-Model and the new distinction that expand and enhance the Meta-Model.

Magic
as described by Bandler and Grinder

"While the techniques of these wizards are different,
they share one thing:
they introduce changes in their clients' models
which allow their clients
more options in their behavior.
What we see is that each of these wizards
has a map or model
for changing their clients' model of the world,
i.e. a meta-model
which allows them to effectively expand and enrich
their clients' model in some way
that makes the clients' lives richer
and more worth living."

(*The Structure of Magic,* 1975, p. 18)

PART IV:

THE MIND-LINES

WORKSHOP

Chapter 14

INTO THE FRAY
OF MIND-LINING

• Are you ready to enter the fray of everyday life and use your knowledge about how we create meaning to invent wild and wonderful *lines* that can change minds?
• Are you ready to use your linguistic skills to more effectively deal with excuses, complaints, irrational arguments, non-sense, manipulation, and objections?

Good. Then let's do it. *Mind-Lines is a model of communication, influence, and persuasion.* As the model presents a structured way to think about the structure of meaning, it gives us a way to shift meaning. It gives us a way to offer new and different perspectives on things.

We call this section *The Mind-Lines Workshop* because these chapters will offer some of what we present in the actual trainings. We have intentionally designed this section to repeat many of the key themes already mentioned. The repetition here is designed to make them even more firmly installed as part of your skills. Welcome then to the Mind-Lines Workshop. Pull up a front row seat and get ready to practice your skills as you develop your competence in handling mind-lines.

Revisiting the first Mind-Line Response
If you remember, we put at the beginning of this book a section that we entitled, *Mind-Lining a Toxic Idea.* Do you remember that (pages 13-18)? In that section we used *the mind-lines analysis* to work over one toxic idea, the morbid belief that "not accomplishing a goal means failure." Now that you have become fully acquainted with the *Mind-Lines model*, we recommend revisiting those pages. We believe that you will now find the mind-line responses richer and more impactful.

In this chapter we have provided two more extensive examples of *mind-lining*. People from all around the world have used these mind-lines as an example for creating all kinds of new neuro-linguistic magic in business, personal relationships, marketing, management, education, therapy, sports, etc.

What can you use the *Mind-Lines* model for? You can use it for excuses, arguments, or even for a conceptual "problem." Any mental or perceptual way of looking at something, a phrase, belief, or statement that bugs the daylights out of you is fair game. When that happens, don't just stand there looking at your *magic wand*—wave it for all its worth!

Twenty Ways to Reframe "Learning Difficulty"
Here is a *toxic thought to reframe:*

> "I can't learn Mind-Lines because they involve too much complexity about the structure of the language patterns."

Mind-Lines analysis of the *formula* governing the black magic in that idea
> "Too much complexity"(E.B.) —>/ = "I can't learn" (I.S.)

1) Specificity or "Chunking" Down
"Complex," you say? How do you know when to judge something as too "complex?" How do you represent "complex?" How do you know it is complexity and not just one layer of simple ideas upon another? How does the complexity stop you from learning altogether?

2) Detailing the Strategy
How is it that you go into this state? What leads you to first become aware of something as a complex subject? If you first see or say something to yourself, what do you do then? And what comes after that? How do you cue yourself that something has enough complexity to stop learning?

3) Reframe the E.B.
How interesting! What I really find complex and difficult to learn are the chaotic "word salads" that a schizophrenic produces... trying to find order and structure in that—now I'd call *that* difficult!

4) Reframe the I.S.
The problem may seem like that you *can't* learn these language patterns, but don't you think that the real problem lies in *how much effort* you feel that you will have to expend to learn them? You can learn them, but the learning may not come as quickly and easily as you would like it to. Anyway, how do you know to label a subject as "complex" and not just the next step in learning?

5) Reflexively Apply To Self
What? I don't understand. Why do you have to make such difficult and complex complaints? I just can't figure out what you really mean by these complicated complaints.

6) Reflexively Apply to Listener

Wow! That seems like a pretty complex analysis of your learning strategy! Where did you learn to think and reason in such a complex way?

7) Counter-Example Framing

So do you mean to tell me that you've never learned anything that once upon a time might have seemed complex to you? Somehow, the existence of complexity itself prevents you from learning?

8) Positive Prior Intentional Framing

I wonder if you see learning in terms of complexity in order to not feel overwhelmed by something? I'm sure it protects you from taking on too much and maybe from feeling dumb. Could it also be that this belief about complexity protects you from failing to learn something new and exciting?

9) Positive Prior Causation Framing

When you described your experiences in the fourth grade with that teacher who pushed you so hard, it impressed me that *that* perhaps was the initial experience from which you made this map about complexity. Being pushed too hard and too fast without proper priming would make a subject seem complex and overwhelming.

10) First Outcome Framing

So if you use this belief and let it run your life, next year you will make no further progress in learning these language patterns. How does that settle for you in terms of your communication and persuasion skills?

11) Outcome of Outcome Framing

As you imagine *not* learning anything about these mind-lines by next year, and remaining unskilled in them again the following year—what will that lack of progress lead to? And after that, what will result from getting that outcome?

12) Eternity Framing

When you imagine stepping into eternity as you leave this world, and think about having avoided learning, and especially from learning things that would improve your communication skills, how much do you think you will have missed out on life, relationships, and effectiveness by having let the idea of complexity govern your life?

13) Model of the World Framing

How interesting to posit learning as dependent upon complexity. Do you know where you got this map? From what experience did you map that difficult or layered subjects in some mysterious way have the power to prevent you from learning? How does it strike you now as you realize that this is just a map, and not a very enhancing one at that?

14) Criteria and Value Framing

How important is that to you to avoid complexity in comparison to taking the time and trouble to learn something that challenges your mind? How important is that avoidance related to developing your highest skills?

15) Allness Framing

Since everybody has encountered complex information at some time, does that mean that they cannot or should not attempt to learn such? Would you recommend this to other people? What would happen if everybody on the planet adopted this belief about complexity and learning?

16) Have-To Framing

Do you *have to* see things this way? What would it feel like if you did not use this belief about complexity to think about learning new and challenging things?

17) Identity Framing

Is this *who you are*—someone who will not challenge yourself or take on something that is involved? Are you not a thinker and *learner* who can think about some things in a step-by-step manner, adding one piece of knowledge to another piece until you master a new subject? Is that who you would like to be?

18) Other Abstractions

What if you discovered that learning complexity actually involves the same mental processes as learning the foundational principles of a field? What if you discover that your labeling of a subject as having "complexity" itself creates the difficulty?

19) Ecology Framing

How well does this belief that you can't learn complex things really serve you? Does it enhance your life? Does it increase your motivation and drive for learning? Does it increase your resilience? Would you recommend this belief to others?

20) Metaphoring/Storying and Restorying Framing

When I first saw a Hebrew text of the Bible, I thought, "This is really a complex language. I don't know if I will ever learn this." Then I began to think about the children born to parents who speak Hebrew and how that they just grow up with that language, and that they learn it with as much ease and effectiveness as children in other language environments learn other languages.

Thinking about that made me realize the error in my conclusion about the so-called difficulty of Hebrew. I then realized that Hebrew isn't complex as much as simply different from what I already knew. So as I began at the beginning, I first learned the shape and names of the Hebrew letters. I learned a little bit here and a little bit more there and eventually I gained a level of competency that I could read a page of a text. Yet what previously would have seemed so complex now seemed natural and easy—a piece of cake!

21) Both/And Framing

Could learning these mind-lines be *both* difficult and fun? What if the learning is challenging enough to be tough *and fun*—fun enough to enjoy the toughness?

22) Pseudo-word Framing

What are you referring to by the term "complex?" That learning mind-lines may involve one thought upon another, even layered ideas about the structure of meaning and how to format that structure, is certainly understandable. But "complex?" What if that term itself creates most of the problem regarding learning?

23) Negation Framing

I used to frame learning as difficult. Then I began thinking about it as development, as increasing awareness, as answers to my curiosity. One day I discovered that the very idea of "difficult" had completely vanished away and I began viewing learning as an adventure and challenge.

24) Possibility and As If Framing

I know this may sound crazy, but what if it were possible to view learning complex things as fun? Or, even as easy? Now wouldn't that be a different point of view?

25) Systemic and Probability Framing

What's the probability that learning will be difficult? Are we talking about a 90% probability, 50%, or only 10%? Could there be contributing factors other than the content that makes it difficult? Are you in the right state? Do you have the right motivation? What are you doing to make the learning more fun?

26) Decision Framing

Is this your decision? Have you decided that you will view learning mind-lines as difficult? Would you like to make a different decision? Would you like to make that decision?

Twenty Ways to Reframe Confrontation

A toxic thought:

"I really dread confrontation. It makes me feel anxious and scared. Confrontation never solves anything, it only turns people against each other and it ruins relationships. That's why it is bad."

The Mind-Line analysis of the toxic formula:

"Confrontation" (E.B.) —>/ = "Anxiety, fear" (I.S.)
"Directly saying words" —>/ = Conflict, "bad."

1) Specificity in "Chunking" Down

How do you specifically think about "confrontation?" When you experience a "confrontation" how big do you picture yourself in relationship to others? If I were to peek into the cinema movie of your mind, what would the picture of confrontation look like and what kind of a sound track would you be playing? How loudly do you code the words in a confrontation? What referent experiences do you use?

2) Detailing the Strategy

How do you know to feel anxious or scared when you picture a confrontation? Does it have to be unpleasant? How have you encoded it in an unpleasant way? In the tonality, volume, facial expressions, or what? What do you do first to create this anxiety creating movie, then what? Why not feel curious and excited to discover the differences as you fully listen to another's viewpoint and then work out a win/win arrangement?

3) Reframe the E.B.

If you think conflict or confrontation ruins relationships, try *not* conflicting or confronting to create resolutions. Then, one day something will occur as "the last straw" so that one person won't be able to take it anymore. Then "out of the blue" (or so it will seem) one confrontation will ruin the relationship.

4) Reframe the I.S.

Yes, speaking up and expressing your ideas can feel scary, yet what really evokes anxiety for me is *not* speaking up or surfacing concerns while they are small and manageable. Letting problems fester until they become large and unmanageable—now that's scary!

5) Reflexively Apply To Self

I feel so very anxious right now, and fearful, as you say those words. Bringing this up will destroy our relationship!

6) Reflexively Apply to Listener

So if I bring up anything to you, you have to feel anxious and scared, and think it will ruin things between us? This means you would prefer that I walk on egg-shells in your presence and not relate to you in an authentic or real way?

7) Counter-Example Framing

Thank you for this confrontation—I really appreciate this. I will use this disclosure of yours to relate to you with sensitivity about how things could go awry or hurt your feelings. Just think what might have happened if you hadn't confronted me about this!

8) Positive Prior Intentional Framing

So in learning to feel anxiety and fear, you probably use those feelings to come across to people in a more gentle way. That's great. And I just wonder what other ways you have also found, or could find, that would allow you to incorporate gentleness into your confrontations?

9) Positive Prior Causation Framing

Thanks for telling me about the way your dad "confronted" you as a child. It now makes perfect sense that you'd feel afraid and anxious about "confrontation" with the way he did it. No wonder you mapped confrontation as unpleasant, dangerous, and unproductive. It's a good thing that everybody does not do it in that way.

10) First Outcome Framing

When you think about how you have walked on egg-shells with people, and fail to express your values and perceptions—how do you like those consequences?

11) Outcome of Outcome Framing

How do you like the consequences of people taking advantage of you and your non-confrontational style and using intimidation to get their way with you because they know you won't speak up for yourself? I bet that makes life a party for you!

12) Eternity Framing

When you look back on your life and see how you couldn't speak up for yourself and how you backed off from every conflict and disagreement because of this belief, and see how you over-cared about what people thought of you—how celebrative will you feel about that legacy? How much joy have you missed by not living with self-integrity?

13) Model of the World Framing

Did someone teach you to think about confrontation in this way? Or, did you come up with this on your own? Are you glad that you adopted this belief as your model of the world? Do you know anyone else who has a different perspective that seems to enable them to produce more productive responses?

14) Criteria and Value Framing

Obviously you value peacemaking and harmony, and yet I wonder how honesty, true self-disclosure, and indepth communication with loved ones play into your value of conflict avoidance?

15) Allness Framing

Suppose everybody felt anxious and fearful in bringing up things to others... would you recommend this style of communication? Would you think it would make the world go better?

16) Have-To Framing

Do you *have to* think this way? What *forces* you to keep this old limiting belief? Anything? What would it be like if you did not equate confrontation with negative encounters? What would you have to think to view it in terms of playfulness, lightness, curiosity, and resourcefulness?

17) Identity Framing

Is this *who you are?* You're just an anxious coward? Is that who you want to be? Isn't part of your self-definition that you are a person with thoughts, feelings, and opinions and that you have the right to express yourself honestly? What if you imagined *the you* who did that with dignity, grace, and effectiveness? Would you like that?

18) Other Abstractions Framing

How interesting that you view confrontation in this manner—do you also view *communication* in a similar way? What do you think about *honestly expressing your viewpoint?*

19) Ecology Framing

How well does this belief serve you? How well does it make your life function to equate confrontation with negative relational consequences? How well does it enhance your life for honest communication with those that you love?

20) Metaphoring/Storying and Restorying Framing

I had just started a new job at the Johnson Factory, and I really didn't know all the ins-and-outs of the business. That really became evident on the fourth day when I started to load the delivery truck by the back loading dock. Having observed how the process went, I assumed that I knew how to do it. So I jumped in the big truck and backed it up to the dock.

Then I began loading the truck. Just then Jim came running up yelling... I couldn't tell what he was saying, but at first I felt humiliated that he would talk to me that way! Who did he think he was anyway? As he got closer I heard him yell, "Get the emergency brakes set! Jump back into the truck—the truck won't hold by itself!"

As I looked at the truck, I saw it beginning to move... slowly, ever so slowly... but moving. That's when I began running, jumped into the slowly moving vehicle, and grabbed hold of the emergency brakes. When the truck stopped, I realized that if Jim had not noticed or confronted me when he did, that truck would have rolled through the glass window at the bottom of the hill and through a daycare center. Thank God he had the courage to confront me when he did! I'll always be in his debt.

21) Both /And Framing

Do you need to frame confrontation as bad and destructive to relationships? What if it only sometimes does that, only when two people fail to manage their states and operate from a win/win perspective? It would then be destructive in that case *and* constructive at other times.

22) Pseudo-Word Framing

Could "confrontation" be a pseudo-word with lots of semantically negatively loaded ideas when the real idea is just being straight with each other? What does it mean other than presenting something in a straightforward "face to face" manner?

23) Negation Framing

Remember when you brought up your views and ideas about the new product and expressed your views about the marketing and how that made a difference in the company? And when you remember that, how much does the fear of confrontation just evaporate as you think of it as just expressing a genuine concern?

24) Possibility and As If Framing
>What if you let confrontation be kind and thoughtful directness? If that were possible, if you could confront with kindness and dignity, would you want that?

25) Systemic and Probability Framing
>So that's all there is to confrontation— being nasty or obnoxious to others? What if we let other contributing resources texture it for elegance?

26) Decision Framing
>Have you decided to treat confrontation as a great evil or dread? Is that your choice? I hope you won't decide to let some possible discomfort put you off. Will you do that?

Mind-Lining for Profit

Not long after the second edition of *Mind-Lines* was published, I was hired to consult with a business consultant regarding two of his Fortune 500 clients. He needed some *lines*. His clients were in a quandary about how to respond to some publicity and commercials from those opposing their endeavors. As a media consultant, my contact knew that the very process of running a statement through the mind-line examples would stimulate his creativity and allow him to come up with new scripts that he could use for commercials, press release statements, and that he could even use in his executive coaching with the CEOs of the company.

So that's what we did. For nearly a week, he would call me every morning for a three-hour conference. He would then provide a statement from those opposing the company, statements that he collected from the debates, press conferences, and court hearings of the other side. We would then use the mind-lines formula to analyze the structure of the meaning and how it was framed.

Once we had the problem framed in that way, we would then begin to *play* with those lines. We would first play with the ideas by pulling them apart and deframing them into the component pieces. That gave us lots of data to play with. From there it was easy to give the behaviors and/or the states new meanings, to give them new labels (content reframing). It was also easy to turn them around on the speaker or the listener, to reverse them, to apply to self. After that we pre-framed and post-framed, then danced away at outframing.

It was not only a lot of fun, it was profitable. I made more in that week than I had made in the previous six months of training and seeing clients. It was also extremely profitable for him, and the lines that we created were valuable enough to the company that they subsequently showed up in commercials, company statements, and court rooms.

Frequently, when we started, we both had a stunned sense of feeling stuck and hopeless.

"What in the world can you *say* to that?!"

Yet in every single case, by the time we finished zapping the line with our magic—we felt a certain touch of ferociousness, "Give me another one! Bring it on! Let me have at it!"

And you can too.

Summary

*   There's a new game in town. Instead of crumbling before excuses and complaints or counter-acting by playing the Blame game, we can now step up to play, "Who sets the Frame controls the Game."

*   Ideas run our lives—beliefs, understandings, decisions, intentions, and so on and yet all of these are just frames. And if they are just frames, then we can subject them to quality controlling them to make sure that they serve us well and enhance our lives and expertise.

Chapter 15

EIGHT THINGS
NO, NINE THINGS
EVERY MAGICIAN
NEEDS TO KNOW ABOUT
MEANING

Secrets of Neuro-Semantic Magic

When it comes to understanding, detecting, and working with *neuro-semantic meaning* in our lives and minds, there is no question but that we deal with a complex topic. Philosophers and psychologists have been searching for centuries for a way to understand the entire *meaning making process*. If the way our mind-body system mapped things and created ideas was simple, we would not need such fields. Yet meaning-making is not simple. Actually, we are just now beginning to understand the mystery of the human brain and the mind that emerges from our embodied consciousness.

On the previous pages, we have described *how* meaning emerges from such processes as representation, linkage, linguistic mapping, and reflexive layering. From this we have postulated the *Mind-Lines model* and described ways of using it to transform meaning via conversational reframing. Now we will attempt to summarize and simplify.

In this chapter in the spirit of simplifying, we will streamline our understandings about the framing and reframing of meaning and how that translates to conversational reframing. The focus here is to answer the question: How can we effectively develop a strategic thinking about frames and reframing?

First we have to be crystal clear regarding how we start with *thoughts,* ideas, and information and then transform them into *beliefs* and higher level frames. From there, we create even higher levels as we layer frame upon frame to create a whole series of embedded frames until we create a robust and empowering Matrix or womb of frames wherein our perceiving, emoting, and responding is given birth. We never entertain an *idea* in simple representational form. There are always thoughts in the back of our mind. Our thoughts are always *embedded* in various mental contexts, and those contexts are within contexts and so on.

There are certain conceptual presuppositions that govern the process of the neuro-linguistic magic in *mind-lines*. The following represent the key supporting beliefs that will enable you to become more elegantly skillful in this domain. In this chapter we seek to explore the subject of *meaning:*

- What do we mean by "meaning?"
- What does meaning refer to?
- Where is it? Where does it occur?
- What does it consist of?
- Where did it come from?

THE INSIDE SCOPE ON MEANING

1) Meaning is not real, not externally real.
2) We make meaning out of the stuff of "thoughts."
3) Meaning slips and slides.
4) It's all invented reality, we construct meaning.
5) Meaning occurs in frames-of-reference.
6) Frames govern meaning.
7) He who sets the frame governs the experience.
8) Meaning exists in multiple frames simultaneously.
9) Even "real" meanings may not serve us well.

---

1) Meaning is not *externally* Real

Meaning has no *reality* "out there" beyond our skin. Meaning *only* arises and coheres within a mind; it only exists as part of our internal world. It emerges as a neuro-linguistic product from our interactions with people, events, ideas, etc. As an internal thing, it does not occur "out there," but it occurs as an interaction of event and thought.

What is the effect of thinking about *meaning* in this way? It puts *meaning* under our control. You can imagine how much of a paradigm shift this is for someone brought up to think that language or meaning "is" real in an external and empirical way. External events only have meaning to us as *we* make them meaningful to us.

2) We make Meaning out of the Stuff of "Thoughts"

The word *meaning came* originally from high German and middle English and referred to the thoughts that we *hold in mind.* Whatever we "hold in mind" as our ideas, representations, thoughts, beliefs, etc. are or become our meanings. What do you *mean* by what you say or do? It depends on what you are *holding* in your mind about things.

Consider that statement. Does that reveal the close relationship of *meaning* to *meta-states*? After all, it is not so much what's playing on the screen of our mental cinema that determines our meanings as it is the thoughts that we *hold,* that we keep in the back of our mind, our frames and intentions. These are the thoughts that we *hold* on to and operate from. These are the thoughts that we carry with us on an ongoing basis. These are the thoughts that make up the Matrix of our mind, the sum of our system of embedded frames.

At the first level of meaning we create our sensory-based movie. Here our internal representations map out in sights sounds, sensations, smells, and tastes. This gives us our first symbols for the language of the mind. At the next level we use meta-representational symbols—words and linguistics. Above that we use even higher levels of abstract language. Welcome to the Matrix.

3) Meaning Slips and Slides

As a dynamic non-*thing,* meaning does not have a static or rigid quality. Instead it keeps moving and shifting. Meaning has such plasticity that it is forever bending, stretching, moving, slipping, and sliding. Realizing this helps us from thinking of it or treating it as static, solid, or permanent. It is in flux. If meaning arises *by* mind and *in* mind, then we can expect it to come and go according to the functioning of our consciousness. It doesn't stay put. Now you have it. Now you don't.

We see this most vividly in the ever-shifting nature of meanings. A customer goes out to buy a new car. But what that "purchase of a new car" means to him or her on a given day may change multiple times. It all depends. It depends upon the ideas, memories, referents, values, and thoughts that flow through consciousness.

At first it may mean "getting a more reliable source of transportation." But as the person shops, other meanings may flow into his stream of consciousness. Now it means, "enjoying lookin' good in a sharp machine!" A little later, "a really smart buy—economical, affordable, solid." And then the next minute, "an expression of my power," "an expression of my masculinity," "the envy of my friends," etc.

What in the world is going on? The plastic nature of meaning causes it to bend this way and then that way. Also, there is the multiple nature of meaning. This highlights the most important factor: *meaning* does not (and cannot) exist apart from a *meaning-maker.* It takes a human mind to create, communicate, and experience meaning. Meaning does not exist "in" the car, it arises in the person's thinking and feeling about the car.

Does this represent an entirely new way to think about meaning? It does for most people. And even for those of us who have thought this way about meaning for a long, long time—it can still feel strange.

Why should this *plasticity of meaning* continue to feel strange even if we know this and have thought this way for a long time? Because even though the structure of meaning functions in this manner, the habituation of our thoughts keep seducing us into assuming a false permanence and stability about meaning.

Are there any "old" thoughts about something, something that may have happened decades ago, that you still "hold" in your mind which do not serve you at all? Have you considered simply *changing the meaning of that event?* Do you have permission to do that? Of course, we actually change meanings to past events all the time. It's how our mind and memory works. Yet sometimes we get in a "rut" with some old meanings, forget that it's just a construct, and *hold on to them* even though they make us semantically reactive, even sick.

If you find this strange and scary, then welcome to the club. Most people do. This explains why we typically have to spend some time with this concept to get used to it. In this way we can get over any insecurity or fear about such. That there is a plasticity to meaning does *not* make it so relative that we can make anything mean anything. But it does suggest that we should expect to discover a *fluidity* to meaning such that it keeps shifting and changing, and never stays put.

4) It's all Invented Reality, we Construct Meaning

Precisely because it takes a meaning-maker to create meaning, meaning emerges in our experience as a human construct. Philosophically we call this constructionism. As we now recognize this, it empowers us as we think about and work with "meaning."

Ultimately, we construct our internal realities. The old biblical proverb expressed this in a simple but succinct way, "As a man thinks in his heart, so he is." What we *are* (our reality) operates as a function of our maps (i.e., our perceptions and constructions). This establishes the foundation of our personal responsibility for constructing useful maps.

5) Meaning Occurs in Frames-of-Reference

As a human construct that arises when we use our consciousness to make sense of things, *meaning always exists in some frame.* This explains the source and meaning of the term "frame" and in the idea of reframing in the cognitive sciences.

What significance does this have? It primarily directs us to search for and identify the frame.
- What frame of reference does this idea occur within?
- What frame is this person using to say or perceive this?
- What frame has to be there in order for this statement to make sense?

Frame-less meanings cannot occur. Where you have a meaning, you have a frame of reference. An idea, thought, or emotion as a personal *meaning* attains much of its "meaning" from the ideas, experiences, events that it references.

6) Frames Govern Meaning

We begin to appreciate the power and pervasiveness of our frames when we realize that our frames govern, modulate, organize, drive, and control our experiences. Our thoughts, feelings, language, behavior, and responses are all expressions of our frames. When we set a frame, that frame becomes the governor of our internal universe and reality. It sets in motion certain consequences and conclusions. Korzybski called this "logical fate."

In frame games, we describe the *logical fate* of our frames as our outer *games.* The games that we play in life in our actions, relationships, talk, even our mental and emotional games, are all functions of our frames. Where there is a frame, there's a game. There has to be. And conversely, where there is a Game, there is a frame. Our frames are our inner games, our behaviors are our outer games.
- There are frames that govern the Games that we play with eating and exercising (*Games Slim and Fit People Play*, 2001).

- There are frames that govern the games we play with the things we deem dangerous (*Games for Mastering Fear*, 2001).
- There are frames that govern the games we play at work, in our career, and with money (*Games Business Experts Play,* 2001; *Games Wealthy People Play*).

7) He who Sets the Frame Governs the Experience

All human experiences occur within frames—cultural frames-of-reference, personal frames, family frames, business and economic frames, etc. Even our native language is a frame. In fact, the *language frame* is one of the largest frames that we all unconsciously accept and live within, and which governs so much of our experiences. If you grew up hearing and speaking English, then English will govern how you think, how you perceive, what experiences stand out and count, which do not, etc.

Similarly, our *cultural frame* typically operates outside of our awareness so that we hardly ever notice it. To notice it, we have to *step out of the frame*, perhaps go to a different culture. Then we suddenly become aware of our assumptions about life, relationships, values, etc.. Driving frames in the American culture that are seldom ever questioned include such frames as "bigger is better," "money is the measure of success," "a person's value is measured by achievements," "entertainment doesn't teach, it's just entertainment," etc.

We have no choice about living with frames, framing, and reframing. It's how we think. So as we realize that whoever sets the frame controls the experience, this describes the heart of what happens in relationships and cultures. Someone always sets the frame. Actually, we all live in the midst of many frames —frames embedded within frames. The only questions now become—

- Do you know the frame out of which you operate?
- Does the frame serve you well?
- Who set the frame?
- Do you want to set a different frame?

It works as simply and profoundly as this. If I walked up to you and started talking about my work of researching human resourcefulness, I thereby attempt to set a frame for our conversation. *Setting the frame* refers to setting either *the content* of the subject matter or *the context* for the subject matter. If I ask, "How resourceful do you generally live on a daily basis?" I have set resourcefulness as *the context* of the conversation. Simultaneously, I have set *the content* of the discussion as exploring your evaluation of your own situation.

A subtly occurs in this. Namely, that while the language of the question gets you to focus on *the content* of your life, at a higher logical level, I have actually set a frame whereby I can elicit your higher values, beliefs, understandings, meta-states, etc. I haven't done so explicitly, only implicitly. This is frame by implication. And if we have "ears to hear" we will learn to discover the neuro-semantic structure of a meaning.

The process of Mind-Lining elegantly means learning how to take charge of conversations to direct and control both the content and the context as we converse. When we know how to embed various contents within higher level contexts we will know how to preclude another person's conscious awareness as well as how to include it.

Though conceptual, these understandings about the structure of human meaning play an important role in developing skill with neuro-linguistic magic as we engage in the process of *transforming meaning*.
> 1) Meaning does not exist "out there."
> 2) Meaning slips and slides in its operations.
> 3) We mentally construct meaning.
> 4) Meaning exists in some frame-of-reference.
> 5) The frame governs the meaning.
> 6) He who sets the frame therefore governs the experience.

The Magic Box or Cube
In *Mind-Lines* we encapsulated all of this information by playfully describing it as the Magic Box or Cube. We have two more important conceptual understandings about meaning that we want to add to these first seven.

These basic and supporting keys unlock our understanding of human *neuro-semantic reality*. So, by understanding and accepting them, we become ready to work with *the magical box*. As a semantic class of life we make meanings. Sometimes we find or discover the meanings that others have created and sometimes we invent, construct, conceive, or construct new meanings altogether.

One of the central ways that we do this involves *a linking process*. We link things up. We associate various stimuli with some response and thus the "stimulus" means or equals or leads to that "response" in our nervous system.

Animals create meaning in this way. The dog sees a piece of meat and moves close to it, smells it, and has a response. His autonomic nervous system *reacts* with a response of salivating which prepares his stomach and organism to eating the meat. All the while, an experimenter *rings a bell*. The first time, the dog doesn't respond to the bell except perhaps to cock his ear. This is *Zero Learning* (Bateson). Yet if the meat and bell ringing occurs *together* at the same time or in close approximation, the dog connects the sound of the bell with the meat. He responds to the bell by salivating. This moves us to *Learning I*. We call *the relationship* between the external stuff and the internal stuff "meaning." This is what we put into the Magic 3-D Box in the conceptual equation.

As we move through life, we *link* things with things. Yet some linking does not create an accurate mapping of things.

In one of the larger earthquakes that shook southern California in the 1980s, just moments prior to the quaking of the earth, a mother became upset with her little 5 year old for slamming a door in the house. Just as she began a new rebuke she told him in no uncertain terms that "something really bad will happen if you keep doing this." At that very moment that the boy angrily slammed the door, the whole house simultaneously shook and trembled. Dishes crashed to the floor. Lamps came tumbling down. The absolutely terrified little boy felt that the world was falling apart. And in his nervous system he connected the "slamming the door," the angry disobedience, the sassying of mom to all of the terror of the earthquake. Now he "knew" that being a bad disobedient boy and slamming the door (E.B.) created the earthquake (E.B.) which is devastating (I.S.). His mind-body system connected, "arguing with mom" means "being terrified out of my wit." It causes really terrible things like earthquakes.

This powerfully illustrates the *"logic"* inside the human nervous system. It is not "logical" in a formal way. Nor does it reflect the best of mature human thinking. The *psycho-logic*s inside the nervous system connect all kinds of things together. To an outsider who doesn't know the whole story, the associations may seem very irrational. Yet once we link one thing with another thing—the brain, nervous system, and all connecting human tissue (which means all of our somatic, physical, and body stuff) "knows" at a neurological level that "sassing mom creates devastating effects!" This creates our "intuitive" knowledge.

We Live in the Boxes of Meaning that we Create
We have used the formal language of causation to create "the formula" in Mind-Lines that captures the semantic magic. We describe the formula as the magic box. This formula, as the meaning-making process, offers a structural way to think about how we connect things.

Formally the formula is: $X \longrightarrow / = Y$
In Mind-Lines we use: $E.B. \longrightarrow / = I.S.$

This summarizes how we take an external behavior (like slamming a door or sassing mom) and link it up in *a Cause*—> *Effect structure* so that we think of one thing as leading to another. Eventually the idea of *leading to* becomes *equated with* the idea of "being equal to" and "the same as." At that point we have a Complex Equivalence. An external stimulus "equals" an internal state or the computation of some significance (i.e., a disaster, terrifying fear, pain, horror, etc.). In this way we linguistically punctuate our experience and then encode it with this structure.

Now we have our 3-D Box into which we put our "magic." Whatever we say *leads to* or *is equal to* or *is the same as* something else, so it is—to us. To model this "magic" we have used three key linguistic distinctions from the expanded Meta-Model:

> **Cause —> Effect** statements (C-E)
>> This X leads to this Y.
>
> **Complex Equivalences** (CEq)
>> This X means this Y.
>
> **Identification** (Id)
>> This X means this Y *about me.*

Life in the Box

In our mind-body system of brain, nervous system, mind, consciousness, etc. saying and thinking that one thing *equals* another thing makes it so.

> When she looks at me with that expression, I feel discounted.
>
> When he talks to me in that tone of voice, I know he is angry with me.

It is in this way that we literally speak our internal, subjective reality into being. We box up this meaning, buy the package, and then we live in that box. Then it runs our emotions, behaviors, and responses.

Behaviorists called this internal *"black box"*—a box that they could not look into or test. This phrase *black box* suggests that most of the time we don't have the slightest idea of *how* we have constructed our meanings, or what meanings operate within us as our "programs."

We live mostly unconscious of our meanings and their structure. We assume them and then live, breathe, and move inside them as our mental atmosphere. As our meta-frames of references they function like a conceptual canopy that governs the weather of our mind-and-emotions.

These languaged equations are central to our experiences, skills, abilities, emotions, etc. because they are our meanings. To change we have to change these equations. When we do change the neuro-semantic equations—magic happens. Suddenly everything becomes transformed and new realities pop into existence. Now, for the last two conceptual understandings about meaning.

8) Meaning exists in Multiple Frames Simultaneously

We are now getting to the heart of the problem that creates the mind-body meaning complexity. We not only have primary level "meaning"—this action, experience, event, set of words *linked to and connected to* this idea, thought, feeling, state, etc., we have embedded layers of meaning equations.

To a salesperson a "customer" may "mean" "a source of income," if the person has linked the person looking to buy a product as having that significance to him or her. Of course, a "customer" may also mean other things: "someone who may reject me," "someone who I may enjoy getting to know," "an opportunity to practice my skills," etc.

Figure 15:1

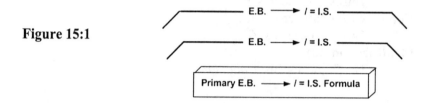

These are the *primary level* connections. "This X means this Y." Yet wouldn't you know that our minds don't stay put. Just as soon as we create a meaning formula, we then entertain another thought about that first one. We think about our thinking. We have feelings about our feelings.

This initiates multiple-levels of meanings. Suppose we begin with *a primary level* thought:

> This person may reject me.

How do you think or feel *about* that? Do you like it? No? Now we have yet another embedded thought:

> I hate my thoughts-and-feelings of feeling vulnerable about being rejected by people.

And how do you feel *about* your *hatred* of your *sensitivity-to-rejection* feelings? You feel guilty about that?

> *Guilty* for feeling *hate/contempt* for *sensitivity to rejection*.

And how do you feel about that? And so on it goes! To understand the *structure* of this word magic in terms of how they work inside our heads, we must understand the reflexivity of our brains. That is, how our brains can have thoughts about thoughts, and then more thoughts about those thoughts. The processing feeds back into itself so that as a cybernetic system, our brain processes its own previous products.

These meta-level meanings refer to meaning *above* other meanings that reference previous meanings. This self-*reflexivity* enables us to move into higher levels of computation as we punctuate our experiences with various understandings.

Self-reflexive thinking creates the complexity and layeredness of thought upon thought, emotion upon emotion. We experience layers of thoughts upon thoughts and these build upon each other to create even more complicated conceptual systems. To add a little bit more complexity to all of this, we then need to understand and realize that consciousness operates simultaneously at many different levels. We can not only have thoughts about something. We can also have thoughts *about* those previous thoughts. This layering of thoughts upon thoughts.creates greater complexity.

Meaning first arises from *the associations* we build (the Cause-Effect linkages in the magic box and then from the contexts (frames) that we put around the box). Associative meaning is the stuff *in* the magic box. Contextual meaning is what we put *around* the box. Recognition of the associating and framing processes enriches our understanding of the magic box.

$$X^2 \longrightarrow \text{ and } = Y^2 \text{ sets the frame}$$
$$\text{of } X^1 \text{ leads to } Y^1, X^1 \text{ equal } Y^1$$

As the equations of equations multiply, we build *systems* of beliefs out of complex equivalent and cause-effect structures. This gives us the flexibility to maneuver around the magic box like a magician as we move in seven directions.

9) Even "Real" Meanings May Not Serve us Well

We know that inside our minds-and-body system, whatever meanings we create become neurologically real to us and put us into state. These meanings then govern our neuro-linguistic states of consciousness and even modulate both our central and autonomic nervous systems.

Though "real" in this sense—*the meaning frames may not serve us well at all.* The meaning may be *sick and toxic* and make us sick and unable to live effectively. Consider the personalizing frame. Many people walk through life personalizing everything that happens.

> Whatever people say to me and whatever events I experience in the world—they are about me. They reflect on me and determine my value, worth, and adequacy as a human being.

Because all frames do not serve us well, we run an ecology check on frames and meanings to check them out and quality control them.

- Does this thought, emotion, state, belief, etc. serve me well?
- Will it enhance my life, bring out my best, put me in a resourceful state, and empower me in reaching my goals?
- Will it enable me to act in a way true to my values?

- Or will it limit me, reduce my effectiveness, and put me at odds with my own highest values and beliefs?

Summary
- *Mind-Lines*, as a model, is all about meaning. It's about the structure of meaning and how we experience meaning inside our neurology as emotions, reactions, and behavioral responses.

- *Mind-Lines* can magically alter meaning precisely because *meaning exists as a half-breed phenomenon of two worlds*—Plethora and Creatura (chapter six). This half physical and half psychical creature pops in and out of our lives—now materializing, now vanishing. Yet with the technology of reframing, we can now tame this beast, we can transform it. We can, in a word, become a master of our Matrix of meaning.

Chapter 16

HOW TO DO WHAT WHEN

Instructions for Magicians

You now know *what* to do in terms of the various reframing patterns for transforming meaning. But do you know *when* to do it? Or *with what?* After you learn the model and become fairly skilled with the patterns for directionalizing consciousness, then we practice our chops so that we can develop artistry with it. Then we become smooth and elegant in our communciations.
- *When* should you use a mind-line?
- *With* whom?
- *Under* what circumstances?
- *Which* mind-line format?
- To accomplish *what?*
- *How* do you decide which one to use with whom?

Recognize the Neuro-Semantic Reality
When we offer someone (including ourselves) a *mind-line,* we do so in order to play around with meaning attributions. As we construct and de-construct the very structure of how we give meaning to things, the mind-lines *change minds.* They alter consciousness. In conversational reframing we are offering the possibility of a new and more enhancing perspective—a new inner game. In doing so, we enter into the realm of that person's model of the world, his or her neuro-linguistic and neuro-semantic reality.

This raises several questions.
- Do I myself have permission to do this?
- Does the relationship we have bear this kind of interaction?
- Do I need to seek permission first?
- What results or consequences might I have to deal with if I offer the mind-line covertly?
- Would I want someone to lay a mind-line on me if our roles were reversed?

- Do I have permission within myself to facilitate a *change* in another person?
- Do I have the skill to do it with grace and elegance?
- Do I know what I'm doing and how to troubleshoot if I get into trouble?

Establish A Clear Sense of the Relational Context

With whom do you want to challenge, question, extend, expand, deframe, or enhance an attributed meaning about something? The person or persons with whom we want to offer a mind-line establishes *the personal context*. As we identify the *relationship* we have with this person, we can begin to address the following questions:

- Do I have sufficient rapport and trust with this person?
- How do I know if I have sufficient rapport?
- Since presenting or delivering a mind-line involves *leading,* have I paced sufficiently?
- Have I proven myself trustworthy, open, and respectful enough with this other person? (If I have not, the *mind-line* will tend to come across and be felt as manipulative.)

Choosing the Right Mind-Line

Assuming that you have the skill, ability, knowledge, internal permission, rapport, trust, and respect with someone (including yourself) to present the gift of a meaning transforming mind-line to magically touch someone with your neuro-semantic wand—*which* mind-line should you go for?

And, *how* will you figure that out? Easy. Go back to the theoretical basis of the model (Chapter 4) and examine *the directions of consciousness* format. This will then empower us to ask ourselves the following questions:

- In what direction would I want to send this person's consciousness?
- In what direction does this person want his or her consciousness sent?
- What default program describes how and where this person now sends his or her brain?
- How stuck is the person in that frame?
- What secondary benefits support the limiting belief?
- Does the old neuro-semantic program first need to be deframed?
- Would a straightforward content reframing work best with this person?
- What conceptual frames would most usefully outframe this person and give him or her a whole new and more resourceful frame-of-reference?
- If I use this particular mind-line pattern, what kind of response can I expect from this person?

Next you will need to determine the person's *frames* and *meta-frames*.

- What directions has the person already sent his or her brain?

- What frames currently create problems or limitations?
- Has the person over-used one particular frame or direction?
- How has this created difficulties or limitations?
- In choosing the right mind-line to use, explore the direction and frame which would counter-act the person's problematic frames.
- Does the person need the current frame deframed?
- Does he need evidence for the current belief to get counter-exampled?
- Does she need the allness of the belief questioned?

What Effect Will Today's Circumstances Play?

Today's events and circumstances constitutes yet another governing influence about which Mind-Line pattern to use. *When* we seek to use our magic wand can make a lot of difference. In consideration of this we ask the following:

- What is the person's current state?
- Is the person in an open or receptive state?
- What degree of openness does the person have at this moment?
- What governs the person's openness?
- Would *now* be a good time to do this? If not, when would be the best time?
- What things has this person had to deal with that might significantly effect the offering of a *mind-line?*

Mind-Lining with Balance

It never hurts, even after delivering a mind-line, to run a quality control on the *mind-line.*

- How has this particular reframing pattern affected this person?
- Has it empowered the person?
- Has it enhanced the person's way of thinking?
- Has it conflicted with other frames?
- How has it fit into or not fit into higher frames?
- Is there any higher frame that seems to or could neutralize this mind-line?

Along the same lines, it never hurts to continually check out your own frames and meta-frames, beliefs, and values. Doing so enables us to take into account the frames that we project onto others.

Use the Present State/ Desired State Algorithm

The most basic NLP algorithm involves a frame-of-reference that considers the gap between present state and desired state. Dilts (1990) put together the S.C.O.R.E. model to incorporate five facets for consideration.

- Symptoms and Causes summarize the current undesired present state description—the problem space.
- Outcome and Effects of the outcome summarize the desired future

state—the solution space.
*   **R**esources specify the processes needed to bridge the gap.

Figure 16:1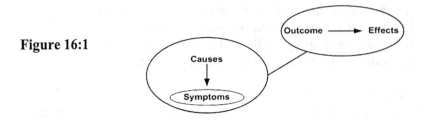

With the SCORE model, we can now begin exploring questions around these distinctions.
*   How strong are the symptoms in the present state?
*   What are the causes and the contributing influences that create the present state?
*   How much does the person really want to move to the desired or preferred outcome state?
*   How much benefit or value does the person see in that?
*   Does the person need more of a sense of aversion to move away from the present state or more attraction toward the desired state?
*   How much of a gap is there between the problem space and the solution space?
*   What, for this person, governs this sense of the gap?
*   Given that the less of a gap, the less desire there will be for change, what increases the sense of the gap?
*   How desperate does the person feel about the gap?
*   Does the person feel that he *can* change?
*   Does she believe she *deserves* to change?
*   What response style meta-program filter does the person have: active, inactive, or reflective?

The Nature of "Problems"
As we think about the nature of what we call "problems," we have numerous perspectives and distinctions that we can use. The SCORE model offers one. We can look at it from the perspective of "time." We can also use the distinctions of *Simple to Complex* and *Unstable to Stable.* I noted these distinctions in *The Sourcebook of Magic* (1998, Chapter 11), picking up on some suggestions from Robert Dilts. Recognizing a problem's structure in terms of simple to complex and unstable to stable offers insights regarding our knowledge about *what* to do and *when.*

Simple—Complex

Sometimes the difficulty that we seek to address involves a *simple* Stimulus—>Response structure rather than a *complex* response involving multiple layers. A phobia involves a simple anchored response. Structurally, a phobia involves a stimulus to which we immediately and automatically respond with a state of fear. X (the stimulus) triggers the Y (response). This leads to that. It's also stable. X *always* leads to Y. Count on it!

Conversely, the state of low self-esteem typically involves more complexity. It depends not only upon *what* associations have gotten connected to *what* stimulus, but also upon the meaning frames (the beliefs, values, expectations, understandings, etc.) that we have constructed around these concepts.

To create a disorientation which therefore gives us a chance to intervene more powerfully, we find the leverage point of the simple S—>R pattern and interrupt it. Or we can make it more complex so that it takes more to create it. Similarly when we reduce the complexity of a complicated problem so that we chunk it down to some simple but workable facet, we again create a point of intervention.

Stable—Unstable

Every experience falls along a continuum of stablility. It's a matter of degree. How stable is this pattern? How unstable? When? Where? What causes the pattern to stabilize or de-stabilize? These terms, *unstable* and *stable,* represent another set of important distinctions that we can use in figuring out what to do when.

- Does the difficulty come and go unpredictably, now here, now gone?
- What are the factors and mechanisms that make for stability and/or instability?

Such instability in the problem suggests that if we first stabilize the problem or some part of it we will be able to work with the current patterns more effectively. A stable problem means that we can count on it. We can predict it, anticipate it, and set our watches by it. Change therefore will start with disrupting that pattern. First we will want to de-stabilize the pattern which puts the person into a more receptive state.

Summary

- The *art* of mind-lining involves learning to negotiate the reframing patterns. Conversational framing emerges from conscious practice, and eventually habituates (as all things do in human neuro-semantic) so that it becomes an unconscious competence.

- *How do we get there?* Richard Bandler says, "By practicing your chops." Become a clinician and walk through each of the processes over and over and over until you not only know the names of the patterns and the questions to ask, but you begin to *think* in terms of transforming the meaning attribution process.

- The playful and deliberate mindfulness that you apply to the process of learning will eventually spring forth in a presence of mind while communicating. At that point, you can consider yourself a master of conversational reframing and ready to rocketship yourself into Neuro-Semantic space.

Chapter 17

GETTING INTO
A MAGICAL STATE

Empowerment for the Mind-Lining

"Why can't I fly, Tinkerbell?"
"To fly, Peter Pan, you've got to find your happy thoughts."

- *What kind of states* will enable us to optimally use the word magic of mind-lines and to do so elegantly?
- Have you ever been in so much of a great state that the idea of performing word magic seemed like a piece of cake?
- Have you ever been in a state where you didn't feel you could reframe yourself out of a paper bag?

States make a difference. Actually our neuro-linguistic states make all the difference in the world with regard to how we perform. That's because, given the nature of *mind-body-emotion states,* our states govern our thinking, feeling, skill level, and everything else that we bring to a situation.

That's why peak performers in every field do one thing in common. They develop the states that are their *top performance states*. Then they cultivate ways to quickly access them so that they can re-access them in a moment's notice.

Regarding conversational reframing, we could actually develop a mastery level of this model and still *lack* the ability to use it effectively. To make the skill level irrelevant all we have to do is be in the wrong state or fail to access the right states. State plays that critical of a role in our lives. To learn the *Mind-Lines model* and to have it at ready access, we must train ourselves in state management skills.

The State for Performing Magic
Our mind-body states as comprised of our *thoughts* and *physiology*. In *Meta-States* we describe these two facets of state as comprising "the two royal roads to state."

Mind refers to our thoughts and ideas that make up our internal representations. These see-hear-feel representations, make up the internal movie by which we encode our understandings. Our internal representations made up of the sensory representational systems, words, etc. provide the cognitive road to state. What do you need to think, see, say, feel, etc. so that you access your best performance state?

Body refers to all of the physical stuff: physiology, neurology, state of health, biochemistry, etc. Our body includes how we stand, sit, move, our posture, how we breath, sleep, gesture, etc. These facets of neurology play a crucial role in our neuro-linguistic states. Together, these comprise our mind-body system—an interactive system that sets the frame for our experience every moment. How do you need to stand, breathe, move, etc. to access your best states?

Empowering States for Mind-Lining
•   What are your top ten states for exploring meaning, playing around with it, and empathizing with the struggles of others so that you can be effectively helpful?
•   What are the states that support your ability to handle the magic of language and meaning so that others recognize that you do it with respect for them?

As we search for the best *states* for conversing, dialoguing, listening, sharing, and presenting, we begin to orient ourselves to this domain. Use the following as a beginning list for your repertoire of high performance states.

1) Energetically Flexible
   "I can vary my responses!"
The most basic and primary state that empower the use of this word magic involves our own personal *flexibility*—i.e, an open, changeable, flexible state of mind-and-emotion. This contrasts with states of rigidity, closeness, and Aristotelian thinking in terms of map/territory confusion, "This **is** that!

How about the flexibility to jump "logical levels" at a single bound? Can you do *that?* Okay, stretch those mental muscles and loosen up your rigid thoughts and get ready to move up and down the levels, to "go meta" to any and every concept (i.e., time, causation, values, identity, ecology, consequences, abstraction, modeling, etc.).

Only when we can jump semantic levels at a single bound are we ready to use the Mind-Lines model. This means we need a mind that has sufficient energy and mental alertness and that suggests taking care of ourselves in terms of eating, exercising, sleep, etc. It's hard to be mentally alert when we are fatigued, worn out, distressed, distracted, or grumpy.

2) Playfully Creative
"Let's play around and see what else this could mean."
The playful state, in contrast with seriousness, reflects a light and easy attitude toward the existence and construction of meanings. You have probably noticed the degree of playful creativity needed to think outside of the box and to come up with other perspectives.

What makes thinking outside of the box hard? Confusing map with territory and thinking words are real. Conversely, when we know, "Everything everybody says are just words. What people say and write are just symbols. None of it is externally real. We are just engaging in a symbolic process, the mapping of our understandings," we have the right state of mind.

So what do you need to do to get yourself into a playful mood about language? To the degree that you think either language or truth is externally real or that they have an existence apart from a human mind, the map/territory confusion will seduce you to *identify* map and territory and to get serious. That's when the game is over. Once we get serious, then we get stupid and our playful creativity goes out the window. Then we're no longer able to play the game of *Meaning Transformation*. We are more likely to be recruited and to play, "My Meanings are Better Than Yours."

Along with playfulness access a state of bantering that allows you to engage in teasing. Have you ever just bantered back and forth with some good friend? Do you know what it means to playfully banter ideas and words? Remember a time or just pretend like you have had such an experience and step into it fully. How much fun do you think you'll have in just bantering back words and frames? Now double that feeling.

3) Un-Insultable
"Come on, throw a term at me."
For a moment just imagine that you have stepped into a state where you feel so centered that nothing, but nothing, could insult you. Once you have fully accessed the state of uninsultability, then imagine receiving the gift of an insult, a good, gut-retching insult. Now as you receive that insult, do so from a feeling of being centered and focused, knowing that it has nothing to do with you as a person, and in the awareness that you can say, "No thanks, I already gave at the office." Now go forth and be playful.

Un-insultability is a high level meta-state that allows us to become un-self-conscious because we can now forget about ourselves. It enables us to get our ego out of the way so that we are not trying to "prove" anything. We can then be graciously proactive, calm and relaxed, centered, gentle, respectful, and loving without fear, apprehension, or worry.

4) Mischievous
What would you say is one of the most mischievous things you've ever done in your entire life? As you step into the state of feeling mischievous, add a dash of seductiveness to it, dip it in charm and stir thoroughly. When you're ready, let all of these feelings pop out in your neurology with a very special smirk, you know, the smirk that your parents used to hate and yell at you about. Remember that one?

When I first studied with Richard Bandler, I discovered that most of his mind-lines occurred as an expression of his mischievousness. He always seemed to thoroughly enjoy taking someone's limited view of reality and twisting it inside out. He seemed to really enjoy getting people going. The problem was that it was often difficult to tell if it was good hearted mischievousness or if he was really going to hurt you.

Actually, I think that his ability to see the world from a tilted point of view is part of his genius. He would not only twist things around and see things from the most ridiculous points of view, but in the early days of NLP he often pushed it so far that he came across in a totally iconoclastic way and so scared a lot of people. Well, while we don't need that much mischievousness, we do need some.

5) Empathy and Antagonism
When you form a *pre-framing* mind-line, you look for positive intentions and try to put the best spin on things. What state will you need when you do that? You will need a sense of care and compassion. You will need states of empathy and thoughtfulness for the person. You will need what is called *agape love* for the person—a genuine sense of wanting the best for the other.

By way of contrast, when you use the *post-framing* mind-lines you will be rubbing the dangerous consequences in someone's face. Then you will need a different state of mind. You will need a more antagonistic state wherein you have the power to provoke and confront, to not let a person off the hook, and the ability to turn up the heat so the person begins to feel that consequential pain of his or her frames.

6) Communicational Knowledge and Elegance
To flexibly play with these mind-lines, you will need a really good knowledge

base of the patterns or at least of the pattern you want to play with. Use your ferocious learning state to read and comprehend the pattern, then make lots of mistakes so that you can learn from all of the marvelous feedback that will come your way. Write out the meaning equation and come up with at least twenty-six reframes.

Problem States which Prevent Word Magic

Because we can get into negative states that undermine our effectiveness, we need to deal with limiting states. While it's best to avoid them in the first place, if we happen to fall into one of them then we have to interrupt them. That's because they are states of mind and emotion that undermine the whole domain of conversational reframing.

It's similar to when a sales person gets him or herself into a state of fearing rejection, down and depressed about low sales, upset about finances, and feeling desperate to make a sale—these are not the kind of states that make one playful, flexible, cognitively alert, etc. So what can we do about such?

> *We can reframe the meaning frames in our minds that create those states in the first place.*

"You mean use this stuff on myself?" Sure it's a wild and crazy idea, but what the hell. It might actually make us more congruent, powerful, human, and authentic. Mind-Lining ourselves makes plenty of sense. We can then take charge of our own frames and frames-within-frames. We can get an inside feel for how the model works. And that will fulfill your own convincer of the relevance and usefulness of Mind-Lines at the same time. Hey, why not?

Self-application will only empower us to work effectively in communication and relationship with others as it will empower us in working much more effectively with ourselves. After all, the existence of our states, the expressions of those states, and the experience of such all result from the meanings frames that we create and accept. So when we reframe our own meanings, we play one of the best frame games around, we play the game of *Running our own Brain*. Try it; it's a real rush.

At the beginning of this work, we provided twenty-six reframes for "failure." Along the way we have suggested other frames for other conceptual realities that frequently create limitations to effectiveness. Use these mind-lines on yourself to provide a way to get the full benefit from the neuro-semantic magic. There's nothing like playing with your own mind, mastering it, and being able to work with it in real time.

Supporting Beliefs for an Empowering Magical State

Above and beyond our states are higher meta-states. These take the form of beliefs, understandings, knowledge, expectations, decisions, values, etc. These meta-level frames either support or hinder our resourceful states. They either enable us to get into the kind of states optimal for learning and using *Mind-Lines* or they sabotage our best efforts at such.

Several years ago, Bob and I began to explore this question and to model each other regarding our ability to create reframes that we could use conversationally. We also began modeling those who seemed skilled in quickly, easily, and automatically producing effective *word magic* in the context of objections, "problems," difficulties, excuses, and such like. From that exploration, we collected the following list of supporting and empowering beliefs.

1) Every statement or objection has within it an answer.
Suppose you believed and knew that no matter what objection a person may raise with regard to a project, product, or service that you offer, that deep within the person's objection you could find an answer for it. Imagine that. Suppose you framed every objection as carrying within it, its own solution?

Believing this, and using it as an operational directive, puts us into states of curiosity, interest, and respect. It empowers us to keep exploring, gathering information, and finding out numerous things about another's model of the world: his or her drives, motives, values, objectives, interests, understandings, etc.

How could that be true? If a statement encodes someone's point of view as just a map, a map of some territory of experience, then exploring that map with the person will do two things at the same time. First it will elicit a fuller representation from the person, one that suffers from less impoverishment, and it will invite the mapper to update the map while he or she is talking about it. The errors in perception then, as mapping errors, self-correct with the right kind of questioning. And, the right kind of questioning can empower a person to map in higher and more exquisite ways because it enables them to directionalize their brain in new ways. In this, of course, lies the magic.

2) It's all feedback and never failure.
This frame expresses one of the key presuppositions in NLP about communicating and about the systemic nature of thoughts and responses. It says that whatever happens in our lives is actually just the next step in some process. It could simply be just communication about how another person perceives or it could be a description of how a process works or doesn't work. It does not have to mean anything more than that. It is just feedback.

This means that we do *not* have to take statements and semantically load them to mean "success" or "failure" in any absolute sense at all. We do not have to personalize it. We can let it just mean "feedback" to a stimulus. Then it becomes only information to us, only a response and in this, we always succeed in getting some response.

Why would we want to do this? In order to stay emotionally neutral when an undesired response comes our way. Then, staying resourcefully curious, we are empowered to keep exploring, seeking to understand, and thinking creatively of other alternatives.

3) Personalizing communication interchanges reduces effectiveness.
Whatever someone says is just words and information. Instead of *personalizing*, I shall recognize that I "am" *so much more* than all of my thoughts, feelings, speech, and behavior. I shall not reduce either myself or others by labeling, name-calling, insulting, or contempting due to some piece of communication that seems disrespectful.

The giving and receiving of information in a communication exchange has really nothing to do with my identity or destiny. Therefore I can refuse to allow myself to put my "self" on the line due to someone else's grumpy state. Sometimes I may have to write down a statement, and play with it for awhile, but eventually I will identify the magic formula within it.

4) Assuming responsibility is an empowering rush.
At first glance almost everybody thinks that by assuming responsibility for the responses we get is connected to blame, accusation, and feeling bad. Could that be an old mind-line equation that someone fed us? I think so. Yet, as a map, blaming others for "not getting it," "being stupid," "not paying sufficient attention," "being obnoxious," "resisting," etc. seldom takes us anywhere useful. It doesn't lead to the building of positive relationships. It doesn't create rapport. It doesn't induce states of openness or receptivity in others.

This is the surprise and magic that occurs in this new map. By assuming that "the response I get is the meaning of my communication" we actually step up into our *power zone*. This gives us more control over things, not less. Now, if I want another response, I alter my behavior and communications.

Applied to conversation and even arguments, it means that because we know that *meaning* is an internal thing, and not an external thing, meaning doesn't exist out there. We use words, signals, gestures, etc. as symbols to convey our meanings, but these symbols do not *mean* in and of themselves. Meaning arises inside of the mind of a meaning-maker. That's why we can say,

> "I really never know what I have communicated. I can know what words I used, what metaphors, what gestures, what tone and volume, etc., but I really never know what I have communicated. I don't know

what the other person heard. That's why I have to constantly ask, calibrate to the other person's responses, seek feedback, and use such to keep adjusting myself to the person's current reality."

And, doing this keeps me *proactive,* involved, engaged, tuned in, and using all of my powers for the communicating feed forward and feed back loops. What a rush! It keeps me from thinking or feeling like a victim. It gives me a sense of control over my own life and destiny.

5) Detecting and recognizing meaning and frames as people talk and interact is simple once you start paying attention.
This belief enables us to not feel overwhelmed by language, by words, by objections, or by statements. Meaning exists *only* as human constructs at best —constructs that we can detect and recognize. As we do, we can formulate an understanding of the meanings involved and *play* with such—framing and reframing to our heart's content.

6) Meaning works by associations and frames. This induces people to live in conceptual worlds of their own making.
This understanding empowers us to understand "meaning" as an internal job, as inside the mind of a meaning-maker, and as an association between things. Recognizing such as a *mental map* and not externally real saves us from the unsanity of confusing map and territory.

This means that just because someone says something, saying does not make it real externally. This is why I do not have to take offense at any word and become reactive. I do not have to feel bad because of the words another person use. At best whatever someone says exists only as a *symbol.*

7) Thinking about my thinking enables me to jump "logical levels" in a single bound.
Knowing that meaning exists at many levels of mind, at the primary level of experience and at meta-levels, empowers us to jump "logical levels" in a single bond. I can now recognize the *about-ness* structure and negotiate the meta-levels. In communication exchanges, the person with the most flexibility in jumping "logical levels" will have the most influence.

8) People deserve the chance to have their maps expanded and will even appreciate the jar after they recover from the dizziness.
Mind-shifting does a person good. In the long run, it makes minds more flexible and adaptable, it develops good ego-strength for facing difficulties, bouncing back from set-backs, and for constructing the most appropriate, healthy, and ecological maps. Most people will love you for it.

These are a few of the initial frames that we found and developed which we felt enhanced our skills in this area. What other beliefs would support you?

Summary

- The Disney Studios put out a new version of *Cinderella* in 1997. I loved the scene where the fairy god-mother started doing some of her magic. First she created the carriage out of a pumpkin, then horses from mice. She made a beautiful gown out of rags, and then performed other wonder-filled transformations. Upon doing all of this, Cinderella was totally awestruck and just had to ask, "How did you do that?" To this the fairy god-mother replied, *"I practice my* magic."

- Magic has to be practiced. So may you also find yourself playfully practicing your semantic magic day by day and seeing all kinds of wonderful transformations popping into existence from the way you frame things and utter lines that change minds! May you create empowering inner games that tkae your performances to new levels of mastery.

Chapter 18

LEARNING MIND-LINES

STEP-BY-STEP

You know the structure of the magic. You know a great many of the secrets of the magic. You have committed yourself to playfully practice your magic. So what is left?

Just a quick summary. And a quick de-mystifying of the magic. In this chapter our aim is to pull apart the magic of conversational reframing and formulate it into a step-by-step process. Doing this will specify *a strategy for learning* the Mind-Lines model. In simplifying it in this way, you will first walk through the pieces consciously and intentionally. You will become a clinician.

Inasmuch as you have reached this place in this book, at times you may have found yourself feeling overwhelmed or entertaining thoughts of the complexity of this subject:

"This is just too difficult!"
"I'll never learn all of this."
"How can anyone master this?"

When you experience these kinds of thoughts and feelings about the learning —you know that you have moved from unconscious incompetence into conscious incompetence which means that you are now at the threshold of the next domain, conscious competence. The best thing to do now is to stay with it. Welcome, even *warmly accept,* the feelings of discomfort that arise at this stage *knowing* that shortly you will move into conscious competence. This is the heart of the learning process. Those who cut off the discomfort, who hate, despise, and reject the awareness of ignorance—end up in the pit of stupidity.

After all, we all have areas of ignorance. And we will always be ignorant about some things. What? Do you think you can *know it all?* How attractive, charming, or warm do you find those who think of themselves as know-it-alls? For *fallible* beings, *ignorance* only means that there's more to discover and will go on without end. As we warmly accept this, we may even learn to *rejoice* in our ignorance—fully knowing that the more we know about our ignorance—the less our stupidity and the greater our humble wisdom.

Stupidity, unlike ignorance, refers to *not using* the brains we have. It not only involves the lack of information (that's "ignorance"), it involves *failing to use* the brains and critical thinking skills that we do have as we try to play it cool as if we did know.

By the way, how you frame "the not-knowing of some information" (ignorance) determines the *meta-state* you create for yourself regarding the primary state of ignorance. Do you accept your-not-knowing and become curious about what you don't know, but can discover and know? Or do you hate and despise the state of not-knowing, and then become stupid by pretending you know, mocking the process of learning-to-know as "being an egg-head," or jeer at those who have spent the time and trouble to know? [And by the way, how many mind-lines did you notice in these paragraphs about not-knowing?]

Step 1:
In unpacking the Mind-Lines model, I think you should first of all thoroughly acquaint yourself with the theoretical understandings about the model. We have incorporated these in Chapters 1 through 4, as well as Chapters 13 and 19. In those chapters you discover the following the framework about meaning:
*   The *magic* of words and how they affect our states, skills, and experiences, how words work as a *neuro*-linguistic process to create our sense of reality in our maps and meanings (Ch. 1 and 2).\
*   How conversationally we can frame and reframe things to create new mappings and states (Ch. 3).
*   The *formula* of the 3-dimensional magic box that summarizes our meaning making (Ch. 4).
*   Using the Meta-Model of language as the framework for the Mind-Lines model (Ch. 13).
*   Nine facets about meaning, what it *is,* how it works, its levels, and the matrices of meaning that we create (Ch. 15).
*   A step-by-step summary of using Mind-Lines as a model for conversational framing (Ch. 18).

Learning the model boils down to distinguishing the things of the empirical world (i.e., the see, hear, feel things) and the things of the mental world. Failing to make this distinction will cause you to confuse "logical levels" and to make category errors in discerning meaning. And when we make category errors, we dis-empower ourselves from effectively engaging in the creativity and flexibility of reframing and from being the master of our meanings.

As meaning-makers, we create meaning in our minds. We create meaning in our minds *by connecting* things of the world (the brute facts of sights, sounds, smells, sensations, events, etc.) with *ideas* in our heads. Doing this creates every magic box that we enter and operate out of.

This describes the heart of every *frame game* that we play in life. Everyday of our lives, whenever we meet *an event* on the road of life, we embrace it with *a thought*. We then embrace and fuse that event with a *meaning* and, lo and behold, suddenly a *belief* in the form of an understanding, model, decision, value, etc. arises.

In doing this, we have used our neurology (i.e., brain, nervous system, and all of its conscious and unconscious functions) to *create something new in the world*. We have created a *felt relationship* between a stimulus and our response. In other words, we *connect* a thought and feeling to a stimulus—and then, magically, that stimulus "is" or "becomes" that response. At least, it "is" to that particular meaning-maker.

Step 2:

Once you know about the structure of meaning magic, don't stop with just knowing about the magic formula (E.B.=I.S.). Pull it apart. Deframe it so that you can then know with precision the specific pieces that come together to make up that particular magic (Chapter 5).

I made a mistake in the first edition of this book. When I organized it originally, I put content reframing before deframing. Then, when I began training the model in workshops I quickly realized the need to switch those chapters around. Why? Because it is through deframing that we obtain the component pieces and the strategy that define every neuro-semantic structure that we want to understand or reframe. Because deframing allows us to see what makes up the original meanings, it increases our insight regarding how the framing works and what new framings will add new resources.

Via deframing we thoroughly acquaint ourselves with *the structure* of the magic. This gives us the advantage of knowing *how* the magic works. Practically, this means that if you ever find yourself having difficulties in identifying and clarifying for yourself *the formula* that governs someone's neuro-semantic reality, then stop, go back to *the specificity* and *detailing the strategy* frames.

Find out how the magic works. Re-discover afresh the very secrets of the magic. Doing this step first enables you to specify the pieces within the linguistic structure. It empowers you to demystify the magical formula itself. This works because the chunking down process uncovers the component pieces of the meaning and its structure. By deframing a person's linguistic and non-linguistic expressions, we pull back the curtains to their subjective "reality." This allows us to see the tricks, the mirrors, and the illusions that support their "black" magic. We can then deal more directly with the Wizard of Oz behind the curtains.

We use *the chunking down* process to *specify*. This shows up in the Meta-Model in the specificity questions which allows us to *index* a reality:
- *Who* are you speaking about specifically?
- *What* did you do specifically?
- *In what way* did that occur?
- *When* did that happen?
- *Where* specifically?

Such specifying enables us to *index* (Korzybski) the specific referents: who, when, where, how, in what way, to what degree, which, etc. This corresponds to a similar process used in modern scientific thinking and journalistic writing. We describe this same process in science in terms of *operationalizing* our terms. In other words, we specify in empirical and behavioral terms (in see, hear, feel, smell, and taste terms) precisely what we mean.

In the Mind-Lines model, indexing accomplishes three things:
1) It provides us the specific E.B. (External Behavior) of the formula.
> Doing this enables us to understand what piece of the world—the plethora to which we have reference.

2) It gives us the specific I.S. (Internal State or Significance) of the formula.
> We consider the internal movements (actions or responses) as behaviors inside the "black box" as well. People outside cannot see, hear, or feel these micro-behaviors since they occur at the neurological level of brain and nervous system functioning. Eye accessing cues and sensory-based predicates as well as other signs do provide some indications of these processes. Through the indexing we may discover that we first made a mental picture in color and close up, then said some words in a sarcastic tonality, and then felt some sensations of tightness in the throat, and then ...

3) It sequences the E.B. components and thereby gives us the person's strategy.
> This tells us how the person created a particular formula and put it all together: first this E.B., then this I.S. of representational sequencing, which creates the response. We use the Miller, et al. TOTE model

format to specify the strategy of the experience.

"Up" and "Down" Simultaneously

In the fall of 1997, I was training the Mind-Lines model in Nottingham, England and met British psychotherapist, Sammy Naden. It was at that time that Sammy insightfully pointed out that *when* we "go down" from the E.B.=—>I.S. formula to get more specifications—*we simultaneously "move up"* a *meta-level.* He found this curious.

*   How can we simultaneous go up and down?
*   How does this *going up **and** going down* at the same time work?
*   Why would we experience a "going up" when we "go down?"

To explore this, consider what is required when we "go down" into the specific sensory components of an experience. What does this presuppose and demand? Does it not require that as we conceptually *step back* from the diving into the details so that we can detect and recognize the component pieces and the strategy? Does it not require that we move to a higher place, a meta-cognitive position, so that we can recognize the representational steps?

In other words, to explore the representational steps and the cinematic frames that we have edited into our mental movie, we have to step back to a meta-position. We do so from a meta-position of *curiosity, exploration, awareness, and understanding* of the process and regarding the subject of our exploration.

This illustrates the systemic nature of consciousness. Our minds are non-linear and go around in circles. We do not do one thing, and then another in a purely linear and sequential way. Rather that *as* we do one thing, we simultaneously do other things. *As* we index the details of a person's awareness, we invite them to step up into a meta-position so that the person can also give us information about what it means to them, their frames. It was via this exploration that Bob and I picked up the scent of something new and different regarding "sub-modalities," what they are and how they actually work. That eventually led us to understand that what we have called *"sub*-modalities" are *not* at a "sub" or lower "logical level" to the representational modalities. They are actually the cinematic frames that we edit into our movies and so operate *above* the representational systems as *meta-modalities.*[1]

To detect and recognize "sub-modalities," to become aware of them as the editorial frames, and to map them over, we have to *step back* or take a *meta-position.* In other words, we have to go meta in order to work with, and transform, the cinematic features. These and many other secrets of "sub-modalities" are detailed in *Sub-Modalities: Going Meta.*

Expanding the Magic Box

With the downward move into the components of the E.B.=/—>I.S. formula, we actually do *not* move outside of the magic cube at all. Instead we go deeper *inside* it and find the symbols that stand for the higher frames. We go within. We do *not* move between "logical levels" at all.

Accordingly, to adjust and to update the original Mind-Lines model, we offer the following chart that more accurately diagrams the process. The two solid lines indicate *the primary level* of experience. The dashed-line indicates going down inside the E.B. and the I.S., but still *within* the box.

Figure 18:1
The Magic Box

$$\text{E.B.} = / \longrightarrow \text{I.S.}$$

V.A.K. ——> V — A — K — V —>   Exit

The unexpected nature of the indexing process within this model explains its power. We "chunk down" (conceptually) *from* a meta-level of awareness. We meta-detail.[2] By this process we then attain the critical insights about several things regarding the structure of meaning. For example, it provides top-notch information about:

• *The strategy* of how we create the meaning we create. We discover the actual sequence of representations in our mental movie as we respond to the external stimulus. This details the internal components that create the experience.

• *The component pieces* in the cinema of our mind that symbolize our meanings and which provide the internal *coding* for those higher frames.

• *How* we have created the meaning or experience from the mixture of the pieces. This generates the subjective experience which we can now choose to keep replicating or interrupt and stop.

Step 3:

As we have moved down to specify the representational components of a person's thinking, and their syntax or sequence which comprise *the structure* of magic inside the box, we have a sense of how the meaning works, how the person has come to think that way, and are ready to reframe the content. *Formula identification* results from the indexing and thoroughly prepares us for engagement in the magical art of content reframing.

In *Content Reframing* we give new meanings, words, labels, and definitions to the two sides of the formula, to the I.S. and the E.B. Linguistically, you can use the following linguistic environments as cues to get you started:

1) "This isn't this I.S. — it is this I.S."

> This isn't laziness, this shows the ability to really relax!
>
> This isn't rudeness, this demonstrates a tremendous skill at being independence from the opinions of others.
>
> This isn't insult, this is bad tonality!

2) "If you really want to see I.S. — look at this E.B."

> If you want to really see laziness, consider if he wouldn't even dress himself. *That* would be laziness!
>
> If you want to see rudeness, listen to Saddam Hussein talk!

3) "What I really consider I.S. is this E.B."

> What I would really consider as rude is if he picked his nose and flipped it at me. That would be rudeness, not being late.

Step 4:

Up to this point we have worked inside the magic cube. We have worked within it clarifying the formula, identifying the elements that lie at its heart, and the sequence of representational steps which create *the magic* inside the box (*Deframing*). We have also worked inside the box to alter the linguistic labels that we have attached to various E.B. stimuli (*Reframing*).

The time has now come for us to step aside from the box entirely. Here we leave *the magic box* intact and no longer seek to change its composition. From this point on we move from *content* reframing into the realm of *context* reframing. We now work to *outframe* the frame. As we move out into the larger *contexts* within which we reference the magic box—the contexts that we apply to, or bring to bear on, the box sets up new and different contexts. This transforms the meaning of the box from a higher "logical level." Like a magician who throws a magical cloth over a box so that we can't see what transformations are occurring, we throw new concepts over the box. We call this *outframing*.

Outframing refers to all of the kinds of ideas, beliefs, and concepts that we can apply to the cube. We do this from *above* the cube. In this book this includes:

- Pre-Framing and Post-Framing (Chapter 8)
- Outframing (Chapter 9)
- Analogous Reframing (Chapter 10)
- Additional Outframing Patterns (Chapter 11)

All of the *context reframing* in these conversational reframes actually involve what we now recognize as the meta-stating process. This means that because we have stepped outside of the belief box into a meta-position to the magic —everything that occurs here involves applying some meta-level frame (or context) to the old formula.

In the Meta-States model, we utilize the principle of layering or embedding. Our self-reflexive awareness allows us to rise up or transcend any thought or emotion that we experience and apply any other thought or emotion to the first one. Yet as we *transcend* the first, we *include* it inside of the second. The second becomes a higher frame to the first and the context of the first. In this way we embed the first into the second. So as we experience thoughts about thoughts, feelings about feelings, ideas about ideas, etc., we can always *loop back* to some other thought, feeling, or idea and bring it to bear on the previous thought. This layers our consciousness. It creates an embeddedness of our ideas. It creates a system of embedded frames within frames, states within states. So what we typically describe as our assumptions, presuppositions, and beliefs are actually meta-state structures.

When we ask, "What idea do you hold *about* this concept?" we get to the frame-of-reference within which the person has embedded the lower idea. We could also ask, "What do you presuppose *about* this experience?" "What comes to mind when you think about that belief?"

When we explore and model the structure of genius in experts we find that they have created and live in a different mental world. The matrix of the frames of their mind are layered in a different way from non-experts. So the magic of their excellence lies in that embedded structure. It's as simple as that; it is as profound and amazing as that.[3]

Step 5:

You now know that you can send a mind in *seven basic directions*. You also now have numerous specific *patterns* within each of these seven directions. This gives you a whole set of ways to reframe meaning and to transform experiences. These seven directions for mind-shifting also describe and illustrate *seven types of mental-emotional functioning* that set up or construct these dimensions.

MAGICAL CUES

Here's a succinct way that summarizes how to think about and remember the *Mind-Line Statements and Questions.* Use the following as cues to prompt your thinking. As you use these, they will eventually become automatic. Use these as *semantic environments and prompters* for your creativity. After you use them for awhile and begin to customize them to the way you talk, they will become natural.

The Deframing Mind-Lines

#1 Specifying the Magic
> What component pieces make up this idea?
> How do you know to call or label this X?
> What lets you know to think, picture, or hear it in this way?
> What do you mean by X?

#2 Detailing the Magical Strategy
> In what order and sequence do these parts occur?
> What comes first, then second, etc.?
> What lets you know to first see this and then hear that?
> When and where do you do this?

The Content Reframing Mind-Lines

#3 Reframing the E.B. Content
> What really is E.B. is ...
> What else would be a case of this E.B.?
> If you want to really see a case of this E.B., consider....

#4 Reframing the IS Content
> This isn't $IS^{\#1}$, it is $IS^{\#2}$
> What other IS could we just as well attribute to this E.B.?
> If you really want to see a case of this IS, consider.....!

The Counter-Framing Mind-Lines

#5 Reflexively Apply the E.B. (X)
> What a X statement!

#6 Reflexively Apply the IS (Y)
> So you are doing Y to me?

#7 Counter-Example
> Has there ever been a time when you did *not* do or experience this?
> When does this magical formula about yourself or life *not* apply?
> So you have *never* experienced the opposite?

The Pre-Framing Mind-Lines

#8 Positive Prior Intention
> You probably did that because of *stated positive intention.*
> Weren't you attempting to accomplish the positive purpose of...?

What would you guess the person sought to accomplish of value to him or her?

#9 Positive Prior Cause

You did that because X or Y occurred, did you not?

What else could have caused the idea or behavior outside your control?

The Post-Framing Mind-Lines

#10 First Outcome

This belief will lead to you experiencing the consequences of ...

What will happen if you run with this idea or behavior?

#11 Outcomes of Outcome

If you experience that outcome, what will it then lead to?

As you get the first outcome, that will then lead to X,

is that what you want?

#12 Ultimate Outcome

Ultimately, this belief will lead to X and Y, how do you like that?

When you look back on your life having experienced all these consequences, how will you think or feel about it?

The Outframing Mind-Lines

#13 Model of the World

Who taught you to think or feel this way?

When you think of this as just a mental map, how does that change things?

#14 Value Outframing

What do you find more important than this?

How does X (some other value) affect this?

When you compare this with X (value), what do you think?

#15 Allness Outframing

Always? To everyone?

Would you recommend this for everybody?

Has there never been a time when you didn't?

#16 Necessity Outframing

What forces you to think this way?

What would happen if you did not?

Do you have to?

What would it be like if you couldn't?

What stops you from doing this other thing?

#17 Identity Outframing

What does this say about you as a person?

When you think or do this, how does that effect your identity?

Who would you be if you didn't believe this?

#18 All Other Abstractions Framing

When you think about A, B, or C *about* that, how does that influence

things?
#19 Ecology Outframing
Does this serve you well?

Does it enhance your life?

Do any parts of you object to this?

The Analogous Framing Mind-Lines
#20 Metaphor Or Story Outframing
I have a friend who just last month...

Carrying over and applying a referent story to the belief.

#21. Both/And Framing
Is this really an either/or situation? Black-or-white?

There are no greys? No middles? No degrees or extent of?

Could it be both and at the same time from different perspectives?
#22. Pseudo-Words Framing
Is this a true word that stands for a real thing or a valid concept?

Could this be a pseudo-word? Just a noise or spell-mark?
#23. Negation Framing
What if this was not real and did not really exist?

What would it be like if this just faded away from your internal cinema? How would that affect things?
#24. Possibility and "As If" Framing
What if there was a possibility of you doing this?

Suppose for the sake of discussion for a moment that you had the resources to ... Would you like that?
#25. Systemic and Probability Framing
What's the probability of this happening? Or not happening?

What other systemic factors or influences affect this?

Is this truly linear or is there anything circular or systemic in this?
#26. Decision Framing
Have you decided that this is so? Is that what you want?

Will you do this? Will you keep choosing this path that doesn't work?

Elegantly Delivering Mind-Lines
Now that you know how to create neuro-semantic magic and how to alter the very structure of meaning, you know how to reframe meaning in a multitude of ways. This gives you the ability to conversationally offer new enhancing maps as you talk with people. Now you're ready to *speak the words and call the new worlds into being.*

Are there any guidelines for doing this? Yes there are. Here are a few.

1) Be congruent in presenting mind-lines.
Depending on the nature, quality, and direction of the mind-line, make sure that your delivery fits with the mind-line itself. Sometimes this will involve a voice of empathy and compassion, sometimes a voice of provocation and aversion, questioning and curiosity, wonderment and amazement, conviction, etc. Access the right kind of state so that it congruently fits the content of the mind-line.

2) Pace, pace, pace, and then lead.
If you're going to use the *pacing and leading* format, then use everything you know in NLP and Neuro-Semantics to first match and pace, verbally and non-verbally. Pace at the physiological level; pace at the conceptual level. Keep testing and checking for rapport and then lead with the mind-line that you've developed. Give plenty of confirmations and affirmations along the way.

3) Adopt a voice of belief, conviction, and matter-of-fact-ness.
Express the mind-line in a way that just makes sense so that it has a "This just-makes-sense" tonality. Anchor the state that conveys the feeling, *"Of course, it makes sense."* This will assist the person to feel that the mind-line is meaningful and significant.

4) Operate from the Being/Behavior difference.
The difference between *being* and *behavior* for reframing is crucial. We *are not* our behaviors. We are more than our actions and the things we do. What we do are but expressions of us. Who we *are* as human *Beings* transcend what we think, feel, say, and do.

This applies equally to others also. People are more than their behaviors. Yet their behaviors make sense given their connections and frames. So how we frame a piece of behavior lies totally and entirely at our disposal. After all, nothing inherently means anything. What is any given behavior? It depends on how we *frame* it.

In mind-lining we are not *playing games* or *distorting* "the truth," or anything of the kind. We are framing and reframing the facts, experiences, events, words, etc. of life to create useful and enhancing maps that allow us to grow, develop, and be all that we can be. Recognizing the difference between person and behavior gives us a new level of flexibility and creativity in framing.

5) Bring your gesturing into conscious awareness
As you communicate your mind-line, notice *what* and *how* you handle the spatial territory around you and the other person. We all externalize our internal maps by means of how we handle actual space. Our gestures and behaviors are

not just "body language." That fails to recognize the symbolic nature of movement and gesture. In gesturing we are engaging in spatial representing anchoring. That is, we are setting up triggers in space and with movement so that how we use movement and location *means* something special.

We do this with our *concept* of "time." Just watch a person. Or, watch your own hands and gestures for that matter and you will see yourself point to such concepts as the "past," the "present," and the "future." The entire domain of time-lines in NLP utilizes this spatial representing. Yet we also externalize many other concepts in space and with gestures—values, beliefs, convictions, levels, etc. Yet it is only the person who has eyes to see who will.

Semantically Pack Your Mind-Lines
For even greater impact, now that you know about a multitude of mind-line patterns that you can use, you can become even more truly powerful and elegant as a Neuro-Semantic Magician if you combine and embed multiple mind-lines into a single statement. I'd recommend that you practice combining three to seven mind-lines into a single statement.

> "I really appreciate your concern for not hurting my feelings (#8) as you *have not* brought up this subject because you have viewed it as 'criticism' instead of just being forthright (#4), since just saying words directly as you calibrate to my state (#1) has typically, in your past, meant something hurtful, although you have at times done so with good results (#7), so I guess as you continue to discover that honesty and being authentic (#14) play as important a role in our interactions, that it will serve you much better than walking around on egg-shells with my feelings (#19, #20), or other negative consequences (#10).

Semantically pack your statements with emotionally compelling terms, images, and suggestions. A semantically packed term has "juice" in it. That is, it seduces you to powerfully represent things in such a way that it *lures* you into the state. So search for such terms ... as you continue in your *explorations* of this *wild and wonderful territory* knowing that you'll get *a lot of mileage* from such terms and be able to *influence* with greater *power and elegance* than ever before.

Summary

*   Add a turbo-charge to your framing and reframing, to your ability to learn and master the Mind-Lines model by simply attending to them, practicing them everyday for awhile and remembering that there is power and magic in *lines* that can change minds.

*   The step-by-step process for learning Mind-Lines enables you to begin to become a neuro-semantic magician. If you need to reframe your own thinking or emoting about the effort and discipline it takes to study, practice, write, play, then elicit whatever lines are in your mind that stops you. Then work those lines through the model.

*   And now, may the magic that you create with the lines that you invent truly be a blessing to yourself and to all of the people that you touch with that magic!

End Notes:

1. See the updated version of our book, *Sub-Modalities Going Meta* (2005).

2. *Meta-Detailing* is one of the prerequisites of genius and is also described in the book, *Sub-Modalities Going Meta*.

3. The book *The Matrix Model* picks up where *Mind-Lines* leaves off to more fully explore the Matrix of all our meanings. Meta-Coaching uses this model as a unifying framework for coaching and many of the newer developments in Neuro-Semantics is also using the Matrix Model as a framework for understanding a complex experience like leadership, wealth creation, resilience, etc.

Chapter 19

THE MIND-LINES
MIND MAP

Pascal J. Gambardella, Ph.D.

How do you learn, apply, and teach potentially complicated subjects? I'm faced with this question each month at an NLP Study Group, which I have run for the last sixteen years. *Conversational Reframing* (or "Sleight of Mouth" Patterns) appeared many times. Yet having never attended a training on "Sleight of Mouth" Patterns, I have had to play the role of a cultural anthropologist in trying to piece together what they were and how to use them.

Using other people's training experiences and artifacts, I tried over the years to construct a picture of the structure of these "Sleight of Mouth" Patterns, and how to use them. Only after I received a copy of the first edition of this book was I able to create a mind-map that I could use to teach this model of *Conversational Reframing*.

Why use *mind-maps?* Sometimes when I show a complicated mind-map to someone and he or she runs away screaming, others will value it as a great learning tool. I suspect, given the varied ways in which we process information, there is truth in both of these reactions. It works for some; it doesn't for others. A colleague of mine, Winnie Conley-Smith uses mind-maps to help children who have difficulty visualizing and remembering.

Mind-maps can show and highlight *structure* in a subject area. Yet this structure may not be readily apparent from looking at the words alone. Knowing (or creating) the structure helps us remember the material. About seven years ago, at the request of the Government, my colleague Glen Ledeboer and I conducted interviews at several large companies to understand how each company develops software. In that project, we developed six pages of questions for each interview.

Glen, with his strong auditory sense, could remember all the questions. Directly after the interview, he could repeat back (on tape) almost word for word what people said. I believe it was panic that led me to convert all six pages of questions to a one-page mind-map the night before the first interview. The mind-map then helped me keep track of progress during each interview. I found this especially valuable since the questions and answers never seemed to come in the same order as in our six-page list. Frequently, people would answer questions that we hadn't asked yet. And sometimes, during an interview, I even caught Glen glancing at the notes on my mind-map to gauge our progress.

Mind-Mapping the Mind-Lines

You will notice in *Figure 19:1* that we begin with a cube into which we put the "content" of some thought. *Content reframing* alters and transforms this content. It changes the formula encoded on the sides of the cube.

- Deframing the I.S.and E.B.
- Deframing

Some mind-lines are represented in the mind-map with related-icons to help us remember them. For example, the cube with "external behavior," "internal state," and "strategy," written on its sides helps us to remember and focus on mind-lines #2 (Strategy), #3 (External Behavior), and #4 (Internal State).

From there we can add *Context Reframing* to the mind-map as shown in Figure 19:2. Context reframing puts the same content in a different context. The mind-lines in this category are further collected in sub-categories.

- Outframing
- Counter-Framing
- Pre-Framing
- Post-Framing
- Analogous Framing

Figure 19:1

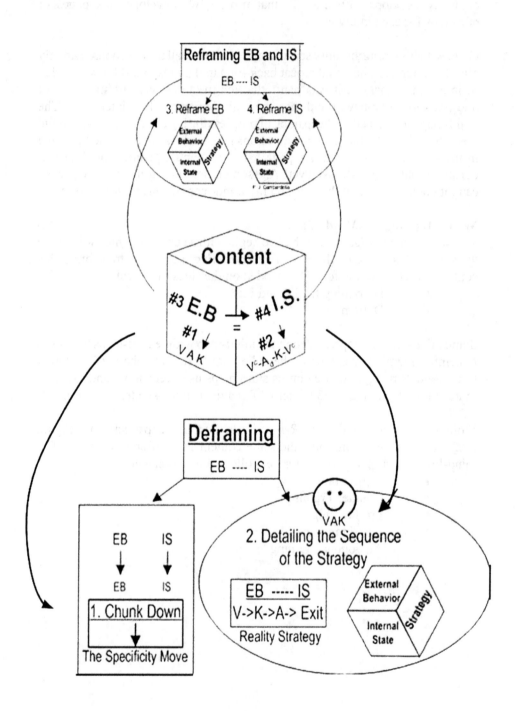

Many mind-lines are represented in the mind-map with related icons and a structure to help remember them. For example, assuming time flows from left to right, mind-lines #8 through #12 are grouped in the direction of time, from "cause" to "eternity." Other mind-lines have icons that can help recall the mind-line. For example, the number "21" in mind-line #21 is situated in the "Both/And" portion of a Venn diagram.

The *mind-map* is still evolving. The mind-lines in the Outframing section still need to be grouped or contrasted in chunks of 7 or less. In the mean time, similar mind-lines, like #16 (Necessity) and #17 (Possibility), are grouped next to each other with icons to help contrast them.

I keep the mind-lines mind-map in my head, trying one mind-line after another with others and myself until I find those valuable shifts in perception. It's like finding that "Door into Summer" that Robert Heinlein once wrote about. During a study group section we usually select one belief like, "Learning a language is difficult and stressful." Then we explore which mind-lines have significant impact on it. Then, we try to guess why those particular mind-lines have impact at all.

As you read this book, I encourage you to create your own mind-map. Make your own special connections and ways of learning *the Mind-Lines Model.*

Pascal J. Gambardella, Ph.D. is a Senior Consultant at Computer Sciences Corporation. He has led an NLP Study Group, *Learning Unlimited,* in the Washington D.C. area for the last sixteen years and is now a NLP/ Neuro-Semantic Trainer.

Figure 19:2

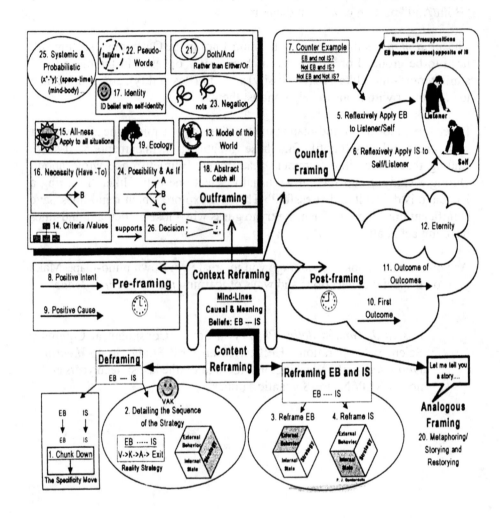

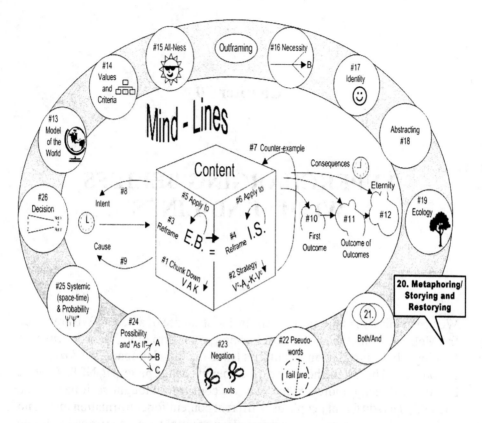

Analogous Framing

Chapter 20

SUPERCHARGING BELIEFS
WITH MIND-LINES

We began this book talking about the inside structure of a belief. We presented the Meta-State modeling of a belief using the confirmation / dis-confirmation framing.[1] In Neuro-Semantics this has led to the foundational *Meta-No / Meta-Yes pattern*. This offers the most explicit belief change pattern in NLP. *Explicit* because it directly addresses the way we confirm a thought so it becomes a "belief." That different people use different content for confirmation makes no difference, the structure is the same, *confirm* a thought, set a confirmation frame over any thought, and it will no longer be just a thought, but a full fledged belief. What any particular person uses for confirmation" whether authority, repetition, familiarity, emotion, etc. is content. It's the dynamic structure of meta-stating *confirmation* that creates the magic.

There are other *belief change* patterns in in NLP, and one of the best in our opinion is Robert Dilts' *Museum of Old Beliefs* pattern.[2] This also is actually a meta-stating pattern as we embed an old belief within a sequence of frames—doubt, openness to change, antiquity ("museum of old beliefs"), etc. In this case it is the *embedding* that does the meta-stating.

Working with Limiting Beliefs
Throughout this book our focus has been on *reframing* a limiting or even a sabotaging belief—an idea that interferes with excellence, that undermines accessing our full range of resources, and that creates a map that prevents us from living and experiencing as fully as possible. When a belief is limiting it invites confusion, sabotages, creates self-doubt, worry, and inhibits action by evoking fears. Within such ideas are frames that make them toxic.

In response, we use the Mind-Lines model to conversationally *re-frame* things.

That is, we communicate in a way to open a mind to new vistas, opportunities, and resources. The conversational reframing invites a new way of thinking by moving the person's focus in seven ways.

- It may invite a deframing of the old frame to loosen it up and give the person a chance to look at things afresh—*deframing*.
- It may provide a lateral shift that invites a new and different perspective—*reframing*.
- It may invite a look at things from the past and so frame things as having positive intentions or positive causes—*preframing*.
- It may zoom out into a future perspective and look back on things so as to invite a consequential framing of things—*postframing*.
- It may flip around and throw some aspect of the current frame back into the speaker's face to test its congruency and universality—*counter-framing*.
- It may soar upward to higher reaches of the mind and perspective and layer one or multiple frames upon the frame thereby changing the psycho-logics of the semantic structure—*outframing*.
- It may do some side-stepping as it steps into the land of metaphor and analogy and covertly, implicitly, and non-directively frame from the side—*analogous framing*.

Supercharging Beliefs

If we can do this with limiting beliefs, what about good everyday beliefs that we already find resourceful? Now the amazing thing is that the *Mind-Lines model* works just as well to enrich beliefs as it does to change beliefs. We can use the same *Mind-Line* questions to intentionally build up, extend, and expand an already powerful and wonderful belief.

When I first considered this, I had serious doubts. Having always used reframing to work with limiting beliefs, applying the same to healthy beliefs struck me as incredible. Yet when I realized that *if* it did work, it would give us a marvelous process for turning a regular but perhaps prosaic belief into a super-charged belief, I gave it a go. The result? I found is that the *Mind-Line questions* which can challenge and reformulate a limiting belief can just as readily empower a belief to make it robust and full of vitality.

How can that be? The reason lies in the attitude and intention we bring as we use the *Mind-Line* questions. If we come with *the intention* in changing a belief, then we set an implicit frame, "Let's change this baby!" If we come with *the intention* of consolidating and supporting a belief, then our frame-by-implication covertly says, "Make this belief more robust than ever before." In both cases we embed the mind-line model and process within a larger frame of either change or enrichment. In other words, confirmation or dis-confirmation. And the magical thing about this kind of meta-stating is that the frame we set will self-organize and create a self-fulfilling process. Consequently for several years we have been using the *Mind-Line questions* in two very different ways. We can use the questions to *pull apart* beliefs that undermine us and also to *glue together*, reinforce, and make robust beliefs that give us a winning edge. You can use this pattern on a belief that limits or sabotages you as well.

Super-Charging a Belief
1) Identify a belief.

>What belief would you like to strengthen and beef up to enrich your life?
>Do you want to transform an everyday belief or a fantastic belief that's too unbelievable?
>What would you want to belief that would empower you so that if you believed it fully, it would truly enrich your life?

2) Express the belief in a clear and succinct sentence.

>Now as you think about a belief that serves you very well that you would like to enrich, extend, and make even more magical, how do you express this belief as congruently and expressively as you can and find it compelling?
>Is that as congruently expressive and compelling as you can express it right now?
>Would you like to make it even more so?
>Have you written the statement down so that you can record it? If not, then do so now.

3) Facilitate the process by asking Mind-Line questions about the belief.

>If you're the coach, use the following questions. As you do, use lots of *confirmation* and *affirmation* statements in the process to create a supportive atmosphere.
>If you're the experiencer, then simply respond naturally and easily to the questions. As you do, fully experience the representations and feelings that the belief elicits, noticing them, witnessing them, and being with them.
>While there is no *right* procedure for asking the questions, the following arrangement gives you one way to begin. As you develop your artistry in this skill, you'll find that you will increasingly follow and pace the energy of the speaker.

The Mind-Line Questions—

>What do you believe?
>What do you mean by X or Y? (X being the external referent, Y the internal one.)
>What do you mean by that?

How do you know that you believe this? And how do you know that?
How do you do that?
How do you represent that in the movie of your mind?
How do you breath, hold yourself, gesture, etc.?
So this means this X to you? (Confirmation with doubting tone for limiting belief, with celebrative tone for empowering belief.)
And does it mean anything else?
How does this benefit you? How does it enrich your life?
How does this serve in a positive way for you?
Did you create this map yourself or did you learn it from someone else?
When did you first learn to think this way?
What does this lead to?
And when you get those benefits, what does that tend to lead to?
When you think this way and use this belief to move through the world, how does it affect your identity or the way you define yourself?
Do you have to do it this way?
Is that all it means to you? Does it mean anything else?
What else could it mean to you that would enrich it even further?
How is that valuable to you?
Is it ecological? When you step back from it, is it productive, healthy, and useful?
What is it like?
What if it wasn't this? If it was not, what would it be?
How does this work within your mind-body-emotion system? And so on as you run through the 26 mind-lines.

Summary

- *Changing* our limiting beliefs is not difficult when we know the thought-belief meta-structure and have some effective tools for influencing the confirmation and dis-confirmation frames that hold the belief in place. *Mind-Line* questions enable us to do precisely that.

- Nor is it difficult to *super-charge* a belief. The Mind-Line questions enable us to solidify and enrich a new belief, to strengthen and consolidate it, and to commission the belief as a command to our nervous system so we can *embody* it in our lives.

End Notes:

1. See *Secrets of Personal Mastery* (1999) and www.neurosemantics.com for several articles and patterns on this.
2. You can find the *Museum of Old Beliefs* pattern in *Changing Belief Systems with NLP* (1990), *Beliefs: Pathways to Health and Well-being* (1990), and also in *The Source Book of Magic* (1997).

EPILOGUE

Let the Magic Begin

You know about framing and reframing,
  you know about the nature and functioning of meaning,
    its structure and levels,
     you know about how we meaning-makers structure our
      neuro-semantic meanings into a Matrix of frames,
     you have explored *seven directions* for sending
    or re-directing consciousness,
      and you have learned about twenty-six ways
       to conversationally reframe meaning.

Now as an apprentice magician
  you only need to get out there
    and get some real-life hands-on practice with the mind-lines.

As you do
  we would love to hear about your forages into the world,
    your experiences of turning frogs into princes,
     taming, slaying, and transforming dragons,
      as you master your own Matrix of meanings
      and facilitate a greater resourcefulness
       in each and every person you meet.

May you frame and reframe with elegance and respect,
  May you walk gently and lovingly as you enter another's world,
    May you spread joy and fun and compassion,
    And may you have wonderful conversations
     that transform you and others.

Go for it!

Appendix A

MODELING HOW WE THINK

REVISITING THE CINEMA OF THE MIND

As a cognitive model of "mind," NLP describes how we "think" in terms of our *representation systems*. This refers to how we have a "sense" on the inside of what we "sense" on the outside. As we see, hear, feel, smell, and taste things, so we *re-present* to ourselves the same referents. We see our dog and can make an internal picture of Spot. We can even see Spot running around in our background, dashing between the trees and over the landscape of newly mowed grass and through the patio and into the garden.

Did you *see* all of that? By using sensory-based words, we evoke in ourselves and others an *internal mental movie*. It is *as if* we have an internal Cinema in our minds and can activate it to recall or create (remember or imagine) sights, sounds, sensations, smells, and tastes. I say it is *as if* we have such because it is only a *phenomenon of consciousness* and not a structure of the brain. In the brain there is no screen.

This is the genius of NLP. Bandler and Grinder used the sensory systems as the foundation of "thought." Yet we do more than just create internal movies in our mind, we say words *about* our movies. We even fill up our movies with words as part of the sound track of the cinema. Yet doing so shifts us to a higher level of mind. While we can *see* words that we write on a surface and *hear* words that are uttered, *words occur as a meta-representational system*. Words are *about* our movies. NLP called the cinema "the VAK representational systems" made up of "modalities" and the finer distinctions, "sub-modalities." That's the jargon of NLP.

By words, we shift to more *abstract* thinking. Words allow us to classify and categorize ideas and to construct ideas, principles, beliefs, and all of the other higher logical levels of the mind. This domain is the speciality of the Meta-States model.

The Cinema that we *re-present* in our mind is a very special type of movie show. What's most obvious is that we encode our cinema with a *sight* and *sound* track. We *see* things and we *hear* things. We reproduce images, sights, pictures, sounds, noises, music, etc. We can also *smell* things, *taste* things, and *feel* things. That means we have a smell track, taste track and sensation track in our mind.

We can imagine a big bright-red and very juice strawberry ... a bowl of strawberries, covered with the coldest and whitest whipped cream ... and imagine bringing a spoonful to our lips ...

The see-hear-feel representations are our *modes* of awareness. The finer distinctions (bright, red, cold, white) are the features and qualities of our *modes*. NLP wrongly labeled these features as *"sub*-modalities." They are not *sub* or lower than the modalities. Actually they operate at a *higher "logical level"* to the sensory systems. They govern how we *frame* the *features* and *qualities* of our sights, sounds, sensations, and smells of our mental movies. They describe the cinematic features of our movie.

Labeling these qualities *"sub*-modalities" unfortunately mis-mapped the structure. These qualities operate at a meta-level and reflect our *conceptual* ideas about our movies. Actually, even to detect these cinematic features of our movies, we have to *go meta* to the see-hear-feel representations. We have to step back and notice them from a meta-position.

- Is my picture in color or is it in black-and-white?
- From what direction does that sound come from?
- How loud is that voice?

Not only is awareness dependent upon the meta-move, so is the ability to work with the cinematic features. If we want to use one of these *meta-level distinctions* ("sub-modalities"), we have to step back from the cinema and then apply the feature to the movie. That's meta-stating. As the internal Director of our Movie, we alter the "location," "intensity," "distance," "volume," "clarity," "focus," "perspective" etc. Yet these terms are nominalizations. They are nominalizations that we cannot put in a wheelbarrow. So inasmuch as they do not exist externally, they are functions of an encoding *mind*.

When we *use* any of these features (or "sub-modalities)" to encode our Cinema, we use them *symbolically and semantically*. We use them as *symbols* that stand for some *idea*.

- What *does it mean* when we bring an image *closer*?
- What does it mean when our pictures are encoded as far away?
- What does a three-dimensional image mean?
- How does that differ from a two-dimensional image?
- What does a serious tone mean? A humorous tone of voice?

As the directors of our internal movies, we use these *features* of representation symbolically. We use them as metaphors. They *stand for* some higher level meaning. They frame the movie to convey different significances and so to create different emotions. It is in this way that we create our neuro-semantic states.

Cinematic Quality	Meta-Programs	Meta-States Evaluative States
Representational systems	Thinking patterns	Semantic states
Sensory based descriptions	Evaluations	Higher Level
The form / structure	Meanings about thought	Evaluations

Visual —>   Representation system

__ Brightness
__ Focus/ Defocused
__ Color/ Black-&-White   —>   **Real, Current**
__ Size   Chunk Size: **Old, Past**
__ Distance: close or far —>   General/ Specific
__ Contrast   Global / Detail   **Compelling**
__ Movement   Options/ Procedures
__ Direction   Sensor/Intuitor; Uptime/Downtime
__ Foreground/ Background   Judger/Perceiver
                                   (Controlling / Perceiving)
__ Location   Self- / Other Referencing
__ Associated/Dissociated   External Reference
__ Changing/ Steady
__ Framed/ Panoramic
__ 2D (Flat), 3D (Holographic)   —> —>   **Real/ Unreal**
__ Speed: fast, slow, normal   Match- Mismatch / Same— Difference

Auditory

__ Pitch   Toward / Away From Values   **Motivation**
__ Continuous or   **Associated/ Dissocated**   **Assoc./ Dissoc.**
   Interrupted   Goal Sort: Optimizing/ Perfectionism
__ Skepticism
__ Tempo: fast/ slow   Value buying: cost, Time, convenience
__ Volume: loud/ soft   Time Tenses: Past/ Present / Future   **"Time"**
__ Rhythm   In Time / Through Time
__ Duration   Affiliation: Independent/ Dependent/ Team/
__ Cadence   Manager
__ Foreground/ Background   Extrovert/ Introvert / Ambivert
__ Distance
__ Location   Convincer—VAK or Words   **Proof**
__ Clarity

Kinesthetic

__ Pressure   MO: Impossibility— Possibility
__ Location & Extent   MO: Necessity — Desire
__ Shape
__ Texture
__ Temperature
__ Movement
__ Rhythm
__ Duration
__ Foreground/ Background
__ **Associated/ Dissociated**   —> **Thinker/ Feeler**
__ Intensity
__ Frequency
__ Weight

This gives us the ability to cue our brains-and-nervous systems to respond to something as "real" in contrast to a "fantasy," and a thousand other key concepts. Most of us will use in color, close, 3-D, and panoramic for "real," and encode our movie as bordered, fuzzy, flat two-dimensional snapshots, etc. for "not real." This is how we use these features as meta-level frames to convey higher level or more abstract *meanings*. See *Sub-modalities: Going Meta (2004)* for extended study.

Experience
Recall some pleasant experience or imagine what a really *delightful and pleasant experience* would be like.

Various things may pop into mind as you do this and just let this happen. Whatever pops up into consciousness, just allow yourself to go with that awareness for the moment. If you don't seem to find the kind of pleasant memory that you prefer, then allow yourself to simply *imagine* a desired pleasant experience that you would like to have. As you do this, you may find that closing your eyes will help.

Once you have this pleasant experience, permit it to remain in your awareness so you can work with it and use it. Now as you do, first just begin to *notice its visual aspects*. As you recall the experience, what do you see? Notice the picture of the memory. If you do not visualize well, then imagine what the pleasant experience *feels* like. Or, allow yourself to just *listen* to some pleasant sounds—words or music and enjoy that kind of an internal pleasant experience.

Now allow the picture of that memory to grow, to become much larger. Let it double in size ... and then let that picture double again ... And notice what happens. When you made the picture bigger, what happens to your feelings of that experience? Do they intensify?

Now let the picture shrink back to normal size, and now notice it as it grows smaller and smaller. Allow it to become so small you can hardly see it ... Stay with this a moment ... Do the intensity of the feelings decrease? Experiment now with making the picture bigger and then smaller. When you make it smaller, do your feelings decrease? And when you make it larger, do your feelings increase? This tends to be typical for most people.

If you had a different experience, just notice that. After all, we code our experiences in unique and individual ways. This describes how we differ from each other. Finish by putting your picture of the pleasant experience in a format that you find most comfortable and acceptable.

With that picture, move it closer to you. Imagine the picture moving closer and closer to you. What happens to your feelings as it does? ... Move the picture farther away. What happens when you move the picture farther away? Do your feelings intensify when you move the picture closer? Do your feelings decrease when you move the picture farther away?

Most people find this true for the way their consciousness / neurology works. When you moved the picture farther away, the feeling probably decreased. Notice that as you change the mental representation in your mind of the experience, your feelings change. This, by the way, describes how we can "distance" ourselves from experiences, does it not?

Suppose you experiment with the brightness of the picture? As you look at your pictures, do you see them in color or black-and-white? If your pictures have color, make them black-and-white, and vice versa if you have them coded as black-and-white. ... When you changed the color, did your feelings change?

Consider the focus of your images: in focus or out of focus? Do you see an image of yourself in the picture or do you experience the scene as if looking out of your own eyes? What about the quality of your images: in three dimensional (3D) form or flat (2D)? Does it have a frame around it or do you experience it as panoramic? Experiment by changing *how* you represent the experience. Change the location of the picture. If you have it coded as on your right, then move it to your left.

We can change our feelings by changing *how* we internally *represent* an experience. This works primarily with the *processes of the mind* rather than with *content*. Here we have changed how we feel about an experience by changing the quality and structure of our images rather than their content. We made the changes at the mental *process* level while leaving the content the same.

What would happen if we made all our *unpleasant pictures* big, bright and up close? What would happen if we made all our *pleasant experiences* small, dim, and far away? We would become an expert at feeling depressed, miserable and unresourceful!

Consider what would happen if we coded our *pleasant experiences* as big, bright, and up close... will that not create for us a more positive outlook on life? What if we made our *unpleasant experiences* small, dim and far away? Would not the negative have less influence over us?

Appendix B
THE META-MODEL

This linguistic model identifies a set of linguistic distinctions that govern how we *model* our internal maps of the world. This may enrich or impoverish our operational models. Questioning the linguistic mapping therefore enables us to recover a fuller representation and to even re-map in more productive ways.

(1) **Unspecified nouns** (deletions):
> Statements lacking a referential index regarding the performer or subject of the action. Unspecified verbs refer to the action or process representation that lacks specificity.

(2) **Unspecified adjectives and adverbs**:
> Qualifiers of nouns and verbs which lack specificity.

(3) **Unspecified relations** (comparative deletions):
> Comparative statements that lack the standard by which the comparison arises. "She is better than him;" "He is smarter than his brother."

(4) **Generalized Referential Index**:
> Words with a generalized referent so that the words do not immediately make the specific reference clear.

(5) **Universal Quantifiers**:
> Words that create representations of allness: all, every, never, everyone, no one, etc.

(6) **Modal Operators**:
> *The modes* of *operating* or style of actions indicating the kind of "world" we live in. Modal operators of *necessity* map a world of laws and rules (should, must, have to, need to, etc.). Modal operators of *possibility* map a world of choice and options (can, may, will, might possible, etc.). Modal operators of *impossibility* map a world of limitations (can't, impossible, etc.).

(7) **Lost Performatives**:
> Phrases and sentences which indicate a value judgment given without specifying who made the evaluation.

(8) **Nominalizations**:
> Noun-like words and phrases that hide or smother a verb. Nominalizing turns a process word (a verb) into a noun and treats the activity as if a "thing" or "entity." This reification of a process or event masquerades the verb to prevent a reader from recognizing it. Relating becomes *relationship,* motive and motivating becomes *motivation,* leading becomes *leadership,* etc. De-nominalizing is the Meta-Model process for challenging nominalizations and turning pseudo-nouns back into the verbs from which they came.

(9) **Mind-Reading**:
> Claiming to know someone's internal state, thought, emotions, etc. without specifying how you attained that information. "You don't like me."

(10) **Cause—Effect**:
> Making a causation statement containing illogical formulations. "She makes me angry."

(11) **Complex Equivalences**:
> Linguistically connecting two experiences so as to make them equal or synonymous. "I know he doesn't like me when he uses that tone of voice."

(12) **Presuppositions**:

The unspoken assumptions, beliefs, understandings, etc. necessary for a statement to "make sense."

Extending the Meta-Model

The following comes from *Communication Magic* (2001, formerly, *The Secrets of Magic,* 1998).

(13) **Pseudo-Words**:
> Written or auditory forms that look and sound like words, but do not actually reference anything. Korzybski described these as "spell-marks" and "noise."

(14) **Static Words**:
> One-valued terms that the speaker has failed to extensionalize.

(15) **Undefined Terms**:
> Like presuppositions, these are terms we can't define except in using terms that make up the meaning of the term. This leads to circular reasoning, defining our terms by the very terms that we use in our definition. Solution? Simply "lay on the table our metaphysics and our assumed structures" recognizing the undefinedness of the terms.

(16) **Either-Or Terms and Phrases**:
> Using an either-or format for representing reality creates a two-valued structure, and typically does not accord with the territory. It generally creates excluded middles and eliminates the both-and thinking of systems.

(17) **Multi-ordinal terms**:
> When we can use a word on different levels without indicating at which level we're using it, its meaning becomes ambiguous. Multi-ordinal terms are nominalizations that are ambiguous in and of themselves. To determine what they mean we have to ask, "At what level are you using this term?"

(18) **Identification**:
> Treating phenomena that occur in different levels or dimensions as if "the same." We identify things, processes, events, etc. when we ignore differences. The *"is" of identity* works in an especially insidious way. Via identifications, we hallucinate concepts as external things, and create a frozen universe.

(19) **Delusional Verbal Splits**:
> When we split or dichotomize phenomenon which cannot and does not exist in those parts (mind-and-body, space-time, etc.) we create an elementalism. Language gives us the ability to analyze and separate things. Yet we often forget that our verbal mapping is only that—at the verbal level and does not actually reflect separate "elements." This can create *delusional* verbal splits, "mind," "body," etc.

(20) **Static or Signal Words**:
> Terms that portray reality as static, definite, absolute, and one-valued give rise to "a legislative semantic mood." Such language leads to the "thinghood of words."

(21) **Metaphors**:
> All language actually works metaphorically. Explicit metaphors describe larger level units of meaning, speaking about one thing in terms of another. Metaphors can involve stories, narrative, poetry, koans, proverbs, "is," "like," etc. Metaphors allow us to map a phenomenon in terms of the structure, function, purpose, etc. of another phenomenon.

(22) **Over-defined and Under-defined Terms.**
> Most terms are *under-defined* extensionally as we fail to point out the *extensional* meanings in sensory-based terms and *over-define intensionally* as

we over-rely upon verbal, dictionary definitions. This leads to unsanity. It moves us further and further away from the sensory based, empirical world and more into a world of words and mere verbal definitions.

THE STRUCTURAL RE-LANGUAGING MODEL

PATTERNS/ DISTINCTIONS	RESPONSES/CHALLENGES

Part I: Deletions

1. PSEUDO-WORDS/ NON-REFERENCING WORDS:

Words with no true referents.	What specifically do you refer to?
Index the Reference.	What specifically do you mean by *failure*?
"That makes him a failure."	Does "failure" refer to anything that actually exists? Does it not merely function as an intensional definition?

2. DESCRIPTIVE/EVALUATIVE WORDS:

Words/language that either empirically describes or that evaluates.	Use see, hear, feel terms.

3. UNSPECIFIED NOUNS & ADJECTIVES:

Unspecified Referential Index; "Simple deletions"

"I am uncomfortable."	Uncomfortable in what way? Uncomfortable when?
"They don't listen to me."	Who specifically doesn't listen to you?
"He said that she was mean."	Who specifically said that? What did he mean by 'mean'?

4. UNSPECIFIED VERBS & ADVERBS:

Verbs that suffer from vagueness	How, specifically, did he reject you?
"He rejected me."	

5. UNSPECIFIED RELATIONS

Comparative Deletions, relations not specified	
"She's a better person."	Better than whom? Better at what? Compared to whom, what? Given what criteria?

6. NOMINALIZATIONS:

Hidden or Smothered Verbs	
"Let's improve our communication."	Who is communicating to you? How would you like to communicate?
"What state did you wake up in this morning?"	Use Co-ordinates to index: what, when, who, where, which, how, etc.?
De-nominalize the nominalization to recover the hidden verb.	

Describe all emotional and psychosomatic words using verbs.

7. STATIC WORDS:

One-valued words.	
"Science says that..."	What science?

Extensionalize the word.

Science according to whose model, theory, etc.?
Does only one "science" speak for all sciences?

8. UNSPECIFIED SPEAKER:
Lost Performative: Speaker of statement deleted.
"It's bad to be inconsistent."

Who evaluates it as bad?
According to what standard?
How do you determine this label of "badness?"

9. UNDEFINED TERMS:
Terms not adequately defined by extension.
"Your egotism is really getting out of
    hand."
State your Assumptions & Presuppositions—

What specifically do you refer to?
What does this mean to you?

Part II: Generalizations

10. UNIVERSAL QUANTIFIERS: Allness.
"She never listens to me."

Never? She never listens to you?
What would happen if she did?

11. MODAL OPERATORS:
Words of State or Mode: Necessity, Possibility,
Impossibility, Desire, etc.
"I have to take care of her."
"I can't tell him the truth."

What would happen if you did?
What would happen if you didn't?
What wouldn't happen if you didn't?
  "...Or what?"

12. EITHER-OR PHRASES:
Indicating two-valued representations.
"If I don't make this relationship
work, I'm done with them."

"See if you can frame that
statement in a non either-or way."
Wave you excluded the middles?
"What in-betweens, grays, stages, etc.
could also enter into this picture?"

13. MULTIORDINAL WORDS:
Word meanings can operate at multiple
levels & depend upon context.
"Science"

"Whose science?" "Science at what time?"
"What kind of science?"

Part III: Distortions

14. MIND READING STATEMENTS:
Statements about another's internal states.
(Thoughts, intentions, motives, motivations, etc.)
"You don't like me..."

How do you know I don't like you?
What evidence leads you to that conclusion?

15. CAUSATIONAL STATEMENTS:
Statements that connect assertions of "cause"
between various processes.
"You make me sad."

How does my behavior cause you to

Counter Example:
How specifically does this work?

respond
with sad feelings?
Do you always feel sad when I do this?

16. EQUIVALENCE STATEMENTS:
Statements of equation and Identity using the "Is"
of Identity. "Complex Equivalence"
"She's always yelling at me;
she doesn't like me."

How does her yelling mean that she doesn't
like you?
Can you recall a time when you yelled at
someone you liked?

Eliminate To-Be Verbs (is, am, are, to be, been
being, was, were) by E-Priming.
"He's a loser when it comes
to business; he just lacks business sense
Extensionalize:

How does him failing at a job turn
him into a loser?
Upon what basis do you make this
evaluation?

Differentiate:
Subscript time, place, person.

How does being a human being
differ from being a loser'?

17. IDENTIFICATION STATEMENTS:
Statements that make the equation that one thing
exists just like another thing in all respects.

18. PRESUPPOSITIONAL STATEMENTS:
Silent Assumptions and Paradigms that lurk
within & behind words and statements.
"If my husband knew how much
I suffered, he wouldn't do that."

This presupposes that she suffers,
that she lets her husband's behavior
cause her suffering, that he lacks
knowledge about her pain, that his
intentions would shift if he knew.

How do you choose to suffer?
How does he react?
How do you know he doesn't know?

19. DELUSIONAL VERBAL SPLIT STATEMENTS:
Statements that split a part of an unsplitable
"reality" into elementalistic parts.
"My depression has nothing to do
with my "mind. "It's just the way my
"body" works."

How can you experience 'mind'
apart from your 'body/?'
How does your mind function
apart from your body?

20. METAPHORS:
Words & Sentences that refer to Analogous relations
Stories.

Tell a story!

Appendix C

THE 'IS' BIZ

What is this business of "is?"

Alfred Korzybski (1933/1994) warned that *the "is" of identity* and *the "is" of predication* present two dangerous linguistic and semantic constructions that map false-to-fact conclusions. The first has to do with identity—how we identify a thing or what we identify with. The second has to do with attribution—how we project our "stuff" onto others and things without realizing it.

E-Prime and E-Choice (a modified version of E-Prime) empowers people to not fall into the "is" traps of language.

E-Prime refers to **English-***primed* of the "to be" verb family of passive verbs (is, am, are, was, were, be, being, been). D. David Bourland, Jr. invented E-Prime and then he and Paul Dennithorne Johnston wrote about it in *To Be or Not: An E-Prime Anthology*.

Identity as "sameness in all respects," does not and cannot exist. At sub-microscopic levels, everything comprises a dance of electrons, always moving, changing, and becoming. No thing ever stays the "same," not even with itself. Nothing "is" static, permanent, or unchanging. Everything continually changes. To use "is" mis-speaks, mis-evaluates, and mis-maps reality. To say, "She is lazy..." "That is a stupid statement..." falsely maps reality. Korzybski argued that unsanity and insanity ultimately lies in *identifications*.

The **"is" of Predication** asserts our responses onto the world. To say, "This *is* good," "That flower *is* red," "He *is* stupid!" presents a language structure implying that something "out there" contains these qualities of "goodness," "redness," and "stupidity." The *"is"* implies that these things exist *independent of the speaker's experience*. Not so. Our descriptions speak primarily about *our internal experience,* judgments, and values. More accurately we would say, "I evaluate as good this or that," "I see that flower as red," "I think of him as suffering from stupidity!"

"Is" statements falsely distract, confuse logical levels, and subtly lead us to think that such value judgments exist outside our skin in the world "objectively." Wrong again. The evaluations (good, red, stupid) function as definitions and interpretations in the speaker's mind.

The "to be" verbs dangerously presuppose that "things" (actually events or processes) stay the same. These verbs invite us to create mental representations of fixedness so that we begin to set the world in concrete and to live in "a frozen universe." These verbs code the dynamic nature of processes statically. "Life *is* tough." "I *am* no good at math."

These statements sound definitive and absolute. "That*'s* just the way it *is*!" Bourland has described "is" "am" and "are," etc. as *"the deity mode."* "The fact *is* that this work *is* no good!" Such words carry a sense of completeness, finality, and time-independence. Yet discerning the difference between the map and the territory tells us these phenomena exist on different logical levels. Using E-Prime (or E-Choice) reduces slipping in groundless authoritarian statements which only close minds or invite arguments.

If we confuse the language we use in describing reality (our map) with reality (the territory), then we *identify* things that differ. That makes for unsanity because t*here "is" no is. "Is"* non-references. It points to nothing real. It operates entirely as an irrational construction of the human mind. Its use leads to semantic mis-evaluations.

Conversely, writing, thinking, and speaking in E-Prime contributes to *"consciousness of abstracting"* so that we make maps of the world which differ from the world. E-Prime enables us to think and speak with more clarity and precision by getting us to take first-person. This reduces the passive verb tense ("It was done." "Mistakes were made."). It restores speakers to statements, thereby contextualizing statements. E-Prime, by raising consciousness of abstracting, thereby enables us to index language. Now I realize that the person I met last week, Person$_{last\ week}$, *"is"* not equal in all respects to the person that now stands before me, Person$_{this\ week}$. This assists me in making critical and valuable distinctions.

E-Choice differs from E-Prime in that with it we use—
> the *"is"* of *existence* (e.g. "Where is your office?"
> "It is on 7th. Street at Elm Avenue."),
> the *auxilary "is"* (e.g. "He is coming next week."),
> and *the "is" of name,* (e.g. "What is your name?"
> "It is Michael." "My name is Bob.").

So we have written this in E-Choice and not *pure* E-Prime as in previous works, thereby avoiding some circumlocutious phrases that we have used in the past(!).

INDEX

Abductions: 49, 199-200
Beliefs: 62-64, 70, 98, 248, 297-300, 322-325
  Definition: 71-75, 80
Cartesian Logic: 135, 137
Change: see Meaning Transformation
Cinderella: 301
Communication: 24, 25, 244-7, 281, 287-292, 312-4
Creatura: 112-3, 286
Chunk Down: 96-102
Deconstruction: 94
Depression: 103-4, 140-2
Ethics: 61
Externalizing: 206
Framing: 100, 259-60, 261, 279, 300
  Analogous: 49, 52, 197-209
  As If or Possibility: 218
  Benevolent Double Bind: 138
  Context: 53, 84, 228, 236-7, 310, 317
  Content: 53, 85, 114-118, 228, 308, 317
  Counter: 48, 125-142, 133, 232-3
  Deframing: 43-44, 47, 93-110, 304, 310
  Layering: 90, 314
  Outframing: 40, 49, 55, 165-196, 311-2
  Pre-framing: 43, 48, 143-152, 233-5, 296, 310
  Post-Framing: 43, 48, 143-145, 153, 233-5, 296, 311
  Overt- Covert: 65-66
  Reframing: 36-7, 48, 76
  Principles: 82, 260, 280
  Realization: 191
  Structure: 42-3, 73, 76, 79, 85, 87, 103, 230, 282-3, 304
  Unreality: 188
  Frame Games: 260

Isomorphic: 199, 204
Hypnosis: 55, 67
General Semantics: 20, 23, 34, 39, 67, 87, 101, 185, 194, 210, 213, 220, 229, 247, 256, 257, 279
  Abstracting: 27, 29, 34

Elementalism: 220
E-Prime: 287, 333-4
Hyphen: 23, 220
Indexing: 87, 96, 305
Semantic Reactions: 87
Logical Fate: 279
Map is not the Territory: 185

Logical Levels: 27, 29, 72, 164, 167, 284, 300, 308
Linguistics: 25, 29, 31
  Neuro-Linguistics: 22
  Sensory-based: 26, 28, 32
  Levels: 27, 38, 71
  Specificity: 31
  Evaluative: 33, 37

Magic: 20, 23, 33, 69-74, 88, 262, 322
  Magic Box: 7, 69, 79, 281, 307
  Magic Cues: 309-312

Meaning: 41-42, 70, 78, 260, 275-286, 299
  Directions: 44, 46, 54
  Formula: 7, 69
  Levels: 27, 39
  "Maybe" story: 77-78
  Plasticity: 277-8
  Transformation: 82, 259, 260, 278, 283, 322-325

Meta-States: 11, 130, 157, 166, 167, 176, 309
  Meta-stating: 11, 157
  Matrix: 70, 91, 277, 315
  Systems thinking, dynamics: 142, 220

Movie Mind: 22, 28, 72, 173, 323-327
  Stepping in: 38
Mind-Lines: 167, 263
  Charts: 46, 56, 109, 116, 128, 126, 196, 231-241, 318, 320, 321
  Examples: failure, 13-18; learning 266-269; Confrontation, 270-2
  List: 50-51, 53, 56, 167-169
  Origin: 57-8, 167-169
  Playground: 95

Sleight of Mouth: 47, 58-62, 229, 316

Mind-Line Patterns:
Specificity: 96-102
Detailing Strategies: 103-
Reframing Content: 114-118
Reflexively Applying: 119-123, 129-130
Counter-Example: 48
Prior Positive Intention: 48, 145-148
Prior Positive Cause: 48, 149-152
Outcome: 153-163
Model of the World: 167, 170-4
Criteria and Value: 175-0
Allness: 168, 179-182
Necessity: 168, 183-184
Identity: 168, 185-187
Ecology: 169, 194-195
Both/And: 211-2
Pseudo-Word: 213-214
Negation: 188, 215-217
Possibility: 218-219
Systemic, Probability: 220-222
Decision: 223-4
Metaphor: 197-207

Meta:
Definition: 29, 188, 199
Levels: 27

Meta-Model: 62, 67, 75, 80-1, 84, 94 200, 228, 247-262, 328-332
Cause-Effect: 80, 86, 112, 124, 257, 283, 328
Complex Equivalent: 80, 86, 112, 124, 257, 283, 328
Identification: 67, 80, 81, 88, 140, 185, 186, 187, 257, 283, 329, 333-4
Lost Performative: 75, 170, 328
Metaphor: 199-207, 329
Modus Operandi: 168, 183, 218, 257, 328
Multi-Ordinality: 101, 108, 329
Nominalization: 24, 30, 175, 257, 328
Presuppositions: 80, 257
Trans-Derivational Search: 202, 258

Transformational Grammar: 255, 258
Universal Quantifier: 179, 242, 328

Mapping: 63-4, 67
Meta-Programs: 97, 173
Milton Model: 99
Modeling: 68, 81, 97, 100, 307-8
Muddle: 43
Neuro-Linguistic Programming:
Description: 20-2
Creatures: 23

Neurology: 63, 76, 251, 257, 259
Questions: 81, 96, 104, 243-6, 254, 256,
309-312

Patterns
Movie Rewind (phobia cure): 21-22, 30
S.C.O.R.E.: 289-290
Belief Change / Enhancer: 324-325
Perceptual Positions: 134, 238
Persuasion: 30
Plethora: 112-3, 286
Psycho-Logics: 10, 40, 45, 69, 132, 252, 282
Psychotherapy: 65, 241, 256
Referential Index Shift / Switch: 96, 119-120, 179, 203
Resistance: 66
Representationally Testing/ Tracking: 85, 256, 262
REBT: 180
Self-Reflexive: 42-43, 119-123, 130, 176, 203-4
Sensory Acuity: 89
Space: 238
Strategies: 103-104, 306
States: 293- 301
Sub-modalities: 25, 89, 91, 97, 171, 178, 306, 324, 325
S.W.O.T.: 234
Stories: see Metaphors
Time: 50-51, 145-163, 189, 239-41, 289
Un-Insultable: 295
Voodoo: 77

Persons:

Andreas, Connirae: 64, 125-126, 171

Bateson, Gregory: 112, 141, 158, 197, 198, 215, 229, 247, 261, 281'

Bandler, Richard: 20, 57-59, 74, 92, 107, 138, 190, 228, 253-4, 259, 291, 296

Belk, Tommy: 69

Bodenhamer, Bob: 131-132, 172, 203, 215-216, 229, 297, 322

Bridoux, Denis: 12, 54, 58, 59, 68, 191,
210, 227, 246

Chomsky, Noam: 200, 253, 255

Coyne, James: 261

Covey, Stephen: 159

Deming, Edwards: 249

Dilts, Robert: 12, 31, 57-59, 125, 165, 198, 204, 229, 289, 290, 322

Einstein: 220

Epstein, Todd: 58

Erickson, Milton: 100, 133, 159, 190, 200, 254

Festinger, Leon: 121

Freud, Sigmund: 69

Gambardella, Pascal: 12, 230, 316, 319

Grinder, John: 20, 29, 92, 94, 138, 190, 228, 253-4, 258

Hall, Chris: 161

Hall, L. Michael: 57, 107, 110, 111, 213, 227, 229, 272-3, 272-3, 297

Huxley, Aldous: 62

Kipling, Rudyard: 43

Kennedy, Suzanne: 69

Korzybski: 20, 23, 34, 39, 67, 87, 101, 185, 194, 210, 213, 220, 229, 247, 256, 257, 279

Kuhn, Thomas: 249

Lewis, C.S.: 164, 166

Lily, John: 69

Miller, George: 99, 231, 305

Naden, Sammy: 306

Orwell, George: 28, 32, 111

Perls, Fritz: 254

Shaw, George Bernard: 125

Shakespeare, William: 75

Senge, Peter: 249

Satir, Virginia: 254

Staten, Henry: 57, 67, 208

Whorf, Benjamin: 261

Wittgenstein: 57

Zink, Nelson: 84

BIBLIOGRAPHY

Bandler, Richard and Grinder, John. (1975). *The structure of magic, Volume I: A book about language and therapy.* Palo Alto, CA: Science & Behavior Books.

Bandler, Richard and Grinder, John. (1976). *The structure of magic, Volume II.* Palo Alto, CA: Science & Behavior Books.

Bandler, Richard and Grinder, John. (1979). *Frogs into princes: Neuro-linguistic programming.* Moab, UT: Real People Press.

Bandler, Richard and Grinder, John. (1982). *Reframing: Neuro-linguistic programming and the transformation of meaning.* Moab, UT: Real People Press.

Bandler, Richard. (1985). *Magic in action.* Moab, UT: Real People Press.

Bandler, Richard. (1985). *Using your brain for a change: Neuro-linguistic programming.* Moab, UT: Real People Press.

Bateson, Gregory. (1979). *Mind and nature: A necessary unity.* New York: Bantam.

Bateson, Gregory. (1972). *Steps to an ecology of mind.* New York: Ballatine.

Bodenhamer, Bobby G. (1993). *Advanced communication course: From neuro-linguistic programming.* Gastonia, NC: NLP of Gastonia.

Bodenhamer, Bobby G.; L. Michael Hall (1997). *Time-lining: Patterns for adventuring in "time."* Wales, UK: Anglo-American Books.

Bourland, David D. Jr. and Johnston,

Paul Dennithorne. (1991). *To be or not: An e-prime anthology.* San Francisco, CA: International Society for General Semantics.

Brunner, Jerome. (1990). *Acts of meaning.* Cambridge, MA: Harvard University Press.

Cade, Brian; and O'Hanlon William H. (1992). *A brief guide to brief therapy.* NY: W.W. Norton and Company.

Coyne, James C. (1985). Toward A Theory of Frames and Reframing: The Social Nature of Frames. *Journal of Marital and Family Therapy, Vol. II,* No. 4, pp. 337-344. Washington DC: American Association of Marriage and Family.

Covey, Stephen. (1987). *Seven habits of highly effective people.* New York: Simon and Schuster.

Dilts, Robert. (1976). *Roots of neuro-linguistic programming.* CA: Meta Publications.

Dilts, Robert. (1990). *Changing belief systems with NLP.* Cupertino, CA: Meta Publications.

Dilts, Robert B. (1999). *Sleight of mouth: The magic of conversational belief change.* Capitola, CA: Meta Publications.

Festinger, Leon. (1957). *A theory of cognitive dissonance.* Evanston, IL: Row, Peterson.

Hall, Michael. (1989). "E-Prime in NLP *Anchor Point,* International Journal for Effective NLP Communicators, Feb. 1995.

Hall, L. Michael. (1995). *Meta-states: A domain of logical levels, self-reflexiveness in human states of consciousness.* Grand Jct., CO: ET Publications.

Hall, L. Michael. (2000). *Dragon slaying: Dragon to princes.* Clifton, CO: NS Publications.

Hall, L. Michael. (1999). *The spirit of NLP: The process, meaning and criteria for mastering NLP.* Carmarthen, Wales, U.K.: Anglo-American Book Company Ltd.

Hall, L. Michael. (1996). *Becoming a ferocious presenter.* Grand Jct., CO: NS Publications

Hall, L. Michael. (1996). *Languaging: The linguistics of psychotherapy.* Grand Jct., CO: ET Publications.

Hall, L. Michael. (2001). *Neuro-linguistic programming: Going meta into logical levels.* Clifton, CO: NS Publications.

Hall, L. Michael. (1997). *Meta-State Magic: Patterns.* Clifton, CO: NS Publications.

Hall, L. Michael; Bodenhamer, Bob G. (1997). *Figuring out people: Design engineering using meta-programs.* Wales, UK: Anglo-American Books.

Hall, L. Michael. (1998). *The secrets of magic: Communication excellence for the 21st. century.* Wales, UK: Crown Press, Anglo-American Books.

Hall, L. Michael. (2000). *Frame games: Persuasion elegance.* Grand Jct. CO: N.S. Publications.

Hall, L. Michael; Bodenhamer, Bob; Bolstad, Richard; Hamblett, Margott. (2000). *The structure of personality: Modeling "personality" using NLP and NS.* Wales, UK: Crown House Publications.

Huxley, Aldous. (1954). *The doors of perception and heaven and hell.* NY: Harper & Row, Publishers.

James, Tad; Woodsmall, Wyatt. (1988). *Time line therapy and the basis of personality.* Cupertino, CA: Meta Publications.

Korzybski, Alfred. (1941/1994). *Science and sanity: An introduction to non-Aristotelian systems and general semantics,* (5th. ed.). Lakeville, CN: International Non-Aristotelian Library Publishing Co.

Kuhn, Thomas S. (1962, 1970). *The structure of scientific revolutions.* Chicago: IL: University of Chicago.

Laborde, Genie Z. (1984). *Influencing with integrity.* Palo Alto, CA: Syntony Publishing Co.

Lewis, Bryon A., Pucelik, R. Frank. (1982). *Magic demystified: A pragmatic guide to communication and change.* Portland, OR: Metamorphous Press, Inc.

O'Connor, Joseph; Seymour, John. (1990). *Introducing neuro-linguistic programming: The new psychology of personal excellence.* Great Britain: Mandala.

Watzlawick, Paul, J.; Weakland, John, and Fisch, Richard. (1974). *Change: Principles of problem formation and problem resolution.* NY: WW. Norton.

Whorf, Benjamin L. (1954). *Language, thought, and reality.* Cambridge, MA: MIT Press.

GLOSSARY OF TERMS

Accessing Cues: The ways we tune our bodies by breathing, posture, gesture and eye movements to think in certain ways.

As-If Frame: Using a pretend or possibility frame of mind to pretend that some event is real or actually happened and to step into that frame of thinking-and-feeling. Thinking "as if" encourages creative problem-solving by mentally going beyond apparent obstacles to desired solutions.

Analogue: A variable that can occur at various degrees between certain limits, like a dimmer switch for a light. An analogue "sub-modality" may vary like from light to dark, while a digital "sub-modality" or cinematic feature will operates in either the on or off position, either a snapshot or a movie.

Anchoring. An NLP technique and process that is derived from the Pavlovian stimulus-response reaction, and so a user-friendly version of classical conditioning. In Pavlov's study the bell became the stimulus or anchor for cuing the dogs to salivate as the meat powder had. When we link or connect a stimulus (external or internal) to a response, the sight, sound, sensation, smell, or word triggers a response or state.

Association: When we are imagining ourselves *inside* of an experience, movie, representation, we are associated into it. We are mentally seeing, hearing, and feeling from inside. We *step into* a state or experience to associate and we *step out* to dissociate. (See dissociation).

Auditory: The sense of hearing, one of our basic sensory representation systems.

Behavior: Any activity we engage in, micro like thinking, or macro like external actions.

Beliefs: A thought that has been confirmed in some way and is now treated as real. When we believe, we hold a generalization about causality, meaning, self, others, behaviors, identity, etc. as true. Beliefs are at a higher "logical level" to thoughts, a gestalt that result from confirming a thought. As frames, beliefs guide us in perceiving and interpreting reality.

Calibration: Tuning-in to another's state via reading non-verbal signals previously observed and calibrated to the person's style of expression.

Chunk and Chunking: A term from computer science about the size of information. When we chunk up, we go up a level, hence, inducing up or induction. This leads to higher abstractions. When we chunk down we go down a level, hence deducing, or deduction to detail more specific examples or cases.

Complex Equivalence: A linguistic distinction wherein someone makes two statements to mean or equate the same thing, e.g. "He doesn't love me because he's late."

Congruence: A state of being internally and externally aligned. What we say corresponds with what we do. Non-verbal signals and verbal statements match to create a state of unity, fitness, and internal harmony, the lack of inner conflict.

Conscious: Present moment awareness. Awareness of $7^{+/-}$ 2 chunks of information.

Content: The specifics and details of an

event, answers *what?* and *why?* Contrasts with process or structure.

Context: The setting, frame or process in which events occur and provides meaning for content.

Cues: Information that provides clues to another's subjective structures, i.e., eye accessing cues, predicates, breathing, body posture, gestures, voice tone and tonality, etc.

Deletion: Leaving out characteristics in a description, the missing portion of an experience in linguistics or representations.

Digital: An off or on distinction. Either the light switch is turned on or off. A digital cinematic feature presents the choice between on or off: a "sub-modality" shift from coded as in color or in black-and-white (see analogue).

Dissociation: The process of *stepping out* of a thought, representation, mental movie, or state and no longer being *inside* it, associated. Seeing or hearing things from outside as from a spectator's point of view (see association). These are relative terms, whenever we step out of one state, we are always stepping into another state.

Distortion: The modeling process by which we alter our representation of something in our neurology or linguistics. This can occur to create limitations or resources.

Downtime: Moving from a state of sensory awareness, to going "down" inside one's own mind to see, hear, and feel thoughts and memories. A light trance state with attention focused inward.

Dragon: A dragon state in the Meta-States model is an unresourceful state that seems to turn its energies against the person. In a primary state, this is too intense or too inappropriate of a state, in a meta-state, it is where a person has turned negative thoughts-and-feelings against oneself. See *Dragon Slaying* (2000).

Ecology: The dynamic balance of elements in a system that produce health, well-being, and balance, in larger contexts and relationships. Asking "the ecology question" is asking about how a belief, state, decision, or experience fits with one's overall set of relationships and its effect on one's health, business, values, etc.

Elicitation: Evoking a state by word, behavior, gesture, or any stimuli. Gathering information by direct observation of non-verbal signals or by asking meta-model questions.

Empowerment: Process of adding vitality, energy, and new powerful resources to a person; vitality at the neurological level, change of habits.

Eye Accessing Cues: Movements of the eyes in certain directions which indicate visual, auditory or kinesthetic thinking (processing).

Epistemology: The study of how we know what we know. NLP, as an epistemology, is based upon the cognitive distinction "the map is not the territory."

First Position: Perceiving the world from your own point of view, associated, one of the three perceptual positions.

Frame: Context, environment, meta-level, a way of perceiving something (as in Outcome Frame, "As If" Frame, Backtrack Frame, etc.). (see *Frame Games*)

Future Pace: Process of mentally practicing (rehearsing) an event before it happens. One of the key processes for ensuring the permanency of an outcome, a frequent and key ingredient in most NLP interventions.

Generalization: Process by which one specific experience comes to represent a whole class of experiences, one of the three modeling processes in NLP.

Genius: This refers to a highly focused state of engagement wherein the world goes away, time goes away, even self goes away, and one is completely present to some engagement, in "flow," "in the zone," and completely there will full access to all of his or her resources. See *Secrets of Personal Mastery* (Hall, 1999).

Gestalt: A German term for something that is "more than the sum of the parts." A gestalt state occurs when new emergent properties arise from a richly textured meta-state.

Incongruence: An inner state of conflict between beliefs, emotions, meanings, hopes, dreams, fears, etc., the lack of total commitment to an outcome expressed in incongruent messages, signals, lack of alignment or matching between word and behavior.

Installation: The process for incorporating a new mental strategy (way of doing things) within our mind-body system so it operates automatically. Installation is often achieved through anchoring, metaphors, parables, reframing, future pacing, quality control questions, etc.

Internal representations: All of the sights, sounds, sensations, smells, and tastes that play out on the theater of our mind as our snapshots and movies.

Kinesthetic: Sensations, feelings, tactile sensations on surface of skin, proprioceptive sensations inside the body, includes vestibular system or sense of balance.

Leading: Pacing and leading describes the essence of excellent communication and hypnosis. We lead by changing our behaviors after we have rapport so the client follows.

Logical levels or types: Two nominalizations that describe how we layer level upon level of thoughts-and-feelings so that one is about another and so classifies or types the lower as a member of that class. A meta-level drives and modulates the levels or layers below it.

Loops: A circle, cycle, a story, metaphor or representation that goes back to its own beginning, so that it loops back (feeds back) onto itself. An open loop: a story left unfinished. A closed loop: finishing a story. In strategies: looping refers to going through a set of procedures that have no way out, no exit.

Map: A model of the world, an unique representation of the world built in each person's brain by abstracting from experiences, comprised of a neurological and a linguistic map. Our internal representations that encode our movie is one level of mapping, the frames about that is yet a higher level.

Matching: Adopting facets of another's outputs (i.e., behavior, words, etc.) to create or enhance rapport.

Meta: A Greek word for "above, beyond, and about." A meta-thought is a higher level thought , a higher "logical level."

Meta-Model: A model with 12 to 26 linguistic distinctions that identifies language patterns that obscure meaning in a communication via distortion, deletion, and generalization.. To each distinction here are questions that we can use to challenge and clarify imprecise language (called *ill-formedness*). When we do this, we reconnect it to sensory experience. Meta-modeling brings a person out of trance. Developed, 1975, by Richard Bandler and John Grinder.

Meta-Programs: The mental and perceptual programs for sorting and paying attention to stimuli or information. The perceptual filters that govern our attention.

Meta-States: Literally, a state about a state, applying one state of mind-body (fear, anger, joy, learning) to another state to set it as a higher "logical level." A meta-state results from self-reflexive consciousness. The Meta-States model was developed by L. Michael Hall.

Mismatching: Offering different patterns of behavior to another, breaking rapport for the purpose of redirecting, interrupting, or terminating a meeting or conversation, mismatching as a meta-programs.

Modal Operators: A linguistic distinction in the Meta-Model that indicate the "mode" by which a person "operates," hence, our *modus operandi,* These include the mode of necessity, impossibility, desire, possibility, etc. We utilize for motivation the predicates—can, can't, possible, impossible, have to, must, etc.

Model: A description of how something works, a generalized, deleted or distorted copy of an original, a template for how to think or act. A complete model has a theory, set of variables, guidelines for using them, and patterns or technologies that result from it.

Modeling: A process of observing and replicating the successful actions and behaviors of others. Modeling involves identifying the variables make up an experience, discerning the sequence of internal representations and behaviors, and presenting as a way to accelerate learning an expertise.

Model of the world: A map of reality, a unique representation of the world via abstraction from our experiences, the total of one's personal operating principles.

Multi-ordinal: Source: Korzybski, *Science and Sanity (1933).* A term is multi-ordinal when it can refer to itself and still make since. Typically only nonminations are reflexive: we can *love* love, we can *fear* fear, we can feel *anger* at anger. At each level the word means something different. The question or challenge is: "At what level are you using this term?"

Multiple description: The process of describing the same thing from different viewpoints using different models or perspectiveness.

Neuro-Linguistic Programming: The study of excellence, a model of how people structure their experience, the structure of subjective experience, how humans become programmed in their thinking-emoting and behaving in their very neurology by the various languages they use to process, code and retrieve information.

Nominalization: A linguistic distinction in the Meta-Model descriing a hypnotic pattern of trance language, a process or verb turned into an (abstract) noun, a process frozen in time by a static noun by the *naming* (nominalizing) of the process.

Outcome: A specific, sensory-based desired result that is well-formed when it meets the criteria in the well-formed outcome pattern.

Pacing: Matching one's reality, gaining and maintaining rapport with another by joining their model of the world by saying that fits with and matches their language, beliefs, values, current experience, etc., crucial to rapport building.

Parts: The full phrase is "a part of one's thinking, feeling, remembering, intending, etc." "Parts" are not real or self-contained entities, but typically disowned and separated functions seem to take on a life of their own by our lack of ownership. A source of intra-personal conflict when incongruous.

Perceptual filters: Any idea, experience, belief, value, meta-program, decision, memory or language that shapes and colors the way we see or experience the world.

Perceptual position: A point of view or perspective. First Position: associated within one's own eyes. Second Position: seeing from the listener's perspective. Third Position: seeing from a meta-position outside self and other, neural observer. Fourth Position: seeing from the viewpoint of the group, system, or organization. Fifth Position: simultaneous and systemically incorporating all four perceptual positions, the "God" or universe viewpoint.

Predicates: What we assert or predicate about a subject, sensory based words indicating a particular representation system (visual predicates, auditory, kinesthetic, unspecified).

Preferred system: The representation system that a person typically uses most in thinking and organizing experience.

Presuppositions: Assumptions, ideas we take for granted that allow a communication to make sense. That which "holds" (position) "up" (sup) a statement "ahead of time" (pre).

Rapport: A sense of connection with another, a feeling of mutuality, a sense of trust, created by pacing, mirroring and matching, a state of empathy or second position.

Reframing: Allowing a frame-of-reference so that it looks new or different, presenting an event or idea from a different point of view or frame so it has a different meaning;. This gives us content reframing or context reframing.

Representation: A *presentation* to ourselves in our mind of what we have already seen, an idea, thought, sensory-based or evaluative based bit of information.

Representation system: The sensory systems of visual, auditory, kinesthetic, olfactory, and gustatory—the VAK which makes up the movie in our mind.

Requisite variety: Flexibility in thinking, emoting, speaking, behaving; the person with the most flexibility of behavior controls the action; the Law of Requisite Variety.

Resources: A source of thought-or-feeling that enhances things or empowers us as persons, a means that helps us to achieve an outcome.

Resourceful state: A mind-body state that enables us to feel and perform at our best.

Satir categories: The five body postures and language styles indicating specific ways of communicating: leveler, blamer, placater, computer and distracter, developed by Virginia Satir in Family Systems Therapy.

Second position: Perceiving the world from another's point of view, in tune with another's sense of reality.

Sensory acuity: Awareness of the outside world, of the senses, making finer distinctions about the sensory information we get from the world.

Sensory-based description: Information directly observable and verifiable by the senses, see-hear-feel language that we can test empirically, in contrast to evaluative descriptions.

"Sleight of Mouth" patterns: The reframing patterns that allow a person to transform meaning conversationally. Similar to "sleight of hand" patterns, we shift to a more enhancing "frame-of-reference that the listener doesn't notice. Reframed as *Mind-Lines* by Hall and Bodenhamer.

State: The full phrase is a state of mind-body-emotoin, the sum total of all neurological and physical processes within individual at any moment in time, a holistic phenomenon of mind-body-emotions, mood.

Strategy: A sequencing of thinking-behaving to obtain an outcome or create an experience, the structure of subjectivity ordered in a linear model of the TOTE.

"Sub-modality:" The cinematic features or distinctions within each representation system which gives us the qualities of internal representations.

Synesthesia: When there is an automatic link from one representation system to another, a V-K synesthesia involves seeing→feeling without a moment of consciousness to think about it, automatic program.

Third position: Perceiving things from the viewpoint of an observer, one of the three perceptual positions, a meta-position for observing both self and other.

Time-line: A metaphor describing how we represent and store our sights, sounds and sensations of memories and imagines, a way of coding and processing the construct "time."

T.O.T.E. A flow-chart model developed by George Miller and associates (Galanter and Pribram) to explain the sequential processes that generate a response. **Test-Operate-Test-Exit** updated the Stimulus—> **R**esponse model of behaviorism, NLP updated by adding representation systems.

Unconscious: Everything *not* in conscious awareness, our experience of our minor representation system.

Universal quantifiers: A linguistic term in the Meta-Model for words that code things with "allness" (every, all, never, none, etc.), a distinction that admits no exceptions.

Unsanity: A term used by Korzybski to describe the stage of poor adjustment between sanity (well adjusted to the territory) and insanity (totally maladjusted to reality). A "lack of consciousness of abstracting, confusion of orders of abstractions resulting from identification ... practically universally operating in every one of us" (1933: 105).

Unspecified nouns: Nouns that do not specify to whom or to what they refer.

Unspecified verbs: Verbs that have the adverb deleted, delete specifics of the action.

Uptime: The state where our attention

and senses are directed outward to immediate environment, all sensory channels open and alert.

VAK: A short-hand for the sensory representation systems of **V**isual, **A**uditory, and **K**inesthetic. The last one (K) includes smells (Olfactory) and tastes (Gustatory).

Value: The ideas, feelings, and experience that we deem as important in a given context. Our values or criteria motivate us and arise from our believing in the value of something.

Visual: Seeing, imagining, the representation systems of sight.

Visualization: The process of seeing images in your mind.

Well-Formedness: The criteria that enable us to specific an outcome in ways that make it achievable and verifiable, powerful tool for negotiating win/win solutions.

Neuro-Semantics®

The field of **Neuro-Semantics**® began with the development of *the Meta-States Model* which models how self-reflexive consciousness works as we jump "logical levels" to think and feel about previous thoughts and feelings. As a description of our meta-cognitive powers, Meta-States describes how we can create frames of meaning within multiple layers of frames which make up the system reality of our Matrix in which we live in and operate from.

Meta-States models the systemic nature of our reflexive mind-body-emotion system and its multiple levels of meaning construction. It specifies how we create *levels of meanings* as we layer level upon level of awareness to create our neuro-semantic states and responses. This maps out our inner game which sets the frames and rules for the outer game of performance and achievement.

Mind-Lines, the first book in the emergent field of Neuro-Semantic, represents *the languaging* of our meta-levels states. The conversational reframing model in this book gives voice to what we create and experience in meta-stating. As we move up *the levels of mind,* layering more and/or different thoughts and feelings about things, we create, nullify, intensify, reduce, texture, quality, and transform our states.

Today there are Institutes of Neuro-Semantics operating under the auspices of the International Society of Neuro-Semantics® or ISNS around the world. These Institutes are training centers offering trainings, coaching, and consulting focusing on closing the knowing-doing gap and enabling people to translate great ideas into muscle-memory and neurological patterns. For more about Neuro-Semantics, see the International website and links scores of other websites. For heaps of free materials (more than 2,000 pages), begin with the following websites:

www.neurosemantics.com
www.meta-coaching.org

About the Authors

L. Michael Hall, Ph.D.

ISNS — **International Society of Neuro-Semantics®**
P.O. Box 8
Clifton, Colorado 81520—0008   USA
(970) 523-7877

www.runyourownbrain.com
www.neurosemantics.com

Dr. Hall is executive director of the *International Society of Neuro-Semantics* (ISNS) having co-founded it with his business partner, Dr. Bob Bodenhamer in 1996. Prior to finding NLP in 1987 and studying with NLP co-founder Richard Bandler, Michael was a licensed psychotherapist in the state of Colorado with graduate degrees in Business, Literature, and Clinical Counseling. He did his doctoral studies in Cognitive Behavioral Psychology with an emphasis on psycho-linguistics in his dissertation at Union Institute University in Cincinnati Ohio.

Upon the discovery of Meta-States in 1994 during a modeling project on resilience, Meta-States won recognition as "the most significant contribution to NLP in 1995" by the International NLP Trainers Association. From there Michael began developing pattern after pattern using meta-states. That, in turn, led to him and associates applying meta-states to facets of NLP itself and finding all kinds of new developments. Meta-States remodeled much of NLP including time-lines, "sub-modalities," the sleight of mouth patterns, meta-programs, etc. This then led to two dozen practical training applications in sales, persuasion, defusing hotheads, leadership, coaching, relationships, wealth creation, etc.

Today Dr. Hall continues his work as a modeler, consulting with businesses, training, and is an entrepreneur in several businesses (real estate, publishing, etc.). He lives part of the year in the Colorado Rocky Mountains and trains internationally the rest of the time. He is a prolific writer and researcher with more than 35 books to his name.

Books by L. Michael Hall

NLP Books
The Spirit of NLP: The Process, Meaning & Criteria for Mastering NLP (1996)
Becoming More Ferocious as a Presenter (1996)
Patterns For Renewing the Mind (w. Dr. Bodenhamer) (1997)
Time-Lining: Advance Time-Line Processes (w. Dr. Bodenhamer) (1997)
NLP: Going Meta—Advance Modeling Using Meta-Levels (2001)
Figuring Out People: Design Engineering with Meta-Programs (w. Dr. Bodenhamer) (1997)
Source Book of Magic (Volume I) (w. B. Belnap) (2004)
Communication Magic (2000) (Originally, *The Secrets of Magic,* 1998)
Sub-Modalities Going Meta: Unmasking their Meta-Levels (w/ Bodenhamer, 2005)
Instant Relaxation (1999, Lederer & Hall)
User's Manual of the Brain: Practitioner Course. Volume I (2001)
User's Manual of the Brain: Master Practitioner Course, Volume II (2002)
MovieMind: Directing the Cinemas of the Mind (2002)

Neuro-Semantic Books:
Meta-States: Self-Reflexiveness in Human States of Consciousness (1995/2000)
Dragon Slaying: Dragons to Princes *(1996, 2000)*
Mind-Lines: Lines For Changing Minds (w. Dr. Bodenharmer) (2005)
Meta-State Magic (2001). From the *Meta-State Journal,* (1997-1999)
The Structure of Personality: Personality Ordering and Disordering Using NLP and Neuro-Semantics (Hall , Bodenhamer, Bolstad, Hamblett, 2001)
The Secrets of Personal Mastery 2000)
The Matrix Model (2002/ 2nd edition 2003)
Sourcebook of Magic, Volume II, Neuro-Semantic Patterns (2003)

Frame Games Books
Frame Games: Persuasion Elegance (2000)
Games Slim People Play (2001)
Games for Mastering Fear (2001, with Bodenhamer)
Games Business Experts Play (2001)
Games Great Lovers Play (2004)

Spiral Books:
Languaging: The Linguistics of Psychotherapy (1996)
The Bateson Report (2002).
Make it So! (2002).
Propulsion Systems (2003)

Coaching Books:
Coaching Conversation (with Duval, 2004)
Meta-Coaching: Coaching Change, Volume I (w/ Duval, 2005)

Bobby G. Bodenhamer, D.Min.
1516 Cecelia Dr.
Gastonia, NC 28054
(704) 864-3585
bbodenhammer@carolina.rr.com
www.neurosemantics.com

Dr. Bodenhamer first trained for the ministry, earned a doctorate in Ministry, and served several churches as pastor. He began NLP training in 1990, studying with Dr. Tad James and receiving Master Practitioner and Trainer Certifications. Since then, he has taught and certified NLP trainings at Gaston College as well as internationally. He has a private therapy practice in Gastonia NC where he lives with his wife, Linda.

Beginning in 1996, Dr. Bodenhamer began studying the Meta-States model and then teamed up with Michael to begin co-authoring several books. Since then he has turned out many works as he and Michael have applied the NLP and Meta-States Models to various facets of human experience.

In 1996 also, Dr. Bodenhamer with Michael co-founded the Society of Neuro-Semantics. This has taken his work to a new level, taken him into International Trainings, and set in motion many Institutes of Neuro-Semantics around the world.

Books:
1) Patterns For "Renewing the Mind" (w. Hall, 1997)
2) Time-Lining: Advance Time-Line Processes (w. Hall, 1997)
3) Figuring Out People: Design Engineering With Meta-Programs (w. Hall, 1997)
4) Mind Lines: Lines For Changing Minds (w. Hall, 1997, 2000 3rd edition)
5) The Structure of Excellence: Unmasking the Meta-Levels of Submodalities (w. Hall, 1999)
6) The User's Manual of the Brain (1999, w. Hall)
7) Hypnotic Language (2000, w. Burton)
8) The Structure of Personality: Modeling "Personality" Using NLP and Neuro-Semantics. (Hall , Bodenhamer, Bolstad, Harmblett, 2001)
9) Games for Mastering Fears (2001, with Hall)
10) User's Manual for the Brain, Volume II. (2002, with Hall)
11) Mastering Blocking and Stuttering (2004)

TRAININGS

NLP TRAININGS

Meta-NLP Practitioner: An intensive 7-day training in the essential NLP skills. *Meta-Masters NLP Practitioner:* An intensive 14-Day Training in mastering three of the NLP meta-domains: Language (Meta-Model; Mind-Lines), Perception (Meta-Programs) and States and Levels (Meta-States), and Modeling.

Basic Meta-State Trainings

Accessing Personal Genius (APG): Introduction to Meta-States as a systemic model about our unique kind of self-reflexive consciousness, 14 coaching patterns applies to our personal genius, accessing the "flow" state at will.

1) Secrets of Personal Mastery: Awakening Your Inner Executive.
2) Frame Games: Persuasion Elegance.

Meta-States Gateway Trainings

1) Wealth Creation Training: Mastering Your Wealth Matrix
2) Selling and Persuasion Excellence
3) Mind-Lines: Lines for Changing Minds
4) Accelerated Learning with NLP and Neuro-Semantics
5) Defusing Hotheads and other Cranky People
6) Instant Relaxation: Stress Management Skills
7) Games for Mastering Fear
8) Games For Mastering Stuttering (Blocking)
9) Games Business Experts Play
10) Games Slim and Fit People Play
11) Mastery Games
12) Matrix Games
13) Resilience Training
14) Prolific Writing
15) Living Personal Genius (LPG)
16) The Leadership Matrix

Advanced Neuro-Semantic Trainings

1) Advanced Modeling Using Meta-Levels
2) Advanced Flexibility Training
3) Neuro-Semantic and NLP Trainers Training
4) The Meta-Coaching® Certification Training system: Coaching Essentials, Coaching Genius, ACMC, ICMC, PCMC, MCMC.